PRAISE FOR
THE BROOKLYN PARAMOUNT THEATRE

"With forgotten information and behind-the-scenes tales, this book invites you to step back in time and experience the magic of an incomparable cinematic cathedral from the golden age of entertainment."

—KEITH WLOSEK, PRINCIPAL ASSOCIATE OF ARCADIS ENGINEERING AND LANDSCAPE ARCHITECTS

"[This book] does a great job documenting those four 'faces' and more about the legendary wonder theatre!"

—GARY GIDDINS, AUTHOR OF *BING CROSBY: A POCKETFUL OF DREAMS*; WINNER OF THE NATIONAL BOOK CRITICS AWARD FOR *VISIONS OF JAZZ*, A LIFETIME ACHIEVEMENT AWARD FROM THE JAZZ JOURNALISTS ASSOCIATION, AND A GRAMMY FOR LINER NOTES

"Wonderful information about the history of the Brooklyn Paramount, a venue I wish I could have played."

—WALTER THEODORE "SONNY" ROLLINS, LEGENDARY "SAXOPHONE COLOSSUS" AND FOUR-TIME GRAMMY WINNER

THE BROOKLYN PARAMOUNT THEATRE

THE
BROOKLYN
PARAMOUNT
THEATRE

AN INTIMATE PORTRAIT

MICHAEL HITTMAN, PhD

THE BROOKLYN PARAMOUNT THEATRE
An Intimate Portrait

FIRST EDITION

ISBN   978-1-5445-5072-5   *Hardcover*
       978-1-5445-5071-8   *Paperback*
       978-1-5445-5073-2   *Ebook*

Front cover image "Sunburst Proscenium" from the Stuart Fishelson Archive
Back cover image of hardcover "Brooklyn Paramount Building" from the Michael Hittman Archive
Interior images and articles: Michael Hittman Archives

"Once in his lifetime a man ought to concentrate his mind of the remembered earth, I believe. He ought to give himself up to a particular landscape in his experience, to look at it from as many angles as he can, to wonder about it, to dwell upon it. He ought to imagine the creatures there and all the faintest motions of the wind. He ought to recollect the glare at noon and all the colors of the dawn and dusk."

—N. SCOTT MOMADAY, THE NAMES

"If a man settles in a certain place and does not bring forth the fruit of that place, the place itself casts him out, as one who has not borne its fruit."

—THOMAS MERTON

"Hope is if home lasts."

—HENRY MILLER

"Now, what I want is facts. Teach these boys and girls nothing but facts. Facts alone are wanted in life. Plant nothing else, and rot everything else. You can only form the minds of reasoning animals upon facts: nothing else will ever be of any service to them... Stick to facts."

—CHARLES DICKENS, HARD TIMES

"To hell with facts, we need theories!"

—KEN KESEY

"The Spirit of the Cinema appears in the American tableau. Here the modern vamp replaces Helen of Troy; Jazz drowns the pipes of Pan; an auto supersedes the chariot; a flying machine outsoars Pegasus; towering skyscrapers overtop the temple-topped Acropolis; the Boy Scout takes the place of the shepherd boy...the composition is the rush hour."

—JAMES DAUGHTERY ON THE LOEW'S STATE THEATRE, CLEVELAND, OHIO (1921)

"They are like Lady Vaudeville's children."

—ANONYMOUS

"Every continent has its own great spirit of place. Every people is polarized and some particular locality, which is home, the homeland. Different places on the face of the earth have different vital effluence, different vibration, different chemical exhalation, different polarity with different stars: call it what you like. But the spirit of place is a great reality."

—D. H. LAWRENCE, *STUDIES IN CLASSIC AMERICAN LITERATURE*

Contents

Prologue

Once upon a time in Brooklyn's former tinsel town, the docents on tour buses paused on the northwest corners of Flatbush Avenue Extension and DeKalb Avenue before turning right and heading back to Manhattan and would point out Junior's "Cheesecake Capital of the World" directly across the way. No argument with that, except to say, that if out-of-towners visiting the Big Apple were lucky, they might also have heard: "Oh, and by the way, also on your right is the Paramount, where Frank Sinatra sang!" And if more knowledgeable— and accurate!—the tour guides most certainly would have added: "The home of Alan Freed's famous Rock 'n' Roll Jubilees in the 1950s!" And possibly stretching their luck, however, they also might inaccurately have entertained folks from as far afield as Peoria, Illinois, and Tokyo, Japan, by adding: "Where Jerry Lee Lewis also set fire to a piano on stage!"

Never mind their failure to name the world's first motion picture theatre built expressly for "the Talkies," which was purchased by Long Island in 1950. An undergraduate between 1959 and 1963, I returned to teach anthropology and Native American studies with PhD in hand for forty-six years. Having graduated in the orchestra a year before the theatre was turned into a gymnasium, I also have to confess that despite full knowledge that films were shown there daily between 3:00 p.m. and midnight, it took all this time for the place's importance to sink in. This Eureka-like shift away from Native American studies occurred. First, I realized that I'd failed to apply what I'd learned about sacred sites from Numus (Northern Paiute) consultants during field studies in Western Nevada to the Brooklyn Paramount Theatre, where I even played basketball for decades on its basketball court; and second, a friendship with a colleague in media arts who similarly "discovered" the importance of this sacred site had also vowed to do something about it. With Stu Fishelson's passing, however, I do no more than account for my changed *weltanschauung*?

Commencing with our employer's decision to purchase an NPR radio station in Southampton on the south fork of Long Island, WPBX 88.3 FM, on what was our alma mater's third campus, I got invited to host an hour-long weekly Jazz radio interview series in 2004. A few words, then, about my love of Jazz seem in order.

After helping get a Jazz club started in 1962 while majoring in sociology and anthropology, this guitarist and my late brother, Jeff Hittman, who became a highly regarded tenor saxophonist, were invited by our music professor, Robert Aquino, to play in his fledging Jazz band. It was years before this great African American musical art form would shed its underground cultlike status and be welcomed into the curriculum of academic institutions like ours. Through Jeff's contacts in the relatively small and obscure world of Jazz, I initially secured radio guests.

The decision was then to base *In the Pocket* on the Brooklyn Paramount, resulting in large part from familiarity with Frank Driggs's often-reproduced photograph of the theatre's marquee advertising an appearance by Duke Ellington's orchestra during its Vaudeville years. So, with piqued curiosity wondering if other Jazz artists also performed on stage here, I headed back to the New York Public Library where I'd done archival research toward my PhD dissertation on opiate addiction among Northern Paiutes in Nevada—a subject that ironically meshed with fateful narcotic addictions in Jazz history. In any event, there I was astonished to learn that nearly every other Jazz great had performed at the Brooklyn Paramount. Armed as such with this revelation, I recall having telephoned my late brother's paddleball partner, Cedar Walton, for an unrelated reason. And thinking to impress that late great Jazz pianist with my "discovery," I inquired if he knew about Jazz at the Brooklyn Paramount. I was flabbergasted by Cedar's reply, "M-F," he said, "I rode an all-night bus from Detroit just to work as an usher and hear Prez (Lester Young) play there!"

Next in recollected chronological order came a telephone call from Long Island University's archivist, Janet Marks, inquiring whether I was interested in meeting a fellow alumnus named John L. Doria Jr., class of '57, who wanted to donate his personal collection of photographs taken of assorted Jazz masters, writers, and deejays he'd apparently invited to perform and lecture on campus a decade before me—including photos of Dave Brubeck, Mal Waldron, and Herbie Nichols, among others, and Jazz writers like Nat Hentoff and Bob Reisner.

Well, that initiated a series of other coincidences that fascinated and puzzled Freud, who called those uncommon. Or, as we call it today, synchronicities (Hittman 2009). Another striking example was a photograph Doria gave me of his father standing in front of my office on the eighth floor of the Humanities building where Mr. Doria Sr. was employed in what was a shoe factory circa 1926. And not only that, but he'd also told his son about having watched Bing Crosby practice his golf swing (or putting) on the roof of Brooklyn Paramount's adjoining eleven-story office building some few airborne yards away in 1931.

Enter Stuart Fishelson, who was also an undergraduate at Long Island University—albeit a decade later than me—returned to teach here as a professor of photography. He independently "discovered" the Brooklyn Paramount and felt compelled to do something about spreading that gospel.

"Wow!" Stu related the same reaction I had with Jazz musicians like Vijay Iyer and Anat Cohen, whom I deliberately led toward the recording studio for radio interviews through the so-called Paramount gym. He similarly led prominent invited speakers like Spike Lee, John Cassavetes, and Gena Rowlands as part of media arts' new major in film in those same years. "How come the school doesn't do something to promote this place?"

Then, much like Jazz musicians "trading fours" after their solos, these synchronicities were exchanged between us:

MH: I went to the (lamented) Up Over Jazz Cafe owned by Bob Myers in Park Slope and chanced to meet Alma Carroll, the widow of Joe "Bebop" Carroll, who sang with Dizzy Gillespie (who also performed here), and she told me about having gone to hear Ethel Waters in 1932 at the Brooklyn Paramount, and I couldn't believe there wasn't a separate "colored seating" section!

SF: Did I ever tell you, Mike, I used to go to Alan Freed concerts here... when Manhattan's Paramount they say didn't allow Rock 'n' Roll shows on account of those powers that were didn't want racial mixing of teenagers in the audience?

MH: Listen to this, Stu. The other day while waiting on Cortelyou Road (near what was my house in Ditmas Park, Brooklyn) for the stalled Q subway train doors to open, the conductor pulled down his window, and after saying he recognized me from that same Jazz club, told of having witnessed an unpleasant marital battle between the Gillespies on Flatbush Avenue Extension after Dizzy's gig, and she was furious because of what borough residents knew in the 1950s, the fact that no yellow cabs were seen to transport them home!

SF: Did I ever tell you when I was a teenager my parents took me to an engagement party where we lived in Bensonhurst (Brooklyn)—for the short-lived marriage of the actors Troy Donahue and Suzanne Pleshette, the daughter of Gene Pleshette, the Brooklyn Paramount's manager at the time?

MH: Right back at you, Stu. When I decided one day to ask Dave, a retired schoolteacher who opened a used book store in Southold, Long Island, where my wife and I own a summer home, if he could locate a copy of *The Amboy Dukes* by Irving Shulman, imagine my surprise when he had a copy, and I found this long-repressed passage in that 1950s early sociological-like study of gangs. As a teenager, I read it for its hot and heavy sexy parts.

> "Want to go to the Paramount?" said one gang member to another. "They've got a good picture." But the real reason wasn't any interest in seeing a flick… He said it was easier to pick up chicks that way without having "to pay for them."

Tough talk between those two then was followed by the author's omniscient-like narrative voice:

> "So for three and a half hours they sat in the Paramount balcony with two high school babes, necking and swapping them as well."

SF: Reminds me of something else… I took a biology class in a sectioned part of that humongous balcony after LIU shut down the movie theatre and used it for that required class!

After conferences about each of the four "faces" of the Brooklyn Paramount, we collaborated, but then Stuart Fishelson sadly died in 2023 following a long, disabling illness. The plans we had made to write two books together, this encyclopedic history and his projected illustrated history, were dashed. My colleague and close friend's untimely death while we learned about the removal of asbestos at the theatre still in progress awaiting Live Nation's anticipated reopening date notwithstanding, I know he would have wanted me to share these additional related synchronicities.

First, a random gift from a colleague in our history department who retired would prove to be Jack Gabel's vintage photograph of the Brooklyn Paramount from 1928. Second, another synchronicity that followed was sleeplessness knowing this book would have to be rewritten and updated from an elegiac-like history of the theatre's earlier history after the amazing news about Live Nation's intentions...which were realized with its reopening in 2024. It was during a random YouTube search that the pop singer Lionel Ritchie rapping with a group of engaged youngsters seated in an auditorium immediately popped up. And in response to one of those kids' transparent boredom remarks—"What do you want to do?"—another, whether scripted or not, suggested, "We can go to the Paramount, maybe?" Only to have a third kid jump in and explain, "The Brooklyn Paramount is gone. It's been taken over by some college!"

Yet a third (new) synchronicity occurred between drafts of this book's rewrites... An email from a Canadian inquired about my father, who directed a settlement house on the Lower East Side for more than a half century, wanted to know about a member of one of the threatening street gangs from my childhood. He was doing a follow-up book on Brooklyn gangs, and David J. Van Pelt was intent on writing it. Short story lengthened, I knew that member of the Sportsmen, an African American who extorted money from me, and about his unpleasant fate. In any event, before securing a copy of *Rumble*, and reading his terrific investigative reporting, Dave said: "I did a book on the Puerto Rican Mau Maus, who shot and killed a Sand Street Italian American gang member in front of a penny arcade very close to the iconic Brooklyn Paramount Theatre, which is now Long Island University!"

A fourth and fifth synchronicity conclude those odd coincidences—the penultimate one closing that circle as it involved my collaborator, Stu Fishelson.

A telephone call from Katheryn Crosby (née Olive Katheryn Grandstaff), Bing's second wife, inquired whether there was interest in commemorating the crooner's seventy-fifth anniversary at "the Paramount." Following her shock that she'd called the wrong place, she expressed interest in visiting and viewing our theatre's remains and continuing the conversation about where her late husband not only shared performance dates but also appeared in the largest number of films of any Hollywood star at the Brooklyn Paramount.

Unfortunately, the meeting Stu and I arranged in our provost's office, joined by Long Island University's president and vice president, prompted thumbs-down from the administration because of an "offer" to perform at that commemorative concert for $7,500; the rest of those costs we would have to contribute. What followed blew my mind. After her gift of her self-published book about Bing Crosby, when we walked that unfazed actress to her limo parked in front of the former box office on Flatbush Avenue Extension and the corner of DeKalb, she thoughtfully invited me to her home in Genoa, Nevada. She was headed there following my disclosure that I, too, was headed to the Silver State a few days later for an annual visit to adopted tribal family members living a short drive's distance away on Campbell Ranch, a federal reservation occupied by Northern Paiutes. The upshot was not unlike the sort of teasing I received from my *beeya* (mother), Ida Mae Valdez, whom I (foolishly though honestly) boasted about having met the lesser-known wife of Bing Crosby and offered to introduce Kathryn to the extended adopted family members in "my tribe." The entire matter comically blew up after we drove sixty miles to Carson Valley, and this *Taivo natsee* (white boy) and I pulled over to call "my girlfriend Kathryn," and her second husband, a medical doctor, as I recall, answered. After he asked the nature of my business, he hung up, saying he didn't know any "Dr. Michael Hittman!"

Finally, let the last laugh, as it hopefully will be, belong with another indigenous tribe, the Western Apache in Arizona, bawdy "wisdom stores" attached to a place by "their" anthropologist, Keith Basso (1996). That book was published before my earliest history of the Brooklyn Paramount and its "second chapter." It transitions to the new theatre manager, Margaret Holmes, who reported this fifth synchronicity: She heard singing in this darkened, gorgeous wonder while opening it in the morning...her Phantom of the Opera being the voice of Julie Andrews singing "The Sound of Music." She asked her docent, me, what I thought. My immediate reply was, "Of course, my older daughter was called 'Little Julie' when she worked for 'Big Julie' at HarperCollins!"

In any event, I make every effort in this book to incorporate what I learned about sacred sites from America's First Citizens compounded by what Basso learned about "wisdom stories attached to place," lest we forget who we are and join the tragic plight of the world's refugees, and also the importance of names emphasized by the Pulitzer Prize–winning Kiowa-poet N. Scott Momaday (1987), which I join with anthropological verities.

PART I

INTRODUCTION

CHAPTER 1

"An Airplane Flies Overhead…"

Amid other banner newspaper headlines like this, the Brooklyn Paramount Theatre opened on November 24, 1928: THE BROOKLYN PARAMOUNT ENFOLDS ITS FIRST 50,000 ADMIRING CUSTOMERS. Although the *Brooklyn Citizen* exaggerated those numbers for the five complete film and Vaudeville shows on that Saturday morning—more like twenty thousand admissions would have rung true—the anticipated opening of the world's first motion picture theatre built from the ground up expressly for the Talkies—though not exclusively, as it was also mistakenly reported elsewhere—would be echoed by other local tabloids.

So, for example, *The Brooklyn Daily Eagle* on that pre-Thanksgiving morning would rave about the new "wonder theatre" in downtown Brooklyn. It joined others as part of the civic-minded and real estate developers' hopes of creating a rival entertainment center to Times Square in Manhattan. Or, as we also frequently read about that goal, "Keeping Brooklynites in Brooklyn."

A broader way of situating that gala opening is by noting important cultural events in our nation in 1928: the publication, for example, of D. H. Lawrence's *Lady Chatterley's Lover*, which led to a firestorm about definitions of obscenity matched by debate regarding censorship in the film industry that in two years saw implementation of the Hollywood Production Code. The racy novel resulted in a landmark Supreme Court decision in 1929 in which artistic merit was privileged over prurient matters. Definitions of "profanity," will also be seen throughout our discussion of all four faces of the Brooklyn Paramount's history—Film, Vaudeville, Jazz, and Rock 'n' Roll.

The year 1928 famously marked world premieres of *Apollo*, an Igor Stravinsky/George Balanchine orchestral-ballet collaboration, and *An American in Paris*, written by another Russian emigrant, George Gershwin (née Jacob Bruskin Gershowitz)—the latter, a film that unfortunately was not screened in our theatre. Yet another major event was Disney's introduction to the world of Mortimer Mouse in *Steamboat Willie* as a scrawny, pugnacious rat transformed over time into the more familiarly recognized iconic round-faced lovable mouse stuck as an adolescent because of "neoteny," a biological process discussed with Mickey in mind in evolutionary adaptive terms by the paleontologist Stephen Jay Gould (1992), defined as succeeding generations of humans appearing younger than their parents and grandparents at comparable ages.

And so, too, did the American Designer's Gallery in 1928 follow a Paris Exhibition that gave birth to "French Art Deco," a term which did not come into use until the 1960s when its bold, stylistic features famously evidenced as the Chrysler Building, for example. It also was responsible for the manufacture of practical objects that included cocktail glass sets (shakers, ice buckets, et al.) during Prohibition referenced by the first film screened in the Brooklyn Paramount (Crisp and Stewart, 2024: 186–88).

Yet another indelible footprint from 1928 must be the negative fact that the "Wizard of Menlo Park," Thomas Alva Edison, whose inventions famously include incandescent light bulbs, the phonograph, and the motion picture camera, impacted every aspect of our theatre. He registered only two patents during a fifty-three-year-long career that, according to his biographer, Edmund Morris (2019: 5–7), saw "one thousand and ninety-three machines, systems, processes, and phenomena patented."

"TODAY IT OPENS" (*The Brooklyn Citizen*/November 24, 1928)

The gala opening of the Brooklyn Paramount occurred toward the end of the "Roaring Twenties," a decade that the great American writer F. Scott Fitzgerald also aptly dubbed "The Jazz Age." Indeed, not unlike Art Deco's alternate moniker as the "Jazz style," a collection of Fitzgerald's early short stories received the title The Jazz Age. Defined as such with these culture markers of flappers, the Charleston and Lindy Hop, Prohibition, gangsters, the commercialization of radio and consumerism fueled by the rise of Madison Avenue following the Great War, World War I, Fitzgerald's short story from 1920 "Bernice Bobs Her Hair" also proved to be emblematic. Since *The New York Times* in 1926 saw that "America's Sweetheart," Mary Pickford, overcame her long-standing objection to Victorian curls and wearing her hair short in the new style seen as news fit to print (Crisp and Stewart, 2024: 155–59).

These three additional cultural markers from that decade were directly and indirectly connected with the gala opening of the Brooklyn Paramount: an airplane stunt, flagpole climbing, and goldfish swallowing.

A year after Lindbergh's historic twenty-fourth solo flight across the Atlantic in the *Spirit of St. Louis* from Roosevelt Field in Long Island, a sister ship of the trimotor Fokker to what Admiral Richard Byrd flew on his historic mission to Antarctica in 1927 was hired to fly back and forth from Curtiss Field. Those reported "throngs" assembled in the streets surrounding Paramount Triangle on the corners of Flatbush Avenue Extension and DeKalb Avenue at noon. The publicist Benjamin Serkowich read (or shouted) through an amplifier the names and addresses from the King's Borough telephone directory of individuals who received free pasteboard admission tickets.

It was nothing unlike the star of George White's *Scandals*, Ann Pennington, who performed in *Everybody's Welcome* at the Brooklyn Paramount, described as the "first Broadway production to come to a motion picture theatre with its original cast (May 21, 1932). She was involved in a unique promotion for Old Gold cigarettes a month before our theatre's opening—when heard singing numbers from another Broadway play in an airplane that flew between Macy's and Times Square, and whose voice was said to have been "distinctly audible" to Manhattan pedestrians in the street below (*The Brooklyn*

Eagle, September 18, 1928). And read not just any American citizens' names during our theatre's unique opening... Serkowich reportedly plastered the area with fliers on every lamppost about our theatre's gala opening. He avoided the abundance of names like Miller, Baker, and Cohen. Whether or not foreign-sounding names like his were deliberately sought remains to be seen.

Whether or not the purported builder of the Brooklyn Paramount, Harold E. Wittemann, piloted that airplane, what we know with certainty is that different versions of flagpole climbing were reported in the tabloids one month prior to the theatre's opening.

Different as well from Aloysius Anthony "Shipwreck" Kelly more famously having perched for twenty-two days atop one near Madison Square Garden in 1924, we read this headline in purple prose in the first of those versions in the *Brooklyn Times-Union* on November 7, 1928: "Disrobes Atop Flagpole: Actress Dares Pneumonia in Paramount Theatre Publicity Stunt." And so we are told "Bee Starr, twenty and shapely" had climbed a forty-foot flagpole atop the eleven-story Paramount Theatrical Building and "disrobed 150-feet in the air." Dismissing for a moment the announced reason she'd lost a bet on Alfred Smith's victory over Hoover in the presidential election, the real reason was publicity for Brooklyn Paramount's opening date three weeks hence. And more: "She took off the tan sweater, skirt and tie she wore, tossed them to the wind and clad only in pink crepe and lace lingerie, she deftly powdered her nose, rouged her cheeks and applied a bit of lipstick to her lips" (*Brooklyn Times-Union*, 1928).

In this second version, illustrating postmodernism's dictum about truth always being contested, we read in the *Brooklyn Eagle* one day later, on November 8, 1928, that she was a former circus performer who reportedly "became immodest" after perching atop a special platform built for her below the flagpole's top. The actress who lived in Leveritch Towers in Brooklyn Heights was photographed after having taken off her dress to expose a "circus costume."

A third variation also appeared in the *Brooklyn Citizen* on November 7, 1928. It said that a nineteen-year-old starlet with the stagestruck name "Bee Starr" climbed "the side of the New Paramount Theatre Building like a human fly," then "scrambled over the cornice" onto the roof, where she reportedly would "shinny up" to the top of that flagpole and "made herself right at home." That is, after waving hello to gaping folks in the street below, she paused to powder her little nose and proceeded to slip off her dress, thus exposing acrobatic attire, and then she sprightly slid down.

A tabulated version saw Rian James, a featured journalist on the *Brooklyn Eagle*, reporting the flagpole stunt in his "Reverting to Type" column on November 9, 1928, as follows: After having been awakened early on that previous Wednesday morning by a telegram from the theatre's publicist, James reportedly did due diligence and zoomed over to the Paramount building a-glitter. Only to discover, however, that other reporters were already assembled with note-taking pencils and pads in hand, gawking up at Ms. Starr, who was to have "emulate(d) a fly" by climbing the yellow brick effacement of the theatre's adjacent building and hoisting herself over the molding and climbing the flagpole onto the roof. As the journalist *au contraire* would report, despite rumors issued by the theatre's publicist about what to expect, Bee Starr instead rode the elevator to the roof with reporters and climbed the flagpole; then posing for the photographers while powdering her nose, she slid back down without promised use of lipstick for smooching the top of the flagpole.

In yet another unsourced tabloid account, we read that after shimmying up the flagpole and removing her clothing, thus revealing gymnast's wear, she clicked her bare heels; and then, yes, the "pretty Miss Starr" reportedly powdered her nose before scribbling her name with lipstick and kissing the flagpole top. Also in this alternate text, the "flapper acrobat" then slid down again to receive a "long-term theatrical contract" from the Brooklyn Paramount's first stage bandleader, Paul Ash—a good sport. He accepted Miss Starr's check for fifty dollars, celebrating the popular New York State governor Alfred Smith's defeat in the presidential election to Herbert Hoover.

Additional details about that decade's flagpole-climbing cultural obsession were found in a typewritten account of the Brooklyn Paramount's opening, generously loaned by John Fontillas, chief architect of H3, which initially was asked to create a plan for the reopening of the Brooklyn Paramount in 2014. We learned that "incidentally, the flag which fluttered above was not the stars and stripes, but a flag specially designed for the theatre." And more: Sixteen-year-old Ginger Rogers (née Virginia Katherine McNath), the movie star, who began as Fred Astaire's second dance partner after winning a Charleston dance contest in Texas, appeared on stage several times during the Brooklyn Paramount's Vaudeville years, which ended in 1934. Not only was it reported outside the theatre next to the ballerina Gambarella who performed that day, but also she was reportedly pointing proudly to the flag. The so-called "Betsy Ross" allegedly sewed a white flag and hoisted it up there; it read BROOKLYN PARAMOUNT.

Before turning to that third culture maker of the Roaring Twenties, goldfish swallowing, we read newspaper accounts nearly a decade before the flagpole stunt that between 1923 and 1927, "America's Premiere Ballerina of the Air" who worked with two sisters as high-wire aerialists in outdoor circus tents in Brooklyn as an adolescent. Also subsequent to our theatre's opening, Bee Starr was reported appearing as herself in Vaudeville aerial performances in the Bedford Theatre (December 16, 1928) and the Fox (December 27, 1931).

Turning next to that third obsession during the 1920s, while there isn't any evidence of anyone associated with the Brooklyn Paramount's earlier history literally swallowing a goldfish, something not completely unrelated can nonetheless be reported.

Turns out a ginormous ten-foot-by-twenty-foot aquarium was found at the base of one of those magnificent winding marble stairs that still lead down to what today is a redesigned resplendent unified basement lounge. But why not let Ben Rosenberg, who was there, relate that near-disaster that occurred outside one of those lounges on the night before our theatre's opening.

BEE STARR FLAGPOLE STUNT (*The Brooklyn Daily Eagle*/November 8, 1928)

"A huge aquarium (was) to be stocked with exotic fish," the retired maintenance man wrote about what happened in front of that recessed parabolic, blue-tiled aquatic motif in a letter to the editor in *Marquee*:

There were large colored spotlights on both sides of the tank, red, blue and amber, to highlight the effects of this large body of water with these spectacular species of fish. The tank was approximately ten feet in height and fifteen in width. The glass which fronted the tank was imported from Belgium.

On the night before the opening of the theater the workmen began filling the tank with water, slowly. The fish would be placed in the water after the tank was filled. The water had reached, perhaps, three quarters of the tank's capacity, representing thousands of gallons. Several of us were watching the procedure. Suddenly there was a tremendous crash: the glass gave way, and an enormous cascade of water came pouring into the lounge, engulfing everything, including us.

Since the glass presumably cracked when cold water was used to fill that heated aquarium, waiting to contain tropical fish, this primary source then described what riotously followed next:

I ran out of the theater to Flatbush and DeKalb Avenues and grabbed every able-bodied man who would agree to come with me, perhaps twenty-five in all. Meanwhile, my colleagues collected piles of rags, pails, shovels—anything which could be used to bail water.

Well, since the show must go on, we happily also read the following:

We toiled all night. Everyone was exhausted. We could not remove the soaked carpet but managed to bail out most of the water. We opened the theater at 10:00 a.m. on schedule, but the lower lounge wasn't used. I think all of us who were involved went sleepless for almost seventy-two hours. We had enormous crowds to handle from the moment we opened our doors. It took weeks to restore the lounge to its intended beautiful state, minus the fish tank. Architects make mistakes.

More than four thousand lucky people gained admission out of thousands, according to a local tabloid. They were lined up between Myrtle Avenue and its elevated subway, two blocks west, and reportedly "all the way to Fulton Street from DeKalb," when the theatre's first manager, John L. McCurdy from the *Brooklyn Eagle*, was cornered and pestered by a reporter to recall the first customer amid that hubbub. The thirty-six-year-old former manager of the Rialto on Times Square, who was described as a veteran following twenty-two years of theatre experience in Chicago, Boston, Detroit, and St. Louis, presumably tongue-in-cheek, identified that person of interest as a "tall, dark, and handsome man." Fortunately, though, for our concerns, when pressed for more information, "Mac" recalled that customers with orchestra seats purchased for twenty-five cents were able to "drink water from marble fountains with elegant cut-glass nozzles" built into opposite side walls of the auditorium. He also reported this incident on opening day: A woman in the lower balcony was so overwhelmed by the gold and marble Grand Lobby, she had to receive first aid after fainting!

The reporter Will Witmore from *Movie World* interviewed our theatre's first manager. Something else occurred on opening day during his visit. At 1:00 p.m. on that Saturday morning, about thirty minutes after the theatre's delayed opening, "suddenly in the midst of the final rush to put in [*sic*] the lights a Wurlitzer mechanic (mistakenly) stepped out onto the big time." That is, he appeared on stage from behind those many sets of curtains just as Henry Murtagh seated at the Mighty Wurlitzer struck up the opening notes of what the journalist identified as Gershwin's "minstrel song," "Swannee," and embarrassedly fled!

Finally, most accounts of the initial impressions of the Brooklyn Paramount reveal its paradoxical mix of glamour and glitz with the theatre's purported working-class family ambience. For example, Sam

Katz, president of Paramount Pictures under the film studio's founder, Adolph Zukor, was quoted on October 4, 1928, nearly two months ahead of the opening date, contrasting ours with its over-the-top sister on Times Square, the Manhattan-Paramount:

> It will not be merely another fine theater but will represent the climax of all our experience in building and operating nearly 300 of the world's finest theaters. The Brooklyn Paramount has everything in it for the luxury and convenience of theater-goers that any other modern theater has, plus the added advantage of the newest of additional months experimentation based on newly discovered scientific building principles and decorative beauties.

Rian James, several months prior, alerted readers in his "Reverting to Type" local newspaper column on February 4, 1928, to expect something more stupendous than the other wonder theatres previously built in downtown Brooklyn: "According to the intelligentsia it isn't art." He wrote that the "deluxer" should be viewed as brash, garish, and gold, a show-off of superstructures and nostrum of the nouveau riche that was intended to be glaring and glittering as well as a show-off. He also wrote that it proved to be without the depth and feeling of genuinely "arty" architecturals [*sic*]. And like the "gorgeous place," which reportedly "ain't art," he curiously wrote that the general public could expect to experience his "yen for beer, believing in Santa Claus" and desire for paring your fingernails with a paring knife.

Edging still closer to the Brooklyn Paramount's opening date, Martin Dickstein in his "Slow Motion" column wrote this three weeks prior on November 4, 1928:

> Already we have been informed that this will be the acme of all that is beautiful and modern in motion picture construction and decoration. Its stage presentations, the management promises, will be the finest obtainable on the five continents.

Yet *Variety's* reviewer, on January 15, 1930, alerted readers of that trade magazine that "over in Brooklyn, the downtown theatre audiences are as family-like as any neighborhood crowd anywhere."

Finally, we turn to our theatre's inaugural dual program: *Manhattan Cocktail*, the first film shown throughout that entire week, which Paramount advertised as a "singing talkie" (it simultaneously premiered at the Manhattan-Paramount, marking the death of Silent Films) and a Vaudeville "playlet," or musical sketch, commemorating another historic event in America's history, titled *At Plymouth Rock*, viewed differently by our nation's First Citizens.

CHAPTER 2

Gala Opening…"What a Show It Was!"

A. Manhattan Cocktail: Comes the Talkies?

Based on a short story by Ethel Doherty, who is said to have been "inspired by" the Greek myth of Ariadne and the Minotaur, *Manhattan Cocktail* was the film selected by Paramount to open the Brooklyn Paramount Theatre. Occasionally called a Talkie, the world's first motion picture theatre was built to exhibit "all dialogue films." It was a Silent Film containing only two fewer songs than Warner Brothers' *The Jazz Singer*, which famously marked that momentous transition (Eyman, 1997; Crafton, 1999). All the same, *Manhattan Cocktail*, which more accurately should be called a "singing film," was simultaneously screened at Manhattan's Paramount, which opened two years earlier as part of the studio's "day-and-same-date policy." Directed by Dorothy Arzner, the first woman in Hollywood to make that cut, the film's treatment credits a Hungarian playwright named Ernest Vadja who adapted the mythical tale of sacrificial youths to a blind cannibalistic monster reimagined on Broadway. *Manhattan Cocktail* aptly begins with a phantom-type ballet whose performers are clad in ancient Greek costuming and leaves off before the culture hero slays the half-bull monster with his magical sword. Along with having directed *Manhattan Cocktail* for Paramount, Arzner lived with Marion Morgan, whose dance company was featured in the Prologue.

DOROTHY ARZNER, FILM DIRECTOR (Academy of Motion
Picture Arts and Sciences, Margaret Herrick Library)

No prints exist for the film, so our initial approach to dissimulating its plot began within a biography of *Manhattan Cocktail*'s singing actress star, Nancy Carroll, by Paul Nemeck:

Along with their friend Bob (Danny O Shea), they (she) embark on Broadway careers after their graduation from college. Renov, an evil producer, complicating their plans, and Fred (Carroll's significant other) and Babs leave the stage for a presumably happy life as a married couple. (Nemeck 1969)

Newspaper film reviews were also quintessential. Sampling some dozen or so, we, for example, read in the *Brooklyn Eagle* (November 26, 1928) about three recent upstate college graduates hoping to make it in "monstrous Manhattan," a. k. a. the Great White Way. There they encounter a preying decadent European producer married to an enabling viper, whose cast couching of young men in turn parallels her husband Renov's Minotaur-like devouring ways of aspiring actresses. Said to lack great originality, the anonymous reviewer drew an object lesson by warning young people apt to patronize Brooklyn theatres...to stay away from Manhattan. Another local reviewer spun a different object lesson: The *Standard Union* (November 30, 1928), which characterized *Manhattan Cocktail* as an "amiable, well-photographed, well-directed, well-titled (romp that)...presents the old argument that New York isn't the only place to live in the world, that people can be happy elsewhere."

The *Brooklyn Times Union* (November 26, 1928) offered a more nuanced motivation for the behavior of the film's female lead, Nancy Carroll (née Ann Veronica Latiff), an Irish ingenue born in Hell's Kitchen on the west side of Manhattan and Paramount Silent Film star, suggesting she is determined to enjoy one last fling (or vamp) before succumbing to the sort of bourgeois middle-class suburban banality described by Sinclair Lewis in his novel *Main Street*. Expressed by Babs singing the provocative lyrics to one of *Manhattan Cocktail*'s two songs written by Victor Scherzinger, "Gotta Be Good," neither would have passed Hollywood's Motion Pictures Production Code two years in the offing (Vieira, 2019).

"Fred" was Fred Tilden played by another Paramount rising star, Richard Arlen (née Sylvanus Richard Mattimor), who also made that transition from Silent Films, and in time would win Hollywood's first coveted Oscar in a remake of *Wings*, which simultaneously played ours as well as our sister's movie theatre during the same week of January 5, 1929. "Another Kiss" was that second risqué song written by Scherzinger, a film director. But more to the point of the preceding film review, we also learn the young wannabe flapper's objection was being placed on a pedestal by her fiancé, who reportedly left Babs feeling "more classic than comfortable." So in modern psychology parlance, she intends to "act out" by flaunting Victorian residual puritanical sex standards that crumbled in the aftermath of the Great War.

The *New York Evening Journal* (November 27, 1928), found *Manhattan Cocktail* a "synthetic entertainment of backstage life." Despite complimenting—or patronizing—its capable director for being a woman, the reviewer chides Ms. Arzner for having Babs "say" through the familiar Silent Film screened dialogue box in response to an attempted rape by the "sophisticated foreign theatrical director," "I'm surprised at you, Mr. Renov, that you would use such an old-fashioned technique." He was played by the Hungarian American actor Paul Lucas, who went on to win an Oscar for Best Actor in *Watch on the Rhine*. Finally, that anonymous reviewer also wrote that he felt *Manhattan Cocktail* had "plenty of speed and bright spots."

According to yet another review from the opposite end of this country, the *Los Angeles Times* (November 26, 1928) characterized the film as "one of the most delightful of recent Paramount pictures" while adding something prescient ignored by others: Professor Fred Tilden's realization that he could earn more money coaching basketball than teaching college! The sport was played on our theatre's stage and replaced Vaudeville killed off by the Great Depression. Also contained in this review was its journalist's expressed delight at being able to hear the taps on Nancy Carroll's chorister shoes; that is, not unlike the sound of those clanking sabers and 127 smooches previously heard as well as seen in *Don Juan*, Warner Brothers' Talkie released in 1926, a year prior to *The Jazz Singer*.

From mid-America comes these two reviews: the *Dayton Herald* (December 10, 1928), whose film critic suggested that after its "shape is ended," an appetite for the film lingers on, and reserved special praise for George Marion Jr., the refreshing title writer of clever comedy captions found in this otherwise Silent Film; and the *Cincinnati Enquirer* (December 2, 1928), which not only spoke about Ms. Morgan's dance school that opened in 1916, and specialized in Greek as well as Egyptian, Oriental as well as Interpretative and Dramatic dancing; but also noted her choreography of the dance number Babs would ultimately receive in Renov's Broadway musical.

Closer to home, the *Hartford Courant* (December 23, 1928) found *Manhattan Cocktail* "entertaining and (that it) holds the interest," a "fast poppy and delightful little picture," which "could sparkle no more" as well as a "realistic picture" depicting Broadway as a "moving thrilling melodrama." Harsh criticism, however, came from the *Baltimore Sun*. Dated December 18, 1928, its readers were put on alert to expect an encounter with the "frustrations of the devilish schemer of a producer of musical shows" in a film otherwise described as cheaply employing the "modern device of sex appeal," and whose "ingredients" were nonetheless "ordinary." As in, symbolically served in a cocktail-like glass "with the cherry." Indeed, *Manhattan Cocktail,* which was also inaccurately described as a Talkie, whose "mediocrity of plot might conceivably contain a 'kick' for the average Midwestern high school girl anxious to make good in the village stage production," while mature viewers would only "find it rather insipid, tasteless and without effect."

If only because of the clout of *The New York Times* in those years, if not these, we read on November 25, 1928, about the film's "ultra-sophisticated direction." But even if its anonymous reviewer found the plot "ridiculous," we nonetheless additionally read the following indictment: "Miss Arzner should be ashamed" because "after what happens to the people in the film it is no wonder that they should rejoice on leaving Manhattan!" And arguably worse, despite having spoiled the ending, was the reviewer's bias: "It is, however, sad to relate the story cannot boast of any degree of human psychology... (hence) interesting only so long as one can pardon the natures and actions of its characters." Finally, and as if symbolically wielding the magical sword Theseus was given to slay the Minotaur in the Greek myth, the anonymous *New York Times* reviewer cleverly likened *Manhattan Cocktail* to "a synthetic cocktail without the cherry."

And so, too, did the film critic of another of New York City's leading tabloids, the *Herald Tribune*, essentially hate what he saw. For, despite writing about "the first-rate quality of the photography and the pictorial brilliance of the modernist set," after expressing his "appreciation" of the film's direction as "clever" and delivering praise for excellent subtitles, he characterized *Manhattan Cocktail* as nothing more than "a trapdoor for the ingénue" and a feature-length photoplay addled by "juvenilia," which offensively depicted the Great White Way in Manhattan as "no place for honest people" in the *Herald Tribune.*

How then did our theatre's initial film offering fare in the major trade magazines?

The *Exhibitor Daily Review* (December 1, 1928) described *Manhattan Cocktail* as a "good comedy drama about Broadway and its heart breaks" with "some good gags," and whose "thrilling climax" provided "laughs and tears for everyone"; hence, it was a "fine sound attraction for all houses." As for Arzner's direction, while we shouldn't be surprised to encounter sexism in its male reviewer's account, although he wrote how she "handled a very old theme refreshingly," the film's female director was ultimately said to have brought "a very feminine softness" to its production that was "ably done and decidedly pleasing," despite her gender!

Photoplay (July–December, 1928) called *Manhattan Cocktail* an "unusually arresting comedy," a film whose reviewer also played off the word "cocktail" in its title by metaphorically viewing the drama as a "stimulating, laugh-inducing, pick-me-up with a kick." And while that fanzine's reviewer would also maintain that the Paramount production proffered a "fascinating review of New York's theater circle," he also praised its actors as "penetratingly delineated by Dorothy Arzner's ultra-sophisticated direction."

Film Spectator (October 20, 1928: 5–6) praised *Manhattan Cocktail* for its "gorgeous...impressive opening sequences." Moviegoers, nonetheless, were warned to be prepared for the "slam indictment" of Broadway, for its reviewer also viewed the film's treatment of the short story on which it was based as "told a little crudely." And critically more, he felt Richard Arlen had been assigned a "wasted part." All the same, *Manhattan Cocktail* was described as being able to "please any audience," which above all "Hollywood should see it." Why? "Not because it was directed by a woman," but "because it was directed so well."

Turning next to *Variety* (November 28, 1928), we find it came down unusually hard on *Manhattan Cocktail*. "Reliable program feature with an expensive symbolic probing meaning nothing but looking good," or so wrote Bige, the *nom de plume* of Joe Bigelow, who criticized the film shot on Paramount's sound stage in Los Angeles as "expensive." Even so, he greatly praised the Prologue as offering "more coin than the picture proper." Then, however, after dismissing what we can only infer was the film's most dramatic moment, i.e., the main character's "best friend" Bob's abreaction to Renov's rejection with a "crazy leap from the proscenium," along with insensitively characterizing his suicide as "just another hole" in the plot, Bige also dismissed the womanizing of that contemporary Minotaur (Renov) as "ridiculous." For, as we learn about the lechery by the film's foremost producer, such behavior reportedly wouldn't last ten minutes in any racket! All the same, Bige wrote that Paul Lukas's portrayal as Renov was likeable while additionally praising the performance of Brooklyn's comedienne Lilyan Tashman as Mrs. Renov, i.e., the "blond and high-stepping wife who recruits boys for her husband" while giving an "excellent accord of herself." No enlightened reader today could swallow *Variety's* film critic's shocking allusion to an attempted rape scene as comic. Bige wrote that *Manhattan Cocktail* was generally "credulous and sweet." And despite complimenting the "excellent synchronization" of Nancy Carroll's voice on both songs with the plot, he sniped she shouldn't give up her day job as an actress! And that is, after having noted the sale of sheet music to both songs in the Paramount lobby, a common practice during those years.

Worse was what the reviewer in *Billboard* wrote on December 1, 1928: Despite rating *Manhattan Cocktail* as "slightly above average," he besmirched the film's storyline as nothing more than "calf-love romance." And writing as well that its plot inexorably led to "the happy ending formula," the reviewer then delivered this hammer: "Doesn't deserve its first-rate houses." Indeed, *Billboard*'s reviewer not only saw it as an "onslaught of New York," he also wrote that the film "breaks and tenders the tender-foot" while predicting an "average first-run," if only since *Manhattan Cocktail* "lends itself happily to exploitation."

Readers left curious about other film reviews are invited to consult *The New York Evening Journal* (November 27, 1928), *Austin-American* (December 16, 1928), *Pittsburgh Post-Gazette* (January 14,1929), *Philadelphia Inquirer* (January 8, 1929), and *Atlanta Constitution* (December 3, 1928). Before summarizing the film's plot based on the screenplay's final treatment, which we obtained, it also remains curious to read that Douglas Eames (1985: 58) in an in-house publication titled "The Paramount Story" described *Manhattan Cocktail* as "trashy but gripping."

A few words about the etymology of that popular mixed drink (vermouth and sweet cordials) from the 1920s during Prohibition, which partially inspired the film's title, seem in order. H. L. Mencken (2000: 151) wrote in his great work about the origins and uses of American language that the cordial traced back to the early nineteenth century, when a mixture of stale beer (or ale) and flour was fed by Irish and English trainers to roosters to heighten those fighting birds for the entertainment and lust of that cruel spectator's blood sport. Called "cock's ale" originally, some unknown person then inserted a "t," and out came "cocktails" in vogue during the 1920s, when the manufacture of "martini glasses" incidentally became popular with the Art Deco vogue circa 1928.

Happily, we located several scripts of the film in the Archives of the Association of Oscar Awards in Los Angeles. Summarizing its plot, then, from its presumed final treatment, *Manhattan Cocktail* began with a commencement celebration in a Greek frat house at fictitious Cranston College. But while the others are singing in close harmony groups still wearing robes if not caps, presumably drunk, "Babs" is blowing off a wedding proposal otherwise sincerely delivered by her fiancé, Fred Tilde...whom she also informs that she and their best friend, Robert "Bob" Markley, have already purchased tickets for the next bus leaving for Manhattan that following morning. Dejected as well on account he's just received good news about having been appointed an assistant professor of Greek history, Fred is consequently forced to unhappily look on while his fiancé cavorts about, leaving him probably to brood how those two could live like one, despite an academician's known low starting salary. A symbolic if not portentous interlude then follows. An elderly married couple quarrels, and Mrs. McGirt tosses Mr. McGirt out in the street while Babs (through Silent Film titles) nonetheless attempts to help alleviate Fred's gloom by reassuring him not to worry about her, because she's heard that despite the city's teaming population of six million people, most Manhattan folks were reported as getting along with each other.

The action shifts next to the Big Apple, specifically the Great White Way, where Bob immediately falls under the spell of the famous Broadway theatre director's wife. And after he stereotypically performs an Irish clog dance at Mrs. Renov's urging, Bob is promised a part in her Russian-born husband's first musical production in the United States. Babs not only can't find work, but by contrast is also seen sitting alone in a YWCA room dejectedly reading newspaper stories about anonymous young girls on morgue slabs, which appear alongside advertisements that seek "new faces" on Broadway.

Meanwhile, back home in upstate New York, Fred nurses his bruised ego by writing a Greek tragedy—with the struggles of a creative writer belied by him tearing page after page out of his typewriter and burning them in a wastepaper basket close at hand while plodding along to finish his play. But after receiving a letter from Bob about his luck, since he's lost contact with Babs, who's also written home albeit with misery and self-pity, Fred will immediately pack and ride the commuter train to his fiancée's rescue—though not without his play, which he hopes to get produced on Broadway.

He's cheated in a scam by proprietors after renting a room from them and is threatened with an arrest, despite having paid a month's advance. Meanwhile, Babs turns to a kindly old theatre manager for help. Armed as such with the director/Minotaur's private hotel address obtained from him, she gets additional support from the elevator girl in Renov's hotel, who suggests they switch clothing pursuant to having sympathetically also learned about the aspiring starlet's dream of obtaining a private interview with Renov. Babs will then obtain a promised part in the director's new production—though not before Renov's attempt to kiss her in the elevator has failed.

Fred and Babs will then meet by chance in the street, and he attempts in vain to convince her to return home with him. Their encounter, however, falls under the scrutiny of a policeman who intervenes thinking she is a prostitute attracting a john as a result of Babs having accidentally dropped her handkerchief, which Fred gentlemanly retrieves.

Back in the theatre again, Bob will inexplicably flub his assigned familiar clog dance and promptly gets fired by Renov, who mercilessly also shames him for allegedly having no talent whatsoever. Whether presumably or not, the result of Renov's jealousy on account of his wife's blatantly overt solicitations toward that virile young man (among others), the next dialogue slide projected onto the screen portends Bob's suicide: "A hero like Theseus." Or so, it apparently read. Arguably worse, Bob's patroness turns her deadly charm on Fred, whom Renov's wife will solicit for her own evil designs by seductively inviting him to read his play aloud. Titled *The Labyrinth*, we also learn it was a Greek tragedy in five acts. As for Bob, he is seen destitute in a cheap cafeteria, yet stubbornly refusing the help of an obese woman, who generously offers him a few cents to eat as well as a job...all before his return to the theatre and ultimate demise.

Then, because of Renov's simmering jealousy, angered that he cannot break up the engagement of Fred and Babs, the Broadway-like Minotaur duplicitously plots revenge by directing his lawyer to hire a detective to trail the aspiring playwright while simultaneously heeding his wife's advice that he hire Fred for a transparent enough reason: as a script consultant. With irony, to be sure, for along with taking him away from his lecherous wife, Renov will convince his new assistant to change the ending of the play—that is, if he wants it produced by him. Then Renov forges his signature on a check for $5,000 and asks

Fred to cash it. That maneuver lands that innocent person in jail when a banker reports back to Renov about the supposedly forged check his caddy is accused of having written. All that goes on while another subplot has Fred attempting to convince Babs that New York isn't really such a bad place at all!

Babs's discovery of her fiancé's arrest prompts her to head directly to Renov's boudoir, where she vows to do anything to help her man. The infamous attempted rape scene then follows; that is, after Renov has agreed to drop all charges and give Babs a part in the chorus line of his new production, though only after she demands to hear Fred's voice as a freed man first. As for that "comical" attempted rape scene, it occurs because Renov is Infuriated when Babs promptly goes back on her word—his menacing pursuit thwarted initially because she crashes the glass plate of a fire alarm with a paperweight while pinned by his hot pursuit against his desk, which in turn alerts the (kindly) stage manager, who informs the fire department, which arrives with a hotel detective and comically hoses Renov down.

The film's action cynically shifts to the final rehearsal of that musical production after Bob has despondingly threatened to kill Renov with a tire iron, only to be thwarted by stagehands whom he escapes from and plunges to his death after climbing a ladder in the flies off stage. This is followed by additional drama when Fred threatens Renov with a gun he's purchased at a pawn shop for revenge. Finally, he and Babs escape after she refuses to take her assigned place in the line of dancers, because it was the same bloodstained landing place of Bob's suicidal leap—cleaned up in anticipation of that evening's opening performance.

Manhattan Cocktail ends in a taxicab transporting Fred and Babs back home to upstate New York while the last screen title projected onto the scrim in effect reprises their frat house "conversation" seen at the film's start: "There are a hundred million people outside of New York and they're getting along alright."

Before turning to the accompanying Vaudeville program, some final words about Dorothy Arzner are also in order:

The 1938 edition of the *World Film Encyclopedia* describes her as five feet, four inches tall, weighing seven stones (108 pounds), and with brown hair and blue eyes. Born in San Francisco, California, she was sent to the Westlake School for Girls in LA after her parents divorced and stepmother worried on account of tomboyishness. Arzner's biographer, Marne (1994: 45), writes about her childhood infatuation with silent screen stars, apparently as a result of her father's managing a restaurant called the Hollywood frequented by them. The grown director then decided against medical school, and dropping out of USC volunteered as an ambulance driver in the states during the First World War. After which she commenced a forty-year career in her beloved film industry at its very bottom, or where women typically were assigned as script typists. Her apparent determination, however, to follow Lois Weber and a relatively large number of Silent Film women directors in 1920 then led to a fortuitous meeting with William DeMille, Cecil's older brother, who happily allowed her to type scripts; she advanced to typing rewrites on sets during film productions. On her own, Arzner learned how to cut or edit films, which caught the attention of James Cruize when she contributed a bullfight scene to Valentino's silent flick *Blood and Sand*, which, as will be seen, was screened at the Brooklyn Paramount during so-called Revivals.

Invited after her promotion in 1923 to work on several of Cruze's other Paramount Silent Films, there was *The Covered Wagon* and *Old Ironside*, before Dorothy Arzner came to the attention of Paramount's founder, Adolph Zukor's partner, Jesse Lasky, who invited her to direct *Fashions on Parade* (starring John Gilbert). One year later after another Silent Film, she directed *Manhattan Cocktail*. Among her subsequent forty screen credits, *Sarah and Son*, "an all-dialogue," also screened here, and about which Lasky said only a woman could have directed that melodrama about a mother's lifelong search for a stolen son—an all-woman's production, nearly, with Ruth Chatterton in the lead role; Verna Mills was listed as film editor; and Henrietta Cohn seemingly the first woman business manager at Paramount Studios. Other films screened here directed by Dorothy Arzner include: *The Wild Party* starring Clara Bow (during the week of May 4, 1929); *Honor Among Lovers*—filmed in the Astoria studio instead of Hollywood (February 27, 1930); *Misleading Lady* (April 8, 1932); and *Craig's Wife* (October 22, 1936).

Of additional relevance is that Dorothy Arzner's prefeminist *Dance, Girl, Dance*, made in 1940, has become a centerpiece of feminist studies since her revival—as a result of its riveting *mise en scene* in which the prim and proper aspiring ballet dancer Maureen O'Hara reproaches gawking men during a burlesque show. She is driven by desperation to perform as a stripper on the advice of her cynical roommate Lucille Ball as a way of earning survival money. This Dorothy Arzner film unfortunately was not shown in our theatre.

Despite having directed tempestuous actresses like Clara Bow in *Wild Party*, which was also a "Revival," Ms. Arzner always maintained that men in what the anthropologist Hortense Powdermaker (1950: 45) called "the Hollywood Dream Factory" were easier to work with. After having convinced Lasky that she could do a man's work as director, he was quoted saying, "Do you know we have tried many women as assistant directors and have found them unsuccessful?" (*Brooklyn Eagle*, August 17, 1928)—despite a successful directorial career in which she admitted years later she often deleted her name as auteur, lest gender discrimination occur. Arzner sadly was forced to grovel for work from men, as evidenced in this undated letter to another major director, Preston Sturgis: "I have had very long years of experience with very real men in this business and from those men I'm sure you will get the best recommendations for my ability to coordinate with a whole company" (Lang and Hall, 2019: 126–27).

This pioneering woman director of a Silent Film whose name ironically was associated with *Get Your Man* in 1927, despite her known lesbian status, would nonetheless retire in 1943 to relative obscurity. She did, however, host a radio program and lectured on films at UCLA as well as direct Pepsi Cola commercials featuring Joan Crawford. Her most prominent student was Francis Ford Coppola, who convinced

Paramount in 2018 to name a dressing room to honor Arzner. David Thomson (2010: 37), a film scholar, is ambivalent. He recently characterized her as " not a great filmmaker...(whose) pioneering should not inflate her reputation." Moot as that remains, Dorothy Arzner and her lifelong partner lived one mansion over from Mary Pickford and Douglas Fairbanks in Beverley Hills before moving to Palm Springs. And while Kay and Perry (1977: 23) would similarly conclude that her contributions to cinematic history were "more important than immortal art is today's art," she wrote that while Dorothy Arzner's career was "not in touch with the gods, but with the contemporary world," it should also be noted she remains famously as the inventor of the film director's main tool in trade: the viewfinder, a cardboard cutout attached to her megaphone, which she ingeniously devised.

Finally, we also note that *Manhattan Cocktail* was filmed by Harold Fishbeck and Paul Juno, who served as assistant director, while Doris Drought received credit as its editor.

B. *At Plymouth Rock*: A Thanksgiving Vaudeville Playlet

The Vaudeville component paired with *Manhattan Cocktail* during the Brooklyn Paramount's opening week also ran the same approximate length of time: an hour or more. This family-oriented type of live entertainment featured major and minor performers in so-called playlets and/or musical numbers that changed weekly until 1934, when reduced production costs occasioned by the Great Depression entirely killed those off. We learn that given the theatre's pre-Thanksgiving date, the opening playlet was built around the Puritans' landing at Plymouth Rock in 1619—as illustrated by the theatre's in-house photographer Lewis Nathan's photograph of those painted backdrops.

So, turning next from the first to the second face in the Brooklyn Paramount's earlier history, *On Plymouth Rock,* a musical overture played by our theatre's orchestra, followed a "Welcome to the Brooklyn Paramount Theatre" speech delivered by Brooklyn's Borough President James J. Byrne on that Saturday morning. It was filmed and rebroadcasted during the four additional shows that day, as well as throughout opening week, but it was also seen in fifteen hundred Paramount theatres throughout the nation and world. According to the version that appeared in that local tabloid two days prior, Byrne grandiloquently stated:

On November 24, 1928, the Brooklyn Paramount Theatre at Paramount Square, Flatbush and DeKalb Avenue, opens its doors to the public at noon. This will give Brooklyn an additional world leadership in a new field, through its consequent possession of the best theater in the world. This theater and its entertainment is of a stature that will bring visitors from all over the world to enjoy its beauty, and thus be an important economic factor in the progress of Brooklyn. I, therefore, as chief executive of the Borough of Brooklyn, do proclaim its worthy purpose and request all citizens to take due cognizance of the Brooklyn Paramount Theatre and to join in the general feeling of welcome to this fine new institution, and to the owners and operators, most of whom are Brooklyn citizens.

Then, after *At Plymouth Rock*, a musical suite presented by the Brooklyn Paramount Grand Orchestra under Josef Koestler written by Boris Morros, a controversial Russian émigré in charge of music for the film studio, which featured a vocal ensemble, "News of the World by Paramount," followed next. The filmed segment featured the arrival of Ottorino Respighi, the Italian composer whose best-known work remains *The Four Seasons*, seen disembarking from one of those luxurious transatlantic liners we used to see on West Side piers in Manhattan during that long mostly gone era of ocean travel, in town for the preview of his new opera, *La Campana Sommersa* ("The Sunken Bell"), an opera making its world debut at the block-long Roxy Theatre, a 5,290-seat truly cinematic-like palace built and named for a larger-than-life impresario, Samuel Rothapfel, at 153 Fiftieth Street between Sixth and Seventh Avenues in Manhattan, which sadly was closed in 1960 and demolished some years later (Melnick, 2012).

MARIA "GAMBY" GAMBARELLI (*The Brooklyn Daily Eagle*/December 31, 1933)

Next came "Gamby." Billed as "The World-Famous Maria Gambarelli," she was a danseuse-choreographer said to have come out of retirement for a starring role in *The Porcelain Clock* as fealty to Paul Ash, who led the Brooklyn Paramount stage band. The ballet was described as an "original dance fantasy" written by the protege of "Roxy," who not only appeared several times on stage with her "precision dancers" during our theatre's gala opening, but getting ahead of our story, Gamby's dressing room would be robbed during her opening appearance.

Another filmed segment followed. It featured the young effervescent, hand-clapping, banjo-eyed, manic-like future megastar of radio as well as TV, Eddie Cantor (née Isidore Itkowitz), who was born on Cherry Street on the Lower East Side, and famously—infamously today—frequently worked in blackface starting out. *That Certain Person* was the name of his filmed musical number; an early George Gershwin composition featuring Cantor was advertised as a "Paramount Singing and Talking Novelty Production."

A Trip Through the Mighty Organ followed next. It featured Henry Murtagh, advertised as a "world famous soloist" performing on the Brooklyn Paramount's "Mighty Wurlitzer," a so-called 4–26 "unit orchestra" that tragically put thousands of musicians out of work. But along with its wondrous sound, it was also employed for what Esther Morgan-Ellis (2018) characterized as "community sing-alongs." And the inaugural program's *Miracle of Magical Harmony* was without hyperbole the name of that number played on what was also called the "Brooklyn Paramount Grande-Organ." Then ending the first half was the "Inaugural Publix Revue," a skit simply titled *Stars.* It was written and staged by John Murray Anderson, a Canadian, whose show business résumé not only included original numbers for the Ziegfeld Follies on Broadway, but also for *The King of Jazz*, a Hollywood biopic about the bandleader Paul Whiteman, whose music is viewed today by critics as a deliberate attempt to "sweeten" the genre of syncopated music invented by African Americans, discussed as another face in our theatre's earlier history of Jazz. Anderson wrote additional Vaudeville skits. His opening skit was said to have featured "maidens in Greek nighties, whooshing with great squares of thin silk into billows over their heads." Whether deliberate or serendipitous, it clearly mimed the Prologue choreographed by Marion Morgan for her dance company as seen in *Manhattan Cocktail.*

The entire second half of the inaugural Vaudeville program reads like an homage to Paul Ash. He was a peripatetic German American émigré and classical pianist who began his show business career in San Francisco's barbary coast and achieved greater success in Chicago leading a small band in wonder theatres like the Oriental—that is, before being recruited further east to perform in both Paramount theatres in our respective boroughs. Morgan-Ellis (2018: 41) would discuss the redheaded Ash whose smiling face appears on the block-long Dekalb-painted mural greeting the audience as follows: "Listen, folks!" The inaccurately listed Vaudeville star called "The Genial Giant of Jazz" relocated from Manhattan's Paramount to ours with his so-called stage band of "Merry Pranksters."

Yet another revealing account of Ash's impactful role as bandleader/emcee is found in *Exhibitor's Herald and Moving Pictures World,* which wrote the following about him on December 1, 1928: "The policy of the new house...will be first-run photoplays with a stage show presided over by Paul Ash, the originator of this policy" (Whitmore, 1928). His silhouette "mounted on a platform high above the stage" that opened the second half of the inaugural Vaudeville program at the Brooklyn Paramount appeared in an elaborately choreographed skit titled *Ten Dancing Fingers.* Each created the illusion of control by strings of ten women in the Gamby-Hale dance troupe similarly wearing white tuxedos, while Maestro Ash (somehow) simultaneously managed to "swing the stick," i.e., waved his baton while also leading "his own Brooklyn Paramount Theatre Stage-Band."

The next musical offering was "I Must Have That Man." A Tin Pan Alley popular song composed by Jimmy McHugh, and with lyrics by Dorothy Fields, it was originally part of *Blackbirds of 1928,* an all-Black Broadway musical starring the legendary hoofer Bill "Bojangles"

Robinson, who would perform on stage here during our theatre's Vaudeville years twice during separate weeks. The Merry Pranksters were positioned on the stage facing theatre audiences, which was a direct contrast with the symphony orchestra, whose members worked with their backs turned to them while its leader faced the packed house while Ash, by contrast, periodically turned around to do the same.

Next up were Maureen and Sonny. Dubbed in the program as "stars from Broadway hits," and in the tabloids as "youngsters," they were acrobatic dancers described as capable of executing "furious turns," a familiar-enough standard Vaudeville act whose reception one reviewer described as "well-received."

The Russian-born violin virtuoso David Rubinoff made his Brooklyn Paramount debut. More frequently known by his surname, Rubinoff, he was hired like so many others largely on a reputation made on radio. *Under Grecian Stars* was the solo performed by that European-trained Western Classical virtuoso on nothing less than a Stradivarius. And similar to Ash, a crowd-pleasing entertainer known as "Dave" would lead the Brooklyn Paramount Orchestra in programs that mixed Tin Pan Alley favorites with Western Classical musical compositions by the likes of Chopin and other canonical figures. Moreover, this first of several musical offerings from Rubinoff was backed by those omnipresent Gamby-Hale Girls.

Lyndon and Farman followed next. Described as "for laughing purposes only," their "terpsichorean number" was also billed as a "popular Apache dance." Despite its title, it had nothing at all to do with those Native Americans imprisoned in Florida under Geronimo for twenty-three years as a prisoner of war for resisting encroachment of their land by Spanish and American conquistadors in the Southwest. Phil DeLoria (1998) wrote about similar cultural appropriations of this nation's First Citizens since Boston Massacre participants were "playing Indians." But the "apache dance"—written always in lowercase letters—was invented by a ballroom dancer and fellow Brooklynite, Maurice Mouvet, who depicted the world of rough-and-tumble Parisian pimps, hookers, and gangsters, not unlike those found in Kurt Weill's famous *Three Penny Opera*. Or, as Lewis Erenberg (1981: 165) described the "apache dance," it was a "passionate lower-class exhibitionist" number metaphorically suggesting the engagement of a male tiger and "loose women created in 1911 by Mouvet as an intensely brutal dance of realism, of primitive passion, as a picture of life in the raw...which nonetheless possesses 'beauty and warmth,' and also as "one of the first major acts in a New York cabaret." And which incidentally would be performed by Maurice Chevalier twice on film: in a segment of *Paramount on Parade*, a 1930 film directed by Ernest Lubitsch "utilizing every Paramount player of the time" (Baxter, 1968: 38–39), and also in the studio's film *Love Me Tonight* directed by Rouben Mamoulian, which was not screened here (Erenberg, 1981: 75). Finally, the *Exhibitor's Herald and Moving Picture World* reviewer wrote in the December 1 issue in 1928 that the "apace [*sic*] dance" staged at the Brooklyn Paramount's opening was "played for laughs." Lydon and Farman were also described in a local newspaper as "costumed ridiculously" during their "burlesque," and as the only "droll" number during that entire Vaudeville show.

Next up was George Dewey Washington. He was a largely forgotten African American crooner discovered by Paul Ash, singing in saloons on the docks of San Francisco during the 1920s, who then followed his mentor to Chicago and further east to Manhattan's Paramount before appearing on our theatre's stage. Washington was a movie star as well of *Cabin in the Sky*, an MGM all-Black cast film made in 1943, based on a successful Broadway show that costarred Ethel Waters, who also appeared here as did Bojangles during our theatre's Vaudeville/Jazz years. George Dewey Washington's opening number at the Brooklyn Paramount was described in a local tabloid as that of a "young colored man who puts his songs over with showmanship," and a "true blue [*sic*] crooner" as well. The Columbia recording artist was dubiously called in newsprint a "colored Pagliacci capable of smiling."

The next part of the second half of this inaugural program was a song titled "There's a Rainbow Around My Shoulder." Written and originally performed by Al Jolson, who never performed on our theatre's stage but was seen in several films screened here, the song performed by Paul Ash's stage band was described as a "new tune you'll (want to) whistle."

Eighth in that Vaudeville olio was another musical number, "Under Eastern Skies," which not only marked the third appearance on stage by the Gamby-Hale Dancers but also introduced an otherwise completely forgotten Vaudeville performer named Jerry Ryan, who sang "Tokio Blues." It was described as a "new song" written by a young tunesmith at the time, the legendary songwriter Irving Berlin...and that's "Tokio" not "Tokyo," as the capital of the rising imperialist power Japan was spelled in those years. A number whose clear allusion to Commander Perry's "opening" of the Land of the Rising Sun to Western trade in 1852 was further suggested by that Irish troubadour dressed like a United States naval officer surrounded by chorines appropriately costumed as well as "Japanese maidens"—the latter, a clear instance of what the Palestinian literary critic Edward Said (1978) meant by "Orientalism," i.e., the cultural appropriation of images from Asia for stereotypical representation.

A pair of "pole artists" then claimed the stage. Evans and Perez were acrobats, who in Vaudeville lingo were a "dumb" or silent act executing "risley work," i.e., the technical term for juggling human bodies in midair by individuals lying flat on their back. Inspired apparently by an Australian gymnast named John Risley, this form of live entertainment was popularized in the museum owned by another great showman, P. T. Barnum, on the Bowery around the time of the Civil War. A lengthy review in *Exhibitors Herald and Moving Picture World* (December 1, 1928) would describe Evans and Perez's acrobatic work as an "episode in poise," which thrilled Brooklyn Paramount audiences who were anxious to see one gymnast standing with his foot in the orchestra pit and the other firmly planted on stage in front of the theatre's sixty-foot-wide main curtain balancing the other acrobat jugging balls while balanced atop a fifteen-foot pole.

They were followed next by the noted American violin virtuoso, as

David Rubinoff was also frequently advertised. His second solo piece was titled "Dance of the Russian Peasant," a number which could only have brought tears to the eyes of new American citizens born in Eastern European countries in the audience familiar with that song, or as a result of habituation with others with similar minor-key signatures.

And for the finale...the entire Brooklyn Paramount ensemble gathered on stage to perform an old-time minstrel cakewalk. Minstrel shows, as readers of this book will probably know, reigned supreme as popular entertainment from post–Civil War years outdoors through the advent of electricity, which allowed nighttime entertainment like Vaudeville after the start of the twentieth century (Bogle, 2001; Erenberg, 1981). "And what a show it was!" A reviewer in the *Exhibitor's World* wrote about that cakewalk, which succeeded minstrel shows with the high-stepping cheerleaders marching to booming bass drummers during football rallies. It originated, as postmodern studies inform us, as subversive forms of entertainment allowed by plantation owners who allowed slaves to mock them on Sundays, their only days off from forced labor (Stearns and Stearns, 1968; Shaw, 1986).

Additional light on the inaugural program in the Brooklyn Paramount's earlier history, however, can also be gleaned from other sources.

Variety's publisher "Abel" on November 28, 1928, repeated mantras about "Your Paramount's easier to reach than New York!" while characterizing this opening Vaudeville program as "disappointing." Excepting, that is, for the short musical film featuring Eddie Cantor—in blackface—which Abel Green called the "hit of the evening." Or, in the lingo from those years, a "laugh wow." We also read that "A Trip Through the Organ" was "demonstrated" on both Wurlitzers by Henry Murtagh and George Johnson—the latter featured on a smaller accompanying pipe organ regrettably called the "slave console" that was dependent on the Mighty Wurlitzer employed by "Popular Concert" down the road every noon at 12:30 p.m. And Gamby was also singled out for praise—the dancer-choreographer further identified as "radio's (familiar) representative with the Brooklynites." Also writing that the hizzoner's "live remarks" were Byrne's twelfth motion picture theatre dedication in the past three years, the trade magazine's reviewer finally wrote that the new theatre's first publicist (Serkowich) plastered the neighborhood with advertisements to fuel anticipation of the Brooklyn Paramount's opening. The ads included these three promotional pieces he might well have also authored, and we continue to attempt to locate: "Brooklyn," a publication by the borough's chamber of commerce; a "Special Brooklyn Paramount" feature that appeared in the *Standard-Union*; and a twelve-page supplement found in the Monday edition of the *Evening Herald*.

Supplemental information from other local tabloids reported that Henry Murtagh and George Johnson also performed two additional organ pieces, "The Poet and Peasant Overture" from the 1846 operetta *Dichter un Bauer* by Austrian composer Franz von Suppe and John Philip Sousa's more familiar "Stars and Stripes Forever," to theatre patrons while an otherwise recondite (or neglected?) fact about that band known for military marching numbers being that Sousa also included Ragtime as part of its repertoire. It was written in syncopated music originally credited to Scott Joplin who, combined with the Blues, became the foundation of Jazz, the third face of the Brooklyn Paramount's earlier history in our theatre.

Yet another local newspaper review indicated that Murtaugh provided the musical accompaniment for the Paramount Singing Quartet: a rendition of "Swannee," the famous—or infamous—elegy about Dixie penned by George Gershwin associated with the amazing career of Al Jolson, who also performed wearing burnt cork and, like other white Vaudevillians, sang so-called "coon songs."

The gala opening contained this comic delight experienced by audiences, which resulted from the playful raising and lowering of both "twin lifts" required for both organs found at opposite ends of the orchestra by their organists. Additional information identifies three songs sung by George Dewey Washington, backed by Paul Ash's stage band: (1) "Memories of France," which a reviewer wrote contained a "dramatic recitation" that reportedly "tore the house down;" (2) "There's a Rainbow Around My Shoulder," the popular song identified with Jolson's early career; and (3) "Keep Smiling at Trouble," which was also said to have contained another "short recitation" colloquially analogized with boxing as a "knockout." And the African American crooner was also reported participating in the "minstrel cakewalk" that might have ended the first half of Vaudeville programs during that initial week, much as it did the grand finale, which reportedly caused the house to go wild.

We were also fortunate to get a typewritten manuscript with annotated comments about that inaugural program from our friend John Fontillas, the head of Hugh Hardy's famous H3 architecture firm. From it, we learned that the Paramount newsreel about Respighi's arrival in Manhattan lacked narration, and that a Krazy Kat cartoon was shown before Paul Ash's introduction. The latter's subject unfortunately remains unknown to us, but still we wonder if it dealt with Jazz, a subject close to the heart of the cartoon's creator, George Herriman. He was born in New Orleans, the birthplace of the third face of our theatre, and his previously hidden racial identity was revealed as "colored" (Tisserand, 2016).

And those original typewritten notes not only characterized the appearances of Henry Murtagh and George Johnson on twin Wurlitzer consoles as "the moment you have been waiting for"; they also reference the Wilfred color organ, an innovation among fifty others employed for lighting up "the alcoves along the balcony with colored changing lights in moving shapes and patterns," thereby animating the theatre's decorative plaster and terra cotta "smilax vines and shrubbery."

The annotated original manuscript also noted that Carmine Vitol was responsible for stage settings memorably photographed by Lewis Nathan, and that costumes for weekly changing Vaudeville shows were sewn by Dolly Tree. Special music for an unknown portion of the inaugural program was contributed by Cliff Hass. The name of ballerina Maria Gamberelli's "assistant" was George Hale. Don Baker, a master organist, was sent by the Wurlitzer showroom in Manhattan to witness the assembly of both pipe organs. He was also described as Henry Murtagh's musical assistant.

Still naming names, we'll identify the personnel of the Brooklyn Paramount Orchestra, which was initially led by Josef Koestner, and who was followed by other maestros. These musicians reportedly were hired after hundreds of hours of auditions by Boris Morros, who was listed as general music director and had been assisted by Paul Ash. It was described as the "most unique assembly of musicians that has ever gathered together in the history of the world" in the *Brooklyn Times Union* (November 18, 1928), which named and characterized most players.

1. Sammy Carr, an accordionist formerly with Paul Whiteman, played "the most difficult concertos and symphonies on his lowly Jazz-inspired instrument";
2. Mouse Beechcraft, a drummer formerly with bandleader Paul Specht's Capitol Gang, was described as able to "make 77 different noises at the same time" on the traps;
3. Seymour Ginzier, a trombonist with the reputed "longest arm reach" was said to have been hired away from Roger Wolfe Kahn's dance band;
4. Homer Green, another trombonist presumably had long enough arms to excel on that brass instrument and was otherwise affiliated with the Arnold Johnson Orchestra, which played dance music for diners during the *Paramount-Prolix Radio Hour* broadcast from the Hotel Paramount in mid-Manhattan;
5. Phil Napoleon, a well-known bona fide Jazz musician, was described as "New York's hottest and sweetest trumpet player from Brooklyn";
6. John Ventry, a trumpet player, was said to belong to "the famous Boston Ventry family";
7. Harold Pepper, was reputed to play "hot trumpet," i.e., Jazz;
8. Kulseppi De Pollio was yet another trumpet player; and these members of the reed section were capable of "doubling," as in

playing other instruments belonging to that family of European musical instruments:

A. Kenneth Moyer,

B. Oroch Kyri,

C. Paul Cartwright,

D. Ladd Bernhardt, and

E. Louis Chagmane, a bassist from France;

9. Tom Hansen played tuba, the brass instrument destined to be replaced by the double bass in early Jazz history;

10. Leeper Norflect was a cellist;

11. Boris Orlowitz was reputed to play a "hot fiddle"; and finally

12. Irving Brodsky was listed as playing piano in this first iteration of the Brooklyn Paramount Orchestra.

We also might highlight the names of the Brooklyn Paramount Theatre projection staff from 1931: Morris Heller, Nat Hewitt, William Paster, George Van Deurs, John Hurley, John Timmerman, William Garbade, Charles Lipman, and I. Sherman. Their successors would figure in labor–management disputes.

Finally, returning again to music, another important name cannot be ignored: Ruth Smith Bingaham (1991), an Ohio native and musical prodigy reportedly able to perform Beethoven's C Major Concerto at the age of ten, who with "helicopter" parents moved to the Big Apple so their talented daughter could study with noted teachers, and made demos for the Weite-Mignon Record Company. However, she met Boris Morros, and he hired Ruth Bingaham as a cocktail-type pianist in the Grand Lobby during our theatre's gala opening.

Boris Miklanowich Morros (1959) was born in St. Petersburg before the Russian Revolution and wrote in his autobiography about having studied with the famous Russian composer Rimski-Korsakov, as well as having taught no less another major figure in Western Classical than the renowned cellist Gregor Piatereseky. He told about leaving his family behind in 1922 after what John Reed memorably described as "ten days that shook the world" to go on tour with the *Chauvre*

Souris (the Bat), a dance company led by Nikita Balieff, named for a Parisian cabaret that formed in Leningrad in 1906, and whose *Parade of the Wooden Soldiers* not only was performed on stage here during the second week of March 1930 but today remains part of Radio City Music Hall's annual Christmas extravaganza.

Morros's subsequent controversial life as a double agent eleven years later in 1947 included recruitment by the FBI for his help exposing a Russian spy cell in the United States. We note a film about him starring Ernest Borgnine, *Man on a String*, that never played here but was discussed in an article about the spy in *Look* magazine, February 26, 1957, and *The New Yorker* on October 19, 1957, as well as in his autobiography. Notwithstanding his additional claims of having discovered Ginger Rogers during his stint as the music director of the Brooklyn Paramount, Morros rigorously auditioned the professor of music at the University of Texas and forced Ruth Bingaham to play what a local tabloid characterized as a mixture of Western Classical and Pop songs, ultimately intended to aid theatre patrons to "glide softly and soothingly…in and out of the theater…(thereby reportedly) furnishing the sympathetic obbligato to their thoughts as they wander about the palatial lobby (while) exploring the art treasures which have been gathered from every corner of the world."

Restated, the young pianist played everything from the pittance profusions of the old masters to the last squawks of Tin Pan Alley during that rigorous audition—a musical hodgepodge she recalled years later not only included Irving Berlin's "All Alone and Fiddle-Up, Fiddle-Up on Your Violin," but also fragments from memory of 167 canonical pieces of Western Classical music, including Chopin's: Waltz in A Minor"; Tchaikovsky's "Patheque Symphony"; a Bach fugue; Scarlatti chorale; sections from Handel's "Messiah"; and a passage from Beethoven's "Fifth Symphony." Indeed, she was also asked to play the popular novelty song in those years, "Yes, We Have No Bananas," which was written in 1923 and that Brooklyn Paramount audiences would have been more familiar with from frequent radio play. The latter, whose contribution to making new Americans from

European immigrants in those years, as discussed by the critic Gilbert Searles, was as follows:

> One hears it on the stage, in the drawing room, in the kitchen, everywhere...the musical rage of this moment...a tribute to the optimism of the newly arrived immigrant; to his earnest fight to master the language of his temporary country. (Seldes, 2001: 368)

Finally, whether or not Ruth Bingham was seated at the grand piano on stage in Lewis Nathan's photograph of "Lady Paramount," which we have adopted as our muse, let the last word about the gala opening of our theatre be given to the controversial Boris Morros, Paramount-Prolix's musical director and composer of film scores, who wrote about his recruited hire's role in our theatre's earlier history, much as would Paramount's founder, Adolph Zukor (1953), hope to accomplish through the studio's films and Vaudeville entertainment: "to satisfy the musical yearnings of every patron, from the simple, pounding rhythm of the dock hand to the intricate, symphonic tone poems of the music lover."

CHAPTER 3

A Wonder Theatre Like No Other?
"Mama, Does God Live Here?"

The Brooklyn Paramount reportedly contained fifty-one innovations. Before examining that claim, these additional words about the theatre's gala opening deserve attention.

So, for example, we additionally read that "extra cops" not surprisingly were hired for crowd control as "thousands and thousands" were lined up between Myrtle Avenue two blocks west "all the way to Fulton Street from DeKalb "hoping to gain admission. Asked by a local reporter if he recalled the first patron, John McCurdy, who was the theatre's first manager probably tongue-in-cheek alluded to a "tall, dark, and handsome man." Fortunately, however, when pressed for additional information, "Mac" recalled customers who purchased orchestra seats—for 25 cents—able to "drink water from [one of four] marble fountains with elegant cut-glass nozzles" built into opposite side walls of the theatre's orchestra as well as an incident involving a woman in the lower balcony who reportedly was so overwhelmed by the "gold and marble grand lobby" that she had to receive first aid after fainting!

And so, too, did a reporter from *Movie World* privileged to be on hand that afternoon relate that at 12:30 p.m. on that historic Saturday morning, i.e., thirty minutes later than everyone was supposed to have taken their seats for the start of the first complete show, "suddenly in the midst of the final rush to put in [*sic*] the lights a Wurlitzer mechanic [mistakenly] stepped out onto the big time." That is, he'd reportedly stepped out from behind the curtains onto the stage when Henry Murtagh struck up the opening notes of what this unnamed journalist identified as Gershwin's "minstrel song," *Swanee*, before fleeing!

Every account of the theatre's gala opening bespeaks the Brooklyn Paramount's glamour and glitz. So, for example, Sam Katz, the president of Paramount-Prolix, which under Adolph Zukor's leadership expanded from Manhattan into the King's Borough as well as built other cinematic palaces herein the 1920s (see Fifteen), immodestly released the following statement in the local tabloids on October 4 1928, nearly two months ahead of our theatre's opening date:

It will not be merely another fine theater, but will represent the climax of all our experience in building and operating nearly three hundred of the world's finest theaters. [For] the Brooklyn Paramount has everything in it for the luxury and convenience of theater-goers that any other modern theater has, plus the added advantage of the newest of additional months experimentation based on newly discovered scientific building principles and decorative beauties.

Yet Rian James, who contributed a daily column to the *Brooklyn Daily Eagle* on February 4 1928, titled a piece "Reverting to Type," also intended to alert his readers they should expect something different from the other wonder theatres in downtown Brooklyn: "According to the intelligentsia it isn't art," he initially cautioned. And yes, it would be "brash, garish and gold" as well as a "showoff of super structures" and "nostrum of the nouveau rich"; and, yes, the Brooklyn Paramount would be "glaring and glittering" and a "show-off," but "without the depth of and feeling of genuinely 'arty' architecturals (*sic*)."

Still closer to its opening date, Martin Dickstein in his "Slow Motion" newspaper column on November 4, 1928, also alerted readers about what to uniquely expect:

Already we have been informed that this will be the acme of all that is beautiful and modern in motion picture construction and decoration. Its stage presentations, the management promises, will be the finest obtainable on the five continents.

Indeed, four years after its closing, an anonymous source described the place:

Romance is not all dead in Brooklyn. Spires of steel and stone rise over night; subways scuttle on their speedy ways; radio loud-speakers bark at you from diverse doorways, Western Union and Postal Telegraph youths have new uniforms, brighter bicycles and cleaner ears; the Squibb Building, in the gloom of night, has, of a verity, gone Joseph Urban, and you can see the sign—now red, now white—of the Brooklyn Paramount Building from the Manhattan side of the Brooklyn Bridge.

All the same, David Naylor (1981: 134) would reiterate Zukor's claim by characterizing its sister theatre in Manhattan, which opened in 1926, as "undoubtedly the richest theater." And while every source (cf. Ben Hall, 1961) raved about the latter as the *paramount* Paramount, the superlative inarguably belongs to the Roxy, which like Manhattan's Paramount was also built in 1926 and before being razed in 1960 occupied an entire block formerly close by.

Notwithstanding Zukor's partiality for Manhattan's Paramount, which he insisted be demarcated from the other theatres with a dash. It should also be noted that among the twelve-to-fifteen hundred other theatres built or leased by that titan's film company initially for exclusive showing of the studio's produced products, these were among those bearing its brand name: the **Paramount** (or Stapleton) in Staten Island, New York; Newark **Paramount**, New Jersey; the **Paramount** in Abilene, Kansas; Fort Wayne **Paramount** in Indiana; Denver **Paramount** in Colorado; Toledo **Paramount** in Ohio; Portland and Seattle **Paramount**(s) in Oregon; and El Capitan **Paramount** in what subsequently replaced the northeast as the emerging film capital of the world, Hollywood, California. But also abroad do we find the

London **Paramount** (a. k. a. London Plaza), built in association with a production studio in Islington, England, in 1924. The Paramount brand name, in any event, was challenged by Warner Brothers, who owned a reported 850 Strand movie theatres in the 1930s out of some 18,000 escapist film venues in this nation.

Alas, the flagship Manhattan-**Paramount** became the Hard Rock café, and Detroit's **Paramount** was turned into a garage. On the other hand, Oakland's **Paramount**, like ours, not only was spared the wrecker's ball but was turned into a viable performance space. And while a full account of the other so-called "vaud-movie houses" in our borough during the 1920s lies beyond the purview of this study, an article titled "Fall and Decline of Thespis in Dodgerland" in *Variety* (January 4, 1956) written by Jo Ranson lists these fourteen Silent Film venues in Brooklyn, which of course once boasted the former home of one of every six American citizens: the Academy of Music, Amphion, Pantheon, Bijou, Columbia, Grand Opera House, Folly, Park & Star, Hyman & Damon House, Montauk, Orpheum, Brooklyn Music Hall, Payton's Lee Avenue, and Payton's Fulton Street (also see Del Valle, 2010).

Of greater relevance to this study are those aptly named "wonder theatres" a. k. a. "cinematic cathedrals" a. k. a. "deluxers," and which more specifically the Brits called "transpontine," alluding to the Brooklyn Paramount's location on the other side of the East River from Times Square in Manhattan back in the day when developers promulgated this competitive seeming mantra, "Keep Brooklynites in Brooklyn." In chronological construction date order, those four are or were:

The Loew's Metropolitan, with its seating capacity of 3,160, built in 1914 on A. D. Matthews & Sons' converted department store on Fulton Street, which showed film through the 1960s, today serves as the Brooklyn Tabernacle Church; the Mark Strand, built four years later in 1918, originally boasting 2,940 seats; the E. A. Albee, built in 1925 (3,246 seats) on the site of the demolished Cowperthwaite Furniture Store closest to the Brooklyn Paramount across Flatbush Avenue

Extension, demolished in 1978; and finally the (Howard) Fox, which originally had 4,044 seats and opened several months ahead of ours on August 21, 1928, and which was demolished in 1971. All of those, like others through the nation, are examples of what Naylor (1981) characterized as "architectures of fantasy that seemingly exploded with the advent of the Silent Film industry throughout the nation since the First World War."

Returning to those purported fifty-one innovations that marked the Brooklyn Paramount as unique when work began on the theatre and its adjoining eleven-story office building on July 28, 1927, a Thursday. It was designed by the Chicago architectural firm of Rapp & Rapp, whom Naylor (ibid: 98) not only called "house architects" of Paramount, but also characterized as "the purists among palace architects," a "special type of soft cement" was poured into its foundation that purportedly functioned as an inlaid tuning fork, which "enhanced" the performances of singers and musicians. Ken Wlosek, whose architectural firm of Leed Green Associates redesigned for Live Nation what originally was inspired by the Boboli Gardens in Florence, Italy, as well as by the Sun King Louis XIV's Versailles Palace and doubtless also by the Paris Opera House, told this author in 2024 that that unique design feature might be likened to poured slabs positioned vertically that in effect "hummed."

And so, too, was visual acuity universally applauded as an innovation in what *Variety* (July 21, 1926) not surprisingly charactered in the Brooklyn Paramount Theatre as a "composite." It was inspired by the Austrian-born movie theatre designer John Eberson's notion of an "atmosphere theatre," which Hall (1961: 136) evocatively described as attempting to create the illusion of sitting in an Italian outdoors garden through special lighting and clouds painted on a blue-domed ceiling. It therefore contrasted with another original major movie theatre designer, the Scottish-born Thomas W. Lamb, whose "staid Adam's elegance to Arabian Nights phantasmagoria" differed with Eberson's reach for "breathtaking meteorological effects" translated on the ground by Rapp & Rapp's reported "eye-bulging opulence" by the absence of columns that might otherwise have impaired the sight lines of our theatre's 1,983 patrons seated eight stories above ground in its cavernous balcony with "acres of seats," and 411 in the cantilevered lower balcony or mezzanine and 1,730 patrons in the orchestra. Which of course adds up to 4,144, excluding some dozen few seated in side boxes in this seat count among others variously given.

Then we read in the *Standard Union* (November 24, 1928) that "double sets of steel girders, with secure, powerful overhead suspension trestles, were [additionally] necessary to ensure absolute safety." And that that innovation with the "absence of pillars and posts to support balconies and ceilings" that proffered "perfect unobscured sightlines within that acre of seats" translated into so-called "democratic airs" that were part and parcel of the new theatre in which so-called "high hats"—public figures—who reserved assigned seating in the mezzanine on opening day similarly as well were able to enjoy unrestricted "speech platforms" from the stage.

Still speaking acoustics, while Rudy Vallée required a megaphone to amplify his self-described "limited crooning ability," Ethel Merman's chops, by contrast, were not surprisingly heard rising sotto voce above the heads of those in the very top row of the balcony. That is, until management finally overcame its resistance to interfere with sight lines caused by freestanding microphones in 1932, when Paul Whiteman's vocalist Peggy Healy reportedly complained to the so-called "King of Jazz" about not being heard after her appearance in a Vaudeville skit during the week of December 2, 1932, with the result being the influential bandleader convinced Brooklyn Paramount's management to install tiny microphones hidden along the front of the proscenium.

Variety (November 14, 1928), in any event, additionally previewed what it identified as two other "exclusive novelty devices": the Clavilux, which it described as "rhythms in color," a device capable of projecting through colored lights "Jazz or symphonic effects"; and the theatre's "unique lighting system."

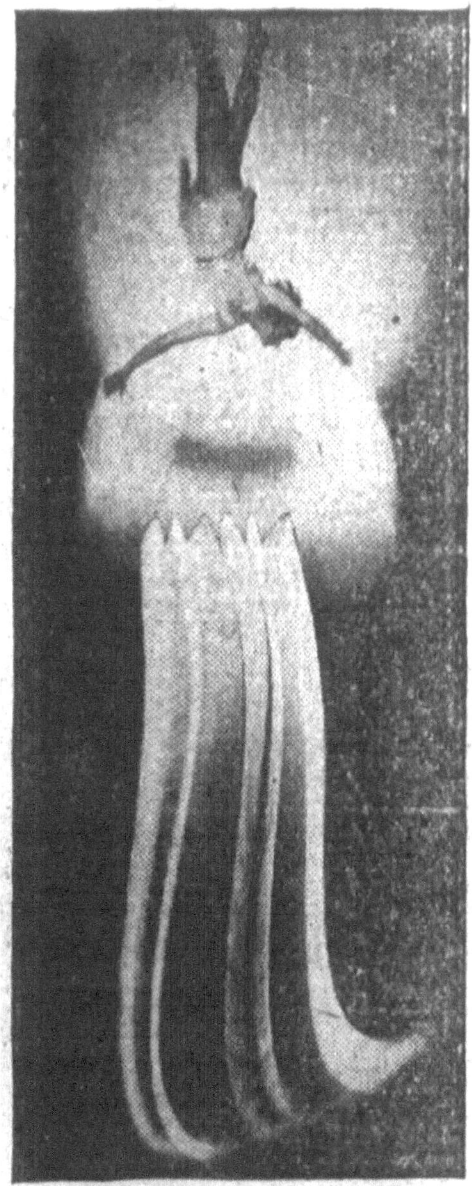

THREE D-CLAVILUX IMAGE (*The Standard Union*/November 24, 1928)

Thomas Winfred, a Danish classical pianist dubbed today "the Father of Psychedelics," invented the "color organ," which allowed a projectionist, through the use of colored lenses and light, to "build stage settings," that is, 3D-like imagery projected into alcoves that could be recorded and replayed like piano rolls, thus augmenting painted sets for weekly changing Vaudeville shows. Only one of three of those misleadingly called "color organs" that Frank Cambria purchased for the Brooklyn Paramount was, in fact, built. Winfred (1966: 467), whose esthetics, in fact, preached silence as well as color imagery over sound, marking him light-years (pun unintended) ahead of John Cage's famous composition titled *4'-33* An article in *Motion Picture News* (December 1, 1928) further described the working of the Clavilux, which was also called the Luminaire, in terms of its inventor's instructions to technicians trained to work that unique innovation by improvising beams of light "from the lowest red to the deepest violet" while creating 3D-like images from soundless keyboards.

As for the Brooklyn Paramount's unique lighting system, while *Variety* failed to report the use of two hundred and forty-eight dimmers manufactured by the Ward Leonard Company in Mount Vernon, New York, Whit Whitlock, a journalist, noted in *Moving Picture World* on December 22, 1928, that our theatre's first manager not only told him those were "the largest number" in use in any theatre "in the world," but that they also required 100,000 kilowatt hours of "juice" during peak hours. And as if illustrating that point, J. L. McCurdy, finally, related the sad story of a stray or in-house feline, which unfortunately leaped onto an exposed live circuit board and was immediately fried. A cat very nearly literally on a hot (tin) roof, that is, if you can forgive this allusion to the Tennessee Williams film starring Elizabeth Taylor, which never played the Brooklyn Paramount.

Back again to the theatre's unique lighting, mention must also be made of its iconic backlit "royal sunburst glow" atop the arched proscenium preserved by Live Nation and used in advertisements for the place as well as the front cover of this book. But there also were (René) Lalique's French Nouveau Art stanchions that additionally contributed to the Brooklyn Paramount's "burnt orange" effect in the auditorium, thus contrasting with more-familiar crimson reds found in other movie houses. Credited to Paramount's chief designer Arthur Frederick Adams, readers interested in our theatre's unique lighting are invited to consult a technical piece cowritten by Cambia & Flage (1929).

And while "Mac"—McCurdy—also maintained for Whitlock that the Brooklyn Paramount's rococo-baroque imitative "composite" design had "very little decoration," the journalist nonetheless quoted him saying this:

The walls have been treated in gold and silver and vari-colored lights are thrown upon the surfaces. **The theatre is decorated with light rather than paint.** We can change the decorations at will by simply changing the lights which play on the surfaces (boldness supplied).

Returning to the notion of an "atmospheric theatre," Rapp & Rapp reportedly added double sets of steel girders to enhance Ebersoll's intention of creating movie houses with the effect of being outdoors at night within the closed confines of an otherwise darkened daytime place around the clock. For along with the orchestra's domed ceiling, the effect of its seemingly painted clouds and twinkling stars was achieved by the Brenograph, which Naylor (1981: 68) describes as a "magic lantern machine" aimed at yet another innovation, a solid heavy steel lattice suspended ten feet below and held by wires—a device also covering those cumulus- and nimbus-like clouds and tiny lights reported in the tabloids as a crowd-pleaser, which were achieved by drawing a strip of negatives projected in front of a 1,500-watt bulb, which suggests those referenced in the lyrics of "American Pie," the ode to three Rock legends sung by Don McLean.

Along with the experience Naylor (1981: 135) described as the original delight of "theatre-goers in the big city [who] need foliage, water displays, etc., to counteract urban congestion"—achieved by plaster potted plants, trees, vines, and birds built into opposite auditorium walls, there were plaster gargoyles and caryatid figures. Among those, we note the angelic representation of Cupid shooting an arrow toward the butt of Psyche in a sculpture that once stood at the head of the stairs between the mezzanine and orchestra.

Yet another innovation was what we learned from Peter Tymus, Long Island University's belated vice president of construction projects and passionate devotee of all things Brooklyn Paramount: a pool of underground water originally installed beneath the theatre's foundation he rhapsodized as having "anticipated the Green Revolution." As discussed in *Motion Picture News* in an October–December 1928 issue, the Brooklyn Paramount was described as having uniquely opened with "manufactured weather...installed by the Carrier System for Air Conditioning." For, indeed, McCurdy also told the aforementioned investigative reporter during their early walking tour de force of the theatre:

Here is a[nother] novel feature for you. In our ventilating system, instead of forcing the fresh air into the theatre for the auditorium floor, we carry it to the top of the theatre and force it down and draw it out from the floor of the theatre (ibid).

Or, as he added: "Some 200,000 cubic feet of air a minute to supply our patrons with the right kind of air." A unique natural cooling system in advance of AC installed in the 1940s and which was discussed in another early review of the place, the *Brooklyn Eagle* on April 13, 1930:

And at that beautiful palace of amusement those Brooklynites who seek comfort with their entertainment will find the climax of their desires. The most complete system for making weather is sheltered in the Brooklyn Paramount. The air is refrigerated, washed and cooled before and will greatly add to the comfort of the audience during the sultry summer days.

By the same token, Keith Wlosek in March 2024 also told this author during an interview following what Live Nation calls the "second chapter" in our theatre's glorious past about another original innovation: temperature-controlling electricity devices installed in the orchestra seats that brought heat in winter as well as cool air in summer.

We reserve for the Epilogue a discussion of paintings valued in 1928 at three million dollars by the *New York Times* on June 9 one year later, which in effect comprised an art museum along with relict European furniture, and a marble statuette valued at $2,500, which our theatre's first manager commented was "more than I make in a year" (ibid). Before turning to outdoor structural features originally adorning the Brooklyn Paramount, general knowledge about this wonder theatre built during the Silent Film–Talkies transitional years deserves a summarization.

So, for example, there was the Brooklyn Paramount's 147-foot-long by ten-foot-wide Grand Foyer, whose Italian Carrera marble floor was also found in the somewhat smaller and narrower adjacent Great Hall (or inner lobby) with its twenty-foot-tall decorated, vaulted ceiling side located directly behind the last row of seats in the orchestra and which provided a passageway between the box office, uniquely built into the theatre on the corner of Flatbush Avenue Extension and DeKalb Avenue, and its rear entrance near an elevator that transported patrons between lounges in the basement and the mezzanine and/or balcony. And that "Grand Lobby," a. k. a. "Great Hall," adjoining the so-called "Great" or "Grand Foyer" by contrast primarily served as a holding pen, as it were, for customers with orchestra tickets forced to line up prior to admission to the next complete show between upholstered cords attached to stanchions whose metal pucks remain set in its marble floor...parallel lines that wound back and forth as Disneyland-goers will surely appreciate, an area which also served as a hangout for smokers during intermissions while being entertained by the cocktail-type piano music discussed in the previous chapter as well as additional extracurricular musical events discussed in Chapter 11. But also for the record, Hall notes that this structural feature was twice the width of the Great or Grand Foyer and decorated with floor-to-ceiling fluted marble columns, grilled arches on one wall that faced seven thirty-foot mirrors on the opposite side, and a pair of ginormous bronze chandeliers suspended from its forty-two-foot ceiling.

BROOKLYN PARAMOUNT STAIRCASE (Stuart Fishelson Archives)

Frank Cambria outfitted the Florentine and Granada basement lounges, whose furniture were displayed according to those distinct national origins and was accessible through semicircular staircases at both ends of the theatre, among those including two antique Florentine Cardinal chairs and an ivory-lined cabinet also apparently purchased from a castle in Florence, Italy.

And that really grand semicircular marble staircase found at the northern end of the Grand Hall contained red leaf carpeted steps leading up and down to the mezzanine level, which for this author prefigured the actress Loretta Young's opening shot on her weekly dramatic TV show in the 1950s—with or without carpeting like our theatre, the thickness of which reportedly allowed cigarettes to be put out without leaving burn traces when that vice was still permitted in movie theatres and other public places.

Gender-based restrooms were also found in the basement lounges, but so, too, does Hall note what only must have been a spectacular Ladies' Lounge on the Mezzanine level. It was located behind an apron overlooking the Great Lobby, which for unknown reason was called the "Vauxhall Hall" as well as the "Music Room"; the latter, insofar as a cocktail pianist was probably hired for auxiliary entertainment during intermissions. The Ladies' Lounge, incidentally, would be renamed the Jonas Boardroom for LIU's founder referenced in Chapter 14. While back in the day, the mezzanine-level Ladies' Lounge boasted comfortable chairs and was decorated with a lavish marble fireplace with inlaid tile peacocks evident in this author's familiarity with what became a meeting place, as well as a disappeared painting like other artworks and clearly magnificent furniture since 1950, when my alma mater took possession of what indigenous people in the nation would doubtless call a sacred place. Then too, there were Greco-Roman-like plaster nudes still found inside gated alcoves, albeit headless, this author's half-century familiarity with what became the Avena Lounge, as well as peacocks stenciled on art deco mirrors still evident.

Finally, the Brooklyn Paramount's stage, according to Hall, used to boast a sixty-foot blue crimson satin (or velvet) curtain also decorated with embroidered images of peacocks, as well as several subsidiary curtains found in other theatres that featured Vaudeville.

Outdoors, two twenty-foot-tall signs spelling PARAMOUNT and THEATRE were stacked four stories high and caddy-corner to each other atop scaffolding on the roof of the movie theatre's adjoining eleven-story office building. Indeed, their very positioning atop what was among the borough's earliest skyscraper was reportedly deliberately angled as such so that Manhattanites in the southern end of that rivalrous borough would be reminded of the Brooklyn Paramount's presence.

Additional signage, however, found in other wonder theatres in those years, include the separate pair of letterings spelling out our theatre's birthname as it were, P-A-R-A-M-O-U-N-T that ran vertically from the roof along both cornered sides of the building down toward our theatre's famous original wraparound marquis referenced below, and which, apropos to this author's reliance on Native American teachings in this book, seemed to end with projectile-like points at the end of seeming fletched arrows that additionally called attention to current attractions.

Still talking signage, nothing comparable seemingly existed in the world like Brooklyn Paramount's "Talking Sign." One hundred thirty feet (or 180 feet) long by twenty feet (or twenty-three feet) tall, this "world's first" dubbed advertisement of place was purchased by Paramount Pictures from the Metro Outdoor Advertising Company and intended to remind recreation seekers in this borough's iconic Coney Island beachside and summer recreational area about coming attractions eight miles north to the theatre. Placed atop the roof of a single-story building near what was Dreamland, which of course tragically burned in 1911, circus-like barkers were employed to climb up there twice a day between 3:00 and 5:00 p.m. and between 9:00 and 11:00 p.m. and announce the names of Paramount studio films and accompanying Vaudeville acts that changed weekly on our theatre's stage. And that signage, which read BROOKLYN PARAMOUNT, reached seventy-five feet into the sky and reportedly could also be seen by ships in the Atlantic Ocean a mile or so away.

The "Talking Sign," furthermore, cost $45,000 to build, and according to *Variety* (June 4, 1930) was dedicated in a ceremony on a Monday two days prior. "Ain't Science Wonderful?" was in fact the heading of a newspaper account in the local tabloid on June 5, 1930, which told about a flag-decked reviewing stand containing these public figures: Henry Hesterberg, the borough's newly elected mayor; Postmaster Albert Firmin; our theater's new—second—manager, Bob Weitman (whose name was misspelled as "Whiteman"); Dr. Phillip Nash, said to represent Coney Island; and, finally Marcus Bergman, the Brooklyn Paramount's new publicist, who was reported having introduced musicians from the theatre that included Bob Shafalow, "the singing usher," as well as the so-called "strolling accordionist," Frank Judnick, a player in Paul Ash's band who not only followed that maestro east from the McIver Theatre in Chicago, but who would also entertain our theatre's patrons in the Grand Lobby awaiting admission as previously discussed.

And what should go without saying is the fact that a movie house the size of the Brooklyn Paramount and that offered five shows of seemingly continuous entertainment daily depended on a large help staff. Not surprisingly, then, one hundred ushers who were said to have been recruited from Columbia and New York University got trained how to escort theatre patrons to their orchestral seats. Indeed, they reportedly "came to attention" when McCurdy unannounced "walked into their dressing room," according to Whitlock. Another journalist, John McElhenny, called those caped and uniformed employees "Zukor's Zouves" in his "Look Out Below" newspaper column on December 3, 1928. And along with reports that they earned $20/week, he mocked what we'd today called their "professionalism," i.e., their accused "unfriendliness" discussed as refusing to accept bribes for better seats.

But so, too, did another *Brooklyn Eagle* beat writer portray those ushers as a "combination of Gene Tunney, Grover Whalen, and General Pershing," and "less than a West Pointer and more like the hunchback of Notre Dame"—his similar objection to their reported stiff and formal manner by which they escorted folks to their seat, which led that journalist also to bristle and be confounded whether or not to return their military-like salutes with bowed genuflection. Hall (1961: 162–169) in fact wrote that Brooklyn Paramount ushers also formed sports teams that competed against other theatres without indicating their martial-like training followed the former United States Marine Roxie's institutionalization of the same in his assorted movie theatre (Chapter 10).

By contrast, however, the *Exhibitors Herald & Moving Picture World* (October–December, 1928) proffered this view of ushers. For along with praising the "us folks/taking the Ritz Out of the Ritz" of the new theatre, its anonymous reporter wrote about the intimate-like "relation of ushers to the public," and how their dealings were not only "less formal and more natural" but contributed to the "relaxation of the service system," i.e., meaning they reportedly took the time to step out of character and answer questions, and "not by script" either. Indeed, reflecting the Jacksonian-like "common man" mantra frequently found in accounts of the Brooklyn Paramount, he also gushed with purple prose about the theatre's ushers with an Apache-like story regarding "wisdom attached to place":

Down with tall millinery in movie theatre! The democratic movies, long gone high hat, what with ramrod-spinal columns, will be democratic again—this time to stay at least in the Brooklyn Paramount.

In any event, returning to the indispensable task of cleaning up after shows, since the theatre employed twenty-four porters and three matrons in the late 1940s, it doesn't seem far-fetched to at least double those numbers when 20,000 tickets were sold daily, filling the ginormous theatre during five complete showings of films and Vaudeville show during those initial two decades since its opening. All the same, we read these numbers in 1948 with regard to material required for cleaning up nightly after each final film shown daily: six dozen radiator brushers, one hundred pounds of detergent, four gallons of furniture polish, six hundred pounds of wash rags, twenty-four feather dusters, twelve "deck brushes," one dozen corn brooms, twenty gallons of bleach, two dozen chamois clothes and twenty-four mops, as well as two hundred gallons of a "special soap" used in the bathrooms. Cleaning supplies were repurchased quarterly.

We also read therein about men presumably hired to work powerful vacuums whose one-hundred-foot-long hoses "sucked out two barrels of grime" while cleaning seventeen thousand feet of carpeting. Other tasks included brushing Heywood-Wakefield manufactured seats containing the letter "P" for Paramount monogrammed on their burgundy-colored backs, buffing those Carrera marble floors in the lobby and foyer, polishing Lalique fixtures, and cleaning those enormous mirrors and chandeliers in the Grand Lobby. At the same time, help staff women presumably attended to the bathrooms and polished furniture and dusted paintings—the latter, as we, for example, read in the caption of a photo about an African American woman cleaning our theatre's valuable art collection had been removed from storage along with the Mighty Wurlitzer in 1946 following the Depression.

But so, too, must these additional quintessential tasks be noted: First, the need for workmen to ascend the mechanical Hi-Lift that enabled them to clean fluted marble columns in the theatre's foyer and main assembly area; second, climbing ladders to take down the sixty-foot stage curtain and others semiannually, so they could be sent out for fall and spring cleaning; and third, inarguably the most dangerous assignment of all, the need for some few brave men in the theatre assigned the arduous task of negotiating catwalks more than one hundred feet above the orchestra in order to change those burnt-out tiny light bulbs installed as for celestial special effects in our "atmospheric theatre."

Now, before posing a variation of that derived anti-intellectual question with regard to how many professors it takes to change a single light bulb, which in the case of the Brooklyn Paramount meant teams responsible for tackling that seeming "endless wraparound marquis," the painted portrait of Paul Ash nearly fully occupied the block-long mural on the brick wall outside the theatre on DeKalb Avenue, and might well also comprise another of those fifty-one purported innovations. A palimpsest today, the naturalized German American's beaming smile and red head found in newspaper ads for hair products, were displayed under the lettering BROOKLYN PARA-MOUNT and one or the other studio motto: THE BEST IN DELUXE SHOWS and/or, IF IT'S A PARAMOUNT PICTURE, IT'S THE BEST SHOW IN TOWN!

Returning, however, to that provocative riddle emblematic of the sort of anti-intellectualism in America famously discussed by Richard Hofstadter (1963), before addressing the "endless wraparound degree" and matter of numbers regarding workmen required to "relamp" it, as changing light bulbs was called nearly a century ago, "Hesterberg's Talking Sign," so-called, reportedly contained 17,500 incandescent light bulbs. Regardless how many men doubtless were responsible for that task, we can at least report that two Brooklyn Paramount staff members from the electrical department replaced those burnt out from twenty thousand light bulbs on the marquee as well as the decorative arch above the box office also advertising current shows.

Finally, there were at least another four innovations associated with the Brooklyn Paramount: First, the Mighty 4–26 "unit orches-tra" and smaller unfortunately named "slave console" with their two thousand pipes discussed in Hall (1961: 179–196) and Chapter 9 of this book.

Second, transportation. And not only free parking initially for theatre patrons in the Paramount Garage recently torn down on DeKalb for yet another high-rise in the seemingly unaffordable apartments in what LIU purchased in the 1970s that originally was a garment factory, but arrangements made with the Dixie Company to run buses to and from West 43rd Street in Manhattan for its denizens wishing to attend shows in the theatre constructed in association with subway lines that promised in situ entrances.

Third, this aspect of the so-called "It girl," Brooklyn's fabled controversial actress Clara Bow, about whom we read the following in *Variety* as part of the hype celebrating the fourth anniversary of the Brooklyn Paramount's opening as "family-oriented as any neighborhood anywhere": the trade magazine's additional view that ours was "the only theater in the world in which the petite star, Clara Bow, whose aversion to personal appearances is nationally known, appeared on the stage for a personal appearance engagement."

And fourth, a device for hearing-impaired theatre patrons discussed in Chapter 13.

Finally, unlike the studio's in-house architect George Rapp's frequently quoted view that Paramount theatres not only "offered escape to working-class new-Americans…into a world of starlit gardens or double damask dignity or temples of Vishnu," where "their stock in trade was a grandeur that spelled m*o*n*e*y to the dazzled two-bit ticket holder" what we find in Ben Hall (1961: 123): a reproduction of a *New Yorker* cartoon by Helen Hodkinson from 1929, which depicts what could only have been that same sense of awe a young schoolgirl expressed to her mother upon seeing the Roxy, which Brooklyn Paramount theatre audiences might well have also asked: "Mama-Does God Live Here?"

CHAPTER 4

Famous Players–Lasky: The Back Story of Paramount Pictures

Adolph Zukor not only founded what became Paramount Pictures in 1913 but remarkably remained in control for more than a half century. Tendered a Golden Anniversary testimonial dinner at the Waldorf-Astoria in 1953, this remarkable entrepreneur, who lived to be 103, was the subject of an in-house documentary screened nationwide in various movie theatres. Recalling Ralph Waldo Emerson's maxim about an institution being "but lengthened shadows of a man," Zukor was one of "six Jews who built Hollywood"—the title of a study of the American film industry by Neal Gabler, who retrieved this memorable earlier portrait of him:

> The most notable figure in the moving picture field today is Adolph Zukor, a young man of medium size, slender build, clean-cut face, keen eyes, of Hungarian birth, who speaks the English language with a marked accent, but whose mind works with all the swiftness and certainty of the mind of a Napoleon. (Gabler, 1988: 114–15)

But so does the founder of what originally was called Famous Players in Featured Plays call to mind the poet John Donne's aphorism "No man is an island." For, without detracting from Zukor's considerable individual achievements, he received help from bankers and other notable figures in the movie industry like Cecil B. DeMille and Jesse Lansky; the latter, whose Silent Film company curiously was similarly named *Featured Players*, would merge with Zukor in 1916. Nearly a dozen years later, Famous Players-Lasky was rebranded Paramount-Prolix on April 1, 1927, a few years prior to a bankruptcy declaration and dissolution of their creative partnership as a result of the Great Depression.

Zukor's early life: Born in 1873 in Risce, Hungary, the Tokay grape/wine–growing region of the former Austro-Hungarian Empire, he was the son of grocery store owners. Orphaned relatively young and placed in care of a maternal uncle whose religious orthodoxy prompted a longing to escape, Zukor was fueled by enthusiastic letters from émigrés in the United States. The sixteen-year-old, who labored to obtain a passport, traveled to Berlin, where he booked passage to New York City with $14 (or $40) earned money sewn into his clothing lining. The title of an article about him in the *Brooklyn Eagle* on April 25, 1935, recounted much of what can also be found in his autobiography, *Penny Collector to Millionaire: Adolph Zukor, Moving Picture Magnate Stretched $25 to $25,000,000 in Forty Years.*

Thus, from floor sweeper in a fur company on the Lower East Side of Manhattan, he became a millionaire by the age of thirty after relocating to Chicago, where Zukor opened Novelty Furs, specializing in hats and capes. And that is a *real* millionaire, not in the sense of the old Vaudeville joke about someone with $10,000 in the bank! And his early fortune largely resulted from an imaginatively realized clasp of a real fox's teeth that closed the collar of a woman's fur coat. Here's another synchronicity which figures into our story—Zukor's lifelong marital partner, Lotte Kaufman, who was raised on the American Plains where her father's trade was also in buffalo skins obtained from the Lakota after the tragic Wounded Knee massacre in South

Dakota following the 1890 Ghost Dance this author has also written about (Hittman, 1997).

Street-toughened from fighting and hardscrabble living in Manhattan's ghetto, Zukor's riches-to-rags story then took a left turn after he viewed a peep show in Mitchell Mark's Edisonia Hall on 125th Street in what was then German-Harlem. For, with religious-like conversion to the Wizard of Menlo Park's so-called "moving pictures," he risked his fortune by entering into his first partnership with another Hollywood icon, Marcus Loew, the former ragpicker and scion of MGM. Sophie Tucker memorialized their relationship while recounting her own humble beginnings:

> I was often engaged to sing…(in the) little ten-cent theater owned by Marcus Loew, Adolph Zukor, and Nicholas Scheck at 116th Street and Lenox Avenue… All they showed was a one-reel slapstick comedy and me in blackface for the ten afternoon shows, and whiteface for the ten night shows. (Tucker, 1945: 38)

So, with permission from this nation's greatest inventor, Thomas Alva Edison, to rent one of his patented film projectors, Zukor and Loew followed the transformation of the Edison Company's penny shows commencing in 1893 into the explosion of nickelodeons from fifty to five thousand between 1901 and 1908 in New York City alone, by establishing the Automatic Vaudeville Company on Union Square in Manhattan (East Fourteenth Street) within the heart of the theatre district those years. Zukor (1953: 12) also writing the "burlesque house in Brooklyn for exclusive showing of movies" he opened with the so-called "Henry Ford of Vaudeville," Marcus Loew, whose surname in time appeared on more marquees than any other early magnate in the history of cinema, i.e., some three hundred movie theatres, including three of them this author nostalgically attended in Manhattan—the Commodore on Second Avenue, Delancey on that same named street, and the Avenue B apparently built in honor of the former ragpicker's mother, each of them gone.

After parting ways with Loew, Zukor next operated the Crystal Hall, also on Union Square, where patrons for the cost of a—buffalo!—nickel could view Edison's longer—thirty-second—films on rented chairs as part the evolution of the film industry. Crediting Loew as the first to combine continuous live action with film, Humanova was the name given to pantomimed actions of actors hidden behind flickering images screened as part of Zukor's early mixed-media experiment. Jesse L. Lasky, seemingly destined to become Zukor's next and main creative associate, described the Crystal Hall (named for a glass stairway) as follows: "Filled with automatic-tellers, strength testers, and other fascinating gadgets...(there was also) a row of peep box dispensers of thirty-second dramas collecting the steadiest stream of coins" (Zukor and Kramer, 1953).

Along with peep shows was Zukor's fascination with *The Great Train Robbery*, an eight-minute action film directed in 1908 by Edwin Porter out of Edison's Black Mariah studio in New Jersey, and with *The Kiss*, according to Whitfield (1997: 139), convincing him to start his own film studio.

Originally located in a brownstone also on Union Square—at 46–48 East Fourteenth Street in Manhattan—Zukor produced his own films, two of them notably starring the greatest of all illusionists, Harry Houdini. In time, however, he ran afoul of Edison as well as the Catholic Church for producing multireel films as well as exhibiting two European films on Broadway discovered while on vacation abroad: *The Greatest Story* and Sarah Bernhardt in *Queen Elizabeth* (Viera, 2019). Pressed additionally with the challenge of distributing his Silent Films, Zukor traveled in 1914 to Salt Lake City, Utah, for a meeting with W. W. Hodkinson, who headed a powerful consortium of Midwestern movie theatre exhibitors. With Hodkinson, who was also the inventor of widescreen film formatting, he formed a 65–35 percent business relationship, which allowed the minor partner to produce and show his own lengthy films; *The Prisoner of Zenda* was the first of what deliberately were successful Broadway plays Zukor transformed into celluloid as part of his agenda to make European immigrants into Americans, such as Zukor had done for himself. Soon after gaining control of their partnership, however, Zukor not only would appropriate Hodkinson's company's name, "Paramount," but joined with other early Silent Film pioneers to defeat Edison's Trust in a Supreme Court anti-monopoly case.

According to his studio's origin story, Hodkinson reportedly told Zukor the studio's name came from serendipitously walking past an apartment building in the Mormon capital with the name Paramount. As for Paramount's iconic logo, it was said to have been inspired by Hodkinson's doodle of those snowcapped jagged Wasatch Mountains framing Salt Lake City on its immediate east, to which an anonymous figure added an array of heavenly stars whose double entendre references the new studio's stable of Hollywood stars Zukor hired (Zukor, 1953: 135–136).

And here we pause yet again to relate another pair of synchronicities involved with this research into the early history of the Brooklyn Paramount: first, the etymology of the name of those mountains supplied by a *Nuuwuvi* or Southern Paiute named Archie Rogers, *Wuhu'Seai*, "Frozen Penis," which not only was another example of a "wisdom story sits in place," i.e., purportedly inspired by the death of a hunter trapped in a blizzard while wearing his moccasins, not cowboy boots, remotely suggesting their distant Great Basin Northern Paiute relation's nickname of me, *Atsa Moosoowee*, "Red Beard," whose bowdlerization I leave for another occasion; and second, F. Scott Fitzgerald's unfinished novel about Hollywood during the "Jazz Age" titled *The Last Tycoon*. It contains a scene involving the Bennington College student, Cecelia Brady, who looks out the airplane window while flying home on school break to see her father, and she muses about her crush on a character inspired by MGM's genius producer, Irving Thalberg, and is described as follows while glimpsing at those same Wasatch Mountains: "Then in the late afternoon, flying over them, the peaks themselves—the Mountains of the Frozen Saw..."

Returning, however, to our backstory of Famous Players, Jesse Lasky was born in San Francisco and was thought to become rich during the Alaskan Klondike Gold Rush—only to return home broke. Teaming up then with his sister in a two-trumpet Vaudeville act, they toured the West Coast. But when Blanche Lasky married another future Hollywood filmmaker, the glove manufacturer Samuel Goldfish-cum-"Goldwyn," also of MGM fame, Jesse Lasky moved east and began performing at venues like Tony Pastor's popular Opera House on the Bowery. But after performing in Pathe musical movie shorts like *Redheads* and *Lasky's Beauties*, he went broke in 1911 attempting to create an American version of the Parisian Folies Bergère on Broadway with a fellow Vaudevillian, Henry Harris. And that prototype nightclub, Erenberg (1981: 115–19) wrote, offered two lavish Vaudeville-like shows nightly combined with food served restaurant style, as well as a late-night special show.

Of greater relevance to this book, however, was that that scholar also wrote about their failed venture: "It is also true that one of the first major acts in a New York cabaret was the Apache dance taken from the slums of Paris and (also?) performed at Louis Martin's in 1911" (Erenberg, 1981: 75)—the same act, which was part of Vaude-ville on the Brooklyn Paramount's opening night nearly two decades later, but which the great star of that middling form of entertainment, Fanny Brice, also performed in early in her career.

Lasky's reversal of fortune included a stint as a Vaudeville theat-rical booking agent; that is, before starting his own film production company with Goldwyn and Cecil DeMille. Contrasting their films with Zukor's Famous Players, Lasky immodestly penned this in his autobiography:

I always claim we made better, if not fewer, pictures than Famous Players in the early days, but I must concede that Zukor knew what he was doing. All my original stars were top actors on the stage, but who remembers them today? Zukor often took lesser lights and from the stage but built them into outstanding screen names. Among his early acquisitions were Mary Pickford, Marguerite Clark, John Barrymore, and Pauline Frederick. (Lasky and Weldon, 1957: 102)

And yet, Thomson (2010: 555–56) wrote that Jesse Lasky was associated with no fewer than 350 Silent Films between 1921 and 1930. Our count, however, records 1,023 between 1916 and 1927 (Eames, 1985). Objecting, though, to the Paramount name—and which Lasky originated in San Francisco not Salt Lake City—he stated, "I didn't like the name at all. I didn't think it suggested film artistry, it sounded more like a brand of cheese or woolen mittens."

Whatever explanation might exist for what Thomson (2010: 556) wrote was that major Silent Film player, second fiddle player to Zukor following the merger of their companies, Lasky then became the vice president of Paramount in Hollywood following their studio's move from Union Square to the Ninth Regiment Armory at 213–227 West Twenty-Sixth Street (between Seventh and Eighth Avenues), which reflected the movement north of the theater district to Herald Square at Thirty-Fourth Street, that in large part resulted from the extension of public transportation before it finally settled on Longacre Square, i.e., Forty-Second Street, a. k. a. Times Square, and then following a devasting fire, Famous Players-Lasky would move to an abandoned horse stable on East Fifty-Sixth Street, and from there to Astoria, Queens. That was a penultimate move across the Fifty-Ninth Street Bridge famously sung about by Simon and Garfunkel's "59th Street Bridge Song (Feelin' Groovy)"into an abandoned amusement park. And while Paramount East continued to turn out Silent Films between 1920 and 1927—between 20 and 25 before its closing year—following its briefer reopening two years later, the renewed production schedule called for fifteen Talkies a year and a hundred shorts; the studio was also home for "most of the scoring for Paramount pictures" (*Brooklyn Eagle*, April 12, 1929). DeMille's discovery of an abandoned twenty-six-acre farm "near a small town named Hollywood" on Vine Street while shooting *The Squaw Man* in Flagstaff, Arizona, led him to relocate to the so-called "Barn," which in turn became today's headquarters and tourist attraction known as Paramount Pictures (Koszarski, 1983).

"You exhibit them, I'll produce them!" That innocuous statement by Adolph Zukor contrasted the personalities of those unlikely business partners: Zukor, the so-called "Killer" with his "icy coolness," who insisted on being addressed as "Mr.," and blue-eyed fixed stares anticipated the so-called "ray" of another calculating genius, the Jazz musician Benny Goodman, and the universally beloved "dreamer," Jesse Lasky, whose temperament was fondly described by his partner's son as "far from Wall Street" and as such:

> Lasky was a dreamer. He was as far removed from Wall Street and what was going on as one could be. The world was a beautiful place to paint pictures... He loved to be with writers and creators. And the money? "So, what!" The budgeting he said (sic), "Well it's true if it's too much, but it isn't too much if you get what you want for it." His attitude was, it wasn't going into anyone's pocket. It was going toward a purpose—a good objective. (quoted in Gabler, 1988: 203)

But let's allow Lasky to draw that contrast with his fiercely competitive partner, who lived by the biblical injunction "Thou Shalt Not Lie," as well as by Zukor's eleventh mosaiclike biblical commandment regarding business practices: "Thou Shalt Not Lose":

> While I was turning out the continuous flow of pictures like a frozen custard machine, Sidney Kent was selling them like hot cakes, and Adolph Zukor was collecting theater chains like postage stamps, a collection that eventually numbered almost 2000 houses, first under the able direction of Harold Franklin, and later managed by Sam Katz. (Lasky and Weldon, 1957: 130–31)

Their collaboration saw some 104 bicoastal-produced Silent Films between 1916 and 1927 before the decision was made to make only Talkies. A decision based on technical innovations associated with Edison's Kinescope and DeForest's Phonofilm, along with more efficient ways of synchronizing amplified sound on disks with film strips that gave way to simultaneously record directly on celluloid (Eyman, 1997).

And whether or not too much has been made about the differences between Zukor's "Mr. Outsider" and Lasky's "Mr. Insider," in most ways, the European-born pioneer who also built film studios in Islington, London, and India, and acquired the UFA-EFA film company in Germany, recruited continental film stars like Maurice Chevalier and Marlene Dietrich, directors like Emil Jannings and Josef von Sternberg, as well as the Canadian-born Mary Pickford, who ironically became known as "America's Sweetheart," contrasts dramatically with his American-born partner, who, for example, discovered the Helena, Montana, actor Gary Cooper, an original Paramount "talking" film star. Zukor hired American-born Broadway actors, writers, and directors, whereas Lasky would be first to recognize the comedic genius of the British-born Charlie Chaplin, whom he immediately signed to contract.

We read that on May 7, 1928, while construction of the Brooklyn Paramount continued in earnest, Jesse Lasky informed the press that Paramount planned on making twenty-eight Talkies, two hundred musical shorts, 104 episodes of *Paramount News,* twenty-six one-reel episodes about the Inkwell Imp, an early cartoon character, twelve two-reel films, a new series titled Great Stars and Authors, and also thirty-two Krazy Kat cartoons.

This little more about sound, which speak ended the Silent Film era, might also be noted before returning directly to the earlier history of the Brooklyn Paramount (Eyman, 1997; Crafton, 1999). Anthony Slide's more recent study, *New Historical Dictionary of American Film and Industry,* speaks about Edison's Kinetoscope in 1894, following his patented inventions of the microphone, amplification, and phonographs quintessential in technical ways to movie theatres originally built for the Talkies, and those which had to be reoutfitted to accommodate those revolutionary technological breakthroughs. For it wasn't Jolson whose voice was heard first in the Talkies in 1927, but Edison's associate, William K. L. Dickson, who famously said these words on Kinescope when talking pictures were promised in 1894: "Good Morning, Mr. Edison. I hope you are satisfied with the

Kineto-phonograph." Their dispute about credit for that revolutionary invention notwithstanding, the totally deaf Edison's voice was also recorded earlier than what was heard in *The Jazz Singer* in 1927—his reciting "Mary Had a Little Lamb" in 1913.

And while the first motion picture theatre in America was built in 1905 in Pittsburgh, Pennsylvania, audiences thrilled to Thomas A. Edison's latest marvel, the Vitascope in Koester and Bialy's Vaudeville House in Manhattan, since it opened in April 1896. Moreover, Jesse Lasky (1957: 212) was featured in an early Vaudeville skit titled *The Planophiends*, which "played the Colonial Theatre in New York on the same bill as a talking picture in 1907." Still other important early so-called "eye-ear films," as Eames (1985: 36) reminds us, included Pola Negra starring in *Bella Donna*, screened in Paramount's theatre the Rivoli on Broadway, whose sound was synchronized by Lee DeForest's Photophone back in 1923; that is, two years after D. W. Griffith's *Dream Street* played Town Hall in Manhattan and contained some dialogue as well as music as a result of another recording device from some ninety-four other systems already in existence...all those a few years in advance of Warner Brothers' two pioneering feature-length experiments with sound: *Don Juan* in 1926, which featured the sound of sabers clashing and 127 smooches joined by an orchestra; and *The Jazz Singer* in 1927 that essentially went head-to-ear against Manhattan's Paramount, which opened on November 6, 1926, with the Silent Film *God Gave Me Twenty Cents*... Al Jolson's memorable words, "You ain't heard nothin' yet!" weren't even the first spoken in *The Jazz Singer*...those or it should be credited to his father protesting "STOP!" while Jolson attempted to sing a Tin Pan Alley number (Sapofsky, 1994).

Restated, the end of seven- to eight-hundred Silent Films made in that year alone, 1927, generating studio incomes of $7,000,000 weekdays and $9,000,000 on Sundays as part of that sixth-largest industry in the nation would pale by comparison with $60,000,000 earned by movie theatres two years later in 1929 during the Great Depression. That followed the advent of the Talkies! Lasky's dramatic announcement in 1928 about Paramount's decision to join Warner Brothers by making only Talkies forced movie theatre owners either to reoutfit—rewire—to accommodate the onrush of those new films—or go out of business...which some thirteen thousand movie theaters reportedly did in 1928, while "deluxers" like the Brooklyn Paramount were built from the ground up for sound. And while *Manhattan Cocktail* was a Silent Film, whose only voice heard was Nancy Carroll singing two songs, *Beggars for Life* screened nearly a month later during the week of January 26, 1929, in our theatre and was Paramount's first "100 percent all dialogue," that is, shot from beginning to end with sound rather than redubbed with added dialogue like *Interference*, for example, a successful London play screened here two years later during the week of August 28, 1931.

Before turning to this first face and survey of our theatre's thirty-four run of Talkies between 1928 and 1962, a few words should be devoted to the Actor's School, which Jessie Lasky started on the Paramount lot in Astoria, Queens, the home today of Kaufman Studios (Koszarski, 1983).

Thomas Schatz (1988: 72) characterized the Paramount East Actor's Studio that opened on March 18, 1926, as modest. Its goal was recruiting and training actors for the studio's relatively few prestige pictures and greater number of low-budget films shot there. Fifteen selected Hollywood aspirants received checks for $500 from which $25 per week was deducted for room and board and promised screen tests following a vigorous curriculum that included physical training in sports like swimming and boxing; mandatory attendance at lectures on literature, sociology, photography, and sobriety; training in etiquette during enforced lunches with tourists and visiting dignitaries; and acting lessons.

Quoting her (second) husband's similarly nicknamed "America's Boyfriend's" recollection about the Artist Studio on the Paramount East lot, America's Sweetheart, Mary Pickford, quoted what Charles "Buddy" Rogers, who was born in Olathe, Kansas, and was unaware that his father had mailed off a required photograph of his handsome son, an aspiring musician with the required application to one of the thirty branch offices in Manhattan, said about the Astoria Studio: "We learned two things—how to fall downstairs without hurting ourselves and how to hold a kiss for three without laughing" (quoted in Whitfield, 1997: 276).

The Paramount Junior Stars, some sixteen young men between eighteen to thirty and women between the ages of sixteen to twenty-five separately lodged in Allerton Hotels in Manhattan comprised that first and only class and were featured in a Silent Film titled *Glorious Youth*, partially filmed in Lake Placid and Red Bank, New Jersey (Kaufman, 1990: 131–51). Since the film school was Jesse Lasky's brainstorm, he was present at its first and only commencement exercise held on March 2, 1926, during which acting certificates and golden cigarettes were presented to each graduate at the Ritz-Carlton in Manhattan (Kenly, 1987: 7).

A former journalism major who graduated from the University of Kansas and appeared in Silent Films—like W. C. Field's *So's Your Old Man* in 1926—Rogers made the transition to the Talkies—starring in *Wings*, a World War I aviation film shot in 1928 that played in both Brooklyn's and Manhattan's Paramount theatres.

Although the Paramount East Actor's School was fated to permanently close in 1927, it temporarily reopened following a disastrous fire in one of the new sound stages built in the studio's future headquarters in Hollywood, California. Prestige films were shot there during its short-lived existence: *Salome of the Tenements*, a Silent Film made in 1924 with authentic locals like Hester Street on the Lower East Side, and these Talkies, which played here: *The Letter*, an Oscar-nominated film starring Jeanne Eagles, was the studio's synchronized version of a previously successful Silent Film titled *Burlesque*; Victor Scherzinger's *The Laughing Lady* (1929); *The Sap from Syracuse* (starring Jack Oakie); Ginger Rogers in *Young Man of Manhattan*; Dorothy Arzner's *Honor Among Lovers* (1931); Paul Robeson in *Emperor Jones* (1933); as well as four of the Marx Brothers' madcap Talkies: *Cocoanuts, Duck Soup, Monkey Business*, and *Animal Crackers*.

A local tabloid reported on April 12, 1929, that the Long Island Studio had turned out between twenty and twenty-five Silent Films annually as a result of its proximity to Broadway. This allowed easy transportation while satisfying Zukor's immodest dream of recruiting actors in dramatic roles, like Walter Huston and Edward G. Robinson, and directors for family-friendly films. Lasky was quoted on May 17, 1932, in the local tabloid saying that one hundred films had been shot there. These films included all of D. W. Griffith's Silent Films, followed by all-dialogue advertised films like the *Gentlemen of the Press*, which also was screened at the Brooklyn Paramount.

Central to those two thousand administered voice tests for aspiring actors held at Paramount East was what sociologists would term as its latent function—the studio's mission of expunging accents—that is, regional dialects. Despite what linguistics has proved to be the beauty of internal diversity within different tongues, a veritable war was waged against that notion. So, for example, a newspaper clipping from April 3, 1933, reported the following about those shenanigans: "No matter how charming they may sound, Southern accents—and accents of any kind—were strictly verboten." And that ukase was issued by George Somnes, director of voice, who in no uncertain terms also stated his opposition to all traces of regionalism.

The famed Virginian-cum-early-Western-movie-star Randolph Scott was forced to shed his Southern accent and speak pure English [*sic*]—that is, if he wanted work at the studio. Apart from wondering what would have happened had *Gone with the Wind* been shot at Paramount East instead of MGM in Hollywood, when the English actress Ida Lupino was interviewed on May 25, 1934, during a screening of *Come On Marines*, she would praise American movies for challenging the Oxford accent. The latter, a Great Britain dialect otherwise connoting snooty upper-class English boarding schools and prestigious colleges like Oxford and Cambridge...an irony of which surely being that African American divas like Ethel Waters trilled their r's and also affected those other phonological sonorities. Still, Ms. Lupino would celebrate the demise of that dialect said to be hoot(ed) into disuse in favor of the American dialect spoken by her husband, Howard Duff, as she further expressed the hope that a small step toward the new international language of all English-speaking countries was inferentially made at Paramount East.

Despite Adolph Zukor's personal love of opera and other examples of so-called high art, his empire of thousands of movie theatres devoted to transforming European émigrés into America's melting pot. Accents or not, Mae West from Bushwick's stereotypical Brooklyn accent reportedly kept Paramount going during those initial years of the Great Depression.

It might also be added that propaganda films on behalf of the Allied cause were shot on the Astoria lot in Queens during the Second World War, and that the renamed Kaufman's Astoria, a tourist attraction today at 31 East Fifty-First Street in Queens, not only became the future home of TV series like *Sesame Street* but of successful films like *The World According to Garp* as well.

MAE WEST (*She Done Him Wrong*) MOVIE ADVERTISEMENT
(*The Brooklyn Daily Eagle*/February 24,1933)

FOUR FACES

CHAPTER 5

Face One: Films

Manhattan Cocktail and *Hatari* were, respectively, the alpha and omega of films screened at the Brooklyn Paramount between the theatre's opening and closing years, 1928–1962. By our count, an approximate additional 1,907 different films were screened during those 1,786 weeks of the theatre's thirty-four years. New releases typically ran for seven days, and many were held over for two or more weeks—also called Revivals, i.e., Silent Films that by definition were anachronistic since ours was the first cinematic-like cathedral built expressly from the ground up for the Talkies and previews. The following overview must also be viewed against the Brooklyn Paramount being shut for thirty weeks during the summer months of 1933 and 1934.

Our tabulation of this primary face comprised of feature-length films commences with fifty-eight different Paramount releases shown—or exhibited, employing that arcane term in the late 1920s— less five Revivals featured along with Vaudeville, our theatre's second face. During the 1930s, five hundred different films during those 490 weeks, whose inflated figure resulted from double bills, commencing June 11, 1935, with *The Case Against Mrs. Ames*, paired with *Florida Special* (with Jack Oakie), and which also included non-Paramount films screened to keep up with rival wonder theatres in downtown Brooklyn. During the 1940s and 1950s, there were 446 and 726 different films, respectively, spread over 1,040 combined weeks. Finally, during the 1960s, there were only 179 different films screened during those 140 weeks, culminating on August 21, 1962, with *Hatari* starring John Wayne.

During the last two years of the 1920s, not only were there six complete shows (e.g., April 27, 1929), commencing at 11:20 a.m., and the last of those startup times being 10:25. And with complete late-night screenings on Saturdays and Sundays commencing at 3: 00 p.m. buIn addition, there were also single-night double features between March 16, 1929 and August 1, 1929, i.e., with reruns of the previous week's feature combined with the current Vaudeville show, as well as other changing opening dates for complete vaude-cine shows ordinarily from Saturdays to Fridays, and commencing on August 8, 1929, before the first Monday Revival on November 1, 1929.

Then, during the tumultuous 1930s, sixteen opening screen dates alternated between Wednesday and Friday nights, and with occasional Saturday and Tuesday openings in 1933 for variety. A single Vaudeville show brought back a second week on October 13 and October 20, which also featured Wednesday previews of the following week's attractions, commencing on February 8, 1933.

While during the 1940s, there were forty-five Wednesday–Friday flip-flops, each of those playing for several consecutive weeks, respectively; seven Monday nights when new films opened here; nine Tuesdays; two different Saturdays for brief runs; and fifteen different Thursday openings double bills, which monopolized all the decade's screen offerings—over 150 weeks by rough estimate. The Christmas bonus was advertised on the night of December 24, 1948, as a triple header.

During the 1950s we not only count thirteen Wednesday–Friday flip-flops during that initial year of that decade—sixteen overall—and other new films screened here on three Tuesdays, two Thursdays, one Saturday, and two Sundays, along with several Tuesday triple headers as was the case on July 29, 1953.

Finally, during the theatre's last two years of operation, there were nine change-of-opening dates rotating between Wednesdays and Fridays, and that included a Thursday (October 27, 1960), as well as three Sundays and a single Saturday (March 16,1962) on through *Hatari*, whose last screening date was August 21, 1962, our theatre's closing date on that Tuesday.

The studio couldn't realistically turn out enough films to satisfy those 1,456 weeks of operation between the end of Vaudeville in 1934 and our theatre's closing in 1962, even if Paramount turned out 1,619 films between 1935 and 1962 (Eames, 1985).

A detailed decadienal breakdown further reveals that while no films were held over during the Roaring 1920s, nineteen and received a second week's run in the 1930s. So, for example, before that Great Divide in 1935, when double bills became the norm, *Tom Sawyer*, starring the child actor Jackie Coogan, opened on December 19, 1930, and was held over a second week. Another example was *I'm No Angel*, which starred the bawdy/brainy film star Mae West, whose blockbuster films are generally credited with pulling Famous Players-Lasky-cum-Paramount-Prolix out of the red during the film studio's Depression years, 1931–1932 (Baxter, 1968: 33). On the other hand, *I Married a Doctor* (starring Pat O'Brien), which opened on April 23, 1936, was shown for two additional consecutive weeks. As was the case with *The Golden Arrow* (starring Bette Davis and George Brent), paired with *The Moon's Our Home* (with Henry Fonda and Margaret Sullivan), which opened on May 8, 1936. Additional films that played here for three weeks included *Rhythm on the Range*, which starred Bing Crosby and Francis Langford, paired with *The Return of Sophie Lang*, commencing August 21, 1936; and *Tovarich* starring Claudette Colbert and Charles Boyer, a Warner Brothers' film that became a Broadway musical in the early 1960s, paired with *Sergeant Murphy* starring the future American president, Ronald Reagan, whose opening date was February 1, 1938. *Racket Busters* starring Humphrey Bogart paired with *Army Girl*, which opened August 17 of that year and was held over for two additional weeks, as was *The Old Maid* starring a newcomer to the screen, the future Oscar winner Bette Davis, and Silent Screen favorite Miriam Hopkins paired with *Million Dollar Legs* starring Betty Grable, a. k. a. Her Gams, commencing August 24, 1938. Those and other non-Paramount films were shown because the studio could not keep up with those production demands.

Films held over for an additional week during the 1940s included: *The Great Victor Herbert* (starring Allan Jones and Mary Martin) paired with *Blondie Brings Up Baby*, whose opening date was January 1, 1940; *George Washington Slept Here* (starring Jack Benny) paired with Ann Sheridan in *I Live on Danger* (November 1, 1942); *Sister Kenny* (starring Rosalind Russell) and *They Were Sisters* (with James Mason), commencing November 7, 1946; *The Perfect Marriage* (starring Loretta Young and David Niven) and *Ladies Man* (February 20, 1947); *Sealed Verdict* and *Anna Karenina,* both starring Vivian Leigh (April 2, 1948); and, *Albuquerque,* a Western starring Randolph Scott, unlikely paired with *Shoe Shine,* a neo-realistic film made by the Italian director Vittorio De Sica, about a pair of street urchins in post–World War II Rome, both held over for a second week following their respective opening dates on April 8, 1948.

The number of films held over for two additional weeks during the 1940s totaled 137. *The Fighting 69th* (starring James Cagney and Pat O'Brian) was paired with *Money to Burn* on February 13, 1940; *Dough Girls* (with Ann Sheridan, Alexis Smith, and Jane Wyman) paired with *Storm over Lisbon,* whose paired opening dates were November 7, 1944; *The Strange Love of Martha Ivers* (starring Barbara Stanwyck, Van Heflin, and Lizabeth Scott) paired with *It Shouldn't Happen to a Dog* (October 26, 1946); and *Red, Hot and Blue,* a musical comedy starring Betty Hutton and Victor Mature with a gangster subplot, paired with *Song of Surrender* (starring Wanda Hendrix and Claude Rains), whose three-week run commenced on October 26, 1949.

Of the twenty-one double features held over for three additional weeks during the 1940s, notably among those was *Casablanca,* the Warner Brothers' World War II classic directed by Michael Curtiz, which starred Humphrey Bogart and Ingrid Bergman, which was paired with *By All Networks* commencing March 10, 1943. Those paired flickers also played the big house in downtown Brooklyn for an entire month during that decade: *The Story of Doctor Wassell* (with Gary Cooper) paired with *Goodnight, Sweetheart,* whose opening dates were September 20, 1944; and *My Favorite Brunette,* which starred Dorothy Lamour, was paired with *Fear In The Night,* a film noir, their four-week engagements commencing on May 8, 1947. While of the four double features held over for four additional weeks during the 1940s, we note for examples Cecil B. DeMille's *Reap the Wind* paired with *Cadets on Parade* (May 13, 1942); *The Perils of Pauline* and *Wild Harvest* (with Alan Ladd), which opened on September 6, 1947, when *I Cover tThe Big Town* replaced the latter during its five-week run; *Love Letters* (starring Jennifer Jones and Joseph Cotton) paired with a comical detective story, *Follow That Woman,* commencing November 23, 1945. Only one film, however, played here for more than five consecutive weeks during the 1940s: *Going My Way,* starring Bing Crosby, who won an Oscar for his portrayal of Father Charles "Chuck" O'Malley—a record-breaking box office blockbuster nationwide, but which played here for ten consecutive weeks after its opening date on May 9, 1944, and was cofeatured with *Silent Partner,* a Grade B murder mystery.

Turning next to the 1950s, our theatre's filmography reveals that thirty-eight double features were held over for an additional week—among those, *Thelma Jordan* (starring Barbara Stanwyck) paired with *There's a Girl in My Heart,* whose opening dates were February 1, 1950; and *About Mrs. Leslie* (with Shirley Booth and Robert Ryan) and *The Limping Man* (with Lloyd Bridges) that opened during the week of August 11, 1954. There were 138 films held over for two additional weeks in that decade. Among those, twenty-nine single features running for three consecutive weeks included *Samson and Delilah,* another Cecil DeMille extravaganza (starring Victor Mature and Hedy LaMarr), commencing April 7, 1950. Double bills held over for two additional weeks include the Hitchcock thriller *Rear Window* starring James Stewart and Grace Kelly paired with *Falstaff's Fur Coat* (starring Paul Douglas) that opened on October 20, 1954; *Jumping Jacks,* which costarred that decade's popular comedic team of Martin and Lewis, paired with *Rio Grande* (with Edmund O'Brien and Sterling Hayden), commencing August 27, 1952. And while no films were held over for three additional weeks, some were screened at the Brooklyn Paramount for five consecutive weeks: *The Greatest Show on Earth*, starring James Stewart and Betty Hutton, which opened on June 25, 1959; DeMille's remake of his Silent Film classic from 1923, *The Ten Commandments*, which opened on April 4, 1958, and starring Charlton Heston as the Biblical Moses in place of Theodore Roberts, its six weeks hardly comparing with the former's incredible run of forty-eight consecutive weeks at the Criterion in Manhattan. The Talkie version, curiously enough, cofeatured with *La Pariesienne*, starring Bridgette Bardot, which returned for another week following a summer run, though otherwise paired instead with *The Fear-Makers*, commencing October 17, 1958. The screenplay for the earlier 136-minute Silent Film Biblical epic was credited to Jesse Lasky and Jeanie MacPherson.

Finally, among the few films held over a second week during the truncated 1960s decade, *They Came to Cordoba* starring Gary Cooper was paired with *Juke Box Rhythm*, whose opening dates were January 4, 1960; and *The Sad Sack* starring Jerry Lewis was paired with *The Delicate Delinquent* (July 18, 1962), a double feature in which he starred by himself, presumably held over as a result of cost-cutting efforts during the waning years of the Brooklyn Paramount's earlier history. There were five double features held over for two additional weeks: *The Big Fisherman* and *Eyes in Outer Space*, which opened on February 9, 1960; *G. I. Blues* (with Elvis) paired with *The Boy Who Stole a Million* (November 30, 1960); and *Sergeants 3* starring both leaders of Hollywood's notorious Rat Pack, Frank Sinatra and Dean Martin, paired with *X-15*, commencing March 15, 1962. And while only two films played here for three consecutive weeks—Hitchcock's *Psycho*, which starred Anthony Perkins and Janet Leigh and opened on August 3, 1960, and *One-Eyed Jacks*, costarring Jack Nicholson, directed by the latter film's star, Marlon Brando, commencing on May 10, 1961— curiously enough, despite the borough's largest concentration then of

Jews in the world, *Exodus* was also held over only for two additional weeks following its opening date on October 25, 1960.

These cinema-graphic facts regarding our theatre's earlier history should be noted:

1. One film was shown in the 1930s and brought back in the 1950s: *Cleopatra*;
2. Three different films were screened here on different dates in the 1950s and 1960s: *Come Back, Little Sheba*, *The Detective Story*, *The Greatest Show Ever*, and *La Parisienne*;
3. *Psycho* was shown twice during the 1960s; and
4. *Come Back, Little Sheba* was the only film shown here on three separate occasions, twice in the first of those decades and a third time in our theatre's thirty-four-year run as a movie house.

Brooklyn Paramount innovations were those curiously titled Silent Film Revivals, which by definition weren't ordinarily screened in our theatre wired for sound from its onset. Thus, on Saturdays or Mondays toward the end of 1929 through the early 1930s, these Silent Films were screened weekly following the last complete new "vaude-cine" screen offering: *The Hummingbird* starring Gloria Swanson, a 1924 Paramount release presented on November 25, 1929, and which inaugurated the Revival series; *The Underground* (December 2, 1929); *The Sheik of Araby* (starring the Silent Film legend Rudolph Valentino) on December 9, 1929; *The Covered Wagon* (December 16, 1929), which was said to be loosely based on Jesse Lasky's grandparents' cross-country trip from New York in the 1840s to California; Cecil B. DeMille's initial *Ten Commandments* (December 23, 1929); and *Pony Express* (December 28, 1929). Carrying over into the next decade we, for example, note DeMille's *Male and Female* revived on the first or second February in 1930. Still others include *We're in the Navy* (January 25, 1930). *Blood and Sand*, however, deserves special attention, for this Paramount Silent Film debuted in 1926 and was revived here on March 15, 1930—it helped launch Dorothy Arzner's film career—followed by *Personal Maid*, starring Nancy Carroll, and a Vaudeville sketch titled *Down by the Bay*.

This early policy anticipated double bills that replaced Vaudeville in 1935.

GEORGE RAFT ("Bolero") MOVIE ADVERTISEMENT (*The Brooklyn Daily Eagle*/February 16, 1934)

Previews need not detain us very long, insofar as those were complete films shown as coming attractions, usually on Thursday nights, similarly. It was another marketing strategy inarguably undertaken by our theatre's management as a result of stiff competition always with the Fox, Albee, Strand, and Loew's Metropolitan, and the other wonder theatres in downtown Brooklyn. As we read on February 8, 1933, DeMille's *Sign of the Cross* immediately followed *Island of Lost Souls* and that week's Vaudeville offerings. Another example being *Go into Your Dance* (starring Al Jolson and Ruby Keeler); which theatre patrons were enticed to attend a 6:45 p.m. Studio (sneak) Preview of *G-Men* starring George Raft, was the coming week's attraction. Two decades later, we read that during the week of September 30, 1952, *Hurricane Smith* (with Yvonne DeCarlo and John Ireland), was scheduled as the coming week's feature attraction between screenings of Abbott and Costello in *Lost in Alaska* twice on that Thursday, at 11:00 a.m. and 9:00 p.m.—that is, along with *Night Without Sleep* (with Linda Darnell) paired with *Holiday for Sinners* (with Gig Young), the theatre's current attractions. Thus, Brooklyn Paramount movie revelers got the jump on the coming week's attractions and could recommend them to family members and friends, thereby gaining another competitive advantage over the other wonder theatres, which meant movie theatre patrons might enjoy three films on those nights.

Finally, during what could only have been a desperate measure twelve months before the movie theatre's closing date on August 21, 1962, management offered a sneak showing of *Most Dangerous Man Alive*, in this instance with the current attraction *The Warrior Empress* not once but twice that week: on the following Saturday, July 24, 1961, between 5:00 p.m. and 9:00 p.m., and Sunday between 1:00 p.m. and 9:00 p.m. (June 22, 1961).

Concluding this statistical presentation, we return to *Hatari*, which for bookend-like reasons was paired with *Manhattan Cocktail* as the omega and alpha of our theatre's earlier history. The former a romantic comedy starring John Wayne that dealt with large game collections from Africa's Serengeti Plain in Kenya sought to stock

American zoos, which by contrast ran for ten days, from August 8, 1962, a Wednesday, until Tuesday, August 21, 1962, our theatre's closing date.

BLUE SKIES (*The Brooklyn Daily Eagle,* December 25, 1946)

Other tabulations reveal that the crooner superstar Bing Crosby, in addition to six record-breaking stage appearances during our theatre's Vaudeville era, also appeared in the largest number of films in our theatre's earlier history: forty-three of them to be precise, which included those popular road films costarring Dorothy Lamour and another emerging superstar, Bob Hope, who along with his lone Vaudeville appearance occupied second place by starring in thirty-four films screened here. Among those, *Monsieur Beaucaire* (with Joan Caulfield) paired with *Swamp Fire* costarring Johnny Weissmuller and Buster Crabbe, commencing on October 17, 1946. The latter movie star headed up the second rodeo on our theatre's stage in 1950. And for another example, Bob Hope costarred in *Son of Paleface* with Jane Russell, and Roy Rogers paired with *The Blazing Forest* during the week of October 29, 1952, which were cofeatured with a Vaudeville-like revue.

Third to sixth places, respectively, in this imaginary competitive listing pitting male film stars against each other went to Gary Cooper (thirty-three), Alan Ladd (twenty-five), Ray Milland (twenty-one), and Fredric March (twenty) in descending order. The laconic early Paramount star, Cooper, significantly appeared in films in all four decades of our theatre's earlier history from nearly its very opening during the week of December 29, 1928, to nearly its closing. *The Naked Edge* (September 13, 1961) with the action hero, Ladd, for example, in his best-remembered film. *Shane*, which played here for three weeks commencing July 1, 1953. The moody Milland (*Lost Weekend*, April 4, 1956) and the TV star of *My Three Sons*, Fred McMurray, made their screen debut in our theatre on July 12, 1935, in *Men Without Names*, a film title not unrelated to the book's commitment to reference the importance of names in its four faces earliest history.

On a parenthetical note, the Irish American former circus performer Burt Lancaster, born in Spanish Harlem, has the distinction of appearing in the same film screened here on three separate occasions: *Come Back, Little Sheba*, costarring Shirley Booth, which opened during the week of April 22, 1953, and was paired with *Ride the Man Down* (starring Brian Donleavy), then was brought back during the week of August 31, 1955, paired with *Houdini* (starring Tony Curtis), and for a final seven-day run commencing January 22, 1960, when it was paired with *The Detective Story*, starring Kirk Douglas.

Also of presumed interest hopefully to film and/or movie theatre buffs, Charles "Buddy" Rogers appeared in seven Talkies in 1928 and beyond, following success in Silent Films: *Someone to Love*, which was the second film shown in our theatre's earlier history, i.e., during the week of December 1, 1928; and *Take a Chance* five years later, during the week of November 24, 1933. And more: Mary Pickford's second husband appeared on stage here during the week of February 28, 1930, and appeared in *Hollywood in Brooklyn*, a revue in which he not only conducted the orchestra but also played several instruments in addition to relating stories of the film capital.

Turning our phantom Klug spotlight next on women who appeared in the largest number of films at the Brooklyn Paramount, Claudette Colbert (née Emilie Claudette Chaucoin) tops this otherwise phantom list with twenty-four films spread over three decades. She was born in France in 1905 and also skirted the noted difficult transition from Silent Films to sound, arguably as a result of Broadway stage credits, and won an Oscar in 1934 for Frank Capra's screwball comedy *It Happened One Night* (costarring Clark Gable), which unfortunately didn't play our house. Ms. Colbert also appeared here in *Young Man of Manhattan*, screened during the week of April 18, 1930, followed by six credits in the 1940s and 1950s, and *Practically Yours* with Fred MacMurray on May 16, 1945.

Second place among all-time leading actresses goes to Barbara Stanwyck, who appeared in eighteen films over three decades—commencing with *Shopworn* during the week of April 1, 1930, and *Crime of Passion* nearly three decades later during the week of January 16, 1957. While third place running these numbers goes to Nancy Carroll, who starred in our theatre's opening film *Manhattan Cocktail* and also appeared once on stage during a Vaudeville sketch on October 19, 1930, and who appeared in thirteen films screened here during that decade, *The Woman Accused*, commencing March 17, 1933, among those. Skipping past third place for a reasons referenced below, fourth and fifth go to two additional Silent Film stars who also effectively made that difficult transition to the Talkies, which often otherwise destroyed the distinguished careers of Silent Film actors like John Gilbert: Ruth Chatterton starred in *Doctor's Secret* that commenced here February 2, 1929, among ten other flicks; and Clara Bow, the controversial redhead born on Church Avenue in Brooklyn, whom Ed Sullivan would have introduced on his popular TV show as a really big star, if not by that ineffable term coined by the English writer Glynnis John as "It Girl," appeared in nine Talkies screened here, commencing with *Three Weekends* (December 8, 1928) and concluding with *Kick In* three years later on May 22, 1931. And finally, back to the second place winner, which somewhat surprisingly goes to Ginger Rogers, who was present during the flagpole stunt associated with the initial opening of the Brooklyn Paramount, and along with appearing three times in original radio broadcasting on stage, starred in eleven films screened here. Among those were *Young Man of Manhattan* (April 18, 1930), *Queen High* (April 22, 1930), and *Sitting Pretty* (December 1, 1933) during the theatre's fifth anniversary celebration in which she sang "Did You Ever Hear a Dream Walking."

John Douglas Eames (1985: ii) would also write in the studio's in-house publication about triumphant musicals made by Paramount during the 1930s. Named among those was *The Love Parade*, which played here during the week of April 4, 1930, and which costarred Jeanette MacDonald along with Maurice Chevalier. And Eames's contention would be supported by the film historian John Baxter (1968: 32–33), who'd previously written the following about *Love Me Tonight*, which played here during the week of October 7, 1932, and costarred Charles Ruggles and Myrna Loy: "If there is a better musical of the Thirties, one wonders what can it be." Others were light dramatic comedies, which cornered the market despite its reported constantly shifting financial structure.

Suffice to note here these obvious thematic subjects in films over time: for example, blockbusters about historical events, whether or not with religious subject matter, and whose popularity was such they often were held over for a second or third week: *Union Pacific*, starring Joel McCray, for example, a film about the transcontinental railroad also directed by Cecil B. DeMille that unusually was shown on a Monday, May 29, 1939, inarguably to get the jump on rival movie houses, when their usual openings were on Fridays. Two other block-busters with religious themes were *The Sign of the Cross*, featuring Paramount contract players like Claudette Colbert, Fredric March, and Charles Laughton, which opened on February 9, 1933, and *The Crusades* (also directed by Cecil B. DeMille) during the week of October 25, 1935—the latter, another remake of his Silent Film classic originally shown in other theatres in 1923.

Westerns were not only an integral part of Hollywood's history, but our theatre's as well. Following the success of DeMille's *The Squaw Man*, which was shown here during one of countless extracurricular-type occasions, others included *The Plainsman*, starring Gary Cooper as "Wild Bill" Hichok and Jean Arthur as Calamity Jane screened here during the week of January 27, 1937. *The Indians Are Coming*, a Western weekly series starring the Silent Film star Tim McCoy screened daily except for Sundays following its debut in 1930 (*Brooklyn Times Union*, September 28, 1930).

Yet another broad thematic genre was swashbuckling pirate films like *The Buccaneer*, starring Fredric March as Jean Lafitte, which opened at the Brooklyn Paramount on March 8, 1938. There were also numerous gangster films, whose popularity was connected with Brooklyn's reputation in the annals of America's organized crime history. A large number of war films were also made by all the major studios during the Second World War. These films curiously attracted audiences comprised mostly of women whose husbands and other family members heeded the call to fight fascism abroad.

Not surprisingly, films about diverse subjects predominated at the Brooklyn Paramount during the 1950s:

1. Teenagers and juvenile delinquency, the latter, a much scrutinized social problem that drew national concern initially in the 1930s, two decades ahead of their alleged cause as a result of the fourth face of our theatre's earlier history, Rock 'n' Roll, famously illustrated by *Blackboard Jungle*, which opened with Bill Haley's anthem from those years, "Rock Around the Clock," screened here on

November 20, 1957, and whose greater concern should have been the nihilism of out-of-control high school students destroying their teacher's precious Jazz collection. That concern was evidenced by these controversial films also screened here: *Teenage Rebel* starring Ginger Rogers during the week of December 5, 1956; *Shake, Rattle and Roll* (November 7, 1956); and a double bill that paired *Dragstrip Girl* with *Rock All Nite* during the week of May 2, 1957—the former sensationally advertised in the *Williamsburg News* on that date as Hollywood's first authentic hot rod picture. It shows crazed modern teenagers in their nonstop thirst for stunts, thrills, chicken races, and Rock 'n' Roll action;

2. sci-film horror films like *Godzilla*, which not only was screened here during the week of May 30, 1956, but curiously got paired with another film dealing with aliens, *Wetbacks*; and

3. flicks during that tumultuous decade whose hidden message was intended to inflame alarms after Russia launched a satellite in space before our nation—*Threshold of Space*, for example, during the week of May 4, 1956.

Eames (1985), in a chapter about Paramount's roller-coaster-like financial history titled "The Mountain Rises Again" discussed the studio's bottom line as follows: How after a downward slump in earnings from $18,381,178 in 1930 to $15,857,544 in 1932 during the Great Depression, Paramount studio earnings would (after a brief recovery once again) drop from $20 million to $6 million following (bankruptcy-caused) divestment. Then after nearly hitting rock bottom with $3 million in profit in 1933, its finances rebounded three years later in 1936 following reorganization and a bailout from the feds. As Eames further wrote, despite back-to-back slump years in 1938 and 1939, the rebranded United Paramount began its steady increase toward stupendous profits.

Still another way of crunching numbers is by examining film production. So, for example, after Paramount-Prolix produced one hundred or so films during the Golden Age of Silent Films, that number precipitously dropped from thirty-six Talkies in 1942 to twenty-nine films in the following year, followed by a slight increase to thirty-one films in the following year, before dropping back down again to twenty films two years later in 1945, and even lower to nineteen films made in 1946, before the studio's spectacular turnabout during the 1950s. Fearing the impact TV might have, Zukor realized greater profits might be made from investments in that relatively new medium.

Apropos, the studio's jackpot year in 1968, six years after the Brooklyn Paramount closed, *The Odd Couple* earned $20 million compounded by more as a result of its TV spin-off serialization. And even greater profits made from films like *Grease* earned $96 million in the 1970s; but that was after the studio's takeover by the conglomerate Gulf and Western in 1966, which resulted in even greater earnings of $290 million—a figure that kept rising to $551 million as a result of globalization, not to mention original films for TV and home viewing as well as commercial profits through advertising that today impact the Internet.

Finally, a decade before the Supreme Court ruled against block booking, additional monopolist practices like exhibiting films owned by studios who produced them violated the Sherman Antitrust Act. Nearly four hundred Talkies made in the late twenties, and thousand from the thirties to the sixties, could hardly fill the policy of double bills, resulting in management's decision to book films from the other major studios at the Brooklyn Paramount.

WOMEN LOVE ONCE (*The Brooklyn Daily Eagle*, June 26, 1931)

CHAPTER 6

Face Two: And That's Spelled V*a*u*d*e*v*i*l*l*e with a Double L, Not Burlesque!

Since Vaudeville alternated with films at the Brooklyn Paramount from its opening early in 1928 until 1934, we identify this popular form of entertainment as the second face of our theatre's history. The term, according to Frank Cullen et al. (2006) derives from *Val-de-brie*, "Songs of the Valley," mid-nineteenth-century compositions credited to a Normandy troubadour, Olivier Basselin, who sang (in French) what were called *chansons du vaud-vire*. So, too, did another scholar, Robert Snyder (1989: 12), traced its etymology from the French—from *voix or vaux de ville*, which he translated as "Voice of the City" and "worthy of city." Bernard Sobel (1961) would add another context for those song sketches, calling them drinking songs and arguing they trace further back historically to the eleventh century Normandy conquest of France under the English Duke of Normandy, a. k. a. William the Conqueror. And Joe Laurie Jr., who worked for many years as a comic during the heyday of Vaudeville in the United States in the early twentieth century, characterized them as songs of the city streets and also added the following:

I do know that originally it was called Variety…(before being called)
Vaudeville, (then) Advanced Vaudeville, Refined Vaudeville, Progres-
sive Vaudeville. And when it was all but dead they called it Glorified
Vaudeville. (Laurie, 1953: 10)

Since anthropologists seek local place-based emic—from phone-
mics in linguistics—understandings of all social and cultural things,
I add what Sophie Tucker offered as an origin story attributed to her
agent, William Morris, founder of the powerful booking agency that
still bears his name, and whom for good reason was called "The Boss."

The way he explained it, vaudeville really began in eating places. Once
upon a time, it seems, there was a miller somewhere in France who
had the bright idea of setting some tables and benches under the trees
by the mill and selling the farmers red wine and homemade bread
and cheese while they waited for their grain to be ground. This mill
was just one of many in the valley of the Vire River. Competition was
pretty keen, and this particular miller counted on his restaurant to draw
trade to his mill. It drew something else as well—the show people who
traveled along the highroad through that valley to Paris. There were
jugglers and acrobats and singers of songs and men with dancing bears
and trained monkeys. When they saw the crowds gathered by the mill,
eating and drinking, they would stop in the road and put on a show for
the customers and then pass the hat. That gave the miller an idea. He
offered them a free meal and a night's lodging to stop at his mill and
put on regular shows for his customers. I don't know what became of
the miller; probably he ended up a millionaire. Anyway, other restaurant
proprietors got the idea that most folks like entertainment as they ate
and started to offer their customers a show. That, the Boss told me,
is how vaudeville began. Even its name is derived from Vaux de Vire
(valley of the Vire). And wasn't one of the great cabarets in Paris the
Moulin Rouge (Red Mill)? (Tucker, 1945: 155–56)

Returning to its history, we read elsewhere that Vaudeville established deep public entertainment roots in Paris by 1792 in the *Theatre de Vaudeville* before jumping the English Channel as a result of diffusion; i.e., another anthropological concept denoting the spread of what the Brits still call variety and variety shows by the 1830s to these shores by 1871, when the earliest use of our term applied to H. Sargent's Great Vaudeville Company in Cincinnati, Ohio. Laurie Jr. would then identify M. S. Leavitt and John W. Ransom as promoters of what in time replaced minstrel shows, whose florescence followed the Civil War (Laurie, 1953). Leavitt, according to another Vaudeville scholar, Alfred McClean (1965: 18–19), claimed to be the first person in America to use the term commercially in 1880, i.e., Leavitt's Gigantic Vaudeville Stars.

Whether or not Arnold Shaw (1978: 37) who worked for song publishers during what we identify as the fourth face of our theatre's earlier history, is correct about the importance of olio minstrel shows in shaping American Vaudeville, i.e., on the basis of similarities between their specialty acts, McClean (1965: 2–7) would additionally write about the myriad ways in which Vaudeville mirrored the "American Myth of Success"; that is, with its "star system, lavish architecture of the theaters—appropriately called 'palaces'—...all (which) pointed to a set of common assumptions about the desirability of making money."

Marcus Loew, as previously noted, might well have been the first to link the presentation of this type of live entertainment with the showing of early Silent Films, but Benjamin Franklin Keith and E. A. Albee formed the earliest powerful booking agency that represented Vaudevillians in our country. Not to be ignored in all this was Antonio (Tony) Pastor, who was born in Greenwich Village in 1832, and ran the gamut in show business from circus ringmaster to minstrel show performer—in blackface—before co-partnering with Sam Sharply and opening Pastor's Opera House on New York's Bowery in 1881. Of greater historical relevance for our concerns, however, is that Pastor abandoned gender-segregated girlie shows called Burlesque for what became clean family entertainment. That was after he purchased a movie theater in Paterson, New Jersey, that attracted women through giveaways of coffee, coal, hams, sewing machines, and silk dresses. It was differentiated as well from the other gender-based form of popular entertainment by signs posted on the walls of Pastor's succeeding Vaudeville place near Tammany Hall off Union Square, which banned swear words, such as damn, slob, and liar, otherwise commonly heard in Burlesque as well as the street. That date in the growing theater district in Manhattan was October 14, 1884. For, as per Sophie Tucker (1945: 106), Tony Pastor should also be credited with playing daily matinees, which depended on women. For, as she additionally wrote, "You had to please the women patrons to be and stay a headliner."

Yet another sociological aspect of Vaudeville's rising popularity was discussed by Snyder (1989: 87). "Vaudeville," he wrote, "was created largely by people from immigrant and working-class backgrounds who supplied it with talent and audiences." And to which, we might add what Snyder (ibid) similarly wrote about Vaudeville as the symbol of the modern American's search for commonality in the Industrial Age...the dazzling wonderland of comfort and convenience brought about by technology and capitalism, which consequently took its permanent place in the popular imagination. In effect, it became the language of the masses with its stereotyped images deliberately and admittedly devoid of artistic quality. Nonetheless, it challenged the needs of heterogeneous American audiences in search of a collective myth of assimilation into the American dream of success.

Before surveying what according to Vaudeville lingo were called Big and Small acts (if not forgotten) of what formulaically also contained animal acts for openers, followed by singers, then short plays with known actors, and so-called "wake 'em up acts" like Apache dancers. Following intermission were penultimate close to closing acts like comics identified in Vaudeville handbooks "as playing to the haircuts," which were aimed to drive out audiences for new customers in this nonstop live entertainment whose motto was "Make it fast and snappy and good."

A capsule account of another ethnic, Belle Baker, who like Tucker played our theatre and also made it in Vaudeville can be presented before our deeper dive.

Dubbed the "Sarah Bernhardt of Song," and fortunate enough to have survived the Triangle Shirtwaist Factory Fire in 1911, after several years of acting in the Yiddish Theater on Second Avenue in Manhattan, she changed her family name from Becker to Baker before transitioning into Vaudeville. Her salary not only increased from five dollars a week to one hundred dollars, but her repertoire expanded in strict accord with ethnically mixed audiences. So, along with singing "Eli Eli" and "My Yiddishe Momma," Yiddish favorites, Ms. Becker/Baker warbled Tin Pan Alley favorites like "All of Me" as well as comic songs like "Come Back Antonio." The latter, a tearjerker about a forty-three-year-old Jewish American woman named Sadie Cohen Jacob who laments her wayward Italian American Roman Catholic husband's desertion by magically attempting to woo her Tony back by singing he should return home and do the right thing, which was to return ASAP to his shoeshine stand and keep his marital vow by providing for his (nagging) wife and destitute (presumably cloying) children! But Belle Baker tugged at the heartstrings of other hyphenated-American audience members in the Brooklyn Paramount and other venues with her renditions of the late-nineteenth-century popular *belle canto* tenor John McCormack's biggest hit, "My Mother's Rosary."—not to mention also playing on their homophobia with another forgotten popular novelty number from those years, "What Did Robinson Caruso Do with Friday on Saturday Night?"

Restated, the dutiful daughter who used bountiful Vaudeville earnings to move her desperately poor parents from the Lower East Side into nicer digs additionally sang "Blue Skies" written by a fellow landsman, Irving Berlin. The song could only have brightened hopes for a better day during the Great Depression, and it became the theme song of her popular radio show toward the end of the Vaudeville era, when some 1,500 acts were said to have folded within a single year. According to the *Times-Union,* Belle Baker was reported as having brought down the house at the Brooklyn Paramount with a few well-chosen jokes. Which, along with sensical and nonsensible phrases employed by others not only were heard on the radio, but in films as well. The phrases got repeated, thereby contributing to what Mencken (2000) discussed as the emergence of a new American language heard among wannabe immigrants anxious to become part of what used to be called the melting pot.

Discussing those one-liners, the comedienne Eve Sully's retort to put-downs from her stereotypically posturing sexist husband/straight man in their mixed gender team, Jesse Block, during those pre–women's liberation years: "Just look at him!" Her retort was uttered on the Brooklyn Paramount stage during at least one of their three appearances—the weeks of November 21, 1930; September 5, 1931; and April 27, 1934.

A pair of nut comics, so-called Weber (Joseph "Joe" Morris) and Fields (Lew), who also performed here, went viral: "Oh, how I luff you, Mike!" Another example being what mad Hungarian comic Joe Penner, who began life as Josef Pinter, must have said during performance weeks of May 8, 1931, and April 23, 1932, while holding his rubber duck named "Goo-goo" for additional yuks: "You wanna buy a duck?" And the other catchy phrase also proffered by Penner for comic effect, "You naaaasty man!"

A final example was Bill "Bojangles" Robinson's recondite declaration: "Everything's copasetic!" A phrase which came to mean "Everything's cool!" in African American speech and derived from jangle applied to a contentious person, such as the personable hoofer who also appeared here twice and always carried a gun was also known to be.

The *Vaudeville Guidebook* reproduced in Snyder (1989) differentiates four subcategories of what it called legitimate acts represented by agents, and illegitimate because those were viewed as derivative:

1. child performers who either began as street urchins—like Eddie Cantor—or received training in schools like the one run by Gus

Edward, which also included Georgie Jessel, who also performed here;

2. youngsters whose early training occurred in family troupes like the one that produced the great sour-faced comic, Buster Keaton, who didn't perform at the Brooklyn Paramount;
3. singers like Sophie Tucker, whose careers began in cafés; and
4. jugglers and acrobats, otherwise dubbed as specialty people or silent and dummy acts.

What follows is an A–Z compendium of those really big stars—as Ed Sullivan said while introducing many of these performers on his Sunday-night TV variety show, which the writer Tennessee Williams acerbically termed "tired Vaudeville." That is, a sampling from the thousand or so described in the local tabloid as providing "a fairyland of light, a wonderland of color, a garden of talented and beautiful girls, all expert entertainers, musical surprises and a blend of the best in popular classical entertainment—a stage show that is more than that—this is the type of public stage show which will appear at the Brooklyn Paramount."

So, turning to the first letter in our Phoenician-derived alphabet, Ethel Cecile Rosalie Allen was the female half of the married comedic team Burns and Allen. "Oh, George, I bet you say that to all the girls!" Was the iconic one-liner authored by the so-called Mrs. Malapropism, whose Spoonerisms defined their act, and who once for fun ran for the American presidency?

ALLEN, Fred (née John Florence Sullivan), previously shucked two other early stage names—Paul Huckle and Freddy James—while beginning in Vaudeville as the "World's Worst Juggler." He famously starred in *Three's a Crowd*, which played in our theatre during the week of March 25, 1932. Billed as a "$5.50 Broadway musical show presented at popular prices," it originally co-starred Clifton Webb and Libby Holman and advertised here as an "entirely new show" produced by Max Gordon, the owner of the Village Vanguard in Manhattan, still among the most famous venues for Jazz, i.e., the third face of our theatre's earlier history.

Quoting from one of Fred Allen's published *Letters* about that appearance on our theatre's stage, he wittily recalled:

At Brooklyn, I was worth 25c at the first show, $35 from two p.m. until six and from then until closing time it cost 65c to see me when I was good and tired. The mentality of the average picture theatre audience is so low you can't call them down unless you are in a sewer, but I am slowly adjusting myself and will eventually find their medium of banter. I have invented such jokes as—"Do you know Andy Mellon?"—and the other fellow says—"No, but I know his brother Walter." That will give you an idea. (McCarthy, 1966: 79–80)

Michele Hilms (1997: 200–202) reminds us, however, that Fred Allen's greatest success was in radio when he teamed up with his wife, Portland Hoffa, whose famous one-liner simply was: "Oh, *Mr. Allen!*" Hilms describes the monologist as a figure of totemic resistance whose acerbic wit in radio skits like the following caused fits for producers and commercial sponsors: "If you want to know who we are, we're the hucksters of radio (and) confidentially all jerks!" Another example was this risqué allusion to Union Station in Hollywood, where Fred Allen also spent years writing scripts and starring in films: "The only train stop In America where aspiring actresses back off the trains!"

ASH (née Ashenberry), Paul was raised in Milwaukee after his family immigrated to the United States from Germany. He achieved great fame in Vaudeville initially as a bandleader in Chicago, and whose abundant energy included jumping onto stages from orchestra pits. His constant good cheer as the Brooklyn Paramount's first stage bandleader led Oscar Door, a *Brooklyn Eagle* columnist, to attempt to comprehend.

In an article on November 21, 1928, titled "Genial Giant of Jazz, Syncopates for Rhythm Mad Audiences," notwithstanding the journalist's suspiciousness, he was genuine and the stage bandleader's boyish over-the-top effusions might be attributed to his redheaded marcel wave. Just how big was Paul Ash, who advertised men's commercial hair products in his day? Along with also having discovered Helen Kane after George Dewey Washington, not only did Ash's portrait appear on the block-long mural on the DeKalb Avenue side of our theatre, there reportedly were 2,400 button-wearing fans in the Greater Paul Ash Fan Club during the 1920s. Ash offered to donate $10,000 to the Chicago Symphony Orchestra's efforts to increase salaries in 1927, provided it went only for salaries—as reported in *The New York Times* on August 4 of that year.

AUSTIN, Lemuel, a. k. a. Gene Lucas, had a million-selling record in 1927, "My Blue Heaven," which he sang on stage here during the week of September 27, 1929.

BECK, Billie (née Hattie Helen Gould) was renamed Sally Rand by Cecil B. DeMille. She titillated audiences with her controversial fan dance, thereby challenging the conventional line drawn between Vaudeville and Burlesque by provocatively wearing ostrich feathers on stage which covered—and exposed—her nudity, and about which she quipped: "Proving the fan is quicker than the eye." The following comes from a review in the *Brooklyn Eagle* about Sally Rand's lone appearance on stage here during the week of March 2, 1934:

Apparently some people had the bright idea to come in early and get front seats, with the result that at 6 o'clock the front half of the orchestra floor was solidly packed. By the time the dancer went on, most of the lower floor was pre-emptied, but this did not prevent most of the latecomers from marching down the aisle to the orchestra pit and then walking slowly back in the hope of detecting some seat in a section where close inspection would be possible. The ushers did their best to check the rush, but they were outnumbered and those in the side section had their view of part of the stage almost continuously interrupted. Practically everyone wanted front seats and would not take the ushers' word there were none. Plenty of room at the 9 o'clock show.

In Billy Minsky's Burlesque theatre on Fulton Street, *Variety* would report that "150 feet from the Paramount box office...ten times as much nudity to be seen." Moreover, its reviewer quipped: "The best Brooklyn did about it was to yelp for the police with business generally pretty poor." And while the trade magazine's journalist ended by likening her provocative performance to moll psychology, he also reported kickers who protested the nudity of Sally Rand...(yet nonetheless came) to satisfy their curiosity. As for the notoriety of that controversy, she was quoted in the tabloid on March 4, 1934, saying:

I created the fan dance in 1929 as an esthetic symbolization of a great white bird flying in the moonlight.

I use the fans to give the impression of wings. Because I depict a bird I create the illusion of nudity. You never saw a bird wearing pants. The entire concept is artistic and beautiful.

BENNY, Jack (née Benjamin Kubelsky) was touted as "Everyone's Favorite Comedian!" Gary Giddins (2000) observed he might still well be the only great comedian in American showbusiness without an identifiable joke. But Jack Benny carved out a stage persona claiming always to be thirty-nine years old and playing the consummate cheapskate as well as the violin. "Well?" He could always draw additional laughter by standing starchily with both arms folded akimbo famously insulted before delivering this demurral to a thief's demand for money: "I'm thinking!"

But Jack Benny really did play the violin; that is, rather than employing it as a prop, as was the case with another comedian, Henny Youngman. Trained to perform Western Classical music as a child, he performed *Zigeneurweiser*, "Gypsy Airs," with numerous orchestras while raising nearly six million dollars for various causes (Fein, 1976: 248–55). As for his lone stage appearance here during the week of May 27, 1932, Jack Benny was advertised as a "popular comedian of stage, screen...who in the past four weeks has established himself as a radio star." And so, too, was *Love Thy Neighbor* among the Hollywood films he starred in, and which was screened here during the week of December 25, 1940. From the cast of Jack Benny's long-running successful radio show, we might note the bumbling Jewish character Mr. Kitzel, played by Artie Auerbach, who'd previously covered the Lindbergh/Bruno Hauptman infant kidnapping case as a professional photographer, and Eddie "Rochester" Anderson, the son of a Black Vaudevillian who always got a laugh at the expense of his straight, white-man boss. Jack Benny's off-stage wife Mary Livingston's cutting lines were also directed at his expense.

BURNS, George (née Nathan Birnbaum) not only went through five professional surnames during his nearly century-long career— Eddie Delight, Billy Pierce, Captain Betts, Jed Jackson, and Jimmy Malone—but he also lived long enough to partner with several comediennes after his real-life unflappable stooge-like wife retired. Lest readers have forgotten, or worse are unfamiliar with the most famous Burns and Allen Vaudeville routine titled *Lamb Chops*, it went like this:

> "Gracie, do you like to love?" "Why, no, George." "Do you like to kiss?" "Why, no, George." "Then what do you like, Gracie?" "Well, you ought to know, George—lamb chops!" "Well, a little girl like you, Gracie, could you eat two lamb chops alone?" Followed by her punchline: "Of course not, George...but with potatoes I would!"

Finally, we note that Burns and Allen performed on stage at the Brooklyn Paramount twice: during the weeks of March 25, 1932, and May 27, 1932. But following Gracie's retirement from their successful TV carryover in 1968, her husband continued working until his one-hundredth birthday! With his cigar serving as a prop.

BERLE, Milton (née Milton Berlinger) became Uncle Miltie and Mr. TV during the formative years of that new medium in the 1950s. A comic who cleverly incorporated what other comedians routinely did, i.e., steal jokes as part of his persona, Berle, like other male performers in Vaudeville, cross-dressing as part of his *schtick*, included four performances on stage here during these dates: the weeks of December 30, 1932, and December 1, 1933; and twice more in 1934—the latter date close to the end of this second face in our theatre's earlier history. Describing his penultimate appearance during the week of February 9, 1934, the *Times-Union* one day later not only praised Berle's "super-specialized stage show," but also pronounced him "the greatest comedian the footlights have ever seen." His appearance during the week of December 1, 1933, in *The World's Fair Frolics* was part of the theatre's fifth anniversary. During Milton Berle's last appearance—the week of March 11, 1934—that power-packed manic entertainer, who appeared on stage here with Bing Crosby and others, was also said to have "mowed down his audience" with running gags, as well as singing and tap-dancing with the Nicholas Brothers, African American performers described as "two sepia youths."

BRICE, Fanny (née Fania Borah) appeared here twice: during the weeks of September 30, 1932, and December 9, 1932, respectively. She achieved show business immortality with *My Man*, originally a French chanson titled *Mon Homme* at the Ziegfeld Follies in 1920, and a subsequent hit identified with the Jazz singer Billie Holiday. A comedienne said to have paid $125,000 by Warner Brothers for appearing in the film with that name that never was screened here, Goldman (1992: 139) also wrote about the life of this radio star of a long-running show who introduced "Baby Snooks" on Broadway. The musical *Funny Girl* in the 1970s starred Brooklyn's Barbra Streisand, who also appeared in *Funny Lady*, its film version. Other songs famously performed by Brice, whose "Dying Swan" ballet satire at the Ziegfeld Follies in 1910 jump-started her comedic career, included "Second Hand Rose." Sophie Tucker (1945: 57) memorably described Fanny Brice as a tall, lanky, funny-faced kid with rubber legs. And finally we note in this brief sketch of that big Vaudevillian, whose romantic involvement with Julius W. Arnstein, on whom she spent a small fortune twice on separate court cases, which resulted in separate sentences of fourteen months for wiretapping in 1918 and an even longer term in 1924 for stealing five million dollars of bank securities prior to their divorce.

FANNY BRICE DRAWING (*The Brooklyn Daily Eagle*/January 28, 1929)

CANTOR, Eddie (née Isidore Itzkowitz) morphed from singing in back of a candy store on the Lower East Side not unlike those owned by this author's maternal grandparents into a singing waiter in Carey Walsh's saloon in Coney Island—occasionally accompanied on piano by Jimmy Durante, no less.

EDDIE CANTOR (*The Brooklyn Daily Eagle,* December 23, 1932)

Cantor's start reputedly has him stealing material from a Black pianist in a Bowery saloon unfortunately named Nigger Mike's. Subsequently famous for "Makin' Whoopee," a song David Weinstein (2018: 144) argues was performed blackface with white-rimmed eyeglasses solely for comedic affect, Eddie Cantor returned here on December 24, 1932, more than four years after his initial screen appearance during the Brooklyn Paramount's opening week. The latter, as described by the *Standard Union* on another date, displays his frenetic energy that included a cross-dressed impersonation of the legendary Silent Film star Greta Garbo in *Grand Hotel.*

Along with four additional return stage appearances—during the weeks of June 5, 1930; September 4, 1931; September 18, 1931; and January 5, 1934—Eddie Cantor also starred in *Kid Boots* (with Clara Bow) screened here. Another reviewer in the borough's leading local tabloid praised Cantor's impersonation of Mae West as a personal hit during the third of those appearance dates. A more detailed review of Cantor's final appearance here appeared in *Variety* (January 9, 1934). It describes the nonstop effervescent performer variously plugging his radio show; joking about the orchestra leader, Dave Rubinoff; calling attention to a forthcoming film; praising the newly formed Film Promotion Censorship Board; riffing on a member of his show, Bob Rippa, whom he introduced as a very good juggler—then proceeding to juggle three balls himself; praising FDR; and finally offering what were termed Jewish similes despite no blackface.

As the founder of the Jewish Actors' Union, Cantor's serious side sought to restore Vaudevillians' wages drastically slashed during the Great Depression (Weinstein, 2018: 99). He also generously sponsored summer camp vacations for city kids at the Education Alliance's Surprise Lake in Cold Spring, New York. Additional political involvements included leading an actor's strike for better wages against Hollywood studios during the early 1930s. After breaking into radio on September 13, 1931, this multimedia big star years later got canned by a commercial sponsor (Camel cigarettes) for an anti-Hitler remark. But it didn't prevent Eddie Cantor in the late 1940s from antagonizing them yet again—in 1946, when that *cause celebre* resulted from defending an African American Jazz singer on his show, Thelma Carpenter, who apparently got fired for refusing to stereotypically sing the Blues.

Among Cantor's other recording hits—performed in blackface— were "Ma, He's Making Eyes at Me," "If You Knew Susie," "How You Gonna Keep 'Em Down on the Farm After They See Paree," and "Ida," the name of his lifelong marital partner. And his famous one-liner was: "Let's sit down and smoke a herring together."

After his supervision of a condensed version of Ziegfeld's "Whoopee" during the week of April 14, 1930, nearly two dozen years after his name had initially appeared in lights while working in 1912 under the headliners (Jean) Bendini and (Roy) Arthur, jugglers/parodists/female impersonators, whose act would be retitled "Bedini and Arthur assisted by Eddie Cantor," this wisdom-type story attached to place appeared in Art Arthur's newspaper column on January 4, 1934. It told about a visit to his dressing room under the stage at the Brooklyn Paramount and an encounter with a bright-eyed old man cleaning up while he interviewed Cantor. He had been part of that team, which gave the comic his initial break in show business, and whom he later met outside in the street, both enjoying the coincidence of sharing their given birth names. Finally, Eddie Cantor starred in *Fog* during the week of January 7, 1934, the film's distinction being that it was among the earliest produced by a different studio than Paramount—Columbia Pictures in this instance.

COLUMBO, Russ (née Ruggeiero Eugenio di Rodolfo) changed the original spelling of his shortened birth name by substituting a "u" for one of those three "o's." And whether or not the TV sleuth Peter Falk, whose detective series was titled as such, could have confirmed the lingering mystery of that crooner's death from a dueling pistol while playing Russian Roulette with his partner, among the highlights of Russ Columbo's relatively brief career was recording with Gus Arnhem and His Ambassadors on Victor. "I Surrender Dear" was the theme song of Columbo, the "Romeo of Song," who performed on stage here a record-breaking eleven consecutive weeks in Vaudeville—from November 20, 1931, through the week of January 29, 1932. He also appeared in the fourth in a series of Paramount films about radio, *The Big Broadcast*, which played our house during the week of October 12, 1932.

Promoted not unlike second-generation white Rock 'n' Roll performers on his good looks and resemblance to Valentino, news of

Russ Columbo's death was held by his doting mother, who received letters from his devoted friends as part of that protective subterfuge!

CROSBY, Bing (née Harry Lillis Crosby) was born in Tacoma, Washington. The subject of a PBS *American Masters*, which in itself belies the magnitude of his importance in popular culture, "El Bingo" began a lengthy career in show business as the drummer in a trio with a boyhood buddy, Al Rinker, the brother of the Jazz singer Mildred Bailey. Along with holding the previously unsung record for the number of films starred in the Brooklyn Paramount's earlier history, Bing Crosby, during the so-called "Battle of the Crooners" appeared on stage here for six consecutive weeks between February 12 and March 18, 1932...but never appeared with his rival, Russ Columbo, who also alternated at Manhattan's Paramount on different dates.

Referencing Gary Giddins's (2001: 46) comprehensive biography of the first half of Bing Crosby's life, these countless firsts might be extracted: a discography of 1,668 recorded songs plus hundreds more heard live on radio, as well as on TV; the first male vocalist ever signed to perform full time with any orchestra; Crosby's "White Christmas" topped American pop charts twenty times and almost annually between 1942 and 1962; the most number one pop hits—thirty-eight; and ranked the number one Hollywood box office attraction on five separate occasions between 1944 and 1948. Finally, we should also note Bing Crosby's three Academy Award nominations, winning one for *Going My Way*.

Our selection for the letter "D" requires DURANTE, Jimmy's separating from Clayton, Jackson and Durante, who played our theatre as a musical/comedic trio twice: during the weeks of February 21, 1930 and June 5, 1931. Née James Francis Durante, he was advertised initially as "Ragtime Jimmy (who) plays (piano) and jokes" before becoming a much-beloved persona because of his gravelly voiced Lower East Side manner of singing, talking, and fabulously outsized nose. Nicknamed as "Schnozzola," Durante was also seen in *The Phantom President*, a Paramount precode film starring George M. Cohan and Claudette Colbert that screened here during the week of September 30, 1932.

The mystery of Jimmy Durante's famous TV media signoff, "Good night, Mrs. Kalabash, wherever you are," has apparently been solved. It was his way of keeping alive the memory of a beloved wife, Jeanne Carson, who tragically died in a plane crash in the Kalaba Mountains near their home in Southern California.

ETTING, Ruth, a torch singer whose marriage to a gangster not unlike Fanny Brice's very nearly defined as well as derailed her career. Indeed, Ruth Etting's ménage-a-trois would prompt her jealous husband, Moe "the Gimp" Snyder, to gun down his wife's lover and piano man, Harry Alderman, on their front door step in 1938! Ruth Etting's biography inspired the Hollywood biopic *Love Me or Leave Me* starring Doris Day, which unfortunately did not play here. Among her hit songs were "Shine on Harvest Moon," "Mean to Me," and "Button Up Your Overcoat." She also started out in the Ziegfeld Follies in 1927, singing an Irving Berlin song, "Shaking the Blues Away," that seemingly was prescient about the coming Great Depression. And while this chanteuse never performed on stage in Vaudeville in our theatre, we further make this exception for that big star in Vaudeville because of her role in a Paramount musical short screen, titled *Follies*, shown here during the second week of the Brooklyn Paramount's operation.

GRAY, Gilda (née Marianna Michalska) was born in Kraków, Poland, and not only successfully made the transition from Silent Films to the Talkies but achieved renown because of her association with the Shimmy. That's the name of one of many dance crazes originating in Harlem that swept the nation during the Roaring Twenties, not Gilda Gray's boyfriend—as Borsch Belt Jewish comedians would joke. She claimed to have invented the Shimmy during a performance of "The Star-Spangled Banner" while reportedly shaking with embarrassment after forgetting the lyrics. Years later, however, Gilda Gray changed her tune: "My entire routine was the result of having decided to shake my chemise," she related.

In addition to appearing in Ziegfeld's *Follies* and George White's *Scandals*, she went from a starring role in the Silent Film original version of *Cabaret* in 1927 to *Rose-Marie*, a popular Talkie about the

Canadian Royal Mounted Police starring Nelson Eddy and Jeanette McDonald, which was filmed in Lake Tahoe and featured Nevada's First People talking Northern Paiute instead of any far northern indigenous people's language—a filmed light opera that never played the Brooklyn Paramount.

HOLMAN, Libby is yet another sadly forgotten former big Vaudeville star today. The torch singer, née Elizabeth Lloyd Holtzman, was born in Cincinnati, Ohio, where as the saying "You can't make this up" goes, that Midwestern city was America's pig industry capital and the birthplace of Reform Judaism, which absolves kashruth prohibitions and allowed eating pork. "Body and Soul," Libby Holman's signature song, was composed by a precious twenty-three-year-old named Johnny Green, who for a month led the Brooklyn Paramount Orchestra and premiered at the Broadway show *Three's a Crowd*, which leapfrogged across the East River from Broadway to the Brooklyn Paramount stage during the week of March 23, 1932. A civil rights activist as well, Libby Holman was initially charged with the murder of her wealthy husband, a tobacco magnate, and years later took her own life. On stage here, the diva sang in a Vaudeville sketch titled *Orange Follies* during the week of June 21, 1931, which, curiously enough, was performed five times daily between screenings of *Confession of a Co-ed*.

HOPE, Bob (née Leslie Townes Hope), another emerging transcendent mega-show-business superstar born in London, was a hoofer at the age of four and went on from being really big in Vaudeville to bigger if not better appearances on radio and TV following his film career. The much-caricatured ski-slope-nosed quipster famously costarred with Bing Crosby and Dorothy Lamour in road films named for different global destinations that played here, before leading a touring troupe of performers that entertained our troops during World War II and the Korean conflict, as well as frequently at home on army bases during peacetime. After appearing at the Brooklyn's Paramount during the waning years of Vaudeville—the week of April 7, 1933, to be exact—Bob Hope returned nearly two decades later on November 24, 1950, with a retro-Vaudeville show.

"Thanks for the Memories" was the theme song of Bob Hope. He starred in thirty-one films screened, second only to Bing Crosby.

JESSEL, George Albert, a. k. a. Little Georgie Jessiel, began in show business as a youngster under Gus Leonard's mentorship. A local tabloid reviewer wrote about Georgie Jessel when he played the famed Palace Theater near Times Square in Manhattan that opened in 1913 and closed in 1932, the following: "Slams a revue together in the face of the audience." But while performing on our theatre's stage with Sophie Tucker during the week of October 17, 1931, a *Standard Union* reviewer wryly praised the former Broadway stage star of *The Jazz Singer* as "one of the comedians willing to change jokes twice a season." And so, too, would Jessel return here during the week of April 2, 1932, as emcee of *Three's a Crowd*, which was reviewed as "acclaimed by thousands of Brooklyn Paramount fans...a musical extravaganza...(brought to) the popular playhouse...(within) the reach of every person's purse."

A noted singer otherwise of specialty or novelty songs, Georgie Jessel performed "Oh, How I Laughed When I Think How I Cried." Then returning here twice more, he headed up his own revue during the week of August 19, 1932, and returned during Christmas week in a show advertised as "Reunited with Eddie Cantor."

KANE, Helen (née Helen Clare Schroeder) appeared in a Vaudeville sketch during the week of May 2, 1930, between screenings of *The New Adventures of Fu Man Chu*. The popularity of her Betty Boop cartoon, singing "I Wanna Be Loved By Only You" was of such enormity that she not only earned between $5,000 and $7,000 weekly in Vaudeville, but she also amassed an unknown fortune as a result of paraphernalia associated with facsimile dolls following its debut in Mae West's blockbuster film in 1933, *She Done Him Wrong*. One year later, however, Helen Kane sued Paramount-Publix for $250,000 for what today would be termed intellectual property rights regarding her alter ego (*Brooklyn Eagle*, April 6, 1934).

LAHR, Bert (née Irving Larhelm) amassed so many performance credits that the best we can hope in a sketch of the King of Laughter is to recount the roles of Zeke, the Cowardly Lion in the 1939 MGM remake of the Silent Film *The Wizard of Oz*, and of Estragon on Broadway in 1956 in Samuel Beckett's landmark surrealistic play *Waiting for Godot*. Both roles followed Burt Lahr's appearance on our theatre's stage in a Vaudeville revue during the week of July 29, 1932, headlined by Smilin' Eddie Lowery.

"Is Everybody Happy?"

We don't intend that as a question, but reprise what the tragedian Ted LEWIS (née Theodore Leopold Leonard), a professional clarinetist by trade who was also dubbed the "clown prince of Jazz," asked. Notwithstanding its nationwide adoption in those years and that the one-liner was co-opted from a Black Vaudevillian named Harry Brown in 1906, Ted Lewis was also famous for "Me and My Shadow," performed always on stage in tux and silk top hat jauntily tilted at a severe angle on his head while baton twirling and dancing "the old soft shoe."

A reviewer in the local tabloid described Ted Lewis's act in 1919 as follows: "His middle name is rhythm, and he fingers a wicked clarinet not to mention does a mean shimmy." Billed, during his two appearances on stage here—the weeks of February 6, 1931, and November 11, 1932—as "Ted Lewis, the hatted tragician [*sic*] of song," the bandleader of the "Musical Clowns" was also advertised as heading up a "red hot stage show with fun and syncopation."

LUCAS, Nick (née Dominic Nicholas Antony Lucanese) not only was dubbed the Crooning Troubadour, but he achieved a level of such technical proficiency on the guitar that Gibson manufactured the Nick Lucas Special in his name. Indeed, Nick Lucas's name remains inscribed in Jazz histories as having recorded the first Jazz guitar solos on "Teasing the Frets" and "Picking the Guitar," recorded in 1922. In addition to performing on the very closing night of the Palace on November 16, 1932, Nick Lucas's signature song was "Tip Toe Through the Tulips," which famously (or infamously?) got reprised a half century later by Tiny Tim, whose short-lived career of kitsch included marrying Miss Vickie on Johnny Carson's late-night TV variety show on December 17, 1969, while, yes, accompanying himself on the ukulele and singing that Tin Pan Alley number.

MERMAN, Ethel (née Ethel Agnes Zimmerman) was reported as having been discovered on the Brooklyn Paramount stage…while earning a commercial diploma at Bryant High School in Queens, New York. She became infatuated with show business as a result of living near the Paramount studio in Astoria near her home. Vinton Freeman, according to Ethel Merman's frequently retold origin story, supposedly discovered the starstruck stenographer singing in our theatre in 1930 and promptly rushed her for an audition in the swanky Riverside Drive apartment of the great American composer George Gershwin… who in turn (reportedly) immediately gave her a small part in *Girl Crazy*, a Broadway production he cowrote with his brother and collaborator, the lyricist Ira Gershwin.

The New York Times related a different origin story on February 19, 1939. It credited her discovery to Lou Irwin, who reportedly heard her singing in Little Russia, a café on Fifty-Seventh Street in Manhattan. He convinced her to give up her $100 a week job at the B. K. Vacuum Booster-Brake Company for a succession of Manhattan gigs before Vinton Freeman purportedly heard the Broadway diva sing. The new personality girl was described in Brooklyn's *Times Union* (July 27, 1930) as having the greatest singing voice of the year. Accompanied by Al Siegel on piano, she originally sang—more like belted out—numbers like "Eadie Was a Lady," "You're an Old Smoothie," and "I Got Rhythm" in *Girl Crazy*, a Broadway musical and song that not only entered the Great American Songbook but also became iconic in Jazz history as a result of its changes, i.e., chord progression of melody improvised upon.

Ethel Merman performed on stage here five times during our theatre's Vaudeville years…six, counting her featured role in *Follow the Leader*, a film costarring the comic Ed Wynn that screened here during the week of December 5, 1930. "And it was from a pew in that transpontine picture palace that producer Vinton Freeman first heard Miss Merman dish it out and saw the patrons' take with howls of delight." We reprise that origin story, which also speaks about her powerful booming voice not unlike our Mighty Wurlitzer on June 25, 1930, sans microphone, and could also be heard crystal clear at the top of the balcony!

Ethel Merman starred in some of the most famous musicals in Broadway's history: *Annie Get Your Gun*, *Gypsy*, and *Call Me Madam*, naming only three.

NEGRI, Pola (née Barbara Apolonia Chalupiec) was a German Polish silent screen star seen in Adolph Zukor's earliest overseas-made films. The imported sultry Paramount-Prolix film star appeared on stage here during the week of March 18, 1932, in what was billed as an "original dramatic sketch by Jack Lait." Advertised on that date as "The Fiery Star of Two Continents," Pola Negri helped launch the career of the violinist-cum-crooner Russ Columbo. In addition, she was advertised as the "Queen of Tragedy," i.e., after Negri's Silent Film debut in 1923 in Paramount's *Bella Donna*, she (apparently) witnessed the still unsolved mysterious death of the wife of yellow journalist newspaper tycoon William Randolph Hearst aboard his yacht.

NOVIS, Donald George was billed as "Radio's Favorite Voice" and "The Sweetest Voice This Side of Heaven" as well as "The Voice the Nation Loves." He, according to the *Times-Union* on December 30, 1933, also stopped the show with his song at the Brooklyn Paramount. The English singer performed here eight times; count them: during the weeks of October 21, 1932; October 28, 1932; November 11, 1932; November 18, 1932; December 9, 1932; and for an additional three weeks in the following year, commencing March 17, 1933; as well as on March 31, 1933; and September 29, 1933. Another glowing encomium about this former big Vaudeville star was issued by the *Standard Union*, whose reviewer welcomed Donald Novis's initial performance on October 23, 1932, following five weeks at the Manhattan Paramount by dubbing him the acknowledged finest voice on the air (radio). His voice was not only heard in *The Big Broadcast*, which was screened here during the week of October 14, 1932, but in Disney's animated film *Bambi*.

OAKIE, Jack (née) Lewis Delaney Offield acquired his stage name in Muskogee, Oklahoma. His beaming smile not only lit up the Broadway stage but was also carried over to the Golden Age of Silent Films and the early Talkies that followed. Jack Oakie's lone stage appearance here occurred during the week of June 27, 1930, in a Vaudeville skit that accompanied Paramount's remake of the Silent Film *Border Legion*.

PICKFORD, Mary (née Gladys Louise Smith) was inarguably Paramount's biggest Silent Film star during the 1920s. The studio's founder wrote about his legendary—losing—battles negotiating contracts with the Canadian film star called America's Sweetheart and her doting mother (Zukor and Kramer, 1953: 99). Along with Douglas Fairbanks, who became her first husband, she joined forces with Charlie Chaplin and formed United Artists, Hollywood's first independent studio entirely run by actors. As part of a special Vaudeville production, Mary Pickford appeared on our theatre's stage in *A Church Mouse* during the week of February 2, 1934; the latter was a sketch drawn from her popular radio dramatic series with that same title. But so, too, was Mary Pickford's lone appearance here timed with the release of her film *All of Me*. And arguably as well implying her commitment to civil rights and racial justice, a local tabloid wrote about America's Sweetheart in that year as follows: "In addition to Miss Pickford the (Brooklyn) Paramount has this week on the stage a number of colored artists from Lew Leslie's recent revue, *A Rhapsody in Black*."

QUILLAN, Eddie was another former big star of Vaudeville whose name has largely been forgotten. Dubbed "the screen's youngest comic" for his lone appearance on stage here during the week of August 16, 1929, Eddie Quillan also went to numerous dramatic minor roles in Hollywood Talkies, such as *Mutiny on the Bounty*, *Young Lincoln*, and *The Grapes of Wrath*, naming only a few. But he also starred in *The Sophomore*, an all-dialogue advertised film about college life, screened here during the week of November 23, 1929. Finally, Eddie Quillan lived long enough not only to appear in televised episodes of *Perry Mason* two decades later in the 1950s, but also in the original TV series *Matlock* some twenty years later.

Mindful as we (unfortunately) remain of our intimidating public-school spinster-teachers' spelling admonition that the letter "U" must always follow "Q" in English words, in lieu of any such named representative, the next alphabetic listing of a big Vaudeville star is awarded to RAFT, George. Born in Hell's Kitchen on the West Side of Manhattan, which inspired the Universal film from 1957 titled *Slaughter on Tenth Avenue,* and whose gangs were additionally drawn upon by Leonard Bernstein in his memorable folk opera *West Side Story*, George Raft not only famously played gangster parts in Hollywood reportedly as a result of having been "connected" in real life, but also maintained a lifelong friendship with the notorious Jewish gangster Benjamin "Bugsy" Siegel of Brooklyn's notorious Murder Inc., and at whose trial he appeared as a character witness. Indeed, Raft's profile in the *Brooklyn Eagle* on April 11, 1934, references his off-screen gangster-like dress and tough-guy demeanor while surrounded by a traveling crew of thugs.

George Raft began in show business as a dancer. Apropos, his starring role in *Bolero* costarring the Silent Film sex goddess Carole Lombard, which played at our theater during the week of February 16, 1934: and that is, two years following the first of his two stage appearances dancing on stage during the Vaudeville years on December 9, 1932. Other starring film roles that also were screened here during our theatre's relatively few Vaudeville years include *Undercover Man* (during the week of December 19, 1932); *If I Had a Million* (with Sylvia Sidney, January 5, 1933); *Pick Up* (March 13, 1933); *All of Me* (costarring Mary Pickford, February 2, 1934); *You're Telling Me* (with W. C. Fields, April 6, 1934); *Marge and Diane* (April 13, 1934); *The Trumpet Blows* (April 13, 1934); *Limehouse Blues* (October 28, 1934); and *Night After Night,* which opened on December 21, 1934, and costarred Mae West with whom Raft was rumored to have been romantically linked. Still others among those fifteen films that played here after the demise of Vaudeville included *Rhumba* (August 8, 1935) and *Souls at Sea* during the week of November 3, 1937.

RUBINOFF, David, the Western Classical violinist, appeared

during the opening week of our theatre's operation. Dubbed "The Radio King," his virtuosity was described in the *Brooklyn Eagle* on March 7, 1932, as having "perfected...(a) unique and original style of playing jazz compositions" coupled with an appreciation of "the best music in the modern popular vein."—and that is, after Rubinoff's catholicity also prompted a *Standard Union* reviewer two years prior on July 5, 1930, on the other hand, to chide those selections performed here as "a little bizarre;" i.e., specifically as the result of the orchestra leader's performance of George M. Cohan's barnburner "Yankee Doodle" in a program that also included Stephen Foster's American iconic songs like "Dixie" and "Marching Through Georgia," whose implied racism was discussed by the noted Jazz writer and cultural critic, Gary Giddins (1998b). Described as a taskmaster who broke sixteen floorboards as a result of his fury during rehearsals in our theatre, David Rubinoff's immense popularity during the Vaudeville years saw him lead to command performances at the White House. Apart from solo performances, Rubinoff wielded the baton for the Brooklyn Paramount Orchestra for two weeks in May 1932; three times in 1933 and 1934, e.g., during the week of February 3, 1933, when they performed a special arrangement of an Irving Berlin tune under his firm grasp, and during the week of March 17, 1933, when a timely medley of Irish airs were offered to commemorate St. Patrick's Day; and finally during the week of February 9, 1934, when the orchestra was featured in *Radio Frolics* starring Milton Berle as well as lesser-known Vaudevillians.

SMITH, Kate (née Kathryn Elizabeth Smith) was dubbed the "Songbird of the South" as well as the "First Lady of the Radio." After starring in *The Kate Smith (Radio) Show*, which began as fifteen-minute segments on NBC on March 17, 1931, and survived against the most popular show in radio history, *Amos 'n' Andy*, that similarly achieved national prominence and expanded to six nights weekly, including Sunday night broadcasts as well (Chapter 10), Kate Smith, like so many other white performers in Vaudeville began as a coon singer. "That's Why Darkies Were Born," was, for example, the title of an explicitly racist song recorded by the warbler, whose popularity, according to Arnold Shaw (1986: 41–44), commenced in 1895. A reviewer in Brooklyn's *Times-Union* might well have snidely alluded to Kate Smith's weight issues by describing her Brooklyn Paramount date on May 23, 1932, as one of the *largest* entertainment bets the theatre has had in ever so long. For the fact also remains that she self-referentially dealt with what sociologists today call a status problem by announcing before performances, "I'm big and I'm fat, but I have a voice, and when I sing, I sing all over" (Dunning, 1998: 382–84).

"When the Moon Comes over the Mountains" was Kate Smith's theme song, as she famously also sang Irving Berlin's patriotic tune "God Bless America," written during the Second World War to raise funds for American troops. Indeed, her recorded version was played at the start of Philadelphia Flyers' ice hockey games as well as during seventh-inning stretches at New York Yankees' baseball home games in the aftermath of 9/11.

Backed by the Nat Brusiloff Orchestra during her revues at the Brooklyn Paramount those weeks of May 22, 1931, and November 20, 1931, respectively, we conclude this brief sketch with the diva's third and final appearances on our theatre's stage during the week of January 27, 1933, when it coincided with the screening of her Paramount film, *Billion Dollar Scandal*, advertised in such a way that it could only have endeared Adolph Zukor (1953), whose autobiography was similarly titled. She, finally, was also reported singing these songs heard in her previous film, *Hello, Everybody*, aptly: "Out the Open Space" and "20,000,000 People Can't Be Wrong."

On to these big three representatives of the letter "T" who also performed here during our theatre's halcyon Vaudeville years.

First, the "Cyclonic Eva TANGUAY," a. k. a. "The I Don't Care Girl," who never changed either birth name, while performing as well as "America's Biggest Drawing Card" and the advertised "Girl Who Made Vaudeville Famous." She, from all accounts brought the same sort of high-pitched, frenetic performance genius seemingly reprised decades later by Carol Burnett on TV. Indeed, Eva Tanguay reportedly covered so much ground with manic energy that our theater's management was said to have feared for the safety of the grand piano sharing the stage! Given her dynamism—i.e., Tanguay was said to run three miles per show—the cultural critic Ann Douglas (1995) likened the dynamism of this highest-priced performer in Vaudeville to "the spirit of the subway," which began in 1904 during America's post-Victorian industrializing years and grew to such extent that its separate lines combined to cover more under- and above-ground miles than even London's Tube. Finally, another of the early feminist's Eva Tanguy's apt songs was "I Don't Care," recorded in 1922.

TRACY, Arthur was born Abba Avran Tracovutsky in London and accompanied himself initially on accordion. The nicknamed "Street Singer" was heard here during the week of December 16, 1932, in which he was also seen in Paramount-Lasky's film *The Big Broadcast*. And that's after costarring in *Limelight* in 1931 with Charlie Chaplin, a Silent Film made *after* the advent of the Talkies. And since Arthur Tracy was featured in Steve Martin's 1981 remake of Bing Crosby's *Pennies from Heaven* thirty years after his performance in 1963 on Ed Sullivan's popular Sunday-night TV program *Toast of the Town*, and as well enjoyed a cameo role twenty years later in *Crossing Delancey*, filmed in 1988 on the Lower East Side, i.e., in a scene at Guss' Pickle Stand, which used to be on Essex Street, Arthur Tracy is among show business's longest continuously tenured stars.

TUCKER (née Abusa), Sophie was formerly a coon shouter who originally worked in blackface because as she wrote in her autobiography she was employed to cover performance insecurities. "The Last of the Red-Hot Mommas" was performed on stage here *au natural* twice during the weeks of February 6, 1931, and November 11, 1933. Born in steerage during her family's emigration here from Russia, she literally sang her way out of the drudgery of work in her family's restaurant in Hartford, Connecticut, toward world fame. Billed initially as the "Mary Gordon of Ragtime," Sophie Tucker worked with the Five Kings of Syncopation, who included Slim Presser, piano; Sam Green, violin; Ralph Herz, drummer; Phil Saxhere, saxophone; and Peter Guinn, cellist and clarinet. Her theme song was "Some of These Days," written by an African American composer Shelton Brooks, whom the diva met through her long-serving Black maid Mollie. Erenberg (1981: 196) described Sophie Tucker's delivery as "music (which) mixed Negro and Jewish inflections with her Jewish speech overlying."

After additionally recording songs with risqué lyrics in 1910 and 1911 like "That Lovin'" Two-Step Man" and "That Lovin' Soul Kiss," she also introduced Tin Pan Alley future iconic songs like "Blue Skies" and "When the Red-Red Robin Comes Bobbin' Along." This Vaudeville big star, moreover, claimed to have worn men's trousers before Marlene Dietrich was credited with that lasting vogue in the 1930s. Decades after touring England—and shedding blackface, which she incidentally claimed to wear out of dissatisfaction with her looks— "The Sophie Tucker Room" would be named for her in Reisenweiser's Rathskeller in Manhattan, where she performed starting out. And discussing those early years, she wrote: "You didn't have to have a mother in Ireland to feel *Mother Machree*." Not unlike Belle Baker, then, Sophie Tucker's extraordinary success among twenty million immigrants to these shores between 1870 and 1910 would lead to weekly salaries of $4,000 per week, even during hard times caused by the Great Depression. "Lord, You Make the Nights Too Long," she might well have sung at the Brooklyn Paramount during one or more of her three Vaudeville appearances on stage here—in the weeks of October 16, 1931; June 24, 1932; and/or November 11, 1932. Even so, a *Times-Union* reviewer on October 17, 1932, would lament:

> Time was when "Dame" [Tucker, the plain, Sophie] used to burst into voluminously tuneful elucubrations concerning the love life of Afro-Americans…[Whereas today] she has returned from London with a certain disregard, as well as weight. She is more sedate, but the old fire is [still] there for Queen Mother with music by Jack Yellin.

In lieu of any performer representing the letter "U," we move on to "V" and VALLÉE, Rudy (née Hubert Prior). Of French Canadian descent, the second stage bandleader in Brooklyn Paramount's earlier history brought along his "Connecticut Yankees" from Yale University as replacements for Paul Ash. Commencing thus on June 8, 1929, we read the following advertisement about Rudy Vallée in the local tabloid: "Good news to the ladies—and to all lovers of good entertainment...(the) blond, curly-headed Yale graduate has arrived in Brooklyn for an indefinite stay." Indeed, the Vaudeville sketch that week was similarly titled *Rah! Rah! Rah!*

Famously stereotyped for use of a megaphone on stage to be heard in lieu of microphones, notwithstanding self-deprecating views of crooning "My Time is Your Time," "The Vagabond Lover," and other early hits, Rudy Vallée was a talented alto saxophonist. How talented? We can only answer by pronouncing him good enough to duet with another Rudy, Rudy Wiedoeft, the first recognized master of that reed instrument heard on an episode of *The Fleishman's Yeast Hour*, the crooner's long-running weekly radio program (1929–1936), and on which Vallée's idealized mentor appeared.

An example of those occasionally enough mixed reviews he received can be found in the *Standard-Union* on November 15, 1930, when another song popularized by the crooner was said to contain worse lyrics than usual. By contrast, however, the sartorial splendor of his frock coat was praised. Reminiscing about those few years on the Brooklyn Paramount stage, he wrote (boasted?) in his autobiography about hitting forty-thousand-dollar average weekly grosses (monotonously, as a matter of fact) in 1931 (Vallée, 1962: 104; 113). Still, other mixed newspaper reviews like the following appeared: "Something he also felt good about doing was impersonating the voice of the great comic Fred Allen... Among deserved kudos to Rudy Vallée besides having had Alice Faye debut on his radio show." And so, too, must there be praise hiring Louis Armstrong as his summer radio replacement—the first African American to host a nationally syndicated radio variety show, hence breaking another unlamented color barrier. We might also note that Nancy Carroll, the star of *Manhattan Cocktail*, reportedly got the best of Rudy Vallée after not only mixing it up with him during her lone Vaudeville performance on stage here but also delivering her impression of the bandleader (*Standard Union*, October 11, 1930).

RUDY VALLÉE (Ron Hutchinson Archives/The Vitaphone Project)

Finally, in addition to appearing in *Glorifying the American Girl* with Eddie Cantor and singer Helen Morgan, screened at the Brooklyn Paramount during the week of January 10, 1930, as well as dozens of other Hollywood musicals, we record these wisdom stories that sit in place about Rudy Vallée: The first involves singer Harry Richman, whose trademark song was Irving Berlin's "Puttin' on the Ritz," and about whom *Variety* reported on January 15, 1930, that applause given the screen trailer's announcement of Vallée's return tripled the reception for Richman when he walked on stage to sing three songs before the finale of the Publix (Vaudeville) unit. There was a second text appearing in *Variety* (September 2, 1930), which reported a supposed holdup that led to Rudy Vallée's kidnapping for the sake of extortion. Sounding more like a PR agent's fabrication, it was said to have occurred after he left work late one night from here, and he was (allegedly) detained at gunpoint while headed toward his Club Vallée on West Sixty-Second Street in Manhattan. And after being carted off to those thieves' hideout in a basement cellar, the notoriously stingy performer wrote that he laughed off their demand for $10,000, even while captors purportedly forced him to remove his shoes and socks and scalded both feet with a hot iron, lest he promise to deliver an even greater sum of $50,000!

As was true for the letter "T," a similar tie for the letter "W" occurred.

So, first in alphabetized order is the nonpareil, provocatively sexy, male-baiting blonde (bewigged) femme fatal, talented, controversial showstopper Mae WEST from Bushwick in our borough, a creative writer who also penned her own gags as well as controversial Broadway plays written under her pen name Jane West. How many Broadway plays? Four, the most infamous in 1926 titled *Sex*; that is, before prurient censors had it shut down, resulting in Mae West's eight-day imprisonment on Welfare Island for writing what the grand jury concluded was obscene, indecent, immoral, and impure. All the same, she will always be remembered for salacious one-liners like these:

"Why don't you come up and see me sometime?" That immortal, sexually ambiguous line from one of her plays was recycled in the Paramount studio film *She Done Him Wrong*.

"I'm not a little girl from a little town makin' good in a big town. I'm a big girl from a little town making it big in a big Town!"

"Is that a pistol in your pocket, or are you just glad to see me?" (The latter, famously delivered like the others, from the corner of her mouth in this instance, while teasing the gangster portrayed by George Raft, in *Night After Night*. And we also might cite this additional hilarious one-liner with its transparent double entendre: "I like a guy who takes his time."

A final memorable line was her real-life quip reported when asked to strip following her arrest and imprisonment for the previously mentioned Broadway play: "I thought this was a respectable place."

All the same, this larger-than-life performer who reportedly—impossibly—drew one hundred thousand audience-goers at the Brooklyn Paramount during the week of March 10, 1933, returned in *She Done Him Wrong* and accompanying original review. Earning $5,000, she performed here five consecutive weeks, which included appearing in another stage revue aptly titled *Night of Love*.

Still other films include *I'm No Angel* during the week of October 13, 1933; *Belle of the Nineties* (October 5, 1934); *Goin' to Town* (June 10, 1934); *Klondike Annie* (commencing with a Thursday preview on March 26, 1935); and *Go West, Young Man*, whose unusual opening date of September 8, 1935, was a Tuesday. And as reported in the *Brooklyn Eagle*: "No other star in or out of Hollywood can even touch Mae when it comes to lining them up in front of the ticket windows of Si Fabian's big movie parlor on Flatbush Ave. and DeKalb." Fabian, an owner of theatres in Albany, Schenectady, and Troy in upstate New York, leased our theatre and two deluxers in downtown Brooklyn for a decade with his brother after Paramount's declarations of bankruptcy during the Great Depression.

Mae West's immodest agreement with what Eames (1985) similarly wrote how she helped create a moratorium on gloom during the Great Depression while simultaneously saving the Paramount studio: "It's a fact that I saved Paramount Pictures...which was going down the drain," she boldly declared. "If they hadn't had me then, Paramount wouldn't be here now... Mr. Zukor told me so himself: 'You saved us, Mae.'... But he didn't say it in front of anyone else" (Chandler, 2009: 220). All the same, we cite these additional Mae West blockbuster films also screened here: *Belle of the Nineties* (during the week of October 5, 1934, which like the others precipitated a firestorm with the Roman Catholic Church that resulted in its placement in the index of banned films); *I'm No Angel* (during the week of October 13, 1933); the aforementioned *Goin' to Town* (June 10, 1935); *Klondike Annie* (March 26, 1936); and *Go West, Young Man* (screened here during the week of December 8, 1936).

Finally, we (reluctantly) leave off this entry by returning to one of Mae West's Vaudeville revues, which included otherwise forgotten performers like Mady and Partner, the Windwork Wonders, and the Brass Button Squadron under the musical direction of George Metaxas. And if only since another pithy token of advice anticipated Yogi Berra's famous one-liner about what to do when faced with a life dilemma metaphorically described as a fork in the road, Mae West's solution, as it were, can be recounted: "Between two evils, I always pick the one I never tried before!"

Our second representative of the letter "W" is one-half of the famous comedy team of Wheeler and Woolsey who'd broken up by 1932, or before Bert Wheeler appeared alone on stage at the Brooklyn Paramount during the week of July 1, 1932. Née Albert Jerome Wheeler, he, like Georgie Jessel, also graduated from Gus Leonard's so-called School for Child Actors. After initially working as a duo with his wife for a short while, following the breakup of their mixed-gender comedic team of Bert and Betty Wheeler, he commenced that longer and more successful partnership with the cigar-smoking Robert Woolsey. And while Wheeler and Woolsey appeared in twenty Silent Films—the most famous among those *Rio Rita*, which was shot in 1927 after 494

Broadway appearances—Bert Wheeler was listed here during that week as an "Extra-Added Attraction," appearing in a revue headed by Smiling Eddie Lowery. But seven years later, he returned during the week of August 5, 1939, after the brief revival of Vaudeville two years prior, as the star of *The Cowboy Quarterback*, a Warner Brothers film screened here as part of a unique triple-header that included *Each Dawn I Die* (with James Cagney and George Raft) and *Sons of Liberty* (with Claude Rains).

WONG, Anna May was born Wong Liu Tsong in Los Angeles. Among this Asian American actress's numerous Hollywood film credits that played our house, she appeared in *Island of Lost Men* during the week of September 20, 1939. Unhappy, however, with stereotypical racial roles in films like *Dragon Lady*, Anna May Wong quit acting for a time and even became an expatriate. Even so, following her return to acting, she was forced to accept resented parts in *Shanghai Express*, a Von Sternberg film, in 1932 that starred Marlene Dietrich and which played here during the week of March 25, 1932. The dominance of Caucasian-Persuasion actors in a film about China—*The Good Earth*, Hollywood's adaptation of Pearl Buck's popular novel—which wasn't screened at the Brooklyn Paramount further encapsulates her righteous anger about stereotypical roles.

All the same, we leave off with these additional bullet points about Anna May Wong:

First, she appeared on stage during the week of April 8, 1932, with a performer named Young China, sensationally described as an "Oriental Syncopatin' Sensation," along with the curiously titled film *The Misleading Lady* with Claudette Colbert.

Second, Ana May Wong's role in *The Thief of Bagdad*, which starred Douglas Fairbanks, was a Silent Film reshot as a Talkie, neither of which was screened here.

Third, in her lead role in a 1951 TV weekly drama called *The Gallery of Madame Liu-Tsong*, she was the first person of Asian descent to appear in a lead role in that new medium. The series, unfortunately, ran only for six months on DuPont's Channel 5 station.

And fourth, finally, if any further evidence is required about racism in the film industry toward Celestials—who were originally recruited as cheap labor in the 1880s to build the railroad, etc., and then physically beaten as a result of competition with whites—this following comment by a newspaper reviewer in the *Brooklyn Eagle* about the purported large number of the pretty and petit Chinese American countrymen during Anne May Wong's lone performance on stage here should hopefully suffice. They were patronized as "able to sing in English as well" in that Vaudeville skit, and about whom we outrageously read: "If the chop suey restaurants fail to give the service you have been accustomed to, blame Anna May-Wong."

Having already referenced George Dewey Washington, his follow-up Vaudeville appearance featured singing "Chloe" during the week of December 8, 1928.

Since we neither could identify any Vaudeville performers with the letter X, whether big or small, the letter Y will be represented by the insult comic Henny Youngman.

Born in London to Russian Jewish parents, Henry "Henny" Youngman was inarguably the quickest rapid-fire master of one-line misogynist insults directed against his wife in Vaudeville, if not beyond. Indeed, his autobiography was misogynistically titled: *Take My Wife*. Henny Youngman got his start on the radio show *The Kate Smith Hour*. And not unlike Jack Benny, he also appeared on stage with a violin, albeit with this difference—Youngman couldn't play at all. All the same, we hope to reduce his sentence from a misogynistic felony to sexist misdemeanor by reprising the one about the old man in a diner who inquires how long it will take to hard boil an egg? And after being informed three minutes by the waitress, Youngman, who returned here during that brief revival of Vaudeville in 1937, instructs her to tell the chef to boil it faster on account of his uncertainty about how much longer he had left to live!

And, finally, since there were no letter Z's in our survey of the big Vaudeville stars who performed at the Brooklyn Paramount during its vaunted Vaudeville years, we move on to a related subject.

Since it doesn't seem fair to ignore others who might qualify as big stars, the following potpourri begins with the mixed-gender comedic team of Block and Sully, whose lively stage battles were characterized as "Dumb Dora and Wise Alec" in the *Standard Union* (November 22, 1930). Jesse Block, a product of Gus Leonard's acting school, married Eve Sully, whose sharp-tongued retorts like "Look at him!" were widely adopted (November 11, 1934). And the singer Harry Richman, who owned his own nightclub, Club Richman, with a cutaway secret entrance from the ladies room to his office for trysts with women, was a top-hat-and-tux-wearing smooth performer featured in George White's *Scandals* who reportedly was among the highest-paid Vaudevillians and whose signature song "Puttin' On the Ritz" was written by Irving Berlin. Still others included the Ritz Brothers, Al, Jimmy, and Harry (comics), who performed on stage here during the week of May 13, 1932; Singer's Midgets' Harry Rose, a. k. a. the Broadway Jester, whose (vulgar) iconic song was "Every Night I Bring Her a Frankfurter Sandwich," which probably was sung here in late April of 1932; and Amos (Freeman Gosden) and Andy (Charles Corell). Nor can we ignore Ginger Rogers, who among other credits won a Hollywood Oscar for Best Actress in a film, *Kitty Foyle*, in 1940.

Other big Vaudeville stars we should include are Smith and Dale, whose ethnic comedy was arguably alluded to in anti-Semitic terms by a *Standard Union* reviewer on February 21, 1931, who identified them as the funny men of Mendel, Inc. following their performances here; and Bebe Daniels (née Phyllis Virginia Daniels) dubbed the "Good Little Bad Girl" who appeared in fifty-one Silent Films, among them *The Wizard of Oz* in which she was cast as Dorothy, according to the *Times-Union* (April 21, 1934) caused a near riot in our theatre by tossing flowers from the stage after singing a Spanish love song from the film *Rio Rita* apparently upon audience request during that week—in a Vaudeville skit titled *The Talk of the Town*—with a reported large cast; Ray Bolger (née Raymond Wallace Bolger), who famously played

"The Straw Man" opposite Judy Garland in MGM's *The Wizard of Oz*, and who was described as a rubber-legged eccentric dance sensation during both weeks' appearances on the Brooklyn Paramount's stage on May 23, 1930, and July 8, 1932; Morton Downey, dubbed "The Irish Nightingale" in 1931, sang on four separate occasions here; Winnie Lightner, the so-called "tomboy of the Talkies" from Buffalo, New York, performed on our theatre's stage during the week of January 29, 1930, and was billed as well as the "Song a Minute Girl;" Gaetano "Guy" Lombardo, a Canadian big-bandleader-cum-New-Year's-Eve-TV-fixture who rang in the new year while the ball dropped on Times Square with "Auld Lang Syne" and performed on stage here during the week of April 15, 1932; Eddie "Smilin'" Lowery was billed as Brooklyn's newest Jester and reportedly known for waving his tongue at the audience while performing in Vaudeville in and out of the Vaudeville sketch titled *Lowery's Nightclub* built around him during the week of August 13, 1932; Gerard Montgomery Monte Blue, an inveterate Hollywood actor, who, like Lowery, also worked as an emcee during these years, and about whom a local reporter sniped that he appeared thinner than on his last visit during his performance here.

Listed here are others who should have been included:

Borrah Minevitch, a harmonica virtuoso, led the zany Harmonicat Rascals on four different occasions at the Brooklyn Paramount, i.e., during the weeks of April 18, 1930; October 14, 1932; and November 10, 1933. He also infamously staged his own abduction for ransom money, apparently to keep his troupe of little people together as a working band.

Ann Pennington was the former Ziegfeld Girl whose airplane stunt was discussed earlier. Her diminutive height (four foot, one inch) gave rise to her nickname, Penny, and she was a dancer with dimpled knees whose performance on stage here was described in *Variety* on August 29, 1930, as follows: "She greeted you with the newest intricate tap routines."

George Price, a. k. a. "Little Georgie Price," was a bulging-eyed, Cantor-like singer who appeared in Warner Brothers' Vitaphone musical shorts made in the Midwood section of Brooklyn, and who eschewed show business by becoming a stockbroker, but not before making his only appearance on stage here during the week of November 17, 1933.

Yet another comedic team were Stoopnagle (née Frederick Chase Taylor) and Budd (Wilbur Budd Hulick), dubbed as "Radio's Gloom Chasers" during the Depression, and whose sole performance dates on stage here were during the week of July 15, 1932.

ETHEL MERMAN (Ron Hutchinson Archives/The Vitaphone Project)

Sylvia Froos began in Vaudeville at age seven as "Baby Sylvia," a. k. a. "The Little Princess of Song." This largely forgotten popular chanteuse replaced Mildred Bailey as the canary in Paul Whitman's famous sweet-sounding Jazz orchestra, and she also appeared in a musical short with Al Jolson. A reviewer in the *Standard-Union* on August 29, 1931, discussed Ms. Froos's performance here by referencing Ethel Merman, whom our theatre's audience knew was touted as having gone on from our Brooklyn stage to sign a $25,000 contract with George White's *Scandals*. Ms. Froos not only appeared on our Vaudeville stage here twice during the weeks of July 15, 1932, and September 25, 1932, respectively, but also costarred in the 1934 film *Stand Up and Cheer* with Shirley Temple, which for better or worse was not part of our theatre's filmography.

Alice White, another former Silent Film star seen in flicks like *Gentlemen Prefer Blondes* in 1927, whose Vaudeville appearances were advertised in 1930 and 1931 as "Hot from Hollywood" as well as the "Blond Blaze, Dancing, Singing Star," was labeled "The Girl Who Helped Institute the Flapper Craze."

And finally, the bandleader Ben Bernie, continued his advertised (faux) battle of the century on radio with the gossip columnist Walter Winchell, a former Vaudeville dancer, complete with their word-to-word combat and seltzer-bottle antics on stage (March 26, 1933). As described at the New York Paramount, their silliness included Bernie's sudden fright that someone in the audience reminded him of Winchell, prompting the syndicated journalist to appear on stage and pun calling the other player in that farce a monster instead of master of ceremonies...whereupon the latter's band greets the conclusion of the former's simulated radio broadcast by rushing the stage with insect repellent.

* * *

Paraphrasing the legendary tenor saxophonist Sonny Rollins's observation about the tragedy of the arts—if not life—that there being relatively few truly greats, and the vast majority of others who were mere ordinary players, a compilation of small stars in Vaudeville who also played the Brooklyn Paramount during its Vaudeville years, 1928–1934, derived two of our borough's important former tabloids.

We read in the *Standard Union* about Stanley House and Bobby Gilbert, described as injecting wisecracks (and flip-flops) on January

21, 1929; Art Frank as a "character impersonator" (June 1, 1929); Renoff and Renova, advertised as "two famous European dancers" (June 22, 1929); John Burke, who was said to have been "featured in Mack Sennett comedies" (June 29, 1929); Vivien Fay, a danseuse whose novel interpretations were described as having run from classical to ultra-Jazz, and which were featured during our theatre's First Anniversary Celebration in a written skit accompanied by W. C. Handy's most famous composition, "St. Louis Blues" (November 9, 1929); *The Ingenues*, an early all-women's band comprised of twenty-five musicians not only said to have performed tremendously well, but each woman was reportedly able to play four instruments musically, and from the standpoint of ensemble, thus like no other band in the metropolitan district (December 28, 1929); Charles Wither who splashed his whitewash on photos during his old-time Vaudeville act and was also described as an old trouper as funny as he ever was, even if it takes a long time; Bernardo De Pace makes his mandolin talk while appearing along with a performer named Bert Gordon, who proves a perfect fool (April 5, 1930); M. Duval, a personable magician with Darlene Walker, said to perform an excellent acrobatic dance, even though Helen Lewis and her girl band reportedly took the honors...because how those girls can play! (April 12, 1930); and Little Mitzi Green, who not only starred in *Young Man of Manhattan* during the week of April 19, 1930, timed with Vaudeville appearance in which she just ran away with things on stage while impersonating film stars, including blacked-up white comics Mack and Moran; Joe Wong was described as the centerpiece of a multicultural-like revue titled *Chinese Whoopee* (June 7, 1930); Nina Olivette, a beautiful maiden who does eccentric dances superbly...worth an act by herself (July 5, 1930); Billy Grayson, a funny comedian (August 30, 1930); Mae Joyce described as a "moaning (torch singer) a la Libby Holman" (December 6, 1930); Auriole Craven, a double threat, as it were, as a result of her warbling and fiddling (December 20, 1930); Lester Allen, who offered his choice nonsense in a lively Prolix revue (March 21, 1931); Helen Ragland, a good-looking songstress said to have carried off top honors that week

(April 4, 1931); yet another torch singer named Lola Lane, said to look attractive while sporting a new hair comb (May 9, 1931); the Madcap Kings providing their bedlamite and thoroughly enjoyable antics (June 6, 1931); The Three Mississippi Misses, who sang Southern melodies as they never have been heard before (August 22, 1931); Miss Janet Reade described as an expert moaner of mournful melodies (September 19, 1931); and finally from that local tabloid, we read on November 20, 1931, about the dancer Buster West, who danced in his mad manner through a diverting stage show.

Culled as well from the Brooklyn Paramount in the borough's *Times-Union,* we also read about these small Vaudeville stars: "Senator Murphy" described on August 3, 1929, as an original monologist; Joe Browning, the serious-visaged individual who reportedly draws laughter with his steady stream of laughter...appearing with his son (September 23, 1929); a stage show...headed by Wendell Hall, radio artist, which included Leon, a magician (October 7, 1929); Dave Seed's impersonations of the cartoon strip character Andy Gump reviewed as "the best we've seen;" Ralph Austin who similarly drew laughs on stage (October 13, 1929); Herschel Henlere, the hit of the stage show, described as a "clever pianist who plays a score or more of popular songs in rapid succession and then winds up his performance on a musical contraption that is amusing" (November 11, 1929); Ana Chang, advertised as the "pretty Chinese star of syncopation" during novelty skits (December 2, 1929); Sammy Cohen, a comedian of motion pictures (March 23, 1930); Paul Small, the boy with the mellow voice (August 3, 1930); Reis and Dunn, called one of the best harmony singing teams on the radio (June 13, 1931); Lester Allen, identified only as the life of the stage show (March 21, 1931); Irene Bensley, the singing gal from Dixie (March 31, 1931); Al Trahan, identified as the "famed... comedian who made the King of England laugh...(and who) certainly had no difficulty in making the audience last night follow His Majesty's example" (August 1, 1931); an unnamed quartet singing an aria from Rigoletto, who surprisedly were reported as having outdone any feature heard by any Jazz band in any Brooklyn theatre within recent memory (September 5, 1931); the two-piano team of Bert Scheffer and Morton Gould performing a novel arrangement of Ravel's *Bolero* (November 14, 1931); Armida, the fiery little star of stage and screen (November 19, 1931); and those advertised "screamingly funny Minchon Brothers" (January 16, 1932); the Three Little Words, a "clever colored dancing group" advertised as worth seeing on January 25, 1932; the Britton Brothers, who destroyed musical instruments and were featured on the same Vaudeville program with Evelyn Hooey, identified as the singing star of the Chevalier film *Fifty Million Frenchmen* (April 30, 1932); Hannah Williams, a Blues singer said to be known for her recording of *Among My Souvenirs* as well as for being the off-stage wife of the bandleader Roger Wolf Kahn (August 6, 1932); and Mildred Feldman, a graduate of Erasmus High School in Brooklyn, who was divorced and coached by Harry Richman (September 3, 1932).

Still other small and mostly (or totally?) forgotten Vaudeville stars were mentioned in that Brooklyn tabloid. It also spoke of Peter Higgins, Brooklyn's favorite tenor, having returned to our theatre's stage for an encore on *Eli Eli*, the Hebrew song described, which "brings down the house" (September 23, 1932); Isa Kreuger, who sang in Italian and French before or after the acrobatic Diamond Brothers got through pounding upon each other with amazing zest; the Three Rogues, advertised as radio stars and also singers (January 21, 1933); Mary Eaton, appearing in a condensed version of the Ziegfeld production of *Sally*, and who sang *"Look for the Silver Lining"* (February 18, 1933); Bernie Arcel and Winchell, described as dancers whose performance not only was cleverly likened to word-to-word combat, but also reported as the highlight of that week's stage show as well (March 25, 1933); the Hill Billy burlesquers, Walter O' Keefe and Chester Fredericks, identified as having appeared with the Gamby's associate George Hale and his Boys and Girls Dance troupe in a sketch toward the end of Prohibition, whose painted backdrop photographed by Lewis Nathan depicts a German biergarten with teams of brewery horses that strain at a beer wagon (April 1, 1933); Bob Davis, seated at the piano throughout an entire miniature revue (September 9, 1933);

Herb Williams's appearance with a Colored Revue (September 16, 1933); Joe Morrison, dubbed the singing Hill Billy, who warbled "The Last Roundup" (September 30, 1933); Fritz and Jean Hubert, labeled "inebriates (?)" (October 7, 1933); the so-called blackface eccentric, Slim Timblin, a dancer in a fast-moving and entertaining show that for unstated reasons was said not to be Vaudeville (October 14, 1933); the Three Olympics on roller skates, featured in a revue titled *Who's Afraid of the Big Bad Wolf?* (November 11, 1933); Dorothy Crooker, described as dancing on one leg (November 18, 1933); Eddie Garr advertised as "one of best (singers) in the business," and who appeared along with the Three X Sisters, otherwise identified as "charming singers of the radio," as well as the six Danvilles, circus acrobats (January 3, 1934); Jack Powell, described as performing with a pair of drumsticks that beat a rat-tat-tat all over the stage in a playlet that included Vera Van, advertised as an "attractive blues singer of the radio" and Cookie Bowers, identified as a "mouthpiece of movie cartoons" (January 27, 1934).

We note the appearance of Will Mahoney, the Poet Prince who danced on a xylophone (February17, 1934), and who returned during the referenced brief revival of Vaudeville in 1937; Roy Smeck, dubbed the "wizard of the strings" (March 3, 1934); Benny Rubino, who simply thrives on dialects (March 17, 1934); Nell Kelly, appearing in a revue written by Earl Carroll titled *Beauty Parade,* and who was said to impersonate Garbo as well as other movie stars (March 24, 1934); Buddy Doyle, singing (imitating?) Eddie Cantor's iconic song "Makin' Whoopee," appearing with another forgotten figure, young Carter DeHaven, who was described as looking classy and acting that way when dancing, although so far as dramatic effort goes, he didn't rate high (April 18, 1933); Zela Santley, a pianist, joined by the Libonati Trio, xylophonists (November 18, 1933); and last in this survey of small Vaudeville performers, Gus Van, said to be famous for character studies and who joined the Miller Brothers that week, identified as colored dancers (December 16, 1933).

Finally, the film star Miriam Hopkins, also appeared on stage here in a scene from her film for Paramount *The Affairs of Anatole* during the week of 8 March 1934.

* * *

Most if not all those big and small Vaudeville performers appeared in one or more of those 250 weekly changing sketches or playlets that were part of Paramount's so-called revolving wheel that promised work on other wonder theatres; those were also dubbed as imitations of life. A sampling of their titles during the Brooklyn Paramount's earlier history include *Romance Isle* (during the week of August 30, 1929); *The White Cap* (December 1, 1930); *White Caps* (December 27, 1929); *Say It with Music*, which was written by John Murray Anderson and performed here during the week of April 28,1929; *Eskimo Whoopee* (February 17, 1929); *Hello, Rudy*, the previously cited welcome-back revue for Rudy Vallée's return from Hollywood, written by Frank Cambria and featuring another forgotten singer, Hal Sherman (October 18, 1929); *The Ingénue* (December 21, 1929), which was said to have been adapted from the Ziegfeld Follies; *Over the Top* (June 29, 1929); *Tin Types* (March 16, 1930); *Modes and Models* (January 19, 1930); *Step This Way* (June 18, 1928); *Bubbling Over* (March 9, 1929); *Galloping*, which was described in advertisements as a *Revue in Three Scenes*, and also said to have been written and staged by Frank Cambria (March 12, 1929); *Laces and Graces*, yet another John Murray Anderson production (April 8,1929); *Rustic Revels* (March 2, 1929); *Happy Go Lucky* (March 17, 1929); *Summer Sport* (March 30, 1929); and *Assyrian Fantasy* (February 4, 1929).

Other contributors to playlets staged by the Marcon-Fanon team included Jack Parrington, Boris Petroff, Bobby Sanford, and Louis W. McDermott. Partington was noted for building stage shows in San Francisco around the bandleader's personality, hence inferentially responsible for Paul Ash's initial success (Hall, 1961: 201). John Murray Anderson was known for miniature musical comedies or pageants complete with plots of their own, in direct contrast to the mood of that week's feature film (Hall, 1961); and finally, the previously cited Frank Cambria, whose contributions to Vaudeville were praised by *The Exhibitor's Herald* (March 2, 1926) as peculiarly his own.

Not to be ignored in this survey was Harry Gourfain, listed for a time as "in-charge of stage productions at the Brooklyn Paramount." And while the names of the artists who painted those gorgeous weekly changing sets remain unknown to us, Lewis Nathan not only brilliantly photographed our muse and other staged settings in our theatre, but also in Manhattan's Paramount.

Returning to the Brooklyn Paramount Orchestra, after Josef Koestner, the baton was passed to subsequent maestros who might also be enumerated: Eddie Paul was listed as conductor from May 22, 1931, through the week of September 11, 1931, and who returned the following year to collaborate on what the *Standard Union* reported was a special arrangement titled *Masquerade* with the Crawfords, the husband-and-wife organ team...and who returned two years later during the week of February 17, 1933, for a special program celebrating George Washington's birthday along with *Sally*, a Ziegfeld's Folly, and on the screen *The Crime of the Century* (starring Stuart Erwin). Paul backed Mae West during the week of February 24, 1934, when he led the Brooklyn Paramount Orchestra performing their celebrated works by Liszt and Chopin.

Still other conductors over those years included Willy Creeger (during the week of January 2, 1932); Rubinoff on March 4, 1932, as well on other occasions as noted; John Waldo "Johnny" Green, the previously noted young writer of music for films shot at Paramount's Astoria, Queens, studio, and who conducted here for an entire month, commencing April 8, 1932; Leonid Leonardi, hired for two weeks and who on August 13, 1932 was said to have led the relatively large orchestra in a *Slavic Rhapsody* while performing on the piano.

Still others included maestro Charles Previn, a cousin of the famed Western Classical pianist André Previn, and who not only made his monthlong debut on September 23, 1932, but would receive *mitzvot* (praise) for conducting a musical program with Hebrew favors that commemorated the start of the Jewish New Year on that date. Still another maestro was the renown cellist Yasha Buncuk, commencing on March 9, 1934, and conducting for that following week, as well as appearing as part of Roxie's original radio gang; Georgie Auld, a Canadian Jazz tenor saxophonist during the week of March 23, 1934; Alexander Olshanetzky, commencing on May 24, 1934; and finally Emil Hollander.

As for the stage band, after Paul Ash and Rudy Vallée were shuttled back and forth between Manhattan's and Brooklyn's Paramount between November 24, 1928, and January 23, 1931, i.e., Vallée and his Connecticut Yankees here during the weeks of June 8, 1929; October 18, 1929; January 17, 1930; September 5, 1930; and April 2, 1931 following Ash's Merry Prankster's opening our theatre and returning during the week of August 23,1929. Still others include Charlie Davis, who initially led his Joy Gang on stage here during the week of January 23, 1931, and who would on several occasions during the following year and during the week of October 11 reportedly give notices that only Phil Davis, a veteran of Paul Whiteman's band, and Franke Parrish, the boy with the sentimental voice, would be retained; Stan Meyers led the Paramount Music Kings on several occasions in 1933 and was billed as Brooklyn's New Rave and Brooklyn's Own Favorite; George Olson, whose wife, Ethel Shutta, sang "Bruno's Bavarian Band" for him during the week of September 29, 1933; Ben Black, California's reputed Rhythm King during March 16,1929; Oscar Baum in 1930; Irving Talbot during the week of December 5, 1931, and who was reported as leading the program of immortal melodies that included some by Ricard Wagner; Benny Meroff, whose stage band was characterized as versatile while he reportedly played every instrument in the orchestra as well as sang, danced, juggled, and did card tricks; a maestro said to have spent five consecutive years in Chicago with his band and just completed an international tour of the deluxe theatres of the Paramount Publix circuit of houses (December 17, 1932); the better-known Eddie Duchin, who led his Central Park Casino orchestra on stage here for a single week, commencing September 9, 1932, and while ostensibly backing the ballyhooed G. I. Nightingale, Julia Frances-Newbern-Langford, a. k. a. Frances Langford, a blonde sexpot torch singer of Vaudeville fame, we probably should also have highlighted as a big Vaudeville star, if only since her career spanned appearances on Rudy Vallée's radio programs in the early 1930s to entertaining American troops as part of Bob Hope's tours; and this fan's favorite, the United States Indian Reservation Band under Pawnée Chief Shunatuna, who reportedly demonstrated conclusively and spectacularly that the tom-tom and the saxophone are sisters under the skin (February 8, 1930); and finally Phil Spitalny's thirty-five-member all-women orchestra's one-month residency in 1934, which concluded the transition of Vaudeville on stage at the Brooklyn Paramount in the 1930s to double film weekly offerings...that is, until the 1950s when Rock 'n' Roll and Jazz shows were famously booked here.

* * *

On April 21, 1933, however, the following announcement appeared in *The New York Times*:

> The Brooklyn Paramount was closed last night (Thursday) following *A Lady's Performance*. It will reopen next Friday on a straight motion picture basis, presenting first-run films simultaneously with the Paramount Theatre in Times Square. The stage shows which have been an integral part of the theatre's programs during the four years of its existence have been abandoned.

Heavy expense of the stage units was what Chester, the aircraft worker portrayed by William Bendix on radio and TV in *The Life of Riley*, would have called that announcement a "revoltin' development." For, even despite a seventy-five-cent top Paramount admission price when Vaudeville was restored that fall reopening, our big theatre was reportedly "not profitably (able to) offer the stage programs which have customarily been booked across the bridge after their presentation at the New York Paramount."

All the same, we read on August 25,1933, that Cecil B. DeMille's controversial film *This Day and Age* joined Vaudeville, which not unlike Mark Twain's famous quip about rumors of his demise being premature, when it returned, but with these major changes: First, according to *Variety* (July 11, 1933), there not only was a reduced price scale of twenty-five cents till 6:00 p.m., and forty cents thereafter, but also our theatre no longer was operated by the Manhattan Paramount, which aptly was still called the kingpin in a news article on September 1, 1933; and second, the old warhorse, Mort Shea, from the Ferber-Shea circuit in the Midwest, was placed in charge of live shows booked by William "Bill" Gaynor. Thus, *Variety* reported fewer big Vaudeville stars appearing on our theatre's stage as a result of another reduction—the end of $20,000 weekly costs replaced by $3,500 shows booked during the 1933–1934 season...which featured a few of those performers like Milton Berle, Eddie Cantor, and Ethel Merman, among others. Or, as the trade magazine in its September 12, 1933, issue further reported, those would be stripped down and just straight Vaudeville!

Somewhat curiously, the *Brooklyn Eagle* three weeks later (September 29, 1933) reported the following: "Fortunately, the new stage show atones for the dreariness of (the film) *Big Executive*." It featured the can't-miss singer identified as little Ethel Shutta and her husband, Brooklyn's own favorite George Olson and his band performing an interpretation of *Getting the Uptown Lowdown* during Christmas Week, when the Brooklyn Paramount theatre's Vaudeville program also advertised on December 22, 1933, the appearances of Mazzone and King listed as dancers; Paul Remos and his Toy Acrobats; the Jack-in-the-Box Trio; Sidney Page, a ventriloquist said to be working with his wooden dummy misogynistically named Girl Stooge; the Seven Picchianis and Twelve Liazeeds (tumblers); Johnny Lee and the Three Lees (a comedy act); Bob Ripa, a Danish novelty juggler; and the return of Zelda Santley, a pianist noted for doing clever impersonations absent at any big performer paired with the Marx Brothers in their latest film, *Duck Soup*.

And that is, after also reading the following on April 21, 1933 in the *Brooklyn Eagle*:

The BT was closed last night following A *Lady's Profession*. It will reopen next Friday on a straight motion picture basis, presenting first-run films simultaneously with the Paramount Theatre in Times Square. The stage shows which have been an integral part of the theatre's programs during the four years of its existence have been abandoned. The reason given for the change was the heavy expense of the stage units. With a $.75 top, the theatre found it could not profitably offer the stage programs which have customarily been booked across the bridge the week after their presentation at the New York Paramount. The theatre will reopen with a reduced price scale of $.25 cents till 6 PM and $.40 cents thereafter, it was indicated yesterday.

Be that as it may, a newspaper report in the new year reported on January 30, 1934, that "the (Brooklyn) theater reverts to the old policy of playing New York Paramount shows the week after their New York date." Then on February 2, 1934, we read that the "N. Y. (Manhattan) Paramount Operates Brooklyn Theater Again" and that Mort Shea was out, whereas Gaynor "remains as manager." And that in addition to the demotion of Boris Morros from the head of music at Paramount to that position at "the Times Square Paramount," and replacement of Lee Dailey by a Cornell medical school dropout, Robert Weitman, as our theatre's manager—with the appointment of Edward Sullivan as his assistant, Fifi D'Orsay, a renown French comedienne reportedly "proved her merit as an entertainer in a satisfying manner" during the fall of 1933.

Fast-forward now to May 19, 1934, when we once again read that "The Theatre will close tomorrow for the summer." It reopened on August 30, 1934, at 9:30 a.m., a Thursday morning, with another Cecil B. DeMille extravaganza, *Cleopatra*, starring Claudette Colbert sans Vaudeville. However, flippantly explained in the tabloid in September 1934 as "incidentally...the new management...has altered its original policy of presenting stage shows...(with) a promised symphony orchestra...as a supplementary replacement" along the continuation of its policy of screening film. In this instance, the twenty-five-piece "full symphony" orchestra was led by Emile Hollander, whose musical offering on September 14, 1934, featured a mixture of Western Classical music selections by Shubert combined with the light opera of Victor Herbert, as well as a purported "jazz piece" that was the familiar "St. Louis Woman." Phil Spitalny's All-Women's Orchestra arrived in mid-October, as with certitude, the following was reiterated: "The stage shows which have been an integral part of the theater's programs during the four years of its existence have been abandoned." Spitalny, we note, was born in the Ukraine and originally led an all-male orchestra after emigrating to these shores before changing over to his first All-Women's Orchestra. Their repertory similarly advertised Western Classical pieces mixed with Tin Pan Alley popular favorites, as during the week of November 2, 1934, when they reportedly played one of Liszt's rhapsodies and Ravel's *Bolero*.

About Spitalny, another "wisdom story attached to place" was shared with us by Vivian Spivey, the drummer, kind enough in 2004 also to send along a packet of promotional information about herself. But during this author's phone conversation with that elderly trouper, she recalled with outrage meeting the bandleader in a hotel room wearing only his underpants. Fortunately, Mrs. Spitalny was present so nothing untoward presumably occurred.

Along with the Great Depression, McClean (1965: 212) explained the demise of Vaudeville with the availability of live music heard on radio combined with the popularity of 78 rpm records and the Talkies. Still "less than a hundred theatres throughout the country" were reporting and then "booking any vaudeville acts at all," while only a dozen of those could be considered big time. All the same, after Brooklyn Paramount abandoned Vaudeville in 1934, that type of family entertainment was briefly revived in 1937.

Thus, "Professional Nights" were announced...a. k. a. "Pro Nites"; they were offered by the Fabian Brothers, who also acquired control of the adjacent Fox and Strand in lease arrangements with Paramount following tumultuous bankruptcy hearings. So along with those at the Fabian Fox, their new manager, Joe "Doc" Lee, was quoted saying in the borough's leading tabloid that the "stars of the stage, screen, radio, nightclubs, and the musical world" would once again appear on those stages. Alas, the revival lasted only ten weeks. Thus, between April 7, 1937, and June 18, 1937, the promoter, Gerald Griffin, who was described as "one of the outstanding featured stars in the vaudeville world, and a composer of the country's leading song hits," optimistically touted the return of Vaudeville as "presenting this novelty composed of all professional artists" who might consequently obtain contracts "with various large nightclubs, radio chains, and theatre circuits."

Unfortunately, that was not the case. We read that the popular dance bandleader Vincent Lopez served as emcee on opening night at the Brooklyn Paramount and was followed by Buddy Walker (April 16,1937) and Don Kerr (April 23,1937)—the latter, a character actor whose voice was heard in episodes of *Flash Gordon*, which starred Larry "Buster" Crabbe, who, like Tom Mix, also headed up a rodeo on our theater's stage some twenty years later.

Among those relatively unknown Vaudevillians during its brief revival in our rebranded Fabian Paramount, we read that on April 30,1937, between the screening of *Racketeers in Exile* and *Swing High, Swing Low*, these performers appeared on ten Friday nights: the father-and-son dancers Pat Rooney and Pat Rooney Jr; cellist Yasha Bunchuk; Ben Yostes's Variety Eight; Ann Lester, a returning Blues singer; and John and George (harmony singers). On May 7, 1937, between the 8:00 p.m. screen offering of *Jim Harvey, Detective* paired with *Married Woman* (with Betty Davis), these performers appeared on stage at 10:25 p.m.: the violinist Al Sayne, advertised as "Radio's Ambassador of Song"; White and Manning, a dance team; and DePaxe (renown mandolin virtuoso). And skipping further ahead to what the tabloids called "another hour of variety stage entertainment" on May 14, 1937, we also read about the appearance of the former big Vaudeville insult comic star Henny Youngman, joined by Mark Plant; White and Manning; June, Joan and Jerry; and the Piccianni Troupe, a trapeze act.

VAUDEVILLE REVIVAL (*The Brooklyn Daily Eagle*, April 8, 1937)

Subsequent programs on May 21, 1937, featured double-bill screenings like *Call It a Day* and *Interns Can't Take Money* (with Barbara Stanwyck and Joel McCrea). These additional performers appeared on stage here: Estelle Taylor, an advertised screen star said to be returning with a new song routine; Charles Carlile (radio tenor); Paul Regan (mimic); the Romano Brothers, a dance act; Jack and Betty (whirlwind skaters); and others. And on that following Friday night, May 28, 1937, following screenings of Mark Twain's novel *The Prince and the Pauper* (starring Errol Flynn) and *The Case of the Stuttering Bishop,* we read about the third appearance of the African American crooner George Dewey Washington, who was listed as a baritone with Cotton Club Revue; Mells, Kirk, and Howard (clowns); Bert Lynn; and also the Three Robins. And finally, we note in a newspaper advertisement on June 3, 1937, that John Steel, a singing star of the Ziegfield Follies, appeared with Ann Lester, described as a Blues singer making her third Pro Nite appearance, as well as Johnny Burke (screen comedian), Gine de Quincey and Lewis, and Angel Velez (musical act).

Music on those Fridays was provided by the Ben Nelson Orchestra, whose conductor was originally part of Paul Ash's band in Chicago, and the dance band alternated with Glenn Miller's more famous band at the Glen Island Casino in New Rochelle, New York. Al Rogers was listed as musical supervisor.

Finally, we reprise the following humorous story from *Variety*. Dated April 7, 1937, after its reviewer discussed a performer named Bob Howard who reportedly scored top honors with his Fats Waller-esque scat singing, we read the following about Vincent Lopez's sales pitch for mattresses sold in Michel's Furniture on Fifth Avenue in our borough, presumably a sponsor of this short-lived Vaudeville revival: It soon became very evident that a paid audience will not go for commercial spiels.

The following terse announcement appeared in the tabloid on July 2, 1937: "Professional Nites Moved to the Fabian Fox." Thus, the policy of screening two films weekly essentially inaugurated at the start of 1935 and continued until the Brooklyn Paramount's closing date in 1962.

Related to the discussion in this chapter was the June 27, 1937, report about a temporary halt in the rivalry between the Brooklyn's Fabian Paramount and Fox involving a Christmas Eve performers' exchange, as it were, between the organists Rube Wolf and Will Osborne from Fabian's Fox and our rebranded theatre's featured performer on the Mighty Wurlitzer in that year, Bob West...that is, during a midnight benefit for the Forty Neediest (Eagle) Cases Fund. In any event, a breaking down of barriers duly reportedly occurred between those usually archrivals, or so we also read in the local tabloid.

As for our committed search for wisdom stories attached to place, three final examples can be given.

First, with all ten retro-Vaudeville shows in our Paramount apparently broadcast on WMCA radio, while their new startup time on Fridays had been moved back thirty minutes and instead began at 9:30 p.m. We humorously also read about theatre patrons sarcastically informed in the local tabloid that they should be thankful because their attendance kept them off the streets for four hours, i.e., Brooklyn's arguably maligned borough as the home of organized crime. Which, apropos, it might be added that the *Brooklyn Eagle*, a decade earlier on October 28, 1933, echoed developers' understandable goals to "Bring Broadway to Brooklyn" contained this cryptic comment: "Brooklynites all flock to Manhattan for their whoopee...(while) most Manhattanites come to Brooklyn solely for their internment."

A second example penned by John Skinner appeared in his "Seeing What You Hear" *Brooklyn Eagle* column about Pro-Nites. "If you are at all acquainted with vaudeville you'll know that there never was a fine Irish comedian who, when pressed by interviewers, didn't admit that his name was something that smacked of anything but the Quid Sob," he wrote. "For, as the Dublin wag Tom Mooney who most likely would turn out to be a gent whose mother's name was Lapchikanowitz...almost all the burlesque [*sic*] stars, despite the O'Connors and Mahoneys to which they attached themselves, would prove to be distantly related to Cohens and Marshufskys who originated variously in Prague and Warsaw." The observation, it might be noted, seems gratuitous when viewed against the coming institutional anti-Semitism of Mississippi Congressman John Rankin of the House Un-American Activities Committee, who some few years later not only accused Eddie Cantor, Danny Kaye, Edward G. Robinson, and Melvyn Douglas as being Communist subversives, but also outrageously demanded their outted Jewish names be read into the Congressional record (Weinstein, 2018: 200)!

Finally, we note Rian James's gossip-like exposé in his *Reverting to Type* column in the tabloid about the Silent Film star Miriam Hopkins's appearance in *The Affairs of Annabel* as part of a Vaudeville skit during the week of March,14, 1934—the wisdom-type story attached to place praising the actress's quest for authenticity, which unfortunately resulted in weight and alcohol consequences, insofar as she demanded real steak and champagne in that skit performed five times daily!

CHAPTER 7

Face Three: All That Early and Modern Jazz, Almost

A. Early Jazz

What is Jazz? An unforgettable answer to that frequently asked question was given—sung—by Louis Armstrong and Bing Crosby in a duet in the 1956 film *High Society* centered on the Newport Jazz Festival in Rhode Island. Notwithstanding their humorous repartee on Cole Porter's clever lyrics, we begin this discussion of the third face of the Brooklyn Paramount's earlier history with its six criteria defined by Kathy Ogren (1989: 25–27):

1. Syncopation or exaggerated emphasis on the second and fourth beats, rather than the first and third still commonly heard in other genres of music;
2. improvisations based on melodies and/or the chord structure of songs that result in countermelodies;
3. call-and-response derived from field chants preserved by slaves during the Middle Passage from Africa, which carried over in Black churches in the South;

4. polyrhythms derived from African drum languages; and

5. the use of blue notes, a. k. a. flattened fifths, on European musical scales as well as unusual tonalities, as in microtones and so-called extensions of familiar 1–3-5 chordal patterns with use of the 7th, 9th, 11th, and 13th notes.

Yet even though we can safely surmise Brooklyn Paramount theatre audiences recognized the difference between Jazz and what its stage bands alternatively played during the Vaudeville years between 1928 and 1934, the term seems to have had a life of its own, if only evidenced by the 1920s being called the Jazz Age. Thus, Paul Ash, for example, was titled the Rajah of Jazz, and his band members similarly identified as Jazz-maniacs. Indeed, they were also advertised on December 8, 1929, as follows: "Hear the finest jazz band in all New York." And so, too, did Vaudeville skits performed on stage here employ the term in their titles: *Jazz Cocktail*, for example, during the week of February 22, 1922, which was also advertised as "Publix Celebration Week." Moreover, the *Exhibitors Herald* and *Moving Picture World* made that distinction in its review of live entertainment during the week of December 15,1928, when an anonymous writer left his impression of the way the Tin Pan Alley tune "Crazy Rhythm" by Kahn-Meyer and Caesar from the Broadway play *Here's How* was played as an Indian War Dance, Minuet, Waltz, Tango, March, and Modern Jazz, a performance described as very well received by the house. All the same, during the week of June 27, 1934, Jack Powell was featured with his educated drumsticks in a Vaudeville playlet titled *Jazz in the Kitchenette.* Yet another was titled *Jazz Preferred* and led by Rudy Vallée during the week of January 24, 1930, which unusually featured a Revival titled *We're in the Navy Now* starring Wallace Beery on the following night after the Vaudeville and film screening of *The Virginian* (starring Gary Cooper), a Silent Film made in 1926, on a Saturday instead of Monday night.

Nor is this the place to discuss the origin of Jazz. It is usually credited to Charles "Buddy" Bolden (1877–1931), whose innovations as a cornetist were heard during the late nineteenth century in its New

Orleans birthplace that became Dixieland Jazz (Marquis 2005). The 1947 film *New Orleans*, which featured Armstrong and Billie Holiday, picks up on this origin myth with the closing of twenty-three blocks of the port city's Red Light District in 1917 by the United States Navy. The movie discusses the music's migration to Chicago. Ken Burns's 2004 epic, ten-part series titled *Jazz* more accurately tells the story.

As for the word's enigmatic etymology, Mencken (2000: 189–190) suggests it derived from three sources: the name of a "dancing slave," Jasper; "Chaz," the nickname of Charles Washington, a drummer active in New Orleans in 1895; and (3) its slang-like euphemistic use for sex by African Americans in the Mississippi Delta. Other etymologies more recently can be found in Crisp and Stewart (2024: 99–100), including "jasm," which purportedly was slang for pep or energy in use even earlier, circa 1860, which could only have fueled subsequent descriptions of Jazz as hot and spasmic music.

Part and parcel of the term's wider use involve its use by futurist art figures like the Italian poet Filippo Tommaso Marinetti, whose search for ways to popularize that movement prompted him in 1909 to advocate two relatively unused English consonants, "j" and "z." And with the popularity of baseball in those years, Ben Henderson, a pitcher, apparently called his wobbly curve a Jazz ball in 1912.

And whether or not another solution was its derivation from jasmine, a tropical flower, as others would argue, a sign painted on a furniture moving truck in 1915 in New Orleans read: "The Tom Brown Dixieland Jass Band." They performed lively improvised music after dirges played, while delivering bodies to funerals. Nor was its popularity easily won. Henry Ford's vitriolic assault on Jewish Jazz Mormon music speaks for itself (Morris, 2019: 61). Still, the fusion of written syncopated music credited to Scott Joplin that came to be known as Ragtime after the turn of the previous century combined with the Blues, the discovery of which is credited to W. C. Handy's interest in the lamentations of former slaves further impacted modern art...as is the case of the Dutch abstract artist Piet Mondrian, who titled a painting *Broadway Boogie-Woogie*—for a relatively early distinctive type of piano playing—and compositions by major Western Classical composers like Igor Stravinsky, who, for example, wrote *Concerto in Ebony for Clarinet and Jazz Band* in the 1940s. And also George Gershwin was commissioned by the so-called King of Jazz, the white bandleader Paul Whiteman to write *Rhapsody in Blue*, which was performed in New York City in 1924. The same big bandleader, who sought to sweeten African American Jazz he problematically wrote, was born in the African jungle to the beating of the *voodoo* [*sic*] drum.

What followed was a debate about this controversial music, which saw the American composer and music critic Henry Osborne Osgood, write a treatise titled "The Anatomy of Jazz" and contribute a piece in a music journal that asked: "Where Is Jazz Leading America?" And so, too, did even as informed as a major white critic, Gilbert Seldes (2001: 99) descry Jazz nearly a century ago by writing, "Nowhere is the failure of the negro to exploit his gifts more obvious than in the use he has made of the jazz orchestra," or so he bemoaned. "For although nearly every negro jazz band is better than nearly every white band, no negro band has yet come up to the level of the best white ones, and the leader of the best of all, by a little joke, is called Whiteman."

A great divide pitted Black intellectuals identified with the Harlem Renaissance against each other regarding the worth of Jazz. So, while noted writers like James Weldon Johnson, Langston Hughes, and Zora Neal Hurston defended it as a genuine part of African American culture, no less daunting than the towering intellectual figure W. E. B. DuBois condemned Jazz in favor of Western Classical composers like Bach, Beethoven, and Brahms. A concern that existed about *The Souls of Black Folks* shared by Joel A. Rogers, who issued a warning in the anthology *The New Negro* in 1925 about the epidemic contagiousness of Jazz.

Nor have essentialism-type racial debates about this genre unfortunately subsided, which trace back to the fact that the first Jazz recordings were made in New York City in 1917 by the ODJB, the Original Dixieland Jazz Band, comprised of Italian Americans from the Big Easy challenged recently by William Kenney (1986), who wrote that the African American clarinetist Wilbur Sweatman, performed in

Vaudeville and was recorded earlier. Suffice to meld this brief survey with our concerns by reprising the fact that while the Warner Brothers revolutionary sound film was inaccurately titled *The Jazz Singer*, it nonetheless ironically contains a Prologue that definitively contrasts what Paul Ash and Rudy Vallée and the other stage bandleaders played with what Duke Ellington and Cab Calloway brought from the Cotton Club, we look forward to hearing it.

CAB CALLOWAY NEWSPAPER ADVERTISEMENT (*The Brooklyn Daily Eagle*/November 6, 1931)

These words at the start of that epic film read: "In every living soul, a spirit cries for expression—perhaps the plaintive, wailing song of Jazz is the misunderstood utterance of a prayer."

So turning first to Edward Kennedy "Duke" Ellington, he was the talented son of a Washington, DC, butler, who chose not to accept an art scholarship to Pratt Institute in Brooklyn in favor of Jazz. After initially performing as a so-called stride pianist, Ellington formed a five-piece band called the Washingtonians that played the Kentucky Club in Manhattan for two years before increasing that number to nine and commencing a five-year run in Harlem's legendary Cotton Club (Haskins, 1977; Vail, 2002: part 1). Duke Ellington's orchestra appeared on our theatre's stage three times in the early 1930s: during the weeks of January 23, 1931; July 30, 1931; and February 4, 1932. Remarkably, they returned in biblical fashion forty years later in 1971 for a Long Island University fundraiser in the former orchestra of the Brooklyn Paramount referenced in the Epilogue of this book.

"This is Ellington's first stage appearance since his rise to fame on radio," or so we read in a local tabloid. Extrapolating from his career, we note the maestro's written suites and sacred music, as well as numerous songs that entered the Great American Songbook. Among the latter, some of these were performed on stage here in front of nearly white audiences: "It Don't Mean a Thing if It Ain't Got That Thing," "East St. Louis Toodle-Oo," "Black and Tan Fantasy," "Mood Indigo," "In My Solitude," "Reminiscing in Tempo," "Sophisticated Lady," and "Prelude to a Kiss."

The intimate relationship between Jazz and dance was discussed by Marion Morgan in her notebooks (Donnell Library). As further elaborated by Marshall and Jeanne Stearns (1968: 231), they wrote that the story of American dancing includes specialties performed to Jazz rhythms. So, for example, we read about the presentation of the four stepbrothers, acrobatic Black dancers, a. k. a. the Eight Feet of Rhythm, as part of one of Duke Ellington's Cotton Club revues at the Brooklyn Paramount; and also that the African American dancer, Nicodemus (née Horace Winston), a Harlem-born-and-raised Back-to-Africa follower of Marcus Garvey, appeared here along with the Harlem Strutters, mixed-gender dancers. Notwithstanding the importance of polyrhythms that marked Jazz as different from other forms of music heard during those Vaudeville years, Duke Ellington titled a suite, *Drum Is a Woman*, presumably intended to subvert gender bias that forbid women from touching percussive instruments in Africa!

Along with what can be taken away from the stability of key musicians like Harry Carney, Johnny Hodges, and Sonny Greer in Ellington's orchestra, we might also note that "Take the 'A' Train," which bandmembers rode from Harlem to the Hoyt-Schermerhorn subway stop within easy walking distance to our theatre, hadn't yet been written by the maestro's collaborator, Billy Strayhorn, for Ivie Anderson to sing.

A reviewer in *The New York Times* (April 29, 1929) wrote that Ellington, for reasons of his own called "jungle music" was a first-rate Black's moor band, come down from the deepest Harlem to provide a series of specialities that ranged from tepid to torrid. Restated, it illustrates the sensationalism prejudicially associated with the other as further evidenced in advertisements containing phrases with other coded racist meanings: "Sizzling All-Harlem Stage Revue" and "Hot Harlem Blues." Yet ironically the title of one of the films screened during Duke Ellington's appearance on stage here more accurately alludes to his and his band's transcendent aura: *The Royal Family of Broadway*.

Finally, lest any lingering doubt remains in the reader's mind about those qualitative differences between Ellington's early Jazz performed at the Brooklyn Paramount relatively early on and what was otherwise heard during our theatre's Vaudeville years, check out any antiquated recordings on YouTube of Paul Ash's music and compare them yourself with Ellington's in *Check and Double Check*, a 1930 film provocatively costarring Amos 'n' Andy.

"He's back!"

That advertisement was for the second of four appearances here by the Heidi-Heidi Ho Man, Caleb "Cab" Calloway. He was born in

Rochester, New York, and similarly led a nine-piece band, the Missourians, that replaced Duke Ellington's at the Cotton Club. The changing personnel of Calloway's band, by contrast, included numerous great Jazz musicians over the years. such as John Birks "Dizzy" Gillespie, co-founder of Bebop, most famously among them, and who returned under his own name on our stage twice during the 1950s.

Yet another contrast with the never-not-debonair and dignified mien of Ellington always seated majestically at the piano was the exhibitionism of Cab Calloway…who did not play any instrument but led by standing while conducting as it were with his straight (or straightened?) hair flying wildly about. Known as well for wearing zoot suits, which he might well have invented, Cab Calloway wrote the *Hepster's Dictionary of Jive* in 1939, a slim volume containing what H. L. Mencken (2000) called "slanguage" employed by Jazz musicians he might well have also invented. Here are the dates of Cab Calloway's four 1931 Cotton Club revues on our theatre's stage, which also were sensationally advertised as "Hot from Harlem/all-Colored orchestra": during the weeks of April 24, July 10, October 30, and November 6, respectively. And so did those feature African American dancers—Bill "Bojangles" Robinson, most notably, this world's legendary best tap dancer who also returned as the star of his own revue.

Inaccurately reported, however, as "the first joint appearance of colored revue stars in a Brooklyn motion picture theatre," Cab Calloway is further immortalized in Jazz history for having sung controversial songs like "Minnie the Moocher," "The Viper Song," and "The Gong"—each alluding to the first opiate crisis in this nation's history.

Still other examples of the sort of racial profiling associated with Cab Calloway's appearances here include "Strutting His Stuff and How!," "World's Fastest All-Colored Show," and "The Hot-Cha Man of Rhythm." But as was also the case with Ellington, we read similar advertisements like these: "They Burn Your Radio Nightly!" Which belies the importance of what we will argue might well be yet another face of our theatre's fabled earlier history, similar to live wire broadcasts from the Cotton Club heard by some of our theatre's audiences. Anyway, their curiosity was to hear Calloway's orchestra in person, not to mention the reason for his booking dates in our theatre.

Finally, the hyper-frenetic hepster also appeared in four feature-length Hollywood films, two of which were screened here: *The Big Broadcast* (during the week of October 14, 1932) and *The Singing Kid* (which starred Jolson) during the week of April 4, 1936. (*The Cincinnati Kid* and *Blues Brothers* were made years after the Brooklyn Paramount's closing.) But we must reference Cab Calloway starring on Broadway as "Sportin' Life" in Gershwin's folk opera *Porgy and Bess*, if only since it also featured Pearl Bailey, who performed here during the 1950s.

These additional relatively early Jazz musicians also performed here as part of Vaudeville shows:

Eddie Eddinborough and the New Orleans Wildcats, African Americans from the Crescent also sensationally advertised as "Harlem's Hotcha Ambassadors," and who performed here during the week of August 14,1931. The little else we could document about them goes to Dan Morgenstern, the former head of the Institute of Jazz Studies at the Rutgers campus in Newark, who told us that those Dixieland musicians performed songs sung by their leader like "Brown Baby" and "Wild Cat's Ball."

Next up, though not in strict chronological order, was Ethel Waters, a. k. a. "Sweet Mama String Bean." She began as a Shimmy dancer nicknamed for her graceful slenderness and led two revues on our theatre's stage during the weeks of June 19, 1932, and November 4, 1932, respectively. As if anticipating Duke Ellington's memorable phrase about nonpareil excellence in the arts, Ethel Waters (née Ethel Howard) was indeed beyond category. A Blues singer as well in the wake of the success of powerful Black divas like Mamie Smith, Bessie Smith, and Ma Rainey in the 1920s, she eventually moved on to acting. And whether or not flattered being dubbed the ebony Nora Bayes, who was named after one of the biggest stars in Vaudeville, Ethel Waters, typically opened her act by declaiming: "I'm not Bessie Smith!" ironically dubbed a Blues moaner while never singing in dialect. She rather trilled her "r's" and pronounced "cahn't" for "can't" with affectations not unlike white stage actors emulating Oxfordian British English.

ETHEL WATERS (*The Brooklyn Daily Eagle*/June 9, 1932)

"The Mighty Sparrow" not only was another nickname but also the title of the autobiography of this major early Jazz singer, who began recording on Black Swann, a white-owned record label, and enjoyed immediate success in May 1921 with "Down Home Blues" and "Oh, Daddy." Indeed, her earliest record label advertised the diva one year later as "the Black Swan Troubadours featuring Ethel Waters—World's Greatest Singer of Blues and Her Jazz Masters, New York's Leading Exponent of Syncopation." She enjoyed greater success singing "Dinah" from the Broadway show *Stormy Town Topics*, which earned her a new record contract with the Columbia Phonograph Company in 1925. Besides risqué recordings like "My Handy Man," Ethel Waters also enjoyed additional crossover pop hits like "Stormy Weather," which was reportedly written for her by Harold Arlen and Ted Koehler as part of her Cotton Club revue in 1933; and, according to her biographer (Bogle, 2001: 210), not only reflected hard times during the Great Depression, but doubled as well as a lament about the men in Ethel Waters's troubled love life. All the same, after commenting on the wonderful results achieved by George Dewey Washington from our theatre's audiences for that fellow Black crooner's rendition of "Eli Eli," she wrote about being inspired to correctly pronounce Hebrew phonetics, insofar as the plaintive dirge she sang "told the tragic history of the Jews...so similar to that of my own people (so) that I felt I...(would be) telling (singing) the story of my own race" (Waters, 1951: 178).

Waters also wrote the following about one of her stints at the Brooklyn Paramount: "The Jewish people crowded the theatre to hear it, and they would tell one another: 'The *schvarze* (black person) sings "Eli, Eli," the *schwarze*!'" After appearing as the first African American star on the Broadway stage in a musical revue, Ethel Waters's initial Cotton Club revue here was "Rhapsody in Black." It was written by the Russian-born impresario Lew Leslie who was married to Belle Baker; it featured her rendition of "Dark Eyes" described as a sad European melody that pulled at the heartstrings of wannabe Americans from Eastern European countries familiar with its cadences. Featured as well in that revue, which previously played Broadway before the start of a national tour were Jimmie Basquette, the African American singer who played Uncle Remus in Disney's controversial film *Song of the South*; Clinton Dusty Fletcher, who years later wrote the popular Rhythm and Blues novelty jukebox song, "Open the Door, Richard" in 1947; the Cecil Mack Choir; and Valeida Snow, a. k. a. the female Louis Armstrong. And as well, it also featured a tap dancer/comedian, Derby Wilson.

While her biographer also wrote that she agreed to appear in that revue, provided only it wouldn't promote stereotypical images of happy darkies, (Bogle, 2001: 184–209) even so, it was advertised in Brooklyn as starring the first colored girl on Broadway. Yet when "Rhapsody in Black" finally went on the road, it was forced to play segregated theatres in Washington, DC. Also sadly, though importantly illustrating the importance given to place in this book, Bogle (2001) would neglect our Paramount by writing only in his otherwise splendid biography that "By June, 'Rhapsody in Black' was back in New York at the Paramount."

Turning next to Lew Leslie's second Cotton Club revue, "Dixie to Broadway," that also played our theatre, it not only costarred the great hoofer, Bill Robinson, but Bogle (2001) wrote featured African American singers like Adelaide Hall and the Mills Brothers. While a contract dispute with its producer ultimately prompted him to remove Ethel Waters's name from advertisements for the show, a local tabloid called it "the greatest of All-Colored Shows," and an "elaborate color affair...with a cast of 100...(featuring) the most outstanding colored talent of the musical comedy stage." Here again, however, we bemoan the constant primacy given to the other (rival) Paramount in town, because as Ethel Waters's biographer also wrote that "another time Leslie changed the title simply to *Blackbirds*...(as when) it played the New York Paramount."

The *Brooklyn Times Union* (June 11, 1932) called Ethel Waters one of the best Blues singers her race has produced. Her first hit song was the political anthem "Am I Blue?" Other hits, however, crossed over from race music to pop charts, including Tin Pan Alley favorites like "I've Found a New Baby" and "Shine on Harvest Moon"—the latter, originally performed by Nora Baynes. Yet another Ethel Waters signature song was "Suppertime," whose lyrics by Irving Berlin agonizingly portray the plight of a Black woman forced to fix dinner for her family after learning that her husband had been lynched!

Finally, F. Scott Fitzgerald's frequently quoted remark about no second acts in American lives, the life of Ethel Waters saw her reinvention as an actress. Along with receiving critical Broadway acclaim as Hagar in *Mamba's Daughter*, whose character Momweezee was said to have been based on Waters's troubled mother, raped as a thirteen-year-old and had a lifelong love–hate relationship with her only child. Additional dramatic roles included Berenice Sadie Brown in Hollywood's adaptation of Carson McCullers's play *The Member of the Wedding*, which unfortunately was not screened at the Brooklyn Paramount. And still other screen credits include *Tales of Manhattan* (1942); *Cabin in the Sky* (1943)—the first all-Black feature-length film; *Stage Door Canteen* (1943); and *Pinky* (1949)—the latter, a controversial film for its time dealing with a young Black professional woman (Gene Tierney) light enough to have passed in the North, but who is outted after returning home to the South. *Pinky* unfortunately was also never screened here.

Not only did Ethel Waters have her own radio show in 1933, but she also helped launch commercial television with a performance on an early demonstration of that new medium at the World's Fair in 1939. Her (stereotypical) role of the Black nanny "Beulah" would be reprised from radio to TV, where Waters enjoyed numerous appearances, including an episode of TV's *Route 66* titled "Goodnight Sweet Blues" that featured numerous famous Jazz musicians. Also seen at home as well as in Edward R. Murrow's *Person to Person* TV interview series, her final role as a member of Billy Graham's worldwide evangelic ministry saw her singing Gospel numbers.

So, for plenty of good reasons, Gary Giddins (1989a) would title an essay about Ethel Waters, "The Mother of Us All." And, finally, returning to *Eye on the Sparrow*, a Book of the Month bestseller in 1951, its title was derived from a lullaby sung by her grandmother, then reprised in the Carson McCullers coming-of-age play and made into a Hollywood film. Thus, she sang to her troubled adolescent ward played by Julie Harris and six-year-old next-door neighbor's son, Brandon deWilde, after he, too, had climbed into her lap: "I sing because I'm free/For His eye is on the sparrow/and I know He watches me."

Continuing then with the Jazz couple "Mr. and Mrs. Swing," who were (relatively) early Jazz artists featured on our theatre's stage during its Vaudeville years, he was Kenneth Norville, a. k. a. Red Norvo, who played vibraphone and xylophone, married to "The Rocking Chair Lady," Mildred Rinker Bailey, the sister of Alton Rinker, a member of Bing Crosby's original band, and who in time became the girl singer with Paul Whiteman. Mistakenly listed as "Red Novel" during the week of July 15, 1933, as part of the ballyhooed "Greatest All-Youth Festival Ever Presented," Red Norvo lived long enough to transition from New Orleans Dixieland to Swing in the 1930s and Bebop in the 1940s and 1950s.

His first wife, however, returned on her own for a second appearance at the Brooklyn Paramount—a one-night-only/Thursday show on March 5, 1934, during which Mildred Bailey appeared along with the sawed-off comedian, Jimmy Savo, touted as Charlie Chaplin's rival. A part–Coeur d'Alene member of that indigenous tribe from Washington State—on her mother's side—despite being able to pass, she would have other dues to pay, i.e., apparent anger when mistaken as Black despite singing in the African American style and as a result of obesity. Still, she enjoyed her own thirty-minute Friday night weekly radio Jazz show on CBS that featured Norvo, along with Teddy Wilson and Roy Eldridge in the studio band, as well as brought other major Jazz artists like Coleman Hawkins to those airwaves.

Another Jazz musician featured on July 15, 1933, was the white Louis Armstrong, so-called; that is, as Louis Prima (née Louis Leo Prima) was initially dubbed. Born in New Orleans, the Italian American trumpet player was known as "Chief" following his marriage to a Native American Jazz vocalist, the mixed-blood Cherokee, Keely Smith (née Dorothy Jacqueline Smith). The deadpan expression contrasted with comic hijinks of her nut musician husband, whose iconic band featured Sam Butera, a Texas-honking (white) tenor saxophonist also from New Orleans who led "The Witnesses" backing Prima on TV variety shows as well as frequent bookings in Las

Vegas, where they performed the sort of jump music pioneered by another Louis—as in, Jordan, Louis, heard here at the start of the 1950s. Along with lending his distinctive voice to Disney's animated version of Rudyard Kipling's *The Jungle Book*—as the orang-u-tan King Louis singing "I Wanna Be Like You"—Louis Prima recorded numerous Italian vocals like *Angelina, Buono Sera, Felicia No Capica,* as well as comic titles like *Please No Squeeze Da Banana.* A far cry surely from his participation in that new-faces program on our theatre's stage in 1933, which dubbed Louis Prima the "World's Hottest Trumpeter."

Finally, and better get ready or not for this next synchronicity: *Lady and Gent* was the name of the film screened that week in 1933 when Prima performed along with Norvo and Bailey!

Returning to Bojangles, in addition to his appearance with Cab Calloway during the week of April 24, 1933, the great tap dancer was back again some few months later leading his own revue *Goin' to Town,* commencing November 3 of that year. Raised in Virginia by his grandmother who'd been a slave, he'd traded his first name "Luther" for "Bill" with an older brother. The consummate raconteur who could neither read nor write enjoyed introducing himself by provocatively declaring, "I used to be colored." Bill Robinson is credited with having invented the step (ladder) dance; the revue he'd headed not only was written for him, but that act, a. k. a. All-Star Colored Revue, also featured Ada Brown dubbed the Sophie Tucker of Vaudeville. Dubbed the unofficial Mayor of Harlem, he entered show business after winning a dance contest at the Bijou in Brooklyn and was also known as the "Dark Cloud of Joy"—for his fiery temper. In addition to holding the world's record for walking backward nearly until the end of his life, this tap dancer who again illustrates the inseparability of dance from Jazz, not only costarred in *Stormy Weather* with Lena Horne, but also chaperoned the much-beloved child actress Shirley Temple in two Hollywood films: *Rebecca of Sunnybrook Farm* and *The Little Colonel.* None of those three screened here.

BOJANGLES (*The Brooklyn Daily Eagle,* November 2, 1932)

We also note that Bill Bojangles Robinson might be viewed as one of a few performers in our theatre's earlier history who appeared in all four of its faces. Along with films and dance/Jazz during those Vaudeville years, he inspired the Rock 'n' Roll song "Mr. Bojangles," written and performed by Jerry Jeff Walker after our theatre's closing. Finally, this assessment by a biographer of Bojangles, who lived in retirement in Brooklyn with his second wife and mother-in-law until death and was eulogized by the TV host Ed Sullivan at his funeral that drew a million fans as well as curiosity seekers in a procession that stretched from Harlem to the King's Borough and included pallbearers like Duke Ellington, deserves recounting:

Bojangles was probably the only black performer to graduate from the pickaninny to star in a duet in Vaudeville, then as a Vaudeville single, then, go on to Broadway performances, Hollywood, and appear on radio. (Haskins and Mitgang, 1980: 266)

Two more names of Jazz performers who appeared on stage here were the Mills Brothers and Boswell Sisters.

THE BOSWELL SISTERS (David McCain Archives)

Harry, Donald, Herbert, and John Mills, Jr. originally comprised the hip quartet of close harmony singers from Piqua, Ohio. They not only famously imitated different musical instruments through improvisations with their voices but were also heard on recordings alongside major Jazz artists, ranging from Louis Armstrong to Ella Fitzgerald. Known for their sibling sound, Brunswick printed this on their recording labels: "No musical instruments or mechanical devices used on this recording other than one guitar." Check out their version of "Tiger Rag" and compare it with the blazing virtuosity of the greatest of all Jazz pianists who also appeared on stage, Art Tatum!

Following their oldest brother's death, the Four Kings of Harmony would be billed Three Boys and a Guitar as a result of the addition of their father. Their amazing career that spanned forty years counted the Mills Brothers among the first African Americans to host their own weekly radio show in 1932 on the CBS network. All the same, they were described in racially coded advertisements as "Thrilling you with their rhythm, melody and hot-cha." The Mills Brothers made six separate appearances on our theatre's stage during the weeks of December 4, 11, and 18 in 1931; and May 6, August 22, and November 4 in the following year.

Among their numerous million-selling records, we note only "Glow Worm," "You Always Hurt The One You Love," "Till Then," "Paper Doll," and "Someday." The Mills Brothers were the first vocal group to sell over a million records. They appeared in the first of four MGM *Big Broadcast* films whose theme was radio, and performed in the *Broadway Gondolier*, one of Bing Crosby's forty-three flicks screened here during the week of July 26, 1935. Featured in seven Soundies, i.e., the earliest two- and three-minute musical videos heard and seen in jukeboxes, the Mills Brothers, finally, were also featured in a Paramount cartoon humorously titled *When Yuba Plays the Rhumba on the Tuba.*

Last, the Boswell Sisters, Helvetia (Vet), Martha and Connie, who were born in New Orleans and gave up promising careers as instrumentalists in the New Orleans Philharmonic Orchestra to sing

Jazz, following a crossroads-like mystical encounter with an African American musician. Linda Dahl (1984) wrote the following about the Boswell Sisters, who like the Mills Brothers also imitated musical instruments: "they established a swinging, jazz-influenced vocal sound that became popular all over the world."

Recording artists since 1925, the Boswell Sisters not only appeared twice on our theatre's stage in 1932—during the weeks of January 8 and May 13, respectively—but also were featured in the Paramount film *Close Harmony* (starring Buddy Rogers) screened here during the week of May 18, 1929. Along with appearances in other Hollywood films as well, the Boswell Sisters were advertised as "Radio's favorite harmony singers." Indeed, their ability to rag melodies—a colloquial abbreviation derived from Scott Joplin's written Ragtime Jazz—was joined arguably by the first instance of scatting, i.e., slang for nonsensical phrases employed in Jazz as coloratura, a term usually applied to Ella Fitzgerald, which was the direct opposite of vocalese associated with Lambert, Hendricks, and Ross, who wrote lyrics to Jazz solos and appeared on stage at the Brooklyn Paramount during the 1950s.

As a result of African American Jazz influences on their performance style, Titus and Boswell Minnerly (2014: 108) wrote in their biography of the Boswell Sisters that they were initially promoted as Creoles following their debut on NBC radio's Camel Pleasant Hour in November 1931—a year during which it probably should not have to be said Blacks were otherwise denied their own shows.

The Boswell Sisters also appeared in four Hollywood films including *The Big Broadcast,* which starred Bing Crosby and was screened here during the week of October 14, 1932. Their largest hit recordings included "You Ought to Be in Pictures" and "I'm Going to Sit Right Down and Write Myself a Letter."

Finally, four months after their second appearance on stage here, during the week of May 13, 1932, the Boswell Sisters broke up. Yet, while both older siblings quit performing—opting for marriage and family life—Connie Boswell not only continued performing as a soloist, but for unknown reasons, she changed the spelling of her first name to Connee. Courageously then performing in a wheelchair after early childhood polio and a wagon accident compounded by a window fall in her early twenties, she continued to record, notably with other Jazz luminaries like the Dorsey Brothers, Benny Goodman, and Don Redman. Among her largest-selling recorded hits as a soloist were "Martha" and "Heebee Jeebies." Finally, Connee Boswell returned to our theatre during a post–World War II fundraiser in 1947.

* * *

Before turning next to what were dedicated Jazz concerts in the Brooklyn Paramount during the 1950s, some additional aspects of early Jazz during the Vaudeville years probably should be noted.

"Most people in the early twenties did not listen to real jazz," wrote Erenberg (1981: 251) in his study of nightlife in urban areas, which was made feasible in large part by Thomas Edison's incandescent light bulb. "Instead," he also wrote, "they might have heard 'nut' jazz, played by Ted Lewis, the clarinetist-comedian who began making his way in the Broadway cabarets from 1919 on. That is, so-called Nut-jazz men (who) picked up the anarchic animal sounds and unusual instrumentation (of the ODJB) but glorified in the comic effects rather than in the music. At the same time, however, the psychological scars that came with being stigmatized as All-Colored should also not be overlooked. As discussed in the *Brooklyn Eagle* on October 27, 1929, in an article aptly titled 'Stage Negro Must Be Good—That's All There Is to It!' Whose anonymous journalist analyzed the schizoid-like dualism of African Americans in those years that impacted 'the Negro (who) has to have merit in double doses to get across.' First, as the journalist also wrote, the inability 'to complain about (sensationalist) billing, dressing rooms, (and) the management of the orchestra,' and second, what he consequently inexplicably characterized was their alleged lack of originality, which supposedly led them to imitate white performers in order to gain acceptance and recognition, hence were debatable 'denigrated as copycats.'"

B. Modern Jazz Goes to College: The '50s and '60s

By the 1950s, however, we can safely assume most—if not all—ticket holders for dedicated Jazz concerts at the Brooklyn Paramount came out for the music. But the title of this section also evidences the strides Jazz made on college campuses, as referenced in the Prologue. Quite a journey from the New Orleans Red Light District origins, which led to its demeaning appellation as whorehouse music! Restated, the subheading of this part of our discussion of the third face of the Brooklyn Paramount's earlier history literally alludes to Dave Brubeck's performance at Long Island University in the mid-1950s, and the title of a recording he made in 1954 with his renowned quartet following a national tour of institutions of higher learning in the United States—*Jazz Goes to College.*

Our survey of these dedicated Jazz concerts booked into the Brooklyn Paramount during the 1950s by prominent promoters began on March 31, 1950, when we read about a "One Time Only/Friday Night Single 9:40 p.m. Show" featuring Jean-Baptiste Jacquet and Ella Fitzgerald. Their promoter's name unfortunately remains unknown to us as yet.

"Illinois" Jacquet was one of the featured performers. He enjoyed a long career as a tenor saxophonist and big bandleader that traced back to Cab Calloway's orchestra. Along with having recorded one of the most memorable solos in Jazz history as a nineteen-year-old member of Lionel Hampton's Big Band, "Flyin' Home"—a tune he wrote still studied by aspiring players—he was a civil rights activist as well. Jacquet's anti–Jim Crow opposition was paralleled by the Jazz promoter Norman Granz, who hired Jacquet to perform in his legendary JATP Jazz tours. He also doubled on bassoon, a rarely used woodwind instrument in Jazz. Finally, Illinois Jacquet appeared in what generally is regarded among the greatest documentaries in this music's history, the cigarette-smoke-drenched, hauntingly beautiful black-and-white *Jammin' the Blues* made by *Life* magazine's World War II Albanian American photographer Gjon Mili.

Also on that bill was Ella Jane Fitzgerald, whose name we proudly note was given a lounge in our restored theatre: Ella's Room. Discovered at the Apollo Theater's Amateur Night in 1934, the "First Lady of Song" had to recover from stage fright before singing Connee Boswell's hit song "The Object of My Affection." Then still as a teenager, she not only performed in Chick Webb's Savoy Ballroom big band, but when the percussionist tragically died young of a congenital condition, this diva was hired to lead it. Early Ella Fitzgerald signature songs were "Clap Hands, Here Comes Charlie," as well as a hip version of the nursery rhyme "A-Tisket, A-Tasket"—the latter curiously filmed at the back of a bus in an Abbott and Costello film, *Rode 'Em Cowboy*, in 1942. She then went on to win thirteen Grammys and record Songbooks of America's greatest Tin Pan Alley composers—from Gershwin, Rogers and Hart, Irving Berlin, Cole Porter, Jerome Kern, and Duke Ellington. Jasen (1988) described this crossover's multi-octave voice, which memorably shattered a wineglass in a TV commercial for Memorex recording tape as "bell-like, with vocal clarity." She wrote about Fitzgerald's "excellent rhythmic sense of time." Indeed, her unique voice on "Lady Be Good" and "How the Moon," for primary examples, as well as heard on dozens of other recordings, was also likened by musicians to an instrument.

Along with Jacquet, with whom Fitzgerald toured since 1946, these performers also shared our theatre's stage that historic night: Timmie Rogers, an African American comedian, who performed during Ella, her breakout concert at the Harlem Opera House in 1935, and lived long enough to transition from Vaudeville to guest appearances on TV variety shows, Jackie Gleason's memorably among those. And more: Timmie Rogers also appeared in the first all-Black variety show on that new medium, *Uptown Jubilee*, albeit it only briefly aired on CBS-TV in 1949. The tap dancer Bunny Briggs, who confirmed dancing's intrinsic ties with Jazz by working with Duke Ellington's orchestra before winning a Tony in 1989 for hoofing in the Broadway show *Black and Blue*. The latter was set in Paris between the two world wars and whose title came from a 1929 political composition by Fats Waller—with antidiscrimination lyrics by Andy Razaf and Harry Brooks.

Port of New York and *Quartet* were the films co-screened that week in 1950 along with that single-night concert.

The second dedicated Jazz concert booked at the Brooklyn Paramount was also a one-nighter. And so it was that in that same year, on May 12, 1950, a Thursday night, the *enfant terrible* drummer Bernard "Buddy" Rich, who began in Vaudeville with his parents as a child dancer aptly nicknamed Buddy Traps, the Boy Wonder, led "The Buddy Rich All-Star Sextet" on stage here with Johnny Morris (piano), Sam Most (flute), Rolf Ericson (trumpet), Mike Manieri (vibes), and Wyatt Ruther on bass. Doubtless because its promoter sought to sell four thousand–plus seats featuring this Jazz legend, whose numerous credits included backing Frank Sinatra in the Tommy Dorsey Orchestra and appearances in Norman Granz's traveling tours, curiously enough also include a demonstration of how to break boards with those presumably insured golden hands on Johnny Carson's late night TV show and also added these performers: the Ames Brothers, Vick, Ed, Joe, and Gene, a barbershop quartet nicknamed the Rag Mop Boys, and whose signature hit was "The Naughty Lady of Shady Lane"; and the comedian Sam Levinson, a former Spanish teacher at Abraham Lincoln High School in Brooklyn, who enjoyed careers as a bespectacled, avuncular-like TV figure dispensing folk comedy, which meant recounting heartwarming vignettes about near-crushing poverty during the Great Depression as the son of Eastern European immigrant Jews, as well as appearances on numerous TV quiz show panels. Sam Levinson additionally wrote several popular books about his life and comedy.

Riding High and *The Great Plane Robbery* were the films screened that entire week.

The next—third—dedicated Jazz concert in our theatre history during the '50s was booked three years later by another promoter unknown to us: "The Biggest Show of '53" also advertised without explanation as the fall edition and fifth in the series. It featured Sarah Vaughan and Nat King Cole during that single 8:30 p.m. concert on another unlikely Thursday night that advertised both as "America's jukebox favorites" voted by "reports from disk jockeys and jukebox operators all over the country."

Sarah Louise Vaughan was dubbed the Divine One. Like most, if not all, African American singers, she came out of a gospel background in Newark, New Jersey. Gifted with a four-octave operatic-like voice and also nicknamed Sassy, she accompanied herself on piano. Indeed, she occasionally shared that bench with Earl Hines in his big band, that is, when she didn't sing with Billy Eckstine, who also performed here. Not unlike her only rival for that crown, Ella Fitzgerald, Ms. Vaughn was also strongly influenced by Bebop, which followed the Big Band/Swing era. Accused too often as well of having sold out as a result of numerous pop crossover hits like "Broken-Hearted Melody" and "Misty," she also began by winning an Amateur Contest at the Apollo.

William Claxton captured Sarah Vaughan backstage at the Brooklyn Paramount during one of her three appearances here. Elaine Haines (2017: 113), sadly, did not count as a career milestone, while instead writing in her biography about Vaughan's first appearance at the Paramount Theatre on Broadway...another of the famed movie palaces, like the Strand...the most prestigious pop venues in town. Mention, finally, should also be made of *Gershwin Live*, a tribute LP with strings provided by the Los Angeles Philharmonic conducted by Sarah Vaughn's long musical friend, Michael Tilson Thomas, that was released in 1982. And "Broken-Hearted Melody" was among her other greatest hits.

Costarring as well on October 15, 1953, was Nat King Cole, whose remarkable career Will Friedwald (2020) wrote would be evenly divided into two halves: the first half of his career as a top-drawer Jazz pianist who led the Nat King Cole Trio (with Oscar Moore on bass and Johnny Miller on guitar originally), and the second half as a pop vocalist. Among many million-seller vocals were "Route 66," "Darling Je Vous Aime Beaucope," "Sweet Lorraine," "Rambling Rose," and "Pretend." Another, Nat King Cole's rendition of "Nature Boy" written in 1948 by eden ahbez (sans capitalization) was used in *The*

Boy with Green Hair, a film starring Dean Stockwell that unfortunately was never screened in our theatre.

As one of the first African American hosts of his own TV variety show, Nat King Cole's in 1957 was bitterly canceled on account of the loss of commercial sponsors as a result of his brushing too closely to a white singer. Asked for a comment, this nonconfrontational nonpareil performer ironically quipped, "I guess Madison Avenue is afraid of the dark." And that's also after having been attacked by white supremacists one year prior on April 10, 1956, while performing in front of a segregated white audience in Birmingham, Alabama, no less—a performance that got criticized by the NAACP for Jim Crow pandering, which understandably left him further shaken.

We might, however, note Nat King Cole's tongue-in-cheek spoof regarding Rock 'n' Roll's real enough threat to Jazz during the 1950s titled "Mr. Cole Don't Sing Rock and Roll" heard on his *Live at Las Vegas* record album.

In addition to their backing by the Illinois Jacquet band, these additional non-Jazz performers were also cofeatured on this one-night-only Thursday show at the Brooklyn Paramount on October 15, 1953: George Kirby and Peg Leg Bates—doubtless stemming from its promoter's hope of selling additional seats in our gargantuan house.

George Kirby was a Black comic who might well have appeared on every major TV variety show through the 1970s. Unafraid as well of calling attention to civil rights issues during those years, he, however, got his show cancelled. This could only have contributed to Kirby's downward spiral into narcotics that led to a lengthy prison term. Although this comic occasionally performed following his release, the Chicago-born native sadly never recaptured his former fame and glory. As for Clayton Bates, the dancer nicknamed Peg Leg—because he really performed on a wooden leg—the result of a cotton gin industrial accident—he not only was old enough to have worked in TOBA, Black Vaudeville, but continue into its TV years. He frequently appeared on Ed Sullivan's Sunday night "Toast of the Town" and returned from a previous engagement during the week of February 23,

1934, when he appeared in *Hot Chocolates*, described as a fast-stepping sepia revue with a reported cast of one hundred, including the Hot Chocolate Creole Chorus and LeRoy Smith band, in effect pitting Jazz against Western Classical music insofar as the Brooklyn Paramount Orchestra reportedly presented *The Concert*, featuring compositions of Chopin and Liszt.

Finally, Ralph Marterie also brought his ABC-TV studio musicians to our theatre a year before their biggest hit, "Skokiaan." Finally, Frank Marlowe emceed—an Italian American as well, who previously enjoyed a Hollywood acting career that continued into radio and TV. His voice was famously heard announcing the start of a radio series like *The Lone Ranger and Tonto* and *Bulldog Drummond Strikes Back*.

Names of the two films screened that week at the Brooklyn Paramount? *Roman Holiday* and *Spaceways*.

In the following year, 1954, Stanley Newcomb Kenton promoted the first of two Festivals of Modern American Jazz in our theatre. Thus, on February 6, 1954, a Saturday night, the silver-haired bandleader, who was quoted by a biographer saying "From age 14, I was all music. Nothing else entered my mind" (Easton, 1973: 37), initially brought his touring progressive symphonic-like orchestra to our theatre's stage backing these legendary Jazz musicians in a Reserved Seats Only/Two Complete Shows at 8:30 p.m. and midnight:

SAM KENTON JAZZ ADVERTISEMENT (*The Brooklyn Daily Eagle*/February 5,1954)

1. Erroll Garner, a self-taught pianist who couldn't read or write music and incredulously credited his iconoclastic style to a hometown older pianist in Pittsburgh sharing the exact same name! *Concert by the Sea* was Garner's bestselling LP, and like so many other modern Jazz pianists, he modeled his successful trio on Nat King Cole's with Wyatt Ruther on bass and Fats Heard on drums. A frequently quoted vignette about this affable and genuinely joyous performer has the diminutive Erroll Garner assuming his seat on the piano bench on a telephone directory enabling him to reach the keyboard before a concert—then abruptly standing again to remove one of its tissue-thin pages. Erroll Garner's bestselling single recording was *Misty*, which he wrote. The late Bruce Ricker, Esq., who made the documentary *Straight No Chaser* about another eccentric modern pianist, Thelonius Monk, and was Clint Eastwood's attorney, told this author during our radio interview show about having been instructed to purchase the rights for its use for $25,000 by his client for the actor and filmmaker's psychological terrifying initial flick about a female stalker...titled *Play Misty for Me*;

2. Charles Christopher Parker was the legendary co-founder of Bebop. The entire oeuvre (including outtakes!) of this larger-than-life alto saxophonist genius nicknamed Bird—shortened from Yardbird—can still be heard on the late Phil Schaap's early-morning radio rebroadcasts on WKCR-FM. Seemingly countless articles and biographies as well as two biopics have been made about Charlie Parker, whose early death memorably resulted in subway graffiti that read "Bird Lives";

3. John Birks "Dizzy" Gillespie was the other co-founder of Bebop. Introduced contrarily by Parker on one recording as my "worthy constituent" as well as the other "half of my heart," he was a fiercely competitive, complex, brilliant, and ebullient trumpet virtuoso. Despite on- and off-stage hilarious antics, Dizzy Gillespie shared Bird's commitment to presenting their new music like the Western Classics, i.e., as serious enough to require seating

for thoughtful listening, rather than being danced to, such as during the era of the Big Bands, which it replaced following the Second World War. Even so, the writer of numerous landmark Jazz songs, such as *Night in Tunisia*, ironically led his big band while dancing! Gillespie introduced Afro-Cuban Jazz with *Manteca*, and he also famously sang novelty songs like *Cement Mixer, Putty Putt*, and *Salt Peanuts*—the latter, in a spontaneous duet with the late President Jimmy Carter on the White House lawn. Along with the sort of mock-serious presidential run that marked Eddie Cantor's and Gracie Allen's careers, Dizzy Gillespie famously wore a beret and goatee, which stereotypically became trademarks of Bebop. But he was also a deeply spiritual figure who became a Bahá'í and led state department tours representing Jazz throughout the world;

4. Leon "Lee" Konitz began as a disciple of the blind Jazz pianist Lenny Tristano. A leader of the so-called Cool School, the alto saxophonist with Miles Davis recorded with Gerry Mulligan and Warne Marsh, the latter also a Tristano protégé, before emerging as a creative innovator active in his own right until Konitz succumbed to the COIVD-19 virus in 2020;

5. Candido is discussed below; and finally;

6. "The Misty Miss Christy" was part of this first of two Jazz shows promoted by Stan Kenton at the Brooklyn Paramount in 1954. Née Shirley Luster, June Christy became the girl singer in his big band. Her whiskey-like drenched chanson "Something Cool" and lively Latin Jazz number "Tampico" remain fixtures in her legacy.

Names of the films shown that week were *The Sins of Jezebel* and *The Man from Cairo*.

Eight months later, Kenton returned here. That date was November 6, 1954, another Saturday night, and his advertised new music was once again described, pretentiously or not, as utilizing the concert form. Notwithstanding Kenton's ironic humor—he, for example, curiously titled one of the band's theme songs "Sunset in a Hairpin

Turn"—his band was on the road for 328 days one year while logging a reported sixty thousand miles with his musicians living on a bus that went from gig to gig, as one biographer wrote (Easton, 1973: 21).

In any event, at 8:00 p.m. and 11:00 p.m. on that Saturday night, Stan Kenton once again presented these additional great Jazz musicians backed by his orchestra and before what the tabloids reported were full houses at the Brooklyn Paramount:

1. Arthur Tatum Jr., the nonpareil pianist aptly nicknamed God! Left blind in one eye and mostly in the other after a vicious mugging as a teenager in his native Toledo, Ohio, Tatum then developed a technique of such profundity as to astonish Western Classical pianists like Vladimir Horowitz. Check out "Tea for Two" and see if you don't agree! The Art Tatum Trio consisted of Slam Stewart on bass and Everett Barksdale on drums, and its leader also recorded an epic number of solo piano LPs for Norman Granz with whom Tatum enjoyed an exclusive contract;

2. Charlie Ventura was voted Best Tenor Saxophonist by *DownBeat* magazine in 1946 and played in Gene Krupa's big band before forming his own. It was dubbed "Bop for the People";

3. Mary Ann McCall was a featured big band singer in the 1940s, who worked with Woody Herman and Charlie Barnet;

4. Milton "Shorty" Rogers played trumpet and flügelhorn and was a transplanted New-Yorker-cum-West-Coast-expatriate. He not only led a group comically called Shorty Rogers and His Giants but also became a much-sought-after studio musician and arranger. Shorty Rogers's Jazz-inflected scores were also heard on a wide-ranging number of TV shows, from *The Partridge Family* to the Mr. Magoo cartoon series. He additionally achieved an Academy Award for writing the music to *The Man with the Golden Arm*, a Hollywood film about a drummer's drug habit based on Nelson Algren's novel, which unfortunately never was screened in our theatre;

5. Sheldon "Shelly" Manne was a fellow graduate of Manhattan's Music and Arts High School. A drummer and expatriate from the

Big Apple, he became a prominent figure in the so-called West Coast Cool Jazz School. Yet Shelly Manne also performed in virtually every Jazz style from Dixieland through Swing and Bebop. *My Fair Lady* recorded by him in 1956 was the first Jazz LP million seller by the owner of Shelly's Manne-Hole, formerly a popular Jazz club on North Cahuenga Boulevard in Hollywood;

6. John Henry "Johnny" Smith was a self-taught Jazz guitarist whose recordings also included hillbilly, a. k. a. country and western, music. "Moonlight in Vermont," which featured the tenor saxophonist Stan Getz, who performed on stage here, can arguably be found in every serious lover's all-time favorite Jazz album collection;

7. Cándido de Guerra Camero was a Cuban conga player who returned to the Brooklyn Paramount under Stan Kenton's imprimatur as promoter. The exclusive use of Candido's first name alone reminded us with unabashed nostalgia what Bob Myers, owner of Brooklyn's belated Up Over Jazz Club, used to say while introducing another Latin percussionist: "You know he's bad, 'cause cats with one name usually are!" Candido not only worked with the famous Cuban bandleader Machito, but Dizzy Gillespie as well.

Finally, we leave off with the controversy surrounding Stan Kenton. Gary Giddins (1998c: 327–30) critiqued the seemingly exponential continuous growth in size of his orchestras over time without appreciable improvement in the quality of the music. Whereas *Metronome* magazine's critic George Simon (1981: 293) ambivalently wrote about those purported progressive sounds from behemoth orchestras in his landmark book about the Big Band Era: how they were responsible for "some of the most thrilling, some of the most aggravating, some of the most impressive, some of the most depressive, some of the most exciting, (yet) *some of the most boring* and certainly some of the most controversial sounds, music and/or noise ever to emanate from any big-band."

JAZZ AT THE PHILHARMONIC ADVERTISEMENT (*The Brooklyn Daily Eagle*/September 19, 1953)

It is also sad to write that in these challenging times when discussions of slavery like the near-holocaust that wiped out most Native Americans following Columbus are under attack in public school curricula, one of Stan Kenton's biographers derided Stan Kenton's rock-ribbed conservative Republican Waspish values such as motherhood, apple pie, and hard work as the gateway to eternal life (Easton, 1973: 90), but despite presenting African Americans in concert, not only were none hired in his vanilla bands, their leader, whether racist or not, was also quoted as being anti-bop.

The name of the single film shown during Stan Kenton's second concert date at the Brooklyn Paramount was the Hitchcock thriller *Rear Window*.

One year later, JATP made its only appearance in our house. The date was September 19, 1955, and this acronym for "Jazz at the Philharmonic" was a Wilbury-like traveling group of diverse all-star Jazz musicians that owed its birth to a concert promoted in LA's Philharmonic Bowl by the former UCLA-film-student-cum-civil-rights-activist Norman Granz on behalf of Mexican gang members wrongfully charged with the death of a rival in the Sleepy Lagoon Murder case in 1942. Their imprisonment (for seven years) is generally viewed today as a racially motivated police riot triggered by anger because those marginalized sons of Mexican farmworkers violated the War Product Code by wearing zoot suits during the Second World War...a police riot joined by naval soldiers anxiously awaiting orders to be shipped off to the carnage in the Pacific (Hershorn, 2011).

In that Monday night concert booked by that major Jazz promoter and record company owner, who, as noted, refused anything less than equal accommodations for Black traveling musicians, these legendary Jazz giants were presented by Norman Granz on our theatre's original stage during that dedicated Jazz concert:

1. Oscar Peterson, a Canadian virtuoso pianist of West Indian descent whose legacy boasts some two hundred recorded albums and eight Grammys. The son of a classical music teacher—his

mother—Peterson primarily worked in a unique trio format with Ray Brown on bass and Herb Ellison on guitar sans drums, and enjoyed an exclusive contract with Granz;

2. "Ella, Ella," as Ms. Fitzgerald was affectionately dubbed, returned to our theatre for her second and final gig at our theatre;

3. Eugene Bertram "Gene" Krupa was famous for his bombastic style of drumming with Benny Goodman's prime-time Swing band heard on Sing Sing Sing, a composition written by Louis Prima. Krupa's gig with JATP pitted him in mammoth drum battles with Buddy Rich...that is, after he led his own big band in the early 1940s. Along with having been infamously set up by the police for possession of marijuana and arrested, Gene Krupa was featured in two Hollywood biopics about other prominent white Jazz musicians from the Swing Era—the big bandleaders Glenn Miller, and Benny Goodman as well. Yet Sal Mineo portrayed him in *The Gene Krupa Story*, a film released in 1959, which like those other two, unfortunately wasn't screened in our theatre, even if Krupa did his own drumming in the biopic;

4. Buddy Rich returned to the Brooklyn Paramount;

5. Stan(ley) Gayetski Getz, who was dubbed "The Sound" for his extraordinary vibrato and improvisatory skills, was a disciple of the ethereal tenor saxophone style of Lester Young, also featured on the JATP slate at the Brooklyn Paramount. A lifelong drug addict and repeat offender, Getz famously recorded "Early Autumn" with fellow saxophonists Serge Chaloff, Herbie Steward, and Zoot Sims as part of the Four Brothers in Woody Herman's so-called Second Herd in 1947; and that's after starting out as a teenager in Jack Teagarden's Dixieland band. During his lengthy career that included stints with Benny Goodman and Dizzy Gillespie, Getz's mid-career musical sensibilities led to a change in the 1960s that saw his introduction of the Brazilian Bossa Nova/Samba, a. k. a. new-sound, recordings with the vocalist Astrud Gilberto performing songs written by Carlos Jobim to the manifold world of Jazz, "The Girl from Ipanema" most famously among those, and it won a Grammy;

6. Illinois Jacquet's appearance with JATP marked his third date on our theatre's stage;

7. Flip Phillips (née Joseph Edward Filippelli) was an Italian American tenor saxophonist from Brooklyn who not only played in Woody Herman's big band and a smaller ensemble called the Wood Choppers, but also participated in two tenor duels for Granz aimed at re-creating all-night blowing sessions in Kansas City in the 1930s. Flip Phillips paired against Jacquet and/or Stan Getz on that magical Monday night in our theatre's earlier history;

8. Roy Eldridge, who was nicknamed Little Jazz—for physical not musical stature—a brilliant trumpet virtuoso, performed on that gig.

Variety (September 17, 1955) reported ticket sales for $4.75 for that night, which netted JATP $24,000. As for the accompanying films screened that entire week, *One Desire*, which costarred Anne Baxter and Rock Hudson, was paired with *Four Ways Out* starring Ginger Rogers.

The succeeding three Jazz concerts were booked by Morris Levy, a. k. a. the Godfather of Music, and Alan Freed's Rock 'n' Roll partner. But in 1955, 1956, and 1957, Levy sent out the Birdland All-Stars to diverse venues on tour apparently inspired by his business partner's success. It was named for the famous Jazz club Birdland, opened on December 15, 1949, with his brother in the cellar of what formerly was the Cinque and purportedly renamed for Charlie Parker. Birdland used to be near Fifty-First Street and Broadway and identified by a street sign that read: "The Jazz Corner of the World."

On the first of those three annual bookings at the Brooklyn Paramount, the "Birdland Stars of '55" included three returnees and three new Jazz arrivals who also recorded on Levy's Roulette record label and were sold in that reputed mobster's chain of Strawberry record stores. Two shows at 8:00 p.m. and 11:00 p.m. were held on that Friday night, February 25,1955, which brought back Sarah Vaughan, Erroll Garner, and Stan Getz, while introducing Count Basie, George Shearing, and Lester Young.

Basie also performed in Alan Freed's Jubilees in the 1950s, and he was discovered by John Hammond during his band's formative years in Kanas City, Missouri. As for George Shearing, he overcame blindness at birth in London by learning to read music through braille. The George Shearing Quintet included Margie Hyams (vibes), Chuck Wayne (guitar), Denzil Best (drums), and John Levy (bass). Commissioned in 1952 by Morris Levy—no relation to its bassist—to compose a theme song for his nightclub, Shearing (2004: 136–138) wrote in his autobiography how "Lullaby of Birdland" with its changes (chord progression) was based on "Love Me or Leave Me," written in a flash after a lengthy gestation, and whose lyrics were added by George David Weiss, a pseudonym (Shearing and Shipton, 2004: 136–38). Its reported history, however, led to a quarrel with Shearing's patron over ownership and was resolved when the pianist agreed to accept the song's publishing rights while (outrageously) signing over its composition rights to Morris Levy.

The other newcomer to our theatre in 1955 was Prez, a nickname bestowed upon Lester Willis Young by his soulmate, Billie Holiday, whom he dubbed Lady Day, i.e., inspired by their much-beloved American president FDR and his First Lady, Eleanor Roosevelt. Young started out playing drums as a youngster in his father's traveling band before changing to the C-Melody saxophone out of admiration for Frankie Trumbauer, Bix Beiderbecke's legendary musical associate. After going out on his own, Lester Young recorded these numbers among others with Count Basie's Kansas City band during the 1930s: "Lester Leaps In" and "Taxi War Dance," which evidence his originality...and also includes Prez holding his tenor saxophone at a forty-five-degree angle while playing, supposedly an accommodation to overcrowded small bandstands. Also reported about him was an original way of speaking—identifying police with the name of a white musician, Bob Crosby, and sartorial splendor as well—the latter notably including Prez's porkpie hat, long trench coats, and ribbons in his hair. Lester Young's life was melded with events from the Bebop pianist Bud Powell in '*Round Midnight*, a Jazz film starring another great tenor saxophonist legend, Dexter Gordon, which is widely regarded as the best Jazz film ever made.

The Bridges of Toko-ri with an all-star cast that included William Holden, Grace Kelly, and Fredric March was cofeatured with *Jamboree* that entire week.

One year later, on February 24, 1956, another Friday night, these Birdland Stars of '56 ventured across the East River to perform on Brooklyn Paramount's stage as part of Morris Levy's second Jazz booking here:

1. The Count Basie Band was back again with vocalist Joseph Goreed Williams, a. k. a. Joe Williams, whose rendition of Memphis Slim's *Every Day I Got the Blues* became the signature song of that former salesman by day, and nightclub doorman by night, who years later played Uncle Al on Bill Cosby's TV sitcom about the Huxtable family;
2. Albert George "Al" Hibbler, who also returned in another context, i.e., replacing Tony Bennett in Alan Freed's first Labor Day Rock 'n' Roll Show in our theater in 1955;
3. Johnny Smith was another returnee;
4. Sarah Vaughan;
5. Lester Young.

These newcomers initially perform on stage here:

6. Earl Rudolph "Bud" Powell, an original Bebop pianist whose savage beating by a cop led to mental illness and shock therapies, with chronic stays in psychiatric facilities. Powell, however, famously wrote "Un Poco Loco" among other enduring Jazz standards;
7. Al Cohn was a swinging tenor saxophonist–arranger, who, like Stan Getz, came out of Lester Young's bag, i.e., played more with Prez's lightness than the more muscular approach of Coleman Hawkins's rival school;
8. Secondo "Conte" Candoli, who played trumpet in leading (white)

big bands of the 1940s and 1950s, including Stan Kenton's, before joining Doc Severinsen's TV orchestra, which famously backed Johnny Carson's *Tonight Show*;

9. Roy Haynes, among the original Bebop drummers able to boast "I played with Bird";
10. Joe Benjamin, a bassist who worked in a variety of big-band settings, ranging from Artie Shaw's Mainstream to Duke Ellington's original Swing orchestras;
11. Jimmy Jones, a pianist;
12. Phil Woods, who married Charlie Parker's third wife, Chan, and similarly played alto saxophone;
13. "K. D.," whose initials stood for Howard McKinley "Kenny" Dorham, a trumpet player, who not only could boast he performed with Parker but recorded an album as a vocalist.

Screened alongside the advertised West Coast/East Coast Septet hyping of that concert, these films were shown during the week in which the Birdland All-Stars Tour of '56 played the Brooklyn Paramount: *Quentin Durward*, a British film based on a history novel by Sir Walter Scott, that got paired with *Mau-Mau*, which dealt with the Gikuyu revolt against British imperialism in East Africa, whose leader, President Jomo Kenyatta, obtained a PhD in social anthropology in Great Britain and became the first president of Kenya.

Then one year later, on March 16,1957, also a Friday night, Morris Levy sent out a somewhat different cast of great Jazz musicians to our theatre. The Birdland Stars of '57 featured this mixture of new and returning Jazz greats:

1. Clarence Henry "Billy" Eckstine (née Eckstein), a. k. a. Mr. B., the African American Jazz crooner probably best remembered for his crossover pop recording of "That Old Black Magic." Initially a self-taught trumpet player from Pittsburgh, Pennsylvania, Eckstine, like his close friend Sarah Vaughan, changed the original spelling of his surname. The sonorous Mr. B., as Eckstine (née Eckstein)

was dubbed by Duke Ellington, also led his own big band, but they played Bebop on Fifty-Second Street, a. k. a. Swing Street, between 1943 and 1947. Known for his deep and mellifluous bass voice, Billy Eckstine was profiled in *Life* on April 25, 1950, in a story about Bebop's originators, Bird and Dizzy, who performed in his big band. These additional biographical facts about his life might also be added: First, Eckstine's photograph in that weekly glossy magazine with a young white female fan resting her head adoringly on the chest of the drop-dead handsome vocalist was met with a racist backlash that reportedly caused the breakup of his big band; Billy Eckstine was also a fashion trendsetter, i.e., with the so-called Mr. B. collar adopted by hipsters back in that day; his recording of "Jelly Jelly," whose controversial sexual innuendo goes without saying more;

2. Count Basie was brought back a third time;

3. Phineas Newborn Jr. made his first and only appearance here. He was the pianist on Jackie Brenston's influential recording of "Rocket '88," which topped the Rhythm and Blues charts in the 1940s and is viewed today by music critics as a prototype for what became Rock 'n' Roll. Phineas Newborn was gifted with innate musical genius at birth. His career, however, was sadly derailed by a hand injury that unfortunately led to emotional problems;

4. Julius Gubenko, a. k. a. Terry Gibbs, was a vibraphonist from Brooklyn who celebrated his one hundredth birthday in 2024 during Live Nation's ribbon cutting at the reopened Brooklyn Paramount. Along with leading a big band, Gibbs also found steady employment on The Steve Allen Show. During his engagement in our theater in 1957, the vibraphonist probably worked alongside Terry Pollard, the only African American woman vibes player during those years;

5. Richard Davis was another newcomer who began in Jazz as a vocalist in a duo with his brother before concentrating on the double bass. Davis not only backed Sarah Vaughn for several years but also found work outside Jazz performing Western classics as part

of Igor Stravinsky's assemblage. He can also be heard on Bruce Springsteen's Grammy-winning Born to Run LP. Talk about Jazz goes to college; the late professor Richard Davis was the first African American head of any major Jazz program at the University of Wisconsin's Madison campus during the 1970s;

6. John Haley "Zoot" Sims was the son of Vaudevillians who often performed as part of a two-tenor group with Al Cohn. The wildly frenzied saxophone-tooting character on TV's *The Muppet Show* is said to have been modeled on Zoot Sims.

Still other new Brooklyn Paramount performers featured in the Birdland All-Stars of '57 included:

7. Al Cohn, the aforementioned tenor saxophonist;
8. Seldon Powell, a much-sought-after African American saxophonist for studio work whose roots in race music made him a member of Lucky Millinder's jump music/formative Rhythm-and-Blues-cum-Rock-'n'-Roll band heard in our theater in 1950;
9. Rolf Kuhn was a clarinetist born in Germany whose technique was favorably compared with Benny Goodman. Although he remained only three years in the United States before returning home, Kuhn was invited to perform on our campus in downtown Brooklyn by John Doria's Newman Club during those years when Jazz literally went to college;
10. Jimmy Jones (née James Henry Jones) was reportedly Sarah Vaughn's favorite piano accompanist;
11. Roy Haynes, who was nicknamed Snap-Crackle—for his use of snares and cymbals—was also brought back. After being heard on hundreds of Jazz albums, he received a Grammy Lifetime Achievement Award for sixty years. And also, Roy Haynes played in the band featured on *The Late Show with Stephen Colbert* at age ninety-one, after having backed the Allman Brothers Band. He had been the subject of a song by the Rolling Stones;
12. Lester Young was also a returnee to our theatre.

An article in the *Williamsburg News* (March 1, 1957) reported that this third—and last—all-star touring Birdland show outgrossed both previous ones. *Voodoo Woman* and *The Undead* were examples of the Grade B films screened here during those years.

No Jazz concerts were booked in our theater in the following year, but in 1959, the founder of Randall's Island Jazz Festival, Franklyn Geltman, rented our cinematic-like palace for eight nights between October 23 and 29. Featuring many of those same performers in the East River, Geltman presented: (1) the Count Basie Orchestra returning here for a fourth time; (2) Dakota (née Smith) Staton, an enormously popular crossover Columbia Records' pop recording singer during the 1950s appearing here for the first and only time. A convert to Islam like many other African American Jazz musicians during those years, Aliyah Rabia performed under her birth name and was reported by *Variety* (October 28, 1959) to be the highlight of this dedicated Jazz concert in the Brooklyn Paramount. *The Night* was the name of Dakota Staton's bestselling album;

(3) The Miles Davis Sextet was also new to our theatre's stage. The great trumpeter's greatest band on those dates showcased other Jazz legends like John Coltrane on tenor saxophone, whose *Giant Steps* album, issued in that year, without hyperbole revolutionized Jazz; Julian "Cannonball" Adderley, as skilled and as soulful as any disciple of Charlie Parker on the alto saxophone; "Everyone Loves Bill Evans," the title taken from an album containing the original music of this great Jazz pianist from Plainfield, New Jersey; Mr. P. C. (née Paul Lawrence Dunbar Chambers Jr.) on bass; and Wilbur James "Jimmy" Cobb on bass.

(4) George Shearing also returned a second time;

(5) The (Dave) Lambert—(Jon) Hendricks (Annie) Ross (née Anabella Allan Short) Trio, scat and vocalese singers, who it still remains difficult to believe performed together for only two years here as part of Geltman's package in 1959.

Variety (October 28, 1959) reported that our house was only half-filled for the first show on that first Saturday night of this eight-day

Jazz all-star concert, whereas the second night sold out. Geltman brought in Don Adams for yuks, the comedian who starred in TV's *Get Smart*, a hilarious sleuth series popular in the 1960s produced by Mel Brooks. Sid Torin was hired as emcee. Née Tarnopol, a. k. a. Symphony Sid and the Frantic One, Sid Torin was a white hipster who broadcast late-night live-Jazz engagements on WJZ radio from Morris Levy's Birdland as well as his Royal Roost and might well have served as a prototype for Norman Mailer's influential essay, "The White Negro."

Variety reported that Jazz fans came out mostly for Dakota Staton, but tickets cost $2.75. The trade magazine's reviewer praised the "bop scatting hip and witty" Lambert-Hendricks-Ross Trio, while suggesting the rest of the music heard that night was "no more fitting for theater presentation than the Jazz instrumentalists, all of whom are looser in the cloudy cellars."

The name of the film screened throughout that one-week-and-a day momentous Jazz show at the Brooklyn Paramount was *The Young Land,* a Hollywood Western featuring John Wayne's son, Patrick, and also *Easy Rider* with Dennis Hopper.

This eleventh dedicated Jazz concert booked here was a ten-day blockbuster two years before our theatre's closure in 1962. Between April 15 and April 24, 1960, these new and returning Jazz greats appeared: (1) Dinah Washington née Ruth Lee Jones, nicknamed the Queen of the Blues, the Queen of the Jukebox, and Queen of the Jam Session, who like Sarah Vaughan, left the church to perform this banned devil's music. After initially working with Lionel Hampton's big band in 1943, Dinah Washington led a tumultuous and much too brief troubled personal life that included at least seven marriages. Best remembered for her recording of "What a Difference A Day Made," i.e., not as commonly titled "What a Difference a Day Makes," she started out in Rhythm and Blues and moved on from Jazz by crossing over into the commercial world of Pop music. Dinah Washington's recording of "Dirty Blues," however, remains as powerful as ever and is controversial for its lyrics. All the same, she was inducted into the Rock & Roll Hall of Fame after sadly dying young at the age of thirty-nine (Cohodas: 2004); (2) Lambert, Hendricks, and Ross returnees; (3) Walter Maynard Ferguson, a high-note Canadian trumpet player who starred in Stan Kenton's band before making his personal debut on stage here, and whom this author was privileged to see at the original Birdland with a young Wayne Shorter in his band; (4) the Jazztet, one of the premier Jazz groups in the late 1950s. Awarded *DownBeat* magazine's prestigious New Stars award in 1960, they were co-led by Arthur "Art" Stewart Farmer (flügelhorn), Benny Golson (tenor saxophone), and Curtis Fuller (trombone). Golson became an important Jazz composer whose most prominent compositions include "Stablemates," and "I Remember Clifford"—the latter dedicated to Clifford Brown, a brilliant trumpet player who tragically died young in a car accident on the Pennsylvania Turnpike. And not only was Benny Golson's place in the Jazz pantheon marked by his inclusion in Jamey Aebersold's famous *Play-Along* series, the lyrical tenor saxophonist's fame was augmented from his key place in Tom Hanks's film *The Terminal*. The other original members of the Jazztet were Jymie Merritt on bass, McCoy Tyner on piano, and Albert "Tootie" Heath on drums. This begs the question: "What happened to trombonist Curtis Fuller who was absent from this gig at Long Island University's Brooklyn Paramount?"

William B. Williams, the silky-voiced radio host of *Make Believe Ballroom*, a Top Forty radio show that for a time only played recordings by Frank Sinatra, was hired as this Jazz concert's emcee… Whatever Willie B. really thought about Jazz during those ten days—not to mention Rock 'n' Roll—the latter was performed here by Dion DiMucci who reunited with his homeboys from the Bronx, The Belmonts, for this blockbuster show, and whose hits like "The Wanderer" and "I Wonder Why" would probably never be heard on his epigonal Martin Block's "Make Believe Ballroom" on WNEW radio. This radio deejay could only have enjoyed introducing Brook Benton (née Benjamin Franklin Peay) on our theatre's stage, i.e., a pop crooner whose "Rainy Night in Georgia" was among his best-known hits, which included a Top Forty record with Dinah Washington, "Baby You've Got What It Takes."

We also must note the appearance of the comedian and Black hoofer Leo DeLyon, a. k. a. Cha Cha Taps, on stage during Easter week in 1960 in a show promoted (and/or booked) by the formidable PR man Sid Bernstein (1993), which, according to *Variety* (April 20, 1960), grossed only $66,400.

The name of the film shown during those days? *Hell Fighters in Pink Tights* starring the Italian actress Sophie Loren, which, despite being billed as a comedy, might make audiences today take offense to the implied gay bashing in the title of this film, which also trivializes the contributions made to Jazz history by the 369th Regiment Band under James Reese Europe, a. k. a. the Hell-Fighter...who saw combat during the First World War and introduced Jazz overseas years before Willis Conover's *Voice of America* radio broadcasts were aimed at the Iron Curtain.

A twelfth mixed Jazz show also played the Brooklyn Paramount in 1960. So, for six nights during the waning days of our theatre's inaugural run, Pearlie May's Intimate Revue, starring the inimitable singer Pearl Bailey, was staged here between October 21 and October 26. *Variety* (October 26, 1960) also listed these Vaudeville-like acts on stage here: the Eight Ambassadorettes, Three Tappaters, Seven Moroccan Gymnasts, Bluebirds, and Alice Grand, who was advertised as a Negro ballerina assisted by a young terp, Mr. Wynn. We see the intimate and intrinsic connection between dance and Jazz in this show headed by the Queen of Show Business, Pearl Mae Bailey, who sang with anything but her contrived lackadaisical stage manner of announcing herself by descrying, "I'm tired!"

Of greater importance is that her husband, the great Jazz drummer Luigi Paolino Alfredo Francesco Antonio Balassoni, a. k. a. Louie Bellson, headed a sixteen-piece band, which backed those performers of this Vaudeville-like retro revue. Not only did Bellson replace Gene Krupa in Benny Goodman's famous Swing band, among his other career highlights was playing drums in Duke Ellington's sacred orchestral suite in 1948.

Back again for another moment to Momma Pearl's show; in addition to having recorded numerous standards, she starred in the Black version of *Hello. Dolly!* on Broadway. Indeed, Pearl Bailey worked in show business for sixty years yet somehow found time to graduate from Georgetown University with a degree in theology when she was sixty-seven years old! A civil rights activist and tireless worker for other humanitarian causes as well, she additionally served as this nation's unofficial Ambassador of Love, an appointment as special delegate to the United Nations annually renewed by different American presidents—while also finding time to write three books, an autobiography among them.

Finally, we note that *Variety* (August 31, 1960) reported that Pearl Bailey's show was booked by none other than the so-called fifth Beatle, Sid Bernstein, through the Shaw Artists Corporation, arguably as part of our theatre manager's stated intention to bring back adults to the Brooklyn Paramount to avoid the violence that followed a tour of Rock 'n' Roll idols led by Alan Freed.

One more instance of Jazz goes to college, however, needs to be included. Presented out of chronological order, Johnny Hartman performed here as part of *The Bob Hope Show*, which, according to *Variety* (November 29, 1950), NBC was willing to televise in that same year Long Island University purchased the Brooklyn Paramount, depending on audience ratings. And so it was that Robert Weitman, who'd moved over from managing our Paramount in 1946 to theirs in Manhattan, probably convinced his former assistant and replacement, Eugene Pleshette, to seek permission to book both of Bob Hope's Saturday night shows, the first set of which, according to the tabloids, lasted one hundred-and-five minutes, while the second had to be curtailed after ninety minutes on account of hurricane warnings. Nonetheless, with reported earnings of over eight thousand for both, we also read that half went to the house, as Weitman was quoted afterward in *Variety* saying his hope of "creating new interest in the (Brooklyn?) Paramount house" might have been realized.

Returning for a brief moment, however, to the African American Jazz crooner John Maurice Hartman, whether or not the close resemblance of his mellifluous voice with Billy Eckstine's explained his relative obscurity, Hartman sang in Earl Hines's and Dizzy Gillespie's big bands in different years, but famously recorded *Ballads* in 1963 with the legendary John Coltrane, an LP we dare say every Jazz aficionado also has packed and ready to go just in case the Saints decide to call the children home sooner than later! Finally, four songs from another Johnny Hartman album titled *Once in a While* were selected by the film director/Jazz buff Clint Eastwood for inclusion in *The Bridges of Madison County*, a steamy romantic drama in which he costarred with Meryl Streep as well as directed.

Sarah Vaughan, Pearl Bailey and Ella Fitzgerald
television rehearsal, Pasadena, CA c. 1979

Photograph by Milton J. Hinton ©

THREE DIVAS (Berger/Maxson/Hinton Archives)

If only because we haven't yet heard the last of Morris Levy, I close with two contradictory wisdom stories about that complex figure so intimately involved with our sacred place during the 1950s.

In the first, this author's closest pal in Jazz, Hank O'Neal, who owned Chiaroscuro Records in the 1970s and promoted Jazz cruises on the *QE2* with his wife, Shelly, wants it known that mobster O'Neal was always pleasant and cordial during business dealings. The second of those, however, is what the late, great Tony Bennett wrote about Levy's questionable closeness with Count Basie in the iconic crooner's immodestly titled book *Just Getting Started*, published in his ninetieth year of life:

> Bill's label, Roulette Records, was another kind of story in the music business. A guy named Morris Levy founded the label as part of a front for the Genovese crime family. Morris would finally be convicted of extortion in 1986; he died before serving any time in prison. (Bennett and Simon, 2016: 39)

Apropos, after then naming two other prominent Jazz musicians who seemingly were also part of Levy's stable—Dinah Washington and Pearl Bailey—Bennett (2016) tempered his view of that enormously successful financial wheeler-dealer:

> (But) I'll say this for him—(he) gave them creative freedom. But Morris Levy exploited his stars, including Bill Basie. He signed many of them to long-term contracts at low wages…(so) any offer that lets you keep your neck sounds like a bargain even despite hiding his money behind intricate accounting tricks… So while Bill Basie liked to gamble… Morris didn't try to get him help; he just got him in deeper…(and) paid off Bill's debts to gamblers, who were all mobbed up, and in exchange put Bill on Roulette's payroll. (So) Bill told me that he never earned any royalties from all those great albums he recorded for Roulette, just small checks from the company store.

* * *

Before turning to the last major face in our theatre's purchase by Long Island University in 1950, which granted permission to the Brooklyn Paramount's manager, Eugene Pleshette, to book Freed's and other Rock 'n' Roll impresarios, a brief sampling of the most important Jazz musicians who played in the coronated figure's various Big Beat orchestras during our theatre's fourth face should also be documented: (1) Sam "The Man" Taylor, a so-called Texas honker tenor saxophonist who'd worked previously in Cab Calloway's and Lucky Millinder's orchestras, and who was also heard on Joe Turner's "Shake, Rattle and Roll" and the Drifters' "Money Honey" pioneering transitional Rhythm and Blues first recordings; (2) Wilbert "Red" Prysock, whose similar down-on-both-knees, wailing tenor solos are still heard (and hopefully treasured) on "Hand Clappin'," an instrumental recorded in 1955 on the Mercury label with his own band; (3) Albert Omega "Big Al" Sears, yet another Jazz tenor saxophonist, who recorded on the Coral label co-owned by Freed's business partner, Morris Levy; (4) David Albert Francis, the percussionist nicknamed Panama who performed alongside a second drummer hired by Freed, and whose drumsticks are probably enshrined in Cleveland's Rock & Roll Hall of Fame; (5) MacHouston "Mickey" Baker who achieved greater fame for his Rock 'n' Roll recordings, and whose guitar this author purchased; (6) King Curtis (née Curtis Mosley), whose raucous tenor is heard on the Coasters' classic Rock 'n' Roll novelty hit "Yakety Yak"; (7) Marshall Royal, an alto saxophonist who frequently worked with Count Basie; (8) Ernie Wilkins, yet another Jazz saxophonist who also became more famous as an arranger; (9) Freddie Mitchell, another horn player with deep roots in Rhythm and Blues; and finally (10) Edward Joseph Bertolatus, an Italian American trombonist who performed under the stage moniker of Eddie Bert, while independently freelancing with Jazz legends from Charlie Parker's Bebop through Charles Mingus's experimental music. Asked by this author why he accepted gigs playing Rock 'n' Roll's universally deemed inferior music, my radio guest, who donated rehearsal photos playing in Freed's Big Beat orchestra, comically replied, "Because Freed called, and so my wife could shop on Fulton Street in downtown Brooklyn during those shows!"

CHAPTER 8

Face Four: The Birth of Rock 'n' Roll on Our Theatre's Stage Is Here to Stay!

While Alan Freed is usually credited with having branded this fourth face of the Brooklyn Paramount's earlier history, an alternate case will be made in this chapter that credit should deservedly go to Tommy "Dr. Jive" Smalls. Restated, our hypothesis is that the Black Alan Freed—rather than the white Tommy Smalls—arguably deserves that credit. Before we mount that case, however, it will be shown that two shows in 1950 and 1951 on our theatre's stage led by Louis Jordan and Lucky Millinder force us to take a longer perspective viewing that sea change as an evolutionary rather than revolutionary event in the history of twentieth-century American popular music.

A. From Race Music...

The multivariate roots of Rock 'n' Roll, according to Robert Palmer (1980: 4), were a complex tangle of gospel-inspired Black church music in the South and Appalachian folk music that morphed into Western Swing and Boogie-Woogie and Stride Piano combined to make it inevitable. This new music was ultimately shaped by drums and harps from Africa and brass instruments from Europe were involved in those tangled roots. Suffice then to begin here with the race music of African Americans recorded on second-class-like citizenship small labels from the 1920s to the 1940s that transitioned into R & B in 1949 before morphing into Rock 'n' Roll before the first of eight Jubilees led by Alan Freed in 1955 on our theatre's stage.

Freed also booked Rock 'n' Roll outdoor concerts with Jazz stars like Lester Young in 1952. According to *The New York Times* (February 23, 1957), the roots of this popular music were:

(It)...began in the levees and plantations, took in folk songs, and featured blues and rhythm. It's the rhythm that gets to the (white) kids—they're starved of music they can dance to after all those years of crooners.

That complex tragic figure who also loved Wagnerian opera famously declared in a *pater postestas*-type speech while appearing as himself in one of five Grade B films, *Rock, Rock, Rock*, one year earlier in 1956:

Rock 'n' Roll is a river of music that has absorbed many streams: rhythm and blues, jazz, ragtime, cowboy songs, country songs, folk songs. All have contributed to the Big Beat.

Variety (September 5, 1956) would also quote that gauntlet laid down against those who charged that Rock 'n' Roll was the cause of juvenile delinquency saying, "Rock 'n' Roll and the youth are the good citizens of tomorrow." One final citation along these lines might be given. In a magazine named *Paget*, Alan Freed in 1957 self-promoted his passion—and source of a lucrative livelihood—as such:

Before Rock 'n' Roll came along, the kids were starved for entertainment; the ballad type of music they'd been hearing was too soupy for dancing. And TV offered them very little opportunity. So when they encountered the power, the affirmative jazz beat of R n R, it was like making a new discovery.

Freed was referring to white teenagers who embraced this Black music. And if any doubts remain about the sort of mass hysteria about juvenile delinquency and its links to Rock 'n' Roll's nihilism, this is seemingly confirmed by Blackboard Jungle which shows predominately white teenagers destroying their teacher's Jazz records. There is also the sensationalism of these films paired on our theatre's screen during the week of May 3, 1957, *Dragstrip Girl* and *Rock All Night*, the latter advertised in the *Williamsburg News* on that date as "the first authentic hot rod filmed in Hollywood...(depicting) crazed modern teenagers in their nonstop thirst for stunts, thrills, chicken races, and rock and roll action."

Alan Freed famously began playing rebranded race-music-cum-R-&-B in 1951 at radio station WJZ in Cleveland, Ohio. And as that story goes—grows—it followed inside information from the commercial sponsor of his all-night classical music program that white teenagers were purchasing popular Black music in droves, which led the former TV sportscaster to obtain permission from his employers to change the format of those broadcasts. Yet despite Freed's biographer, John Jackson's (1991: 32–39), recitation of history of the new music, this headline in *Billboard* on August 29, 1949, provides a different understanding: Teen-Agers Demand Music with Beat Spurs That Rhythm and Blues.

Leaving aside the anthropologist Rick Coleman's (2007) argument in his biography of Fats Domino, one of the seminal figures involved in those changes, he wrote that rhythmically propulsed music was simultaneously being listened to by white teenagers in the South. He also argued it spurred the civil rights movement...that new music, so to speak, was infused by the addition of electric guitars and honking tenor saxophones in R & B, substituted for race music in 1949 by the Atlantic Records A and R man Jerry Wexler (1993: 62), who wrote that he resented the second-class citizenship accorded to the music he loved, and consequently sought its fuller equality with pop music. Even so, writing about those racially divided years whose large recording studios maintained race-music labels, Reebee Garofalo (2002: 124) noted that between 1947 and 1949, while the former lost $50 million, "not a single black performer was found on the year-end pop charts in 1949." And illustrating her felicitous phrase "black roots, white fruit," a Top Forty Countdown prominent (white) radio deejay pronounced that "All Rhythm and Blues records are dirty and as such bad for kids as dope!" The deejay's allusions to R & B titles like "Work with Me Henry" sung by Etta James, which carried over into Rock 'n' Roll in the early 1950s with songs like "Baby Let Me Bang Your Box" by the El Chords, an innocuous song about a piano also banned, its double entendre title notwithstanding.

So, turning to Tommy "Dr. Jive" Smalls's Rhythm 'n' Blues seminal show on our theatre's stage on that Sunday night, September 12, 1954, some six months prior to Freed: this confirms our hypothesis about his rightful title, King of Rock 'n' Roll. These African Americans performers were probably booked by Moe Gale, whose talent agency exclusively represented African Americans were featured here:

(1) Roy Hamilton, a former gospel singer who enjoyed Top Forty blockbuster crossover recorded hits on Columbia's subsidiary Epic race label, like "You'll Never Walk Alone" and "Unchained Melody"; (2) Faye ("Hurts Me to My Heart") Adams (née Fanny Tuell), who recorded on Herald, a white-owned Indie label in Elizabeth, New Jersey; (3) LaVern Baker, a. k. a. Little Miss Share Cropper, a. k. a. Miss Corn Shucks (née Delores Evans), whose recording career began in 1948, and her R & B hit, "I Want to Rock," three years later and recordings like "Tweedledee" and "Jim Dandy to the Rescue" were part of this sea change. Indeed, Marv Goldberg wrote in his online *R&B Notebooks* (2001 and 2009) that *Tweedledee* was so successful as to prompt Mercury to assign one of its white Pop stars, Georgia Gibbs, to record a cover version, whose use of the same arrangement lifted from its original subsidiary Sepia label without permission prompted the Black diva to petition Congress for an antitrust-type law, thereby

becoming the first known entertainer to have brought a suit of this kind. So outraged was LaVern Baker of that white cover, she bitterly named Miss Nibbs, a. k. a. Georgia Gibbs, as the beneficiary in a pre-flight insurance policy, such as were available in those years, before her departure for an Australian tour. Finally, along with the fact that Ms. Baker would also appear in two of those five Freed films, *Rock, Rock, Rock* and *Mr. Rock 'n' Roll*—the latter screened in the Brooklyn Paramount three years later during the week of November 13, 1957. She also previously appeared on Ed Sullivan's "Toast of the Town" Sunday night TV show along with other R & B performers on November 29, 1955. That fifteen-minute segment devoted to R & B that was intro-duced by Dr. Jive following the initial flush of Rock 'n' Roll, has been viewed by Rock historians as involved with the widespread popularity of rebranded race music among millions of young white viewers; (4) Big Maybelle (née Mabel Louise Smith), who enjoyed a hit with the ballad "Candy" recorded on the Savoy Jazz label in 1955, and whose biggest hit, "Whole Lot of Shaking Going On," became an iconic Rock 'n' Roll song after it was famously covered by another of its pioneers, Jerry Lee Lewis in 1958; (5) the Spaniels, who arguably were the pre-mier R-&-B-cum-earliest-so-called-Rock 'n' Roll-a-cappella harmony singing group, formed in 1952 at Roosevelt High School in Gary, Indi-ana, and were led by Thornton James "Pookie" Hudson, considered by many Rock critics as the greatest of all male singers…a performer said to have been able to entrance young African American women in the Apollo Theater and prompt some to salaciously scream, "Ride my alley!" "Good Night, Sweetheart, Good Night," not only was the Spaniels' signature song, but also the title of their collective biogra-phy by Richard Carter (1994: 49–50), who quoted Hudson's account of the Spaniels' dispute with Alan Freed as follows: "He never played our records—none of our records—and he never had us back on his concert shows." And the reason was because Pookie refused to allow the powerful celebrity Rock 'n' Roll deejay to affix his name as cowriter of the Spaniels' signature song, thus prompting Freed to retaliate. Or, as Hudson's words in his biography about that dispute merit being reprised, if only for what they (additionally) reveal about the way things were done in the record industry during those pre payola years:

> Well, I mean some people would say: "Hey look man, here's the biggest man in New York and you get the record played, you get the record sold and all he wants is to put his name..." (But) if you're realizing really how lucrative the writing end of a song is that's recorded into a big hit...if you don't understand that, you do it because you might say, "Hell, that ain't nothing, I'll write another song..."

> (But) Freed just did it for the money. For whatever the royalties were. It might have been three writers on the song, so he'd be down as number four. Might have been two, and he'd be number three. He wasn't but one. If it wasn't but one, he'd be number two, and he'd get half the money.

That practice traces back to Irving Mills's representation of Duke Ellington in the 1930s, for example. "Goodnight Sweetheart" enjoyed sweet revenge by ultimately becoming a Doo-wop revival Rock 'n' Roll all-time favorite, which was covered like so many early Rock 'n' Roll hits...by the McGuire Sisters, in this instance, a close harmony white singing girl's pop group in the 1950s.

The birth of Rock 'n' Roll during Tommy Smalls's first of three shows also included (6) The Counts, another African American (male) singing transformative group whose single major hit was the ballad *Darling, Dear* recorded in 1953, which also remains among so-called Doo-wop's all-time favorite Rock 'n' Roll classic hits; (7) the Drifters, led by Clyde McPhatter (née Clyde Lensley McPhatter), a smooth high-tenor initially featured on *The Bells* with Billy Ward's gospel group, the Dominoes, in 1953, and music Palmer (1980: 12) characterized as thinly secularized gospel often with the stomping beat and rasping saxophone style of "jump blues." Additional Drifters' recordings that featured their lead singer, Clyde McPhatter, were "Money Honey," "White Christmas," and "Honey Love," recorded on Atlantic;

and (8) Royal Gordon "Rusty" Bryant, a largely forgotten African American tenor saxophonist who recorded "All Night Long" on Dot in the early 1950s, before moving over to Prestige, a major Jazz label.

Mention should also be made of the Erskine Hawkins Orchestra, a mainstay previously of the Savoy Ballroom, which was owned by Moe Gale, a mob-related figure during those years, who backed those African American performers...and a Jazz trumpet player, who'd previously recorded "Tuxedo Junction" on RCA in 1939, and enjoyed greater fame when it was covered by Glenn Miller's Casa Loma Orchestra, known as the twentieth-century Gabriel as a result of Hawkins's virtuosity that allowed him to blow one hundred consecutive high C's!

Films shown during the week of September 12, 1954, between Tommy Small's seminal shows booked at 5:00 p.m. and 8:30 p.m. were *Crossed Swords*, starring Errol Flynn and Gina Lollobrigida, and the *Weak and the Wicked*, starring the English actress Glynis Johns.

Tommy "Dr. Jive" Smalls hosted two shows between Alan Freed's eight Jubilees. Before turning to those, however, mention of jump music forces us to pause and discuss two pre–Rock 'n' Roll earlier shows whose rock scholars transformed from R & B.

First, Lucius Venable "Lucky" Millinder brought his big band from the Apollo Theater's stage to ours for four glorious days and nights between December 29, 1950, and January 1, 1951, inclusively. About this often-overlooked figure, Dizzy Gillespie (1979: 162), who played in Millinder's Jazz-oriented dance band during the 1930s, riffed about his firing complex, i.e., penchant for firing the entire band and then having to start over, which in one comical instance led the bandleader to realize he was the only one left!

Born in 1910 in Anniston, Alabama, Lucky Millinder did not play any musical instrument yet reportedly possessed an extraordinary ability to memorize and direct relatively complex musical arrangements. "Biggest ears of anybody!" as Gillespie (1979: 162) further recalled...whose name band, according to the Jazz historian, Alyn Shipton (2001: 31), was a rung or two below Cab Calloway and Ellington's, and whose leader had a unique style of directing at the time, i.e., Millinder's ability to jump up high in the air and land on the lid of a grand piano...and leap off again onto the floor without missing a beat of the baton.

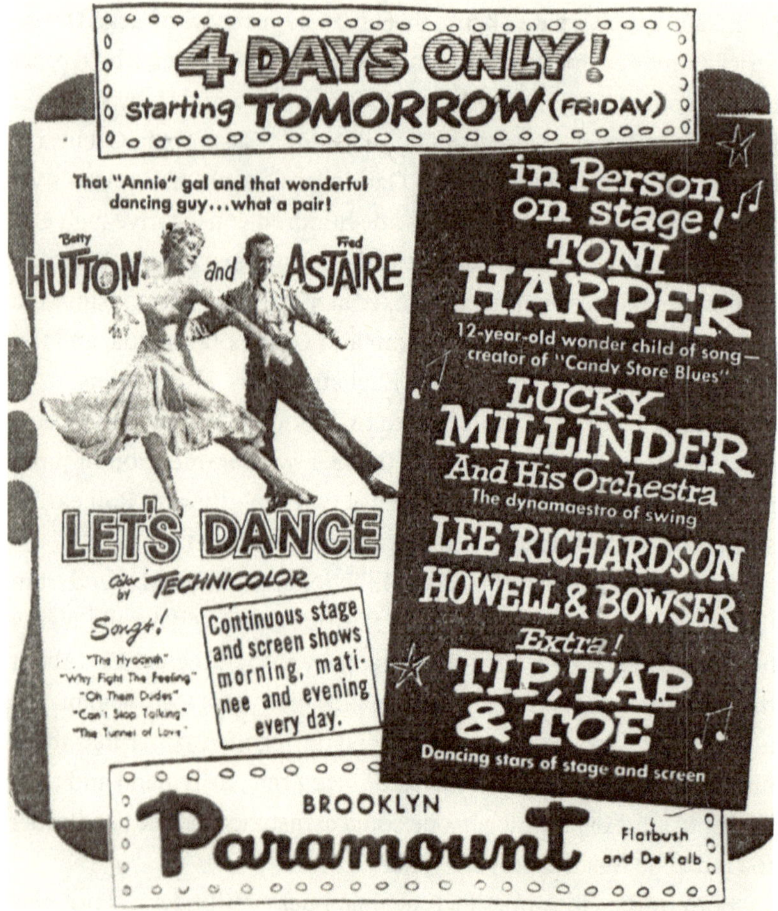

LUCKY MILLINDER (The Brooklyn Daily Eagle/December 29, 1950)

Mindful of George Bernard Shaw's warning about semantic labels becoming forms of libel, and what the transcendental philosopher, Ralph Waldo Emerson, cautioned against the foolish search for consistency being the hobgoblin of small minds, the fact also remains that

Lucky Millinder's musical assemblage over time featured other prominent Jazz musicians like Charlie Shavers, Henry "Red" Allen, Harry "Sweet" Edison, Freddie Webster, and Panama Francis, who played drums in Alan Freed's "Big Beat" orchestra. At the same time, however, the show Lucky Millinder brought to the Brooklyn Paramount four and five years prior to Smalls and Freed was also a retro-Vaudeville show. These additional performers were Toni Harper, who began as a twelve-year-old singer and enjoyed a huge early success with her recording of "Candy Store Blues" in 1946; Howell and Bowser, formerly Black Vaudeville hoofers; and Lee Richardson, a journeyman R & B singer.

Lucky Millinder's band, which recorded on Decca and RCA, major white labels, and who formerly played their lively jitterbug dance music in the home of happy feet, the Savoy Ballroom in Harlem, during the late 1930s and early 1940s, featured these two powerful R & B singers during his gig here: Wynonie Harris and Rosetta Tharpe...who, label them as you might or must, were also dubbed "blues shouters," and respectively cut controversial songs banned from commercial radio play on white stations like these: "Like My Baby's Pudding" and "Wasn't That Good?"

Née Rosetta Nubin, Sister Rosetta Tharpe initially enjoyed successful recordings of gospel songs like "Strange Things Happening Every Day." Noted as well as the first woman to play electric guitar, "Rock Me," which despite its earlier recording date of 1938, might well also qualify among the first Rock 'n' Roll songs in the never-ending challenging search for that Holy Grail. Finally, another Rock 'n' Roll figure, Little Richard, covered "Rock Me" nearly two decades later after Tharpe, who was dubbed the "Godmother of Rock 'n' Roll," and a subject in the PBS *American Masters* series whose visage also appeared on a thirty-two-cent United States stamp in a Gospel Singer series.

The name of the film screened that week, whether or not coincidental along with Lucky Millinder's pre–Rock 'n' Roll appearance at the Brooklyn Paramount Dance, which starred Betty Hutton and the legendary ballroom danseur/tap dancer/singer Fred Astaire, again illustrated the connection between dances like the Charleston and Lindy Hop that were inspired by the famous transcontinental pilot and various genres of popular music.

This second pre–Tommy Smalls/Alan Freed's Rock 'n' Roll booking in our theatre was the subsequent five-day appearance of Louis Jordan and the Tympany Five between June 8 and June 12, 1951.

Dubbed the "King of the Jukebox" as well as "Grandfather of Rock 'n' Roll," Jordan's wider popularity in African American smaller communities was said to be attributed to Bill Randle, a white deejay who once played the alto saxophonist's "Saturday Night Fish Fry" every fifteen minutes on radio station WERE in Cleveland, while otherwise promoting race music before Alan Freed. Louis Jordan's booking agency was probably forced to curate a retro-Vaudeville show when tasked with the challenge of putting four thousand fannies in our theatre's seats several times over those five days while presenting the jump blues music of this important figure, who played a silver alto saxophone that Sonny Rollins has said influenced his decision to play Jazz as well as doubled in Chick Webb's band by singing with Ella Fitzgerald. Among Jordan's racially mixed consequent cast of thirty-five at the Brooklyn Paramount were: (1) Peggy Thomas (Miss Personality of Song), a white singer whose career traced back to the Ziegfeld Follies; (2) Hortense Allen Jordan and the Eight Beautiful Jordanettes, who were African Americans advertised as choristers; (3) "Tiny" Teddy Hale, an African American tap dancer whose long career in show business not only extended further back into the early years of TOBA, Tough on Black Asses, in Black Vaudeville during the 1920s, but also included appearances on TV variety shows in the 1950s; (4) Coco, an internationally known British (white) clown; (5) Steve and Eddy, no, not the married white pop singers on count-less TV variety shows throughout the 1960s, but instead a same-sex male comedy team; and finally (6) the African American Jazz vocalist Johnny Hartman.

LOUIS JORDAN (The Brooklyn Daily Eagle/June 7, 1951)

As for the real star of this Rock 'n' Roll show in the Brooklyn Paramount in 1951, Louis Thomas Jordan, who began as a child star with the famed Rabbit Foot Minstrels in Black Vaudeville, consequently got to play behind legendary Blues divas like Mamie Smith and Ma Rainey in tent shows before becoming a member of Chick Webb's Savoy Ballroom dance band, in which his Tympany Five smaller grouping containing seven musicians played what was also called the "shuffle-boogie beat."

Among their numerous crossover popular hits recorded in the 1940s, we cite only "Knock Me a Kiss," "Caledonia," "Is You or Is You Ain't My Baby," "Reet Petite" and "Gone"; "Choo-Choo Ch'Boogie," and "Keep A-Knockin'." The latter was sung by their leader in 1957 as an Rock 'n' Roll blockbuster hit by Little Richard. And along with those million sellers probably recorded on Decca's subsidiary Sepia race label, Jordan and the Tympani Five previously recorded "Blue Light Boogie" in 1950, a number one hit identified as R & B by a leading Rock critic (Palmer, 1980: 11). And while they also appeared in numerous musical Shorties, they were primarily geared toward Black audiences. Louis Jordan's "Buzz Me, Baby" became a popular jukebox play. Along with being described by his biographer as feeling gypped about not being credited as the founder of Rock 'n' Roll, if only since Bill Haley & His Comets replaced the Tympani Five on Decca, there were additional hit recordings with Ella Fitzgerald's "Stone Cold Dead in the Market" and "Petite Pie" (Koch, 2014). Finally, Louis Jordan also appeared as a dramatic actor in several films—*Meet Miss Bobby Sox* and *Follow the Boys* among those screened here. He was nearly fatally stabbed by his (jealous) wife in Pasadena, California, after having been caught cheating with another woman, and he was also called the original Rock 'n' Roller on his very first album for Atlantic...and that's also having recorded the "Rock and Roll Call" on RCA Victor several years earlier on October 18, 1955, or after Alan Freed's debut, also on our theatre's stage.

The name of the screen offering during Louis Jordan's five-day retro-Vaudeville transitional R & B/Rock 'n' Roll show at the Brooklyn Paramount was *Navy Bound*, starring Tom Neal.

In summary, Ed Ward (2016: 63–65) in his encyclopedic history of Rock 'n' Roll wrote: "the period of 1952–1953, in retrospect...(was the) stylistic watershed for rhythm and blues." And his view—or bias—regarding those origins of Rock 'n' Roll credits the old-style jump blues played by Louis Jordan in the 1940s, which he also wrote predated the R & B contributions of Big Joe Turner, Roy Milton, Charles Brown, and Willie Mae Thornton among other progenitors... particularly, Big Momma Thornton's recording of "Hound Dog" in 1953 covered years later by the reputed King of Rock 'n' Roll, Elvis Presley. And while another prominent Rock historian references Louis Jordan's jump blues as a trendsetter in rhythm and Blues (Winner, 1980: 38), we return to our hypothesis regarding Tommy "Dr. Jive" Smalls's transformation of R & B from race music at the Brooklyn Paramount. We now discuss his two additional shows in our theatre following Freed's influential Easter Jubilee in 1955.

B. Tommy "Dr. Jive" Smalls's Other Shows and the Invention of Rock 'n' Roll on Stage at the Brooklyn Paramount Ahead of Alan Freed

Following his advertised "Biggest Rhythm and Blues Show" on September 12, 1954, Tommy Smalls, who relocated his R & B radio show begun in 1947 in Savannah, Georgia, to New York City five years later to WWRL, included hip banter like "heard on the high spot (1600) all the way at the end of the radio dial from three-oh-five to five-three-oh" and who signed off "Listening to Doctor Jive" musically with "Goodbye, Farewell, So Long" by Tommy Edwards with two additional shows after Alan Freed's inaugural Easter Rock 'n' Roll Jubilee in 1955.

The first of those would interestingly be titled "The Rock 'n' Rhythm Thanksgiving Week Show." It played here between November 23 and 26 that year. Evidencing the importance of middle-class white teenagers with cash (like me) to purchase rebranded African American popular musical 45 rpms, Smalls, who also instructed his radio listeners daily to "Sit back, relax, and enjoy the wax," featured these Black and white performers: (1) the Clovers, who formed in 1946 at Armstrong High School in Washington, DC, and returned with hits like "Fool, Fool, Fool."

Writing about them, Billy Vera, an Rock 'n' Roll musician employed as an A and R man for Lew Chudd's Specialty indie record label in Los Angeles, contextualized that transformative group as follows:

> By 1952, a change was in the wind in the music business. Specialty's front line of stars—Roy Milton, Camille Howard, Joe Liggins and his brother Jimmie—were slowing down sales-wise, and Percy Mayfield was hospitalized, fighting for his life. People were going for a rougher and more youthful sound. Some of the year's bestselling records were the Dominoes' "Have Mercy Baby," Ruth Brown's "5–10–15 Hours" and "Mama, He Treats Your Daughter Mean" and the Clovers' "Ting-A-Ling" and Fats Domino's "Goin' Home." But it wasn't until 1955 that the Clovers struck gold with "Blue Velvet," a song written in 1950 and that Tony Bennett covered one year later and which for Bobby Vinton went gold in 1963. (Vera, 2019: 59)

We might add that Marv Goldberg (*R&B Notebooks*, 1999 and 2009) called the "Mighty Clovers one of the most enduringly popular R & B groups." That is, with their twenty-one recorded charted entries between 1951 and 1955, nineteen of which reached Top Ten, and their popularity was being such that seventeen of those also charted for 190 weeks. Indeed, "Fool, Fool, Fool" sold five hundred thousand copies after its July 1951 release and would be covered in the following year by Kay Starr—albeit minus its original salacious lyrics. A final note about the Clovers, whose additional hit "Devil or Angel" remains a favorite of mine, they illustrate other links with various genres of African American race music, i.e., what the Jazz musician/Western Classical composer David Amram reported about what the co-founder of Bebop Charlie Parker told him: "If you want to understand my music, Dave, listen to the Clovers!"

LaVern Baker was part of this groundbreaking show at the Brooklyn Paramount, singing R & B hits like" Great Day in the Morning" and "Play It Fair," if not her most famous transitional Rock 'n' Roll hit, "Jim Dandy to the Rescue."

RHYTHM 'N' BLUES (Tommy Smalls) (*The Brooklyn Daily Eagle*/September 12, 1954)

The Orioles recorded "It's Too Soon to Know," yet another of their transcendent hits, and appeared on the famous Dixieland guitarist Eddie Condon's TV show in 1949 singing the Dixie Cups' "Crying in the Chapel." The Drifters were also back again as the vocal group that formed in 1953 as backup singers originally for Clyde McPhatter after he left the Dominoes. Marv Goldberg (*R&B Notebooks*, 2009) has touted them as "probably the most amazing R & B group that ever existed."

As for those early white Rockers showcased for Brooklyn Paramount audiences by Smalls, Bill Haley & His Comets appeared along with the popular (white) singer Johnnie Ray.

Starting as John Alvin "Johnnie" Ray, he was born in Dallas, Oregon, and enjoyed worldwide fame though these Top Forty: "Cry" and "The Little White Cloud (That Cried)" on its B-side. Both were recorded on October 15,1951, during a session engineered by Mitch Miller for Columbia records, the oboist and A and R man who wrongly prophesied Rock 'n' Roll was just a passing fad. "Please Mr. Sun" and "Whiskey and Gin" were additional blockbuster hits for this over-the-top performer born with a hearing impairment that forced Ray to wear a prosthetic device until he became totally deaf in both ears. Performing with Al Jolson's adopted expressiveness, Johnnie Ray's meteoric amazing career in Pop music was launched in Detroit's legendary African American Flame Bar and sadly ended in Vegas lounges and strip joints. Yet during his heyday, he was credited as a major influence by Rock 'n' Roll giants like Elvis Presley, Jerry Lee Lewis, and Mick Jagger of the Rolling Stones.

Given our concern with wisdom stories attached to place, Johnny Whiteside (1994: 128) relates the following benign example in his biography: A fourteen-year-old dungaree-clad Brooklyn teenager named Renee Magrisso and fan club president Toni Adama, also from the King's Borough, were invited to Ray's wedding in Manhattan. Tony Bennett wrote the following about the bisexual singer scandalously arrested for sexual preference and who also maintained a public affair with Dorothy Kilgallen, the syndicated journalist/gossip-monger/TV quiz show panelist and cohost of *Dorothy and Dick*, a popular morning radio talk show with her husband:

> He was (after Sinatra and before Elvis) the first to charge an audience. He had to rip the curtain down, bang on the piano, or jump on the piano because he just couldn't stay cool enough... And I really consider Johnnie Ray to be, in that sense, the father of rock and roll. (Bennett, 2016: 68)

Finally, here is more relevant biographical data. First, Johnnie Ray's biographer wrote there was "little else in the trade more debilitating than a failed run at the Paramount"; that is, in Manhattan, another example of our theatre's neglect (Whiteside, 1994: 130). And, second, that Johnnie Ray acquired more nicknames in his career than any other figure in show business history: Cry Guy, Prince of Wails, Mrs. Emotion, the Atomic Ray, the Nabob of Sob, the Golden Tearjerker, the Anguished Bard, the Cheerful Tearful, the Howling Success, the Violent Ray, Million Dollar Teardrop, the Song Wringer, Master of Misery, Johnnie Jolt 'em, and The Man the Girls Strip and also The Guy with the Rubber Face and Squirt Gun.

Bill Haley & His Comets also made their first appearance on our theatre's stage as part of Tommy Smalls's show. This Western Swing Rock 'n' Roll group's impactful recording of "Rock Around the Clock" on April 12, 1954, at the Pythian Temple on Manhattan's West Side—on Decca for Milt Gabler—was blamed as the root cause of juvenile delinquency nationwide following the song's dramatic numerical countdown that opened *Blackboard Jungle* one year later...when read on July 30, 1940, in Jo Ranson's *Radio Dial Log* column in the local tabloid about a current series titled "Why Children Come to Court" on WNYC, the municipal station. More importantly for our concerns, William John Clifton Haley, who was born outside of Detroit and worked as a deejay and music director at a radio station in Chester, Pennsylvania, while performing in a small combo initially called the Saddlemen, enjoyed these firsts with His Comets:

- •"Rock Around the Clock" as the first Rock 'n' Roll song to reach number one in *Billboard*;
- •"See You Later, Alligator" climbing to number six on Pop charts while simultaneously holding the number seven place on R & B charts;
- recorded the first Rock 'n' Roll video ("Roundup of Rhythm");
- His Comets as the first Rock 'n' Roll group to perform multiple times on prime-time TV, e.g., Ed Sullivan's Sunday night TV *Toast of the Town*, as well as Milton Berle's *Texaco Star Theatre* and *The Ray Bolger Show*;
- first Rock 'n' Roll group to perform at Carnegie Hall;
- •"Rock Around the Clock" as the first Rock 'n' Roll million-seller in Great Britain;
- winner of Jazz magazine *DownBeat's* "Best R & B group";
- they also topped Black performers like Dinah Washington and Ruth Brown;
- having recorded the first live Rock 'n' Roll album *At the Roundtable* on the Roulette label owned in Manhattan by Morris Levy;
- Record sales "over 85 million."

Finally, also about this Western-Swing-cum-Rock 'n' Roll impactful pioneering group, Bill Haley didn't wear his Superman-like spit curl for affectation, but rather to serve as a distraction from people noticing the blindness in one eye.

Additional Black *and* white performers in Tommy Smalls's "Rock 'n' Rhythm Thanksgiving Show" at the Brooklyn Paramount in 1955 included the (vanilla) Cheers, who recorded "Bazoom, I Need Your Lovin'" as well as "Black Denim Trousers and Motorcycle Boots," written by two of the most famous wordsmiths in the early history of Rock 'n' Roll, Lieber and Stoller. The song was concerned with the rebelliousness of teenagers in the 1950s additionally blamed on James Dean in *Rebel Without a Cause*; and finally, the Four Step Brothers, hoofers originating in Black Vaudeville as far back as 1927, dubbed the "Eight Feet of Rhythm."

Along with music curiously provided by Art Mooney's orchestra—whose only Top Forty hit was from the 1940s, the widely popular song, "I'm Looking over a Four Leaf Clover," and whose leader obviously attempted to remain relevant—if not cash in!—with a two-sided MGM recording titled *Tribute to James Dean*—the film ironically screened that week as a chaser in the old Vaudeville sense of emptying theatres with flicks so that new patrons could become part of that sort of continuous family entertainment inherited by radio and TV to maximize profits was *Count Three and Pray*, starring Van Heflin.

Then one month later, Tommy "Dr. Jive" Smalls was back for a third at the Brooklyn Paramount with another show. Dubbed Christmas the "Rock 'n' Rhythm 'n' Blues," it went head-to-head against Alan Freed's Rock 'n' Roll show at the Academy of Music near Union Square in Manhattan. The major Black performers brought to our theatre's stage were:

(1) Bo Diddley (née Ellas Otha Bates McDaniel), a guitarist known for stylistic reliance on the so-called hambone rhythm, and whose signature songs were "Hey! Bo Diddley," "Hand Jive," "I'm a Man," and "Who Do You Love"; and (2) Ruth Alston Brown (née Weston), a. k. a. the Mama Girl, who'd previously recorded R & B hits like "Momma, He Treats Your Daughter Mean" that contributed to the Black diva's title as the "Queen of Rhythm and Blues." Indeed, since those and other songs by Ruth Brown were recorded on Atlantic Records, it cleverly called itself "The House That Ruth Built," i.e., a play (pun unintended) on baseball's legendary player from the 1920s and 1930s, George Herman "Babe" Ruth, and the original Yankee Stadium. Along with twenty-four recorded hits on that label, six of which eventually crossed over to Pop charts, she'd previously recorded "5–10–15 Hours" in spring of 1952, whose title alluded to Billy Ward and the Dominoes' controversial "Sixty Minute Man," resulting in that small record label's decision to distract from its salacious lyrics by retitling it "5–10–15 Minutes." A civil rights activist finally as well, Ruth Brown would win a Tony for Best Actress in the Broadway musical *Black and Blue* more than three decades later in 1989.

Still other performers in Smalls's Christmas show were the Four Fellows, Teddy Williams, Jim McGowan, David Jones, and Larry Banks, African American Korean War veterans from Brooklyn, New York, whose a cappella singing group formed in 1953, and they enjoyed a single smash hit, "Soldier Boy," recorded two years later, that got covered by Elvis Presley; the Five Keys, who, according to Marv Goldberg's extensive interviews (2000, 2009), formed in Newport News in 1944, and by 1951 waxed their most famous song (on Aladdin), "The Glory of Love," a cover of a 1936 Swing hit by Benny Goodman; and Doo-wop favorite the Turbans, one-hit African Americans, who, yes, wore those while performing "When You Dance" with its catchy Latin mambo-type feel that contains the first onomatope use of the phrase "Doo-Wop." After switching record labels several times, however, the Turbans, like other Rock 'n' Roll as well as Jazz artists, recorded on Morris Levy's Roulette label, whose studio address was 1790 Broadway in Manhattan.

Finally, we note the remarkable inclusion of Tommy Smalls's third and last show here of Patrick Charles Evan "Pat" Boone, inarguably the most vanilla and financially successful of all those many other white Rock 'n' Roll singers. A former college speech instructor, Boone was famously known for wearing white bucks and cardigan sweaters on stage. In addition to reportedly selling forty-five million cover versions of early Rock classics originated by Black pioneers—not the least being Little Richard's "Rootie Tootie"—thirty-eight of Boone's recordings placed on Top Ten pop lists. Small wonder he then didn't correct the grammar of one of Fats Domino's greatest hits by singing "Isn't" instead of "Ain't That a Shame!"

The *Williamsburg News* (December 23, 1955) advertised "50 famous Rock 'N' Roll recording and radio stars" for Smalls's Christmas show, whose sixteen-piece orchestra was headed by Willis "Gator Tail" Jackson and featured the guitarist Mickey Baker, who recorded "Love Is Strange" (on Groove Records, an RCA Victory subsidiary race label) with his student Sylvia Vanderpool as Mickey and Sylvia.

The name of the film screened during Tommy "Dr." Smalls's

Christmas in our theatre in 1955 was *Storm Fear* costarring the husband-and-wife team of the former gymnast Cornel Wilde and Jean Wallace, a United Artists' release.

C. Alan Freed's Eight Jubilees at the Brooklyn Paramount (1955–1958)

Until such time as a biography of Tommy "Dr. Smalls" might disprove our hypothesis, we focus primarily on Alan Freed and the fame he deservedly has, if only for his eight blockbuster Rock 'n' Roll shows in our theatre.

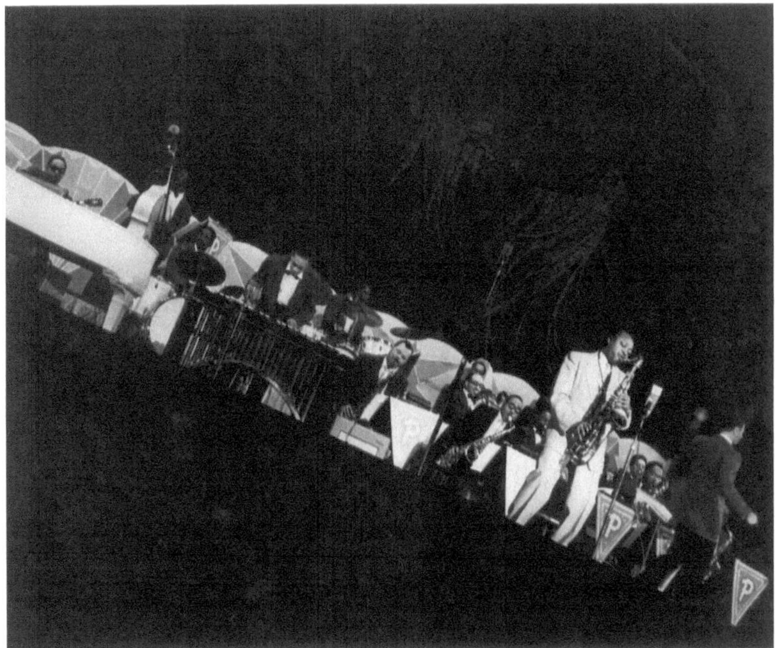

ALAN FREED BIG BEAT ORCHESTRA REHEARSAL (Eddie Bert Archives)

Freed was born in Youngstown, Ohio, and moved to Cleveland following military service. He then studied mechanical engineering in college. Notwithstanding his love of African American popular race-

music-cum-R-&-B, he also was passionate about Jazz as a youngster...
which led to longing to play trombone in Duke Ellington's band after
performing in Salem High School's Sultans of Swing. But following
an ear infection, he went from sports broadcasting to becoming the
Moon Dog after changing over from playing the Western music classics to R & B on his radio show, He called it the Moon Dog Rock 'n'
Roll Party in 1953, a year before Tommy "Dr. Jive" Smalls launched
his R-&-B-cum-R-'n'-R show on the Brooklyn Paramount stage. While
pounding on a telephone book with a gloved hand, enthusiastic shouts
fueled his discovery that white teenagers were avidly devouring R &
B. Freed also hosted Moon Dog Coronation Balls in 1952—the most
famous or infamous among those, a scheduled public dance in Cleveland's outdoor civic center featuring only African American R & B
performers originally intended for Blacks, but which drew an over-
flow crowd of white teenagers hoping to secure tickets, which led to
chaos. Thus, the canceled show was also humorous, featuring Freed's
first wife and children as Mrs. Moon Dog and the Moon Puppies, and
would be rescheduled in a larger venue in the city, which years later
opened the Rock & Roll Hall of Fame in 1989.

Freed's subsequent move to WINS in Manhattan occurred later.
Relaunched on September 8, 1954, he was paid a whopping seventy-
five dollars as a salary, and the celebrity deejay's initial hours were
7:00 a.m. to 1:00 p.m. including Saturday morning hours as well...
which this author faithfully listened to. Along with continuing to play
R & B exclusively—Billy Ward and the Dominoes, "Money Honey" by
the Drifters, and "Shake a Hand" by Faye Adams, with "Blues for Moon
Dog" by Todd Rhodes as the theme song of what he interestingly called
the Blues and Rhythm Moon Dog Radio Show. Freed's relocation to
the Big Apple was anticipated by more public concerts, including: the
Eastern Moon Dog Coronation Ball held at the Sussex Armory in New
Jersey in May 1954, which reportedly drew eleven thousand Black and
white teenagers. Freed's biographer John Jackson (1991: 85) wrote
about a successful two-night show on January 14 and 15, 1955, booked
by his newly acquired partner, Morris Levy, at the St. Nicholas Arena

on West Sixty-Ninth Street. It was a midtown venue otherwise used for ice hockey, professional basketball games, and boxing matches notoriously known to be controlled by the mob. Despite its limited seating capacity—seven thousand to eight thousand—the potential for greater earnings accompanied by Freed's successful WINS radio whose gate receipts from twelve thousand teenagers on both nights totaled between $27,500 and $38,000 could only have fueled the tragic deejay's partnership with "the Turk," a nickname derived from Levy's Sephardic Jewish ancestry (Dannen, 1991: 43). Their "Moonlight Jubilee of Stars Under the Stars," scheduled for August 6, 1954, at Ebbets Field in Brooklyn, where our borough's beloved Major League Baseball team still played, was canceled for unclear reasons.

But alongside their merry way is what our late friend John Jackson also reported in his biography of Freed: a costly court case lost to the blind composer we used to see peddling his poems and music in Viking headgear on Avenue of the Americas, Louis T. Harding, a classically trained musician from the Midwest, who coincidentally also called himself Moon Dog:

The night of Justice Walter's decision (in 1955) that barred Alan Freed from continuing as Moon Dog, the disc jockey and a companion drank at P. J. Moriarty's, a local Manhattan saloon on Fifty-First Street. The two spoke of Freed's (and WINS) (radio) decision to emphasize rock and roll in the wake of the deejay's lost nickname. Sometime between drinks, they decided to copyright the phrase rock and roll. Such copyright would protect Freed from further courtroom shenanigans concerning his radio program's new name—The Rock 'n' Roll Party—but there was another motive involved in the copyright decision. Rhythm and blues, the music Alan Freed now called rock and roll was entering a new era. Whoever held the copyright on the phrase rock and roll would stand to collect royalties each time the phrase was used. (Jackson, 1991: 84)

Along with being denied that moniker, chronic debt that hounded Freed for the rest of his life apparently forced him to borrow money from the owner of Chess Records to pay some of those legal fees and rebrand himself as the King of Rock 'n' Roll. He agreed to play Chuck Berry's "Maybellene" recorded on that Chicago small label in exchange for permission from the record company's owner for royalties to add his name to that blockbuster Rock 'n' Roll written by that Rock 'n' Roll pioneer...whose lawyer in 1986 finally convinced the courts that the late deejay hadn't had any part in its composition while one of Chuck Berry's biographers wrote that Alan Freed's playing the 45 rpm repeatedly on his WINS radio program in 1955 was largely the reason for its success...the sort of illegal shenanigans that resulted in the payola scandal four years later (DeWitt, 1985: 39).

A somewhat different version of this origin story exists about Rock 'n' Roll, whose nouns derive from those bodily assaults, whether riding in horse-drawn carriages or from motion sickness associated with water travel in boats, before their allusion to sex. Thus, Frederic Dannen quoted Freed's business partner, Morris Levy, as follows:

> Alan was having a few drinks and bemoaning the fact that he had to come up with a new name. To be honest with you, I couldn't say if Alan said it or somebody else said it. But somebody said "rock and roll." Everybody just went, Yeah, *Rock and Roll!* (Dannen, 1991: 42)

Variety in that year was already knighting Alan Freed as the "great white father of the controversial rock n' roll (music)," and Steve Waxman (2022: 228) recently uncovered Freed's initial WINS contract in 1955, which stated that the radio station's owner, the Gotham Broadcasting Corporation, owned the compound term's exclusive right for the music he'd been playing for several years prior. And while Bill Haley reminds us that his group's first hit titled "Crazy Man, Crazy" in 1953 (on Essex)—inspired by hearing the Beatnik-like shout at concerts also found in Jack Kerouac's novels—was played by Freed on his WJZ radio show (Haley and Benjaminson, 2019: 57), another caveat found in his biography published shortly before Haley's death in 1981 before turning to the first of Freed's eight Jubilees here should be added to this search for origins: "We played (what became Rock 'n' Roll) back in 1947, 1948 and 1949...a combination of country and western, Dixieland and the old-style rhythm and blues" (Fuchs, 2016: 559). Similarly the R & B Dominoes' "60 Minute Man" was recorded in 1951 ahead of Freed's Moon Dog Radio offerings, those lyrics containing a male's domineering boast about women.

Finally, after having covered Jackie Brenston's "Rocket 88," which many Rock critics call the first Rock 'n' Roll hit, Haley also recalled how very much Alan Freed enjoyed the Comets' other transitional early hits—"Rock This Joint Tonight" recorded in 1952 and "The Rock-a-Beat-in Boogie." Or, as Bill Haley recalled, "He loved it, and kept saying, 'We're gonna rock this joint!'" That is, while "beating his fingers with a pen or ruler on his desk and shouting, 'rock, rock, rock, roll, roll, roll'" (Fuchs, 2016: 559–60). Freed also reportedly took radio requests to play what Haley identified as a rock 'n' roll song.

Since the issue of race figured in all aspects of these sea changes, the explanation given by John Jackson for why our Paramount in Brooklyn was selected over theirs in Manhattan is relevant:

Freed demonstrated that rock and roll was too big an enterprise for seedy, smoke-filled buildings such as the St. Nicholas Area. It was time to bring rock and roll to a more respectable setting. Morris Levy, with strong connections within the American Broadcasting Company's entertainment complex (which included the Paramount Theater chain), wanted to book Freed's next rock and roll show into Manhattan's famed Paramount Theater on Broadway near Times Square. But there were problems. Paramount, concerned with the lingering racial stigma of the music, was cool to Levy's proposal. "Who the hell wanted rock and roll on Broadway?" asked Jack Hooke. A sell job by Levy (however) produced a compromise... Instead of Manhattan, the site of Freed's first theater engagement (in NYC) would be Brooklyn, at the Paramount Theater located at the corner of Flatbush and DeKalb Avenues. Not only would this arrangement enable Paramount to keep the integrated crowds away from Times Square, but it would also take some financial pressure off promoter Levy. (Plus) the Brooklyn Paramount was secured for a much lower fee than would have been required to book Manhattan-Paramount. (Jackson, 1991: 89)

With 1954 as clearly the tipping point for the purported first Rock 'n' Roll hit, some Rock historians awarded that distinction to "Shake, Rattle and Roll" by Bill Haley & His Comets, a cover of Big Joe Turner's original R & B version in 1950 recorded on Decca and covered in turn by the Crewcuts, a Canadian (white) group that recorded the Billboard listing and probably lip-synced those lyrics such as was the custom on TV's *Your Hit Parade* in July 1954, a show that otherwise played pop music (Shaw, 1974: 77).

Ted Groia, on the other hand, argued that Holy Grail belongs to street singing, which he wrote became a way of life on 142nd Street in Harlem among teenage African American a cappella singing groups who made Black music history. His selection for that chimerical song was "Gee," recorded in 1953 by the Crows, comprised of Bill Davis, Daniel "Sonny" Norton, Harold Major, and Gerald Hamilton, about whom he wrote:

Davis had written a song called *Gee* that was recorded by George Goldner (on Rama). The song became the first recording of black street corner singing to transcend the realm of R and B into the white pop market. It was a million-seller and the first Doo-wop record to be recognized by the white media. In hindsight, it has often been referred to as the first Rock 'n' Roll group record. (Groia, 1983: 84)

Other Rock historians, however, conferred that distinction on these pre–R & B transitional tunes: "Gloria," recorded by the Cadillacs and also released in 1954, a cover of the Mills Brothers' version recorded in 1948, and which traces even further back in time to barbershop quartet recordings by white singers in 1915; and "It's Too Soon to Know" by the Orioles from Baltimore who recorded on the Indie label Jubilee in 1948. Those young Blacks among the earliest groups employed bird names, e.g., the Swallows, Meadowlarks, Falcons, Wrens, Robins; and that is, before the Impalas and Fleetwoods were drawn from American car manufacturers. Another candidate was "Count Every Star" by the Ravens with its lead by their bass singer, an R & B group which performed on Ed Sullivan's influential Sunday night TV show on January 2, 1949, and enjoyed other hits like "Old Man River."

Ignoring the earliest use of the phrase "Rock 'n' Roll," the title of the Boswell Sisters' MTV-like video appearance featuring them in sailor suits and wearing nautical caps in a rowboat amid cardboard-simulated waves during a staged hurricane in the 1934 film *Transcendental Merry-Go-Round* and our other late friend, the multi-Grammy winner and legendary host of *Bird Flight* heard weekdays on Columbia University's radio station WKCR, Phil Schaap, who not only attended one or more of Freed's eight Jubilees in our theatre but told this author's students in 2004 that in his considered view, the first Rock 'n' Roll song was "Castle Rock," written by Big Al Sears and recorded twice by Duke Ellington's mainstay alto saxophonist, Johnny Hodges, in 1951 and 1952. Nothing disrespectful intended, but if the opening bars of Count Basie's "Red Wagon," recorded earlier in 1938, doesn't sound like the opening bars of Bill Haley's pioneering "Rock Around the Clock," we'll autograph copies of this book at no extra charge!

In any event, returning the dates of Alan Freed's first Jubilee/Easter show at the Brooklyn Paramount, April 8–14 in 1955, he went head-to-head with Tommy Smalls simultaneously hosting what "Dr. Jive" still called R & B at Harlem's Rockland Palace...a concert that, not unlike his rival, continued to blur the lines between Jazz by, for example, showcasing arguably the greatest of all Jazz singers, Billie Holiday. Reflective of the racial change in the composition audiences in those transitional years, Freed presented these five African American R & B performers and two Caucasian Persuasion performers on stage at the Brooklyn Paramount in 1955:

DeLoris LaVern Baker, a returnee from Smalls's previous show;

The Penguins who famously recorded "Earth Angel" on Dootone one year prior, were African-American teenagers from Los Angeles who did not draw inspiration for their group's name from those flightless aviary wonders in Antarctica, but rather from Willie the Kool, a cartoon penguin created by Madison Avenue for tobacco manufacturers' efforts to convince smokers (viz. our parents and ourselves) that mentholated brands like Kools and Newport cigarettes were less likely to cause throat cancer than the beloved favorite filtered and unfiltered brands like Camels and Du Maurier we also smoked; Daniel Dorsey "Danny" Overbea, a largely forgotten guitarist; The Moonglows, who Marv Goldberg (*R&B Notebooks*, 2007, 2009) reported had in late 1952 "auditioned for Freed over the telephone with a song they were working on called "I Just Can't Tell No Lie," and the deejay defended his right to affix his name as co-author of their signature song "Sincerely" written by lead singer, Harvey Fuqua in 1953—on the basis of allegedly suggesting their name change from The Midnighters."

As for those two vanilla performers hired in recognition of that sea change, which included white teenagers (like me!) with purchasing power to spend on Rock 'n' Roll 45 rpms, the Three Chuckles, who presumably named themselves after those delicious five-flavored sugar-sprinkled licorice candy delights that used to be sold for a nickel on subway station platform columns, with their all-time hit "Runaround," and who were led by Allesandro Carmelo "Teddy" Randazzo, arguably the first in a succession of young white males promoted for sex appeal, born in Sheepshead Bay, Brooklyn, and who would also play the male lead in *Rock, Rock, Rock* (co-starring Tuesday Weld); and finally Eddie Cochrane, whose so-called "rockabilly" major hits "Rock Love" and "Cool it Baby" not only were recorded on a Levy-Freed co-owned label, but their pre-Punk prototypical '50s looks consisted of blue jeans and pompadours atop slick-backed hair that ended in a "D. A.;" that is, a Duck's Ass, which opponents of this music wished instead could have stood for District Attorney.

Program Notes characterized Cochrane's performance as "really (of the) raucous Frankie Laine School"—the latter, an Italian American big band singer, who like Sophie Tucker (and other white Vaudeville performers) began as a coon shouter, yet would pioneer Rock 'n' Roll on the *Shower of Stars* TV show on April 12, 1955, while covering for William Lundigan.

Freed's first Easter Jubilee here reportedly attracted ninety-seven thousand kids and grossed $107,000, thus shattering our theatre's previous record held by Russ Columbo in the 1930s. And if any doubt remains about the continued policy of racial integration at the Brooklyn Paramount stemming back to Ethel Waters's appearance in 1932, check out William PoPsie's oft-reproduced photograph in *Life* magazine of Black and white teenagers enjoying themselves in the balcony less than a decade after Jackie Robinson shattered the color barrier in Major League Baseball in 1947.

The name of the featured film shown when the Sieg Organization, a three-person corporation that included Lew Platt along with Freed and Levy, charged ninety cents for admission was a title that still remains apropos for ongoing problems associated with total racial equaling in the United States: *The Americano,* starring Glenn Ford.

Alan Freed's second show dates in our theatre were from September 2 through 8, 1955. This advertised "First Annual Labor Day Show" portended even greater changes in Rock 'n' Roll history, insofar as its headliner was the recently deceased, beloved, legendary crooner/JJazz song stylist. Despite—or because?—of his pop star status with Top Forty hits like "Boulevard of Broken Dreams" and "Because of You," however, Bennett not only was rudely booed off stage while singing "Stranger in Paradise," but teenagers also expressed displeasure by knocking over his life-size cutouts in the lobby. He was attempting to save face by claiming laryngitis while also attempting to be heard during the first show. Tony Bennett quit in favor of Al Hibbler *Variety* (July 20, 1955) curiously advertised Tony Bennett's appearance on stage here as follows (Evanier, 2011: 1): "An unusual aspect of the Fall bash is that pop singer Tony Bennett will headline the rhythm and blues package." Blame it on their youth, as it were, but the contrast with his treatment at Manhattan's Paramount four years earlier couldn't be any more dramatic: For, during the week of September 19, 1951, we read this about one of those shows that cofeatured the Jazz trumpet player/singer Louis Prima, who as we saw in the last chapter also performed here during the early Jazz years in the Vaudeville era in 1932—skywriting over Times Square advertising TONY BENNETT: NEW YORK PARAMOUNT! Even so, that superstar born in Astoria, Queens, and whose stage name was apparently suggested by Bob Hope, ironically titled a chapter in one of his books, "Rock and Roll Is Here to Stay," (Bennett, 2012: 230).

As for Al Hibbler, whatever the reasons for his apparent audience-friendly reception, the blind African American who previously sang with Duke Ellington's orchestra, like Tony Bennett, enjoyed a block-buster pop crossover hit with "Ebb Tide," recorded in 1953. Hibbler was also called back on stage by applause from that predominantly white audience of teenagers for an encore and sang the Irish ballad "Danny Boy" recorded by Jackie Wilson.

Most famously among the other Rock 'n' Roll performers during Alan Freed's second show/first Labor Day Jubilee in our theatre (that reportedly earned $154,000) was Charles Edward Anderson "Chuck" Berry...who not only was making his debut in our theatre, but regarded his performance as a racial triumph; that is, cryptically coded with bitter racial memories of having been banned as a youngster from attending the Fox, a segregated cinematic palace in St. Louis, Missouri. For, as Chuck Berry (1987: 112) memorialized that hurt in his autobiography:

After we had worked our way through New England, and on through the Capitol area, I accepted a very important contract for one week at the Paramount Theater in New York [*sic*]. It was my debut as an artist in New York with my little three-piece-group, and one of my first acts on arrival was to order three pairs of brown suede shoes totaling thirty dollars and three rayon suits totaling twenty-seven-fifty each to make sure we looked sharp for New York. The big marquee was glittering with names of stars. Headlining the show was Tony Bennett, the most pleasant and gentlemanlike artist I have ever yet come to know in show biz, followed by Lillian Briggs, Nappy Brown, the Four Voices, Chuck Berry and Red Prysock's Orchestra…

Never before had I confronted more than a thousand people watching me perform, and I had never seen the inside of a theater as enormous as the Brooklyn Paramount. My hometown's answer to the Paramount was the St. Louis Fox, but the time had not yet come when a black person could patronize the big Fox in St. Louis. (Berry, 1987: 112)

Along with performing his first blockbuster hit, "Maybellene," a Country and Western song originally titled "Ida Red" he famously recorded on May 21, 1955, in Chicago on Chess, Chuck Berry either launched his iconic duck walk on our theatre's stage or during a Manhattan-Paramount subsequent show hosted by Freed—albeit named instead as the chicken dance. Too bad "School Day" (not Days!) was two years in the offing, insofar as it might have made our transition from those proverbial lazy hazy days of summer vacation to the grind of public school less stressful!

All told, however, the songwriter-cum-poet-laureate-of-Rock wrote only two songs that made *Billboard*'s Top Ten: (Gimme Some of That) "Rock and Roll Music" and "Johnny B. Goode"—the latter, according to one of Chuck Berry's biographers, R. J. Smith, qualifying as the "first protest Rock 'n' Roll song" (Smith, 2022: 133). Berry's largely autobiographical lyrics about the aspirations of a colored boy and his protective mother then prompted a money-savvy white record producer to convince him to change those lyrics to a country boy (Christgau, 1980).

Then, too, the Moonglows returned during Alan Freed's Labor Day Show. Still other legendary African American singing groups included the Harptones, who formed in 1953 and enjoyed Rock 'n' Roll immortality with "Life Is but a Dream." Led by Willie Winfield, they became another staple of Doo-wop revival shows until 2021, or until his death. No matter that Marv Goldberg in his encyclopedic online *R&B Notebooks* (2004, 2000) wrote about the Harptones' lack of a number one hit, they "placed more songs (14) in the top 500 than any other group." "A Sunday Kind of Love" was written by Louis Prima in 1946 while the Harptones were additionally noteworthy for their original choreographed dancing. This was evidenced in *Rockin' the Blues*, a film made in 1956 at the Sunset Studios in Harlem.

The Flamingos were also on hand. They formed in Chicago in 1952 and appeared to have been the only pioneering African American Rock 'n' Roll group with a Black member. Originally the Swallows, upon discovering that the ornithological-inspired (totemic) name had already been taken, they became the Flamingos. "That's My Desire" was among several of their R & B hits. In 1956, they also recorded another all-time Rock 'n' Roll iconic song, "I'll Be Home," three years prior to enjoying their biggest hit in 1959, a recording of the 1934 Tin Pan Alley song. Other songs were the Flamingos' recordings of "I Only Have Eyes for You," a ballad written by white composers Harry Warren and Al Dubin for the 1934 film *Dames*, which, yes, also played the Brooklyn Paramount. And not only that, the prolific scholar of popular music employed by music publishers Arnold Shaw (1974) also wrote that the African American Rock 'n' Roll singers typically earned more in royalties in the long run by covers, provided they lived long enough to collect!

We also note the appearance of the Cardinals out of Baltimore on stage at this Freed Jubilee. Discovered in 1951 by the co-founder of Atlantic, Herb Abramson, who promptly signed them to contract, their rollicking "Come Back My Love" was among the Cardinals' biggest hits; another was "Wheel of Fortune," covered by Kay Starr, another hugely popular pop singer in the 1950s.

Pausing for a moment on that lingering hot button, Shaw (1986: 194–95) wrote that whites in twenty-nine instances not only covered in R-&-B-cum-Rock 'n' Roll hits that enjoyed larger sales than their African American originators—"Ko-Ko-Ko" by Perry Como on RCA, and "Fever" by Peggy Lee on Capitol joining "Sh-Boom" by the African American group called the Chords covered by Crew Cuts cited among those flagrant examples. He also reminded us that for all the understandable righteous anger regarding that practice by African American performers, the sword cut both ways.

Stay for the moment with the influential "Sh-Boom" originally recorded by those young African American street corner singers from the Bronx, in 1954 on Cat, a subsidiary of Atlantic. Herb Cox, lead singer of the Cleftones, maintained during our telephone radio interview in 2006 that the song title "Sh-Boom" had nothing to do with collective fears of nuclear annihilation in the early 1950s. Instead, it concerned innocent puppy love among teenagers. "Thirteen Women" by Bill Haley & His Comets ominously sang about thirteen survivors of nuclear annihilation, twelve women and one man no less! "Sh-Boom" was the title of a song by the Chords, as well as a book by Clay Cole.

The performance of another pivotal African American R-&-B-cum-early-Rock 'n' Roll singing group during Alan Freed's first Labor Day show in 1955 was by The Nutmegs, who were named after their home state of Connecticut and enjoyed a single blockbuster hit, *Story Untold*, recorded in 1955 on Herald.

Finally, these largely forgotten white performers were also booked here during that summer-ending/fall-beginning transition of Jubilee in 1955: Eddie Cochrane (née Edward Reardon), whose rockabilly hits were performed in *The Girl Can't Help It*, a 20th Century-Fox film starring Jayne Mansfield and Tom Ewell released in 1956. It included performances by Little Richard, the Platters, and Fats Domino. Other early white rockers on stage that week were Eddie Fontaine, Gene Vincent and the Blue Caps, and Lillian Briggs, a. k. a. the Blonde Bombshell, who was also advertised as the "White Queen of Rock 'n' Roll." And while under contract with Freed/Levy, she recorded the Tin Pan Alley standard for them, "I Want You to Be My Baby" on their Coral label.

Still others included the Rhythmettes, who were among the first white girls' group in Rock 'n' Roll history, and whose two big hits on RCA Victor were "Seventeen" and "Only You"; and the Four Voices ("Honest Darling, Believe Me" on Columbia).

In addition, these African American performers were also part of Freed's second Jubilee: The Treniers and Nappy Brown (née Napoleon Brown). The Treniers are still frequently overlooked R & B performers, who sing and strut in "The Girl Can't Help It." And the largely forgotten Nappy Brown as well, born in Charlotte, North Carolina, made the transition from R & B with his novelty Rock 'n' Roll song "Piddly Patter-Patter," which was covered by Patti Page on Mercury.

Foxfire, starring Rory Calhoun, was the film shown those eight days and nights, and it broke our theatre's previous all-time earnings ceiling of $125,000.

Freed's third Jubilee was his second Easter Show in our theatre. Staged between March 30 and April 8, 1956, these future and already acknowledged Rock 'n' Roll stars performed.

(1) The Willows from Harlem, whose single hit was "Church Bells May Ring," released on the Melba label in that year, led by Tony Middleton, who expressed anger during a radio interview that it was covered by the white pop singer Sunny Gale in 1960. But he also shared that the chimes heard on that song were played by none other than a second generation, as it were, future Rock star Neil Sedaka. (2) The Platters from Los Angeles were a mixed-gender African American singing group that formed in 1952, and who, according to Marv Goldberg (*R&B Notebooks*, 2009), remained "the most successful black group of their time." Forced to rename themselves from the Flamingos after a recording disc, the Platters were led by Samuel Anthony "Tony" Williams and his falsetto voice. With their fortunes guided by Samuel "Buck" Ram, a Black attorney who apparently advised they should emulate the Ink Spots, world-famous singers literally discovered on Manhattan's Paramount—while cleaning up—and similarly record Top Ten hits, their greatest hits were "My Prayer, Only You (and You Alone)," "Twilight Time," "(You've Got the) Magic Touch," and "The Great Pretender"—the latter not only initially reaching number one on R & B charts, but also crossing over to Rock 'n' Roll listings before (briefly) soaring to the top of pop charts in 1956. Finally, those fan favorites who sang "You'll Never Know" in the Rock 'n' Roll

film *The Girl Can't Help It* recorded Tin Pan Alley standards...like Jerome Kern's "Smoke Gets in Your Eye" and Rudy Vallée's "Harbor Lights."

(3) Yet another new group linked with Freed/Levy performing here for the first time were the Cleftones, who closed out the first half of this show. A fan favorite presumably of every Rock 'n' Roll devotee, the late Herb Cox told this author on his radio show in 2006 about their group's origin as high school classmates from Jamaica, Queens, who learned that their original name had already been taken, so this legendary Rock 'n' Roll singing group adopted a new name inspired from the Clef Club. Among the Cleftones' biggest—and hopefully immortal—up-tempo joyous hits, we happily reprise these favorite titles: "Can't We Be Sweethearts," "You Baby You," "Heart and Soul," and "Little Girl of Mine." On the other hand, "Please Say You Want Me Too" was a dreamy ballad we frankly couldn't wait for the lights to be turned down during so we could slow dance—grind!—at dances sponsored by a settlement house in the 1950s. And from a two-part telephone interview with Herb Cox from his home in Atlanta, Georgia, we can add two more wisdom stories remotely attached to place, i.e., the Brooklyn Paramount:

Life seemed complete... We'd listen to Alan Freed playing our song "You, Baby, You" on the radio and felt we were famous. Remember, Mike, we were just teenagers; we'd gone to Freed's shows and stood in line like every fan at the Brooklyn Paramount, and now here we were on stage performing for him...famous, you could say. Kids who wore black plaid corduroy jackets with charcoal gray pants and white buck shoes and red ties when we performed those four or five shows a day and were hot... but we traveled back and forth from Jamaica on the subway, because we were still living at home! Warren (Corbin) even wore that outfit on the train, and we'd call him Grands—for grandstanding.

I also remember our show for Freed at the Fox in Detroit, a theater almost exactly like the Brooklyn Paramount. We didn't really know anything at the time, but LaVern Baker taught us how to bow! "I will be your show biz Momma," she said to us. She was older than any of us, and we shared a dressing room with the Cadillacs, they were also older. But Richard Barrett from their group was another important influence. I remember he taught us so much about the business because we didn't really know anything... Didn't know for example George Goldner who eventually signed us, was like Freed and was attached at the hip to Moe Levy, so to speak.

The second example of a wisdom-like story is from the lead singer of those renamed Silvertones about an Rock 'n' Roll festival in South Carolina. The Cleftones were denied entry due to their lateness, which was caused by Woodstock-like lines of traffic after a long bus ride from New York...that is, until Herb Cox dropped the name of the mobster Morris Levy, which gave them immediate entry and their contractual guarantee to perform!

Teenagers made their initial appearance on stage here during Alan Freed's second anniversary Easter Jubilee in March 1956. They were led by the incomparable thirteen-year-old Frankie Lymon, and despite the enormity of the teenagers' impact on early Rock 'n' Roll history, they remained together only for eighteen months. As for their origin story, I return again to my telephone interview with Herb Cox of the Cleftones, who was there with his group similarly awaiting an audition for George Goldner in his Rama label studio housed on Broadway in Manhattan. He was asked what he thought of Herman Santiago's singing lead in that blockbuster hit "Why Do Fools Fall in Love" that was covered by two different Caucasian Persuasion pop artists, Gale Storm and Gloria Mann, as well as the Diamonds of modest Rock fame. Herb recalled hesitating before dishonestly answering that he felt his pal sounded good. "You don't know shit, Cox!" Or so that legendary early Rock 'n' Roll record owner and astute instinct regarding talent forced to chronically sell recording labels to Morris Levy to cover gambling debts exploded and overrode Cox's loyalty to a friend before instructing the Teenagers' youngest member to sing lead on their future ginormous hit. And the rest, as they say, was history. Frankie Lymon and the Teenagers also scored big on "Please Be Mine" found on the "B" or flip side of their iconic million-selling signature song released in January 1956, and another title apropos for those years, anyway, "No, No, No, I'm Not a Juvenile Delinquent!"

Finally, and not unrelated to the sordid side of Rock 'n' Roll's payola scandal in 1959, was the long court battle over intellectual property rights regarding "Why Do Fools Fall in Love"...which was finally adjudicated in 1984, when the Circuit Court of Appeals (*Jimmy Merchant and Herman Santiago v. Morris Levy, Big Seven Music Corporation and Roulette Records*) ruled in favor of those original Teenagers singers. Asked why each hadn't attempted to sue for their rightful royalties until 1969 and 1977, respectively, both responded with fear of the Godfather of Music, Morris Levy. His influence was such that Dannen (1991: 32) not only dubbed him "octopus," but also wrote that his amassed personal worth was estimated at $75 million at the time of his death.

Along with (5) the Flamingos' return appearance, this fan-friendly early Rock 'n' Roll foundational group performed here during Alan Freed's third Jubilee. (6) The Valentines, who formed in 1952, had personal best hits after they transitioned from R & B to Rock 'n' Roll. "Lily Mae Bel" was an up-tempo number factually named for one of their friends, Lucille Mabelle. It was recorded in 1955 on the Rama label owned by George Goldner. In another synchronicity, those were the first names of a pair of hookers in Irving Shulman's *Amboy Dukes* who one of the novel's gangs sent to rivals as a truce gesture following a rumble...alright, to Rock 'n' Roll them!

Lesser known if not also unfortunately largely forgotten performers included (7) Ruth McFadden, another established R & B performer who also made that cut, so to speak, with her crossover hit "Darling, Listen to the Words of the Song." She, according to those indispensable Marv Goldberg's R&B Notebooks, cleverly appeared online with marbleized looks of public school composition notebooks as their frontispiece and backed the Moonglows on several recordings; and (8) the Jordimars, a. k. a. Foggy Boys, an obscure Canadian (white) singing group whose biggest hit was "Well Now, Dig This," and will probably remain better known for backing Elvis Presley, commencing in 1956; (9) the Royaltones, an African American vocal group from Dearborn, Michigan, whose biggest hit was "Poor Boy"; (10) Cindy and Lindy ("Let's Go Steady"); (11) the Rover Boys, yet another obscure vanilla group, whose hit song in 1956 was "Come to Me"; and finally (12) Dori Anne Gray, whose biggest hit was "Tears for Me" recorded by Morris Levy. Popularity was achieved as a result of also receiving frequent radio plays from his business partner and Alan Freed's WINS influential program. While hardly qualifying as wisdom stories attached to Brooklyn Paramount, we want to mention these from Alan Freed's third Jubilee in the theatre.

First, Count Basie's swingingest Jazz band in the land slotted incredulously as an intermission band as the result of Freed's love of Jazz or Levy's ownership of Roulette and patron-like friendship with William Basie from Red Bank, New Jersey. While Basie's band, curiously enough, wasn't booed off the stage by those same rowdy audiences of predominantly white teenagers as occurred with Tony Bennett a few months prior, Basie's Territory Band featuring the All-American Rhythm Section (with Freddie Green on guitar, Walter Page on bass, and Papa Joe Jones on drums) was fired a few months later on June 30, 1956, from the celebrity jock's "Camel Rock 'n' Roll TV Dance Party." And while disapproval ratings expressed that their music by a teenager to her father who was the TV show's producer was outrageously given, Basie was quoted in a tabloid saying people were dancing before Rock 'n' Roll and that he had quit.

Second, *Variety* reported on April 4, 1956, that they had received $204,000 from gate receipts. Doubtless in part because the initial price of tickets whose sales understandably slowed on Good Friday and Easter Sunday were raised from $1.25 to $2.00.

And, third, teenagers tore up a subway car as well as assaulted its passengers after leaving that initial Monday morning Easter Jubilee, some of them who might well have stood in line since 6:00 a.m. for tickets, and their misbehavior notwithstanding our theatre's manager in its original incarnation, Gene Pleshette, having taken the precaution of hiring extra security to work alongside assigned NYPD uniformed cops.

The name of the film screened that week was *Battle Stations*, seemingly apropos, which starred John Lund, William Bendix, and Jack Palance, who achieved greater fame as TV's *Paladan*.

Alan Freed's Second Labor Day/Anniversary show, the fourth of those eight Rock 'n' Roll Jubilees by count, ran from Wednesday, August 28, through Thursday, September 6, 1956. With the Jazz saxophonist Jimmy Wright heard on Frankie Lymon and the Teenagers' recordings now leading the Big Beat Orchestra, they backed these major rebranded performers during those ten days and nights:

(1) The Fat Man, a. k. a. Fats Domino (née Antoine Dominique Domino Jr.), made his Brooklyn Paramount debut and was hailed as "simply the most consistent predictable hit maker of them all over a period of twenty years," sold sixty-five million records, and nearly as many gold records (fifteen or twenty) as Elvis or the Beatles in their respective days (Guralnick, 1980: 45). The New Orleans barrelhouse boogie-woogie-style piano-player-cum-Rock 'n' Roll-foundational-figure originally recorded the "Fat Man" and "Junker's Blues" before his signature song "Blueberry Hill" in 1956. That was nearly two decades after the Big Band leader Glenn Miller had covered Gene Autry's earliest country and western version. In the tribute by Domino's recent biographer, Rick Coleman (2007: 78–79), he wrote that Fats Domino effectively opened "the door to America's genuine traditional music...(while) freeing it from its longtime domination by European culture." Indeed, Shaw (1974: 78–79) employed 1953 as the year of Domino's beginning transformation to Rock 'n' Roll notoriety. These additional crossover hits also charted in *Billboard*'s Top 100: "Blue Monday," "I'm Walking," and "Ain't That a Shame."

Notwithstanding the revolutionary nature of this musical sea change, Fats Domino was voted the top-selling R & B artist one year later in *Billboard's* 1954 Jubilee Operators Poll...those many years before his induction into the first class of the Rock & Roll Hall of Fame in 1983. (2) Frankie Lymon and the Teenagers were back again from 165th Street and Edgecombe Avenue in Washington Heights in New York City. They were originally the Premieres who performed here together during this show for the last time. (3) Joseph Vernon "Big Joe" Turner, who for good reason was called "The Boss of the Blues" and about whom our friend, the prominent Jazz writer and culture critic Gary Giddins (1985: 93), said that basso transitional figure famously drew customers off the street to the Sunset Cafe in Kansas City from his station as a bartender, belting out race music tunes in 1939. Giddins significantly told audiences during his appearance at Tramps in Manhattan on August 27, 1987: "We do some rock 'n' roll, some jazz, and some blues." And that's decades after his R & B hit "Shake, Rattle and Roll" that became the earliest Rock 'n' Roll song.

And these returnees were also a part of Freed's fourth Jubilee in our theatre: (4) the Cleftones; (5) Harptones; and (6) the Penguins... the all-time classic hit "Earth Angel" was the B-side of "Hey Senorita," the bigger seller.

Glossing over the other performers who left minor footprints in this music's early history and who were whites, included: (7) Jimmy Cavallo and His House Rockers, listed, whether errantly or not, as "The House Wreckers" and who appeared in Freed's first of five films, *Rock, Rock, Rock*; (8) Jean Chapel (née Opel Jean Amburgey) whose only hit was "Welcome to the Club," which was immediately covered by Elvis Presley during his dramatic rise to superstardom—she, with reverse English, was unfortunately dubbed The Female Elvis; (9) Cirino and the Bow Ties from Brooklyn and apparently under contract with Freed/Levy for whom they recorded "My Rosemarie"; (10) the Shepherd Sisters; and (11) DeMillo Sisters.

African American performers were part of that sociologically significant Rock 'n' Roll show: (12) Mabel Elizabeth King ("Symbol of Love," "That's the Way It Goes," "Three Wishes," and "Second Hand Love" recorded on George Goldner's Rama label, became better known after transitioning into an actress and became Evaline in *The*

Wicked Witch TV series as well as the good witch—as if there ever were such a thing—by starring in Broadway's Black production of *The Wiz*; and finally (13) the Joytones, among several better-known Black girl's groups during those years...who Greil Marcus (1980: 160) described as creating the warmest and most affecting music in early Rock 'n' Roll history...and who were also discovered by Goldner. "The Love That I Give to You," "Gee," "What a Boy," and "Is This Really the End" were among the Joytones' modestly successful recording hits.

Raw Edge, finally, was the film screened during those five and six daily shows, which, according to *Variety* (September 5, 1956), earned $222,000 because ticket prices once again were doubled from $1.25 after the one o'clock show. However, the trade magazine's reviewer complained about the rowdy behavior of the teenagers during his visit, some of whom were promptly thrown out of the theater.

Alan Freed's fifth Rock 'n' Roll show in the Brooklyn Paramount was his first Christmas Jubilee. Running between December 23 and 30, 1956, it also featured an array of new and returning legendary Black performers, as well as several new and largely forgotten white Rock n' Roll performers.

(1) The Moonglows came back for a third time, and they were introduced by the Old Moondogger's cawing as follows: "Hey, kids, here's what you've been waiting for—the Moonglows singing their latest and greatest new hits, "See Saw!" and "Over and Over Again." They also appeared in "Rock, Rock, Rock," which Marv Goldberg (ibid) called "the first true R and R film"; (2) the Dells, whose biggest hit was "Oh, What a Night," seemingly predestined, as it were, to become a Golden Oldie and Doo-Wop favorite. According to Clay Cole (2009: 180), it was created in 1967 by Robert Charles "Gus" Gossert, who was found shot dead in his car in 1976 in Tennessee after hosting his nightly radio show heard on WKOI-FM in Knoxville. It presumably still remains an unsolved crime in Rock 'n' Roll history. "Close Your Eyes," a lush ballad by the Five Keys, which contains the phrase "doo-wop" in the lyrics. Finally, the Doo-Wop Museum might still be located in Wildwood, New Jersey; (3) Jesse Belvin, born in San

Antonio, Texas, was tragically killed along with his wife and another passenger in a car crash three years shy of his thirtieth birthday in 1960. That suspiciously followed a clash with white supremacists at the first integrated rock concert in Little Rock, Arkansas, along with "Earth Angel," another Rock 'n' Roll song. "Mr. Easy," as Belvin was nicknamed, was groomed as the next Nat King Cole.

(4) Shirley and Lee (née Leonard Lee and Shirley Pixley) were dubbed the "Sweethearts of the Blues." They wrote and recorded another Rock 'n' Roll gold standard song in 1956, "Let the Good Times Roll." Despite minor hits featuring her unusual voice, which Winner (1980: 41) wrote scandalized popular music, those included "I Feel Good" on her own; (5) "Screamin'" Jay Hawkins (née Jalacy Hawkins), who was born in Columbus, Ohio, and as a young man became a professional welterweight boxer. Following his love for R & B, however, he then morphed into one of Rock 'n' Roll's truly unique performers. Since his performances which began shocking audiences by leaping from a coffin on stage, "Screamin'" Hawkins sang "I Put a Spell on You," which became his signature song; (6) Lee Andrew and the Hearts, who as devoted fan(atic)s of this great music might or might not know, also began as a gospel-influenced African American singing group with "Long Lonely Nights" as their biggest Rock 'n' Roll hit after having formed in 1952 as a R & B group. They charted by recording Tin Pan Alley standards like "The White Cliffs of Dover" and "The Bells of St. Mary."

Turning next to largely forgotten white performers who were also part of Alan Freed's fifth show in our theatre, they included: (7) Mac Curtis, a Western Swing singer not unlike Bill Haley, who unfortunately was promoted as the next (male) Elvis. Curtis's song "In the Ghetto" was more famously covered by Presley; (8) George Hamilton IV (1937–2014), yet another Country and Western singer booked in 1956 to perform during the Christmas Jubilee in our theatre. Born in Winston-Salem, North Carolina, he not only performed at the Grand Ole Opry but recorded his biggest hit as a nineteen-year-old: "A Rose and a Baby Ruth," which crossed over into pop where it charted, and he was never really considered an Rock 'n' Roll singer; (9) Lillian Briggs (née Biggs) was another Freed-friendly performer. Teenaged audience members who took the time to read their Program Notes consequently learned that she was (presumably) the deejay's personal discovery. And she was a truck driver as well...alright, so not an eighteen-wheeler, but a laundry truck driver all the same; (10) Eddie Cooley who probably led the Dimples singing their signature hit "Priscilla," who was a prolific songwriter as well, hailed from Atlanta, Georgia, and cowrote "Fever" with on of Brooklyn's legendary songwriters, Otis Blackwell; (11) Barbie Gaye sang the rollicking and unforgettable "My Girl," and "Lollipop." A fourteen-year-old sensation at the time, she reportedly was discovered on the beach in Coney Island by Gaetano "Corky" Vastola, one of Morris Levy's reputed gangland associates who got to manage her brief career. "My Boy, Lollypop," was the song's original title. And the writing credit went to the Cadillacs' lead singer, Robert Spencer, who for reasons one can easily imagine, surrendered its copyright to the mobster Morris Levy. In any event, the shuffle rhythm heard in this song, as it turns out, reportedly came at the suggestion of Panama Francis, the Jazz drummer in Alan Freed's Big Beat orchestras. All the same, another singer enjoyed the more famous version (cover) of "My Boy, Lollipop." It was Millie Smith who spiced it with Jamaican Reggae for additional flavor.

(12) The Three Friends were formerly the Chuckles, and they sang "Blanche" minus their former lead singer, Teddy Randazzo. Finally, we note (13) the largely forgotten G-Clefs, an African American group composed of four siblings and a friend from Roxbury, Massachusetts, with "Ka-Ding Dong" as their lone hit.

The name of the film shown that week? *The Cruel Tower*. And *Variety* (December 26, 1956) reported that $240,000 was earned during Freed's fifth show here, while no mention was made either of rioting in the theatre, if only because of Pinkerton Agency security guards hired to assist NYPD for crowd control were armed, as they were, with special flashlights. And finally, we report the following wisdom story recounted by the trade magazine: the report that a rumor of Elvis Presley's film *Love Me Tender* being shown nearly turned into a riot, when an estimated fifteen hundred belated bobby-sockers discovered their idol wouldn't appear in person (Haley and Benjaminson, 2019: 104). Or, as those biographers of Bill Haley Sr. quoted a fifteen-year-old named Carol Olsen who was there, expressing their additional anger to a *Journal American* journalist also regarding allegedly being promised gifts to the first thousand anxious for a sighting of Presley: "It'll be a miracle if this theatre is in one piece when we get out."

This sixth Rock 'n' Roll Alan Freed Jubilee booked in the Brooklyn Paramount was aptly dubbed the Easter Jubilee of Stars '57. These nineteen acts comprising sixty performers thus were booked between April 19 and April 28, 1957, for that third Easter show in a year characterized by Shaw (1974: 200) sociologically as a white year, with more white singers breaking into R & B charts than Black singers into pop:

> He wanted to manage me...you could be a disc jockey *and* manage someone... Freed was forceful, a tall, imposing-type guy, who had an ego and a half. All attitude, because he knew he was the guy...a true innovator in radio programming...(who became) the scapegoat...(despite the fact that) everybody did it—you could barely walk into a men's room in the Brill Building without seeing someone handing a deejay a big envelope of bills...(Still) he was a revolutionary deejay and rock impresario who did more than anyone to promote rock 'n' roll...(and) ended up a kind of tragic figure, getting caught up (in the payola scandal)...a common industry practice. (Anka, 2013: 86)

Among the other white performers at this curiously genre-mixed Easter show were: (3) Buddy Knox from Happy, Texas, whose biggest hit was "Party Doll," cowritten with the next performer in the coming Tex-Mex sound; (4) James Albert "Jimmy" Bowen, who was born in Rio Rita, New Mexico, and appears unique as the only pop music performer to obtain a graduate degree from the prestigious Wharton School of Business, whence Jimmy Bowen changed careers and became a record producer; (5) Little Billy Mason (née Walter Sobolta) not only was another newcomer to our theatre's stage, but another white Canadian singer as well. "Make Me Your Own" was the song performed by Mason and the Rhythm Jesters; (6) the Rosebuds recorded "Kiss Me Tonight" on Lancer, Alan Freed's record label named for one of his sons; (7) Charles Anthony Graci used the stage name "Charlie Gracie" and was the first in a line of Italian Americans from South Philadelphia who was promoted by the host of *American Bandstand*'s TV Rock 'n' Roll show. They featured teenage dancers. This author remains ashamed to report he ran home from Seward Park High School to watch. Jackson (1997: 44–46) also wrote that Gracie's "Poor Butterfly" was his biggest hit, and he appeared in *Wages of Sin*, a documentary about the payola scandal in which he discusses his losing battle with Dick Clark regarding ownership rights to that song.

And while these major Rock 'n' Roll groups, like (8) the Cleftones (9) Harptones, and (10) Bo Diddly were also brought back, (11) were the newcomers, the Del-Vikings. They enjoyed two stupendous hits recorded while they were still in the air force—"Come Go with Me" and "Whispering Bells." Not unlike the Crests, they were also among a handful of mixed-race successful Rock 'n' Roll singing groups; (12) Johnny and Joe were an African American duo born and bred in the Bronx who contributed to Rock 'n' Roll history. That's why they were voted into its hall of fame. (13) The Cellos, who sang "Rang Tang Ding Dong," were a one-hit singing group, African Americans in this instance; (14) the Pearls sang "Shadows of Love"; (15) the G-Clefs sang "Ka-Ding Dong"; (16) The Solitaires, who must have sung their catchy solitary hit "Walking Along," recorded on Argo; (17) Oscar James Winston, known professionally as Bobby Marchan, began as a female impersonator, as did Little Richard in New Orleans before enjoying moderate success in Rock 'n' Roll history with his recording of "There Is Something on Your Mind." And finishing up, we also note the appearances of (18) Anita Ellis and (19) the Teen Chords at Freed's sixth Jubilee in our theatre.

Of French-Canadian descent, Ellis was a singer-actress and also the daughter of Orthodox Jews. While she had a minor hit titled "Forbidden Fruit," as a result of paralyzing stage fright, Anita Ellis carved a successful career doing voiceovers for Hollywood stars. Most famously among those was the voice for the steamy sexpot Rita Hayworth, lip-synching "Put the Blame on Mame" in the (steamy) film *Gilda*, made in 1946, and which was screened in our theatre. But Anita Ellis came back by singing on *The Red Skelton Show*.

As for the Teen Chords, they featured Lewis Lymon, who was Frankie's younger brother (by two years), and who bore a similar soprano-like voice—until puberty. Aptly dubbed the "Kid Sound" by Marv Goldberg (*R&B Notes*, 2008), the Teen Chords achieved modest fame with "I'm So Happy" and "Lydia," recorded on the Whirlin Disc label in 1956. But they answered The Teenager's rhetorical question, "Why Do Fools Fall in Love" on stage at Manhattan-Paramount in 1957 with "I Found Out Why." It was recorded along with a few other songs on George Goldner's short-lived Juanita label before disbanding.

The name of the film screened during that Easter week plus three extra days in 1957 was *The Big Boodle* starring Errol Flynn.

Alan Freed's seventh Rock 'n' Roll blockbuster show at the Brooklyn Paramount was also dubbed the Third Anniversary Labor Day Show. Advertised without much hyperbole as "Starring the Greatest Rock and Roll Radio, Recording and TV Stars," these major Black and white performers appeared on our theatre's stage between August 30 and September 5, 1957, inclusively; and that is, performing as was usually the case between five and seven times daily between 11:00 a.m. and 2:00 a.m. for the admission price of one buck.

(1) The incomparable Rock 'n' Roll pioneer Richard Wayne Penniman, a. k. a. Little Richard, backed by his own orchestra, a. k. a. the King and Queen of Rock 'n' Roll, controversially covered "Tutti Fruiti," Italian for all flavors. His lyrics about anal sex were then changed by Specialty Record's owner Art Rupe from "good booty" to "aw rooty" as a way of avoiding its ban otherwise from commercial radio play (Ribowsky, 2020: 49). The New Orleans lyricist hired to rewrite "Tutti Fruiti" amazingly earned $50,000 in royalties two or three times each

year (Ribowsky, 2020: 49). For another irony, that most vanilla of all ersatz Rock 'n' Roll performers, Pat Boone, also earned more than Little Richard covering his version. One of the greatest ironies in Rock 'n' Roll history is the fact that Chuck Berry's provocative "My Ding-A-Ling" proved to be his biggest seller!

Still other ginormous hits by Little Richard were "Rip It Up," "Slippin' and Slidin'," "Long Tall Sally," "Lucille," and "Good Golly Miss Molly." His lifelong sexual identity conflict, as is well known, combined with guilt stemming from his early Pentecostal Church indoctrination against Rock 'n' Roll as the Devil's Music contributed to tortuous inner conflicts that ultimately prompted his quitting a second time to become a minister condemning homosexuality. But during an earlier hysterical episode, Little Richard reportedly tossed $8,000 worth of jewelry (including diamond rings) into the Hunter River on an abortive tour of Australia following his witnessing a plane engine burst into fire, which was taken as a foreshadowing of his early demise.

Among those seemingly countless outrageous stories told about this disarmingly honest yet never-not-flamboyant figure who inspired performers like Boy George and so-called Glamour Rock, as they pertain to the Brooklyn Paramount, Tommy James (2010: 202) of the Shondells, whose biggest hit "Crimson and Clover" was performed here in 1972 after our theatre was shuttered, recited the following:

> The Brooklyn Paramount was one of Morris's old stomping grounds, where he first had his rock and roll shows with Alan Freed in the fifties. Morris was still doing shows there in the early sixties when he had a famous screaming match with Little Richard, which ended when he pulled Richard's wig off his head in the elevator at the back of the theater and told him if he didn't shut up, "I'll tear your fucking face off."

Another X-rated wisdom-type story that the Apache would have approved is this: (2) Buddy Holly, lead singer of the Crickets, according to a biographer, Phillip Norman (1996: 139), participated in a *ménage à trois* in Little Richard's dressing room between performances. As related in graphic terms, we read:

> ...(so) when we walked in, Richard was there with his girlfriend, Angel, and Larry Williams. Richard was masturbating and Larry was making love to her from behind. None of them took any notice of us (Crickets) standing in the doorway. They just carried right on with what they were doing. Through a window we could see straight across the street, where there was some kind of hospital or institution for the elderly. When Richard had finished what he was doing with Angel he fastened his robe, walked over to the window, and looked over to this home or hospital or whatever it was. I mean its windows were full of those old people in bathrobes, with doctors and nurses looking at them. "Oh, gee," Richard said. "I wonder if the folks over there would like me to go and witness with them." (Norman, 1996: 141)

Well, since precious truth often remains stronger than imaginative fiction, notwithstanding the additional claim that the influential second generation white rocker (Buddy Holly) very nearly missed a curtain call after being forced to run straight on stage to perform, still with a gaping open fly after having been joined in sex with Angel (Norman, 1996), I'm sorry to report that no way Cumberland Hospital, the birthplace of Tony Fauci and both Mikes, Jordan and Tyson, still located on the corner of Ashland and DeKalb Avenue, could have been seen from any windowless dressing room in the basement of our theatre! All the same, this is another less salacious story about the appearance of Buddy Holly and the Crickets at the Brooklyn Paramount with an implied moral lesson.

In it, after commenting on the publicity photo of Buddy Holly (née Charles Hardin Holly) and bandmates Jerry Allen and Joe Mauldin taken on the roof of our theatre for their first record album, *The Chirping Crickets*, Holly's biographer invites us to examine that shot more closely. The lead singer has a cosmetically treated blackened eye that resulted from fisticuffs with a jealous bandmate regarding the married woman whom the rock icon was having an affair with, and had flown to New York for their debut. And so we read the following:

> I mean it swelled up real big. Right after that, we had to go up on the (Brooklyn) Paramount's roof and have pictures done for our first album The Chirping Crickets. They had to retouch the shot to try to hide Buddy's swollen eye but you could [*sic*] still see it. You could still see it to this day. (Norman, 1996: 142)

We add to the record album's cover graphics that the artist did an excellent job of airbrushing out the urban smog caused largely by coal-generated furnaces and replaced it with a blue sky!

Back again to Holly, however, whose group earned $1,100 per week for a minimum of twenty-nine shows. He began performing after being all shook up (pun intended) while attending a show by Elvis Presley in Lubbock, Texas, during his tumultuous beginnings. In any event, while their rockabilly sound was a main influence on the Beatles, who changed their original name in homage to the Crickets, Buddy Holly not only developed a baby-like talk style of singing with catchy repetitions as well as hiccup-like interruptions (Cott, 1980: 78), he personally influenced John Lennon as well as other British "Teddy Boys" who imitated black-rimmed eyeglasses. Finally, among the Crickets' major hits recorded in their manager Norman Petty's studio in Clovis, New Mexico, were "That'll Be the Day," which their lead singer said was inspired by John Wayne's film *The Searchers* (Cott, 1980: 79); "Peggy Sue," adapted as the title of a Francis Ford Coppola film starring Kathleen Turner in 1986; "Oh, Boy, Every Day"; and "All My Lovin'." Buddy Holly's tragic early death in that fatal plane crash in 1959 with two other Rock 'n' Roll stars was unexpected.

These additional minor Black and white newcomers and returnees were also booked in Freed's seventh Rock 'n' Roll show in the Brooklyn Paramount: (3) the Del-Vikings, who hailed from Pittsburgh, Pennsylvania, sang their only hit "Come Go with Me"; (4) Mickey (Michouston) Baker and Sylvia (Vanderpool Robinson), back again for a third time: (5) the Diamonds, a group of white performers whose all-time classic Rock 'n' Roll song, "Lil' Darling," was spiced with some of that Latin Tinge the legendary Jazz pianist Jelly Roll Morton famously said was intrinsic to early Jazz; (6) the Five Keys singing their biggest hit, "The Glory of Love," yet another Doo-Wop classic; and (7) Larry Eugene Williams.

Facts about that controversial performer seem in order. After employment as a valet by his cousin, the legendary Rock 'n' Roll singer Lloyd Price, a pianist born in New Orleans, successfully forged his own singing career with recorded hits that included "Short Fat Fanny," "Boney Maronie," and "Dizzie Miss Lizzie"—the latter, a cover of Little Richard's hit. Another, "Lawdy Miss Clawdy," was a cover of Lloyd Price's smash R & B hit from 1952. Despite frequent run-ins with the law for illegal gun possession, Larry Williams remained a regular on Freed's shows. All the same, Specialty Records' A and R man/Rock 'n' Roll performer, Billy Vera (2019: 125–30) left a memorable impression of that Bad Boy by writing that the singer-pianist was a great in-person act, and the very essence of the rebellious side of Rock 'n' Roll.

Indeed, we can only imagine Larry Williams showcasing his faux faint and pratfalls off the piano during performances—show business schtick, to be sure, but Vera (2019) also made him a hard act to follow. And not only that, but Larry Williams was also known to appear on stage with chimps that caused their own mayhem, i.e., by tossing feces about—animal acts were intrinsic to classic Vaudeville. Etta James, who appeared here in a subsequent Rock 'n' Roll show, was his close friend. She related the following about that second-story man, i.e., burglar, Larry Williams, who was also known to drive a Toronado with a gold bull medallion on its hood and to wear an eighteen-karat gold watch on his wrist and a ruby necklace around his neck. Etta James also wrote:

He stepped out with huge sparkly silver platform shoes with live gold-fish swimming inside the see-through heels. He'd sport enormous furry hats with colored feathers reaching to the sky, red silk shirts with collars as long as airplane wings, rings on every finger, an overcoat of fire-red leather. (James, 1995: 164–165)

Finally, Larry Williams owned a nightclub in LA called the Bossa Nova after being released from prison for narcotics. He was as complicated a figure as any in Rock 'n' Roll who staged an amazing comeback as an A and R man for Okeh Records. That happened before being found shot to death in 1980 with a bullet in his head in his Rolls-Royce that was parked in front of his home on Mulholland Drive. According to James (James, 1995: 233), it was not a suicide, but she felt it looked suspiciously mob related.

Other minor figures also appeared on Freed's seventh Rock 'n' Roll show in the Brooklyn Paramount that Easter: (8) Jo Ann Campbell, a diminutive singer featured in another of Freed's Rock 'n' Roll films, *Go, Johnny Go*. A country and western singer, she was born in Jacksonville, Florida, and was also advertised as a blonde bombshell. "Rock 'n' Roll Love" was Jo Anne Campbell's biggest hit, and it was recorded at a session supervised by the legendary Phil Spector of the "wall of sound" fame; (9) Shaye Cogan (née Helen J. Coggins) was a New Englander who entered show business as a child star in an act with two brothers toward the end of the Vaudeville era. She was also connected at the hip with Freed/Levy as a result of her marriage to the co-owner of Kahl Music Publishing Company, Phil Kahl, who was another shady associate of theirs. Shaye Cogan's (minor) hits were "The Get Acquainted Waltz" and "Pathway to Sin," recorded on Morris Levy's Roulette label, and she also appeared in Alan Freed's film *Mr. Rock 'n' Roll*; (10) Ocie Lee Smith was also new to our stage. He was an African American singer who went gold (if not platinum) with his religious-inspired, sentimental single blockbuster hit, "Little Green Apples."

These crowd-pleasing, pioneering Rock 'n' Roll stalwarts were brought back for the third Labor Day Alan Freed Jubilee: (11) The Cleftones; (12) Bo Diddley; and (13) Chuck Berry, who was not only listed as an "Extra-Added Attraction" but aptly also dubbed the folk poet of the 1950s in newspaper advertisements.

Gunsight Ridge (starring Rory Calhoun) was the name of the film shown during Freed's Rock 'n' Roll show in the Brooklyn Paramount.

Except here, we must break off for breaking news before discussing Freed's eighth show on our theatre's stage. Because on November 21, 1957, another major promoter rented it from Long Island University. Thus, on that Thursday night, Irvin Feld, the head of General Artists Corporation, a booking agency and a co-owner of the Ringling Bros. and Barnum & Bailey Circus, staged a blockbuster concert with two shows here—at 7:30 p.m. and 10:30 p.m. This first of two planned annual tours, which kicked off in Pittsburgh, Pennsylvania, and lasted eighty days with bookings in other wonder theatres in twenty-eight cities in the United States as well as five Canadian provinces, was aptly dubbed the Biggest Show of Stars of '57. A frequently overlooked promoter who also owned a national chain of Super Music Stores as well as the Super Disc record label, Feld began by playing race music as early as 1942 on a radio station in Washington, DC, nearly a decade before Freed and Smalls (and other deejays) championed what became Rock 'n' Roll. Indeed, no less an authority than the lead singer of the Cleftones, Herb Cox, was quoted saying Irvin Feld had "more of an impact than Alan Freed" toward breaking down segregation barriers through both promotions (quoted in Coleman, 2007: 148).

These familiar dozen major and minor Black and white returnees were presented on our theatre's stage by that frequently overlooked figure, whom Coleman also credited with launching "the first super-concert by any promoter" (Coleman, 2007: 247): (1) Fats Domino (and his orchestra); (2) LaVern Baker; (3) the Everly Brothers; (4) Frankie Lymon sans the Teenagers; (4) Clyde McPhatter; (5) the Crickets minus Buddy Holly; (6) Chuck Berry; (7) the Diamonds; (8) Paul Anka; (9) Eddie Cochran; (10) Buddy Knox; (11) Jimmy Bowens; (12) the Moonglows; and (13) the Drifters.

Returning to Freed and what was his eighth and final Rock 'n' Roll show at the Brooklyn Paramount, it was a two-day affair that launched as a national tour and was expected to last sixty days in forty-six northeastern theatres.

And so it was that on March 28 and March 29, 1958, our theatre was selected for symbolic reasons as the kickoff for Freed's latest ambition—albeit with only these thirteen acts drawn from a package of thirty-five returnees and newcomers performing on stage here in five complete shows: two on that Friday night at 8:00 p.m. and 11:00 p.m., and three more on Saturday, commencing with a 2:30 p.m. matinee followed by 8:30 p.m. and 11:30 p.m. sets.

(1) Jerry Lee Lewis, arguably Peck's Baddest Boy in Rock 'n' Roll's early history, the controversial singer-pianist from Faraday, Louisiana, made his first (and only) appearance on our theatre's stage. Until his career came to a dead end later in that year when he married his fourteen-year-old cousin and was banned from bookings in England, Lewis enjoyed two blockbuster hits, "Great Balls of Fire" and "Whole Lot of Shakin'"—the latter, previously also reaching number one in 1957 on country and western and R & B charts. His legendary quarrel with Chuck Berry, who was also part of this show, not only stemmed from their battle about who would or should close those shows, but fictitiously also gave rise to one of the longest-lasting myths in early Rock 'n' Roll history—the white rocker's rage after losing that battle, which allegedly prompted him to set fire to the grand piano and exit the stage triumphantly, and not without a purported racist sneer toward Berry, the ultimate closer and winner.

Well, surely, any fire inside any public theatre, whether large like ours or small, might have caused a stampede and shut down of performances presumably following a visit from the neighboring fire department. Notwithstanding a newspaper strike, which could have resolved the problem, Stuart Isacoff, a classical pianist, perpetuated that myth in his history of the pianoforte:

Of such is the rock 'n' roll movement... Jerry Lee did as he was bid that night; he went on before Chuck Berry. He had the crowd screaming and rushing the stage, and when it seemed that the screams had grown loudest and the rushing most chaotic, he stood, kicked the piano stool away with violence, and broke into "Great Balls of Fire." As the screaming chaos grew suddenly and sublimely greater, he drew from his jacket a Coke bottle full of gasoline, and he doused the piano with one hand as the other hand banged out the song; and he struck a wooden match, and he set the piano on fire. (Isacoff, 2012: 119–20)

"And the hands"—he finishes up with his account—"much like the hands of a madman, did not quit the blazing keys…(whereupon) the kids went utterly, magically berserk with the frenzy of it all" (Isacoff, 2012).

Now, Rick Bragg also recycled this myth in his biography of Jerry Lee Lewis, albeit reporting the torching took place outside of Cincinnati. Still, in his words supposedly quoting that literal firebrand, we read:

Then he did something that has been written about and celebrated and denied ever since he reached inside the piano, took a small Coke bottle of clear liquid, and poured gasoline across the top of the instrument, then struck a match and set it aflame. "I just sprinkled a little bit on it," he says, "but it went up with a *whoosh*." (But) Instead of walking off stage, he just kept playing and playing as the piano burned, and the crowd screamed. Jerry Lee played, hunched over the flames, the smoke in his face and hair, until the song was done, and then he swaggered offstage towards Chuck Berry (Bragg, 2014: 254).

Another biographer recycled that myth (Tosches, 1982: 149–50). Ignoring the fact that *Variety* on April 2, 1958, reported that Jerry Lee Lewis "was able to reach new heights of frenzy in his vocalizing and banging on the piano," Hollywood also perpetuated that myth in its biopic of Jerry Lee Lewis (starring Dennis Quaid). Ignoring those broken ivory keys caused by the fury of his piano pounding—with fists and shoe heels included—and these earlier and later examples— Brooklyn's Britton Brothers, Frank and Milton, who weren't related, reportedly "signed a pledge to break 150 fiddles over the heads, necks, and backs of their bandsmen, so the public may enjoy a good laugh" during their Vaudeville appearances here in 1932 and 1933. Lewis's purported mayhem occurred before Jimi Hendrix burned his guitar on stage outdoors fourteen years after Peter Townsend of the Who. And notwithstanding Little Richard's biographer's account of him setting fire to a piano outdoors in another time and place (Ribowsky, 2020: 148), no way the Brooklyn Paramount's manager, Eugene Pleshette, and Long Island University's CFO, Mary Lai, who signed off on those booking engagements, would have permitted anyone setting fire to one of the Brooklyn Paramount's three grand pianos on or off stage! Let the final word on this persisting matter, however, be given to Arnold Shaw (1974: 190), who reported what its alleged perpetuator replied with a proverbial "wink and a blink" when asked if the story were true...anything presumably for public attention by entertainers being good for business!

Along with (2) Chuck Berry's return to our theatre's stage, (3) Jimmie Rodgers was also featured during this abbreviated final Jubilee in our house. A former lumberjack, Rodgers became the hapless victim of a savage mysterious beating by a hired goon posing as highway patrol, who pulled him over on the Pacific Coast Highway in California for some alleged driving reason. Left with a steel plate in his head, the singer of "Honeycomb" was unable to perform for a quarter century following what is believed to have been retaliation for asking (demanding?) his rightful pay from the owner on the Roulette label who recorded that blockbuster hit.

Yet another newcomer booked for the tour was (4) Ritchie Valens (née Richard Steven Valenzuela), a Chicano from East LA, who also died in that infamous small plane crash in Iowa on February 3, 1959, along with twenty-two-year-old Buddy Holly and the Big Bopper en route to a gig in North Dakota. Having just charted with "Donna," a paean to the impossibility of a relationship between a member of La Raza and a white woman during those years, the song became iconic along with "La Bamba," the B-side, a traditional Mexican wedding song. During Valens's tragically shortened career, he appeared in *Go Johnny Go*, one of five Alan Freed Rock 'n' Roll films. He was also the subject of a Hollywood biopic, *La Bamba*, with Lou Diamond Phillips portraying the singer.

Still other performers included these returnees: (5) Buddy Holly and the Crickets reunited; (6) Frankie Lymon still without the Teenagers—their separation, according to Marv Goldberg (*R&B Notebooks*, 2001, 2009), following a spring 1957 tour of Great Britain, when tensions resulted from his invitation to record on his own. "Pushed into a pop career," as Goldberg put it...the Teenagers officially parted ways with Frankie Lymon on August 14, 1957, after they recorded only twenty-two songs... Its former lead singer might well have performed "Thumb, Thumb" during Freed's final show here, a song recorded on Levy's Roulette label, and following what occurred on Freed's nationally syndicated Saturday-night TV Camels-sponsored *Rock 'n' Roll Dance Party* when the effervescent youngster spontaneously invited a white girl to dance on July 17, 1957, and commercial sponsors, fearing economic boycotts in the South, forced the show's cancellation!

Other returnees included (7) Larry Williams with his additional showmanship that included playing the keys of the piano while lying atop it flat on his back; (8) Screamin' Jay Hawkins; (9) Jo Ann Campbell; (10) the Diamonds, back again with their new hit, "The Stroll," performing what was originally recorded by Chuck Willis, tamer versions of the Cakewalk, and also in the Ritchie Valens biopic filmed in part in the Grand Lobby of the Wiltern Theatre in Los Angeles, another Rapp and Rapp over-the-top design, employed because of its similarity to our theatre's Grand Lobby.

But (11) Danny and the Juniors were making their only appearance here in 1958. They were Italian Americans from Philadelphia, who enjoyed only two huge Rock 'n' Roll perennial classic hits: "At the Hop" and "Rock 'n' Roll Is Here to Stay." Controlled by Dick Clark Productions, the deejay who like others defended his right to affix his name to the former song he alleged to have renamed "At the Bop." Be that as it may, lifelong depression suffered by this group's leader, Danny Rapp, led to his suicide in an Arizona hotel in 1983 (Jackson, 1997: 89–92).

Other nearly completely forgotten minor Rock 'n' Roll performers included: (12) Billie (Ford) and Lillie (Bryant), Black singers in the Mickey and Sylvia "Love Is Strange" mold who enjoyed moderate success with novelty hits like "La-De-Dah" and "The Monster"—each associated with touted new dances, a hybrid Cha-Cha called the Chalypso, for example, in the case of the former. And not only was their career also controlled by Dick Clark, his biographer related how that song bounced into the national top ten as a result of exposure on *American Bandstand* (Jackson, 1997: 99); (13) Dickie Doo and the Don'ts, a Caucasian Persuasion singing group from Philadelphia who enjoyed moderate success with "Click-Clack" and "Did You Cry" as a result of embeddedness within Clark's empire, was named for that powerhouse's deejay's children; (14) the Pastels, another little-known group of white singers whose lone (pop) hit was "Been So Long"; and the legendary pair of African American girl groups (15) the Chantels, who performed their all-time classic rock hit, "Maybe," and (16) the Shirelles, who were from Passaic, New Jersey.

The reporter at *Variety* (April 2, 1958) sent to the Brooklyn Paramount to review one of those shows issued a handful of pluses while otherwise bashing the rest as having no talent. Whatever he felt about Larry Williams doing a modified strip on stage following the half-hour intermission, the Shirelles were shockingly called small-time amateurs and he also snidely suggested that Alan Freed's Big Beat Orchestra leader, Sam "The Man" Taylor, who also recorded on Coral, ought to be investigated by Local 802 of the Musicians Union for what they played! The only other wisdom-type story about this Jubilee we found was the Big Bopper's playful hiding of Ritchie Valens's guitar without which he refused to go on stage...and which was returned in time during a backstage visit from him.

The name of the films shown at the Brooklyn Paramount during Freed's final show in our theatre were *Scared Stiff* paired with *Jumping Jacks*, both starring the '50s most famous American comedic team, Martin and Lewis.

D. Clay Cole and Others: Subsequent Rock 'n' Roll Shows at the Brooklyn Paramount

CLAY COLE (2009) (Clay Cole Archives)

"The Brooklyn Paramount is going after a new disk jockey."

That statement was how our theater's manager was quoted in *The New York Times* on November 12, 1958; that is, some months after the riot accompanying Freed's touring show in Boston on May 3, 1958, that stemmed from a quarrel between rival gang members spilled over into the street during a stampede of teenagers toward the exits and the stabbing of an innocent bystander. Despite Eugene Pleshette's abreaction that he wouldn't rent our theatre to the controversial deejay again, he booked several Rock 'n' Roll shows with other promoters... the first on Thanksgiving weekend.

Thus, for five days between November 26 and November 30, 1958, Ted Steele, a big-band leader was advertised in the *Williamsburg News* (November 14,1958) as promising "rock and roll favorites." Despite that the former radio host of a variety-type show on NBC's Blue Network in 1942, he went on to host *Teen Bandstand* and a TV quiz show on WOR during the 1950s, which refused to play Rock 'n' Roll records, Shaw's (1974: 155) ironic comment explained what followed: "Rock 'n' Roll had largely won the day." About Ted Steele's show here, *Variety* (November 12, 1958) discussed the mixed bag of known and unknown pop and Rock 'n' Roll performer.

(1) Barbara Evans recorded *Souvenirs* on RCA Victor the following year; (2) the Kalin Twins, Herbie and Harold, from Port Jarvis, New York, enjoyed a single modestly successful hit titled *When* in 1958; (3) the Shields, an otherwise obscure African American Doo-Wop-like singing group whose biggest hit was "You Cheated"; (4) the Clusters, yet another little-known African American group who'd covered the Mills Brothers' 1944 hit "Till Then"; (5) the Royaltones, similarly obscure (white) performers whose biggest Rock 'n' Roll hit song was "Poor Boy"; (6) Jerry Butler, who began as lead singer with the Impressions, probably singing "Your Precious Love," and who *Rolling Stone* counted among the magazine's Top 500 all-time Soul songs; (7) the Solitaires, an African American close harmony quintet whose single blockbuster (swinging) Rock 'n' Roll hit was "Walking Along"; and (8) the Big Bopper, who made his only appearance in our theater's earlier history as part of this mixed musical genre show.

The Big Bopper, née Jiles Perry "J. P." Richardson, a. k. a. Jape Richardson, was born in 1930 in Sabine Pass, Texas, and not only started out as a deejay and radio station program director in Beaumont, Texas, but also wrote Rock 'n' Roll songs as a sideline. "White Lightning," for example, recorded by the legendary country and western singer George Jones, among those...then after possibly still holding the record for broadcasting music for 120 consecutive hours, the Big Bopper came to occupy a permanent place in Rock 'n' Roll 's burgeoning history with his recording of "Chantilly Lace"—a humorous, largely spoken telephone conversation narrating the breakup of a romance. As part of his stage persona, the Big Bopper wore a Stetson and tentlike leopard-skin jacket and was comically addressed as Melvin. His tragic death along with Buddy Holly's and Ritchie Valens's in that fatal plane crash on that snowy night in an Iowa cornfield on February 3, 1959, while traveling to a gig was memorialized by Don McLean's elegiac song, "American Pie." Finally, the B-side of "Chantilly Lace" qualified as a Trivial Pursuit question: Name of its crowd-pleasing song? "Purple People Eater Meets Witch Doctor."

Still other performers presented by Ted Steele included: (9) Donnie Owens, whose birthplace was the same as Bill Haley's, Chester, Pennsylvania, and who had a single hit titled "Need You"; (10) the famous soul singer Lloyd Price made his first and only appearance... immortalized for his 1958 blockbuster hit, "(You've Got) Personality," and whose version of the folk classic "Stagger Lee" was retitled by "Stack A-Lee"; (11) Johnny Love; (12) Dickie Doo and the Don'ts, returnees, who incredulously charted that year with the novelty song "Née Née Na Na Na Na Nu Nu," no kidding, recorded and owned by Dick Clark, and which sold well thanks to that powerful figure's promotion; (13) Clyde McPhatter, who was back again a third time, possibly singing two of his biggest hits, "Treasure of Love" and "A Lover's Question," released in the following year. But what seems certain is that Steele wouldn't allow him to do "Sixty Minute Man" with its salacious lyrics.

(14) Jimmie Clanton, a. k. a. the Swamp Singer, was born in Baton Rouge, Louisiana, and was promoted as another white heartthrob by A and R men in those years. His good looks led to an appearance in Alan Freed's Rock 'n' Roll flick *Go Johnny Go*, and he was featured as part of

Dick Clark's touring Cavalcade of Stars (Jackson, 1997: 147–48). Clanton's two biggest Rock 'n' Roll hits were the dreamy ballads "Venus in Blue Jeans" and "Just a Dream"; (15) Concetta Rosa Maria Franconero, a. k. a. Connie Francis, who enjoyed a greater international pop status after Rock 'n' Roll recordings like "Who's Sorry Now" and "Stupid Cupid" during the 1950s and 1960s—and whose contralto was dubbed for Tuesday Weld in the *Rock, Rock, Rock* film; and finally (16) Francis Thomas Avalon, a. k. a. Frankie Avalon, began as a trumpet player in Philadelphia, and good looks alone were reportedly the reason he was recommended to Dick Clark by a close business confederate. A crossover star eventually, Avalon went on to a spectacular singing career with pop hits like "Venus." He also enjoyed acting roles in beach flicks alongside the most famous of all TV's Mouseketeers, Annette Funicello (Jackson, 1997: 62–64).

Those sixteen acts were backed by Ted Steele as the "Rockin' Band." The drummer role was nonetheless filled by William Randolph Cole, a. k. a. Cozy Cole, who began playing in Dixieland Jazz bands and lived long enough to engage in fierce drum battles with Gene Krupa at the Metropole Café in midtown Manhattan after the big band era. A review of Ted Steele's purported Rock 'n' Roll concert in our theatre in the *Williamsburg News* on December 1, 1958, spoke about the comedy of errors during the opening show. In addition to the reviewer's observation of four thousand empty seats—doubtless disappointing to all concerned—he also wrote about the bandleader's failed attempt to establish the correct tempo on one number, and that is counting it off for his band through handclaps as musicians frequently do, and which was then apparently followed by Ted Steele's embarrassingly redressing an unknown bandmember in full view of the band, which drowned out Lloyd Price's first song.

Gun Runners starring Audie Murphy was the title of the flick screened during that Thanksgiving week, and the *Williamsburg Times* (November 21, 1958) advertised Steele's mixed menu featuring seventy rock 'n' roll favorites. Our theatre's manager was quoted saying he refused to allow any advanced ticket sales for reserved seats, purportedly so those shows could be seen by the greatest number of holiday theatregoers.

Then after the payola scandal took down Alan Freed, Tommy Smalls, and several other prominent deejays in 1959, Clay Cole and Murray "the K" were involved in the promotion of three additional Rock 'n' Roll shows shortly before the Brooklyn Paramount's closing in 1962.

Née Albert Franklin Rucker Jr., Clay Cole was born in Youngstown, Ohio, and after precocious work as a youngster on local TV, he moved to the Big Apple hoping not unlike the characters in *Manhattan Cocktail* for success on Broadway. Instead, however, the twenty-two-year-old was hired to host *The Clay Cole Record Wagon* in 1960, an hour-long Monday–Saturday night 6:00 p.m. pop music show on WNTV (Channel, 13), during which teenagers not only rated songs from a variety of musical genres, but also danced to the music.

Recruited, as it were, to head the so-called fifth Beatle, Sid Bernstein, who booked those British mopheads' historic first concert in the United States, to emcee an Rock 'n' Roll show at the Brooklyn Paramount during what previously had been Freed's intended annual Christmas Jubilee. These mostly new (white) Rock 'n' Roll performers were featured between December 23, 1960, and January 2, 1961, by Clay Cole, whose curious explanation for the birth of Rock 'n' Roll deserves recitation: "Rhythm and Blues knocked up Country and Western music and produced the bastard child called Rock and Roll" (Cole, 2009: 57), and he credited an early Blues singer named Daniel "Honeyboy" Edwards as the honorary father of what Little Richard loved to describe Rock 'n' Roll as speeded up R & B, which he also claimed stood for "Real Black!" These performers appeared on stage here during Clay Cole's first of two Rock 'n' Roll shows at the Brooklyn Paramount.

(1) Bobby Rydell (née Robert Ridarelli), a nineteen-year-old musical phenom who not only created hits like "Lonely Teenager" and "Volare"—the latter originally titled "Sway"—but he also led the house band. In addition to having been discovered by Paul Whiteman on

former big-band leader's *TV-Teen Club* program while performing in an Rock 'n' Roll group called Rocco and His Saints that also featured Frankie Avalon on trumpet, Bobby Rydell went on to stardom by appearing in the enormously popular—and commercially successful—film *Bye Bye Birdie* in 1963. Given his south Philly roots and marketable good looks, he was also part of Dick Clark's stable of young white singers (Jackson, 1997: 149–50). Finally, Rydell successfully charted twenty singles that Arnold Shaw (1986: 97) wrote that dealt with the "self-contained world of ponytail and transistor radios, centered around high school." Those students' greatest concerns "were on the order of who would be going with whom to the dance"; (2) Dion Di Mucci, a. k. a. Dion, who was born in the Bronx and formerly led the Belmonts with these neighborhood Italian Americans cronies, Angelo de Aleo, Freddy Milano, and Carlos Mastrangelo, on their greatest hits "Wonder Why, A Teenager in Love," and "Runaround Sue," Dion appeared alone; (3) Neil Sedaka was born in Brooklyn, and after abandoning his earlier Julliard goal of performing Western Classical music as a pianist, he became one of Rock 'n' Roll's important second-generation stars...as a double threat singer and composers with "Calendar Girl," "Breaking Up Is Hard to Do," and "Oh, Carol" among successful recordings of his compositions and "Stupid Cupid" written for Connie Francis, "Since You've Been Gone" for Clyde McPhatter, and "I Cried For You" for LaVern Baker; (4) the Drifters, back again, though with Ben E. King as their lead singer, i.e., with chestnuts like "Under the Boardwalk," "Stand by Me," and "Up on the Roof"; (5) the Coasters making their first and only appearance on our theatre's stage as part of the Clay Cole Christmas Show in 1960–1961. Those former R-&-B-cum-Rock 'n' Roll-Hall-of-Fame singers from Los Angeles originally named the Robins enjoyed enormous success recording novelty hits written for them by Lieber and Stoller, e.g., "Smokey Joe's Cafe," "Along Came Jones," "Poison Ivy," "Charlie Brown," and "Searchin," and who Shaw (1974: 206) called the "most important of the black groups that crossed over...from black ghettoes into the pop teenage (white) world"; (6) the Shirelles, back again with wisdom stories by Clay Cole about this legendary African American girls group, whose major hits on Florence Greenberg's Tiara label include "Tonight's the Night," "Soldier Boy," "Dedicated to the One I Love," and "I Met Him on a Sunday"; (7) the Skyliners, new to our theatre and arguably as mellifluous as any close harmony singing group and whose signature hit was "Since I Don't Have You"; (8) Johnny Burnette, from the South, who made his debut probably with "Train Keep A-Rollin'," if not his biggest hits, "Dreamin' and You're Sixteen," "You're Beautiful," and "You're Mine"—the latter recorded live on stage here during one of these shows, and which was covered by Ringo Starr of the Beatles; (9) Ernest Evans, a. k. a. Chubby Checker, who remains indelibly identified with the Twist, a dance that inspired a national craze, but which was initially recorded by Hank Ballard (of the Moonlighters) two years earlier in 1958. Checker got to duel Clay Cole as dancers in a 1961 film titled *Twist Around the Clock*; (10) Kathy Young, a teenaged singer whose biggest—and most memorable—hit was "A Thousand Stars," a cover of the Rivileers' earlier original recording from 1954; (11) Bobby Vee (née Robert Thomas Velline), who was born in Fargo, North Dakota, a one-hit wonder with his Rock 'n' Roll hit "Run to Him"—lip synched on numerous occasions, such as on Dick Clark's *American Bandstand*, but who also holds the distinction of having given Robert Zimmerman his professional debut, i.e., allowing Bob Dylan to play background guitar in Bobby Vee's first band—the clean-cut latter replacing Buddy Holly at a gig the day after that fateful plane crash; (12) Jimmy Charles, who studied with the legendary Jazz crooner "Little" Jimmie Scott, and sadly was another forgotten Rock 'n' Roll one-hit performer with the ballad "A Million to One"; (13) Bo Diddley, back again for the fourth time and possibly heard on another single signature tune we neglected to cite, "Say Man"; (14) Dante and the Evergreens, a short-lived vanilla vocal group from Santa Monica, California, who became popular with their novelty song "Alley-Oop"; (15) Little Anthony (née Anthony Gourdine) and the Imperials, making their Brooklyn Paramount debut... the rebranded Duponts from the Fort Greene Housing Project in plain sight of our theater boasting having attended Alan Freed shows while attending Boys High School also in Brooklyn...with "Tears on My Pillow" and "Shimmy, Shimmy, Ko-Ko-Bop" among their greatest songs; (16) Brenda Lee (née Brenda Mae Tarpley), all four-foot-tall of her, began as the nine-year-old Little Brenda Lee, a rockabilly sensation from Atlanta, Georgia, whose biggest Rock 'n' Roll hit "I'm Sorry" would also chart as a country and western song...and whose music she would devote herself to for the rest of her career; and finally (17) Ray Charles, the megastar who lost his eyesight as a youngster and went on to incomparable success performing every popular musical genre...a sampling of his tunes including "Georgia," which was written by Hoagie Carmichael, "Hit the Road, Jack" and "What I Say"—the latter, belying Brother Ray's Gospel roots in the South. And this perennial future favorite about whom Duke Ellington could have been thinking while musing about great music of any ilk always being beyond category...the enormity of his success implied by the biopic starring Jamie Foxx in 2004, which only dealt with the first half of Ray Charles's life!

Illustrating Ellington's notion, Charles was quoted by a biographer:

Something else happened in this time slot: rock 'n' roll. I have a hard time defining schools of music, and I've been one to even try. I've been arguing against this my whole life—I hate it when they're slapped on me... I never considered myself part of rock 'n' roll. I didn't believe I was among the forerunners of the music... When I think of the true rock 'n' roll, cats like Chuck Berry and Little Richard and Bo Diddley come to mind... My stuff was more adult. It was more difficult for teenagers to relate to; so much of my music was sad or done... I don't want to put down the others, and I don't want to butter myself up...(but) They sold to whites by the truckloads. Rock 'n' roll was also music that the teenagers could play themselves... My music is more serious, filled with more despair than anything you'd associate with rock 'n' roll. (Charles and Ritz, 1978: 176–77)

Variety (January 11, 1961) reported that what was planned as a ten-day show did so well that two additional concert dates were added, and gate receipts totaled $180,000. *Thunder in Carolina* was screened during Clay Cole's Christmas show in 1960–1961.

Before discussing what was supposed to have been a second show emceed by him, these wisdom-like stories attached to place were found in Cole's memoir published in 2009, which this author was asked to proofread.

In the first of those four, we read that having arrived early in the morning during a bitterly cold December morning, he couldn't believe seeing a long line of young people anxiously awaiting admission to the theater, whose doors did not open until 10:00 a.m.

A second vignette purports to explain why he and Chuck Berry were allegedly banned from Junior's Restaurant located directly across the Flatbush Avenue Extension from the Brooklyn Paramount. As a result of being assigned a street-facing table with full view of the theatre, hordes of teenagers recognized the more famous of them and very nearly broke through the restaurant's window to get at Berry! "We had to do Chinese!" Or, so Clay Cole explained their alleged banishment from the restaurant.

Yet another has him treating the stagehands on Christmas Eve to drinks in a local pub out of gratitude for their hard work presumably at the Brooklyn Dodgers formerly on the southwest corner of DeKalb Avenue directly across from Junior's entrances. He also used to habituate and was known for "tipping the stagehands, the sound and light men, the fire marshal and the four spotlight operators from a paper bag with $10,000 in tens and twenties" (Cole, 2009: 153).

A fourth has that gregarious TV-quiz-and-teenage-dance-show host also telling us about having had to rush from his job in Newark to our theatre in time to repeat his number with the Dominoes. A stagehand pointed out that while hurriedly dressing in a tux, he'd left his fly open. "Now the world knows Clay Cole is circumcised!" was what he then humorously wrote while zipping up (Cole, 2009: 154)!

The next example involves the Shirelles, who Clay wrote with obvious nostalgia about having partied all night with Addie "Micki" Harris, Shirley Owens, Beverly Lee, and Doris Coley in their room at what was formerly the Granada Hotel on Lafayette Avenue. It was only a few blocks from his lodging in Brooklyn Heights, the former with its rooftop ballroom that featured a band and dancing on Saturday nights in the Forsythia Room, with advertisements of a "million dollars worth of entertainment." It was where Clay was presented with a red velvet smoking lounge given to him out of gratitude for the gig (Cole, 2009: 153–54).

Finally, Clay Cole wrote about another gift presented to him by the show's booking agent, Sid Bernstein, on behalf of gratitude for the financial success of the Rock 'n' Roll show's backer, Abe Margolies—a sapphire ring with twin diamonds (Cole, 2009).

That gift ironically proved to be a Judas-like offering...for what was supposed to have been a follow-up Clay Cole show in our theatre in 1961 from his purported close friend Sid Bernstein, who delivered this hammer during a Hansom cab ride around Central Park: regret that their wealthy benefactor had decided to replace him with Alan Freed's factotum, Murray "the K" Kaufman, on account that Clay Cole had lost his TV show after its station was taken over by public television, and hence, couldn't offer free advertisements for this upcoming 1961 blockbuster show as that other celebrity deejay could because of his successful radio show!

"Extra-added Attraction" was how Clay Cole consequently got listed in advertisements for that "Gala Easter Parade of Stars," which ran from March 31 to April 9, 1961, and was headed by Kaufman, who featured these essentially new second-generation Rock 'n' Roll performers.

(1) The Marcelles with their number one hit of the Tin Pan Alley standard "Blue Moon"; (2) Carla Thomas, a. k. a. the Queen of Memphis, a Stax record R-&-B-cum-Rock 'n' Roll singer, whose Doo-Wop song "Gee Whiz (Look at His Eyes)" was recorded with her father; (3) Rosie and the Originals, performing their biggest hit, "Angel Baby"; (4) the Capris ("When I Fall in Love"), another one-shot hit; (5) Mau-

rice Williams and the Zodiacs ("Stay"); (6) guitarist Del Shannon (née Charles Weedon Westover), who had an unusual instrumental blockbuster hit with "Runaway"; (7) the Olympics, yet another one-hit (vanilla) Rock 'n' Roll group singing their catchy number "Western Movies"; (8) The Isley Brothers, Ronald, O'Kelly, and Rudy, from Cincinnati, a nonpareil white group whose biggest hit was "Twist and Shout," performed in their imitative Black style ringlike shout; (9) Maxine Brown, a genuine throwback R & B performer who enjoyed a single Rock 'n' Roll hit, "All in My Mind"; and (10) Little Anthony and the Imperials, back again singing their newest hit, "I'm Alright."

Appearing only during the first five days of this ten-day show were the following seventeen advertised guest stars:

(11) Ben E. King, another returnee; (12) Chubby Checker, ditto, albeit with his newest dance promotion, "The Pony"; (13) the Shirelles, back for a third time; (14) Chuck Jackson, an R & B singer whose biggest Rock 'n' Roll hit was "My Pride"; (15) Dion, also returning as a soloist; (16) Bobby Vee ("Suzie Baby" and "Take Good Care of My Baby"); (17) Freddy Cannon (née Frederick Picariello), another vanilla one-hit wonder with "Tallahassee Lassie"; (18) Ray Peterson, singing his only immensely hit song, "Tell Laura I Love Her"; (19) Andy Rose ("A Rose and a Thorn"); (20) Johnny Burnette ("You're Sixteen"), yet another returnee; (21) Jimmy Clanton, also back again with his new song, "Down the Aisle"; (22) Johnny Tillotson, who had nine top hits, "Poetry in Motion" and "It Keeps on Hurting" most famously among those; (23) Frank Gari (née Frank Daniel Garafola), a songwriter who sang his biggest hit, "Utopia," and would write for those all-time famous British Rockers, Roger McGuinn and the Byrds; (24) Bobby Rydell ("Cloud Baby" and "Wild One"), another returnee who apparently appeared only on three of those five dates, April 7, 8, and 9; (25) the Landon Sisters ("I'm Flipped for You"); (26) Bobby Bongard; and last, though hardly the least, (27) John Royce Mathis. Born in Gilmer, Texas, the former high school track and field star—high hurdles and long-distance runner—who went on to become a mega pop recording star in the 1950s with a cascade of top ten hits

like "Wonderful, Wonderful"; "It's Not for Me to Say"; and "A Certain Smile" were called by Mathis his trinity. The same was true for "Misty," "Twelfth of Never," and "Chances Are"...but Johnny Mathis missed his first two scheduled sets on account of inclement weather during his scheduled flight to New York from Miami Beach and was reported as promptly leaving for San Francisco after fulfilling the other half of his contractual obligation.

Beyond All Limits (starring Jack Palance) was the featured film screened during this Rock 'n' Roll, which *Variety* (April 12, 1961) reported to have netted $173,000 during those ten days—for the music, not the film!

Finally, we arrive at this last Rock 'n' Roll show during the Brooklyn Paramount's fabled thirty-four-year beginning history. Called the "Big Boss Holiday Show," the allusion was to Murray "the K," an over-the-top deejay who dropped out of high school and was a six-time married World War II veteran who replaced Freed on WINS. The host of concerts he called soirees, Kaufman employed jive talk on the radio and the stage that famously included expressions like, "What's happening, baby?" His epigonal Alan Freed–like Labor Day show that ran between August 25 and September 5, 1961, and which advertised these seventeen smash acts while remaining sociologically interesting as a result of the predominantly white performers at this Rock 'n' Roll show.

(1) Clarence "Frogman" Henry, a New Orleans singer whose falsettos imitate a woman's voice and a Tibetan-like monk's singing method by inhaling rather than exhaling, as described by Winner (1980: 40), who also described his voice as sounding like a frog croaking. Henry's single popular Rock 'n' Roll hit in 1958, "Ain't Got No Home," was recorded on Lew Chudd's Imperial indie label in Cosimo Matassa's famous studio in the Crescent City. Finally, Frogman Henry opened for the Beatles on sixteen or more occasions; (2) the Vibrations, also newcomers and whose biggest hit was "The Watusi," which *Variety* questionably described as a "wily Negro dance group that also clowns around"; (3) the Regents, another vanilla group, who sang their big-

gest hit, "Barbara Ann"; (4) Val Donner, also an arriviste and another largely forgotten performer, performing "You Don't Know What You Got till You Lose It"; (5) Frank Gari ("Lullaby of Love"); (6) Brian Hyland, who did the enormously popular novelty hit in those years titled "Itsy Bitsy Teeny Weeny Yellow Polka Dot Bikini" as well as the lush ballad "Sealed with a Kiss," recorded a year after his performance here; (7) Bruce Bruno ("Venus in Blue Jeans"); (8) Curtis Lee, still another newcomer, whose short career contained hits like "Pretty Little Angel Eyes" and "Under the Moon of Love," famously recorded by Phil Spector; (9) the Chantels from the Bronx led by Arlene Smith, who recorded one of Rock 'n' Roll 's all-time classic hits, "Maybe," four years prior; (10) Michael Anthony Orlando Cassivitiss a. k. a. Tony Orlando, whose major hits were "Tie a Yellow Ribbon 'Round the Old Oak Tree," the accumulation of its penny-like royalties jumpstarting Morris Levy's wealth...that before the singer formed Tony Orlando and Dawn, a crowd-pleasing popular duo; (11) Dion and the Belmonts reunited for this return engagement in our theatre; (12) Linda Scott, who went gold with "I've Told Every Little Star"; (13) Ral Donner, whose birth name was Ralph Stuart Emmanuel Donner, and who had a single hit titled "You Don't Know What You've Got (Until You Lose It)"...an Elvis-like impersonation that would in time land him the starring role as the King in Presley's biopic titled *This Is Elvis*.

Four Rock & Roll Hall of Famers complete the list of seventeen acts: (14) Jerry Lee Lewis, also a returnee; (15) the Cleftones, back again for a record-setting sixth appearance; and (16) Etta James and (17) Jackie Wilson, each of whom also deserve special mention.

Etta ("At Last") James (née Jamasetta Hawkins) was the powerful R-&-B-cum-Rock 'n' Roll-singer-cum-Jazz-diva, who previously recorded "Betty and Dupree," "I Hope You're Satisfied," and "If It Ain't One Thing" in duets with Harvey Fuqua of the Moonglows on Chess in 1959, and also "If I Can't Have You and My Heart Cried" on her own in the following year. A Blues shouter, Etta James (1995) wrote in a powerful autobiography about her overcoming a lifelong drug addiction that led to multiple arrests and her conversion to the

Nation of Islam. More importantly for our concerns, however, not only was her account of friendship with Larry Williams but also the spat with Murray "the K" during this show. After being talked out of quitting by the show's closer, Jackie Wilson, this blunt-talking woman, who happened to be the daughter of famed pool hustler Minnesota Fats, wrote:

> When Murray "the K" was about to kick me off the bill at the Brooklyn Paramount for talking back to him, Jackie stepped in, called his valet, Frazier—who came from the Midnighters—and said, "Pack my bags, I'm leaving with Etta." So Murray "the K" shut up quick. (James, ibid: 92)

Finally, Jack Leroy "Jackie" Wilson, dubbed "Mr. Excitement" as such, if only as a result of modeling his act on Al Jolson's hyperfrenetic performance style. Indeed, one of Jackie Wilson's twenty-nine recorded albums was recorded by the previous show-business megastar. His agility as a dancer while performing was influenced by his few years as a professional boxer. Wilson replaced Clyde McPhatter as the lead singer of the Drifters before launching a solo career, which saw "Lonely Teardrops" as the first of a string of successive, blockbuster crossover hits. However, his up-and-down career was initially managed by Nat Tarnopol, another reputed mob-affiliated figure in early Rock 'n' Roll history followed by an involvement with Morris Levy (Douglas, 2001: 126–27). Other huge hits included "Your Love Keeps Lifting Me Higher," which contained the proverbial cry in Jackie Wilson's inimitable singing voice. But after recovering from a gunshot wound by a deranged female fan, this nonstop dynamo performer unfortunately never recovered from a stroke experienced on stage at the start of a nostalgic Good Ol' Rock 'n' Roll/Doo-Wop concert in New Jersey in 1975 organized by Dick Clark (Jackson, 1997: 263).

Film shown that week? *Posse from Hell*, costarring Audie Murphy and John Saxon, as *Variety* (August 30,1961) reported that Murray "the K's" second soiree at the Brooklyn Paramount netted $149,860.

Despite the trade magazine's account of its successful bottom line, Gene Pleshette was quoted in a tabloid saying the earnings from Murray "the K's" Rock 'n' Roll show here were disappointing.

MURRAY THE "K" (*The Brooklyn Times*, April 7, 1961)

A fitting end to the longest chapter in this book about the fourth face—unintended as it were, though arguably proper if only as a result of the association of Alan Freed's Jubilees at the Brooklyn Paramount, we close with what the late Mary Lai, Long Island University's lifelong forever CFO, told us about her financial arrangements with the manager regarding those and other shows here owned by our alma mater since 1950.

Our knowledgeable and trustworthy consultant told us how she decided to tear up their original contract, and instead of charging Pleshette an extra 15 percent above their agreement to pay $100,000 for each booking depending on ticket sales, she said they settled on a flat rental fee of the theatre for $125,000 plus costs incurred for heat and/or air-conditioning, accordingly, as measured by special meters Mrs. Lai installed in the theatre for those purposes. These divergent (though not necessarily contradictory) views were from Eugene Pleshette, who traded in his background in music publishing and record production for employment at Paramount in 1934 and became house manager at Manhattan's Paramount in 1940 before taking over the Brooklyn Paramount in 1945... First, Mrs. Lai's affectionate recollection recalled how he charmingly addressed her as "Marie, Marie, My Dear Marie" while transacting business, and did not fail to send confirmation gifts for each of her two sons' baptisms; the second being Clay Cole's characterization of him as "a stylist showman of the old school and tyrant who intimated dollar-a-day uniformed ushers about keeping order among teenagers in the theatre" (Cole, 2009); last, the following from Sid Bernstein:

> Gene Pleshette was not a guy to be crossed. In Yiddish, we'd call him a no-*chochomas* guy. No fooling around. What you see is what you get. When Gene told the ushers and staff to control the kids, that's exactly what they did. There was no jumping on the seats (like) at the New York Paramount. (Bernstein and Aaron, 1993: 164)

Whether Smalls or Freed ultimately should be credited with effecting the sea change discussed and hypothesized in this chapter, the safer course might go to that insider from those years, Jerry Wexler (1993: 62), who wrote "it's as though he (Freed) lit the fuse that exploded R & B into full-force Rock 'n' Roll."

PART III

OTHER "FACES"

CHAPTER 9

The Mighty Wurlitzer and Community Sing-Alongs

A case can also readily be made that "The Mighty Wurlitzer" and community sing-alongs were another distinctive face of the Brooklyn Paramount's earlier history. Esther Morgan-Ellis (2018: 130) claimed as much in her study of that popular audience-participation event commencing in 1928 when Paramount introduced community singing to Brooklyn, i.e., our wonder theatre.

Custom built for the theatre with apparent input by Jesse Crawford, the Wurlitzer 4–26 Opus #1984 in the "Publix 4" style was similar to two other so-called unit orchestras, one of which apparently vanished, while the other sat disused in the Boston Metropolitan Theater. Ours not only proudly remains, but in addition to retaining mostly original parts, it until recently was still played. An excellent chapter titled "Apotheosis of the Mighty Wurlitzer" can be found in the incomparable history of wonder theatres like ours written by Ben Hall (1961: 178–95). Another invaluable published source dealing with the complexities of this dinosaur-like extinct musical instrument was an article titled "Organ Equals 200-Piece Symphony Calling Upon 800

Instruments" by Raymond Puckett (1928) found in so-called "Pep-O-Grans," an in-house Paramount publication. Readers are also advised to consult YouTube for lecture-demonstrations of the technical complexities of our pipe organ by Joe Amato, the current crew chief of a team of volunteers from TOSA, the Theater Organ Society of America, which formed in 1964 and remains committed to keeping these relics playable. Finally, yet another invaluable resource is or will be this author's interview with the Mighty Wurlitzer's previous caretaker, Warren Liberati, whom we interviewed in 2009 at the console when we also videotaped one of its four pipe chambers high atop the wings of the stage, which will be dropped on YouTube after the publication of this book.

A useful starting point is found in Puckett's (1928) account:

> The organ at the Brooklyn Paramount equals a two-hundred-piece symphony. Wurlitzer the organ builder considers the organ his masterpiece. Each of the five [*sic*] manuals of keys has a double touch that multiplies its sound possibilities. Nearly eight hundred instruments can be called into play through its intricate mechanisms which cover both walls.

Continuing as such, our consultant, Warren Liberati, insisted that Brooklyn Paramount's management work a deal with Wurlitzer to purchase two consoles for $35,000, i.e., rather than the usual $60,000 price. Both rolltop-like desks were reportedly built with instructions from Jesse Crawford, a mainstay performer in subsequent years. Be that as it may, ours not only are outnumbered with more than two thousand pipes but are also dominated both in size and number by Manhattan-Paramount's three pipe organs. In any event, we can only briefly sketch some of our theatre's Mighty Wurlitzer's technical marvels from what we learned from that twenty-year dedicated craftsman as well as what we additionally learned from Joe Amato, before discussing ways in which it, along with the unfortunately smaller slave console, was used during the Brooklyn Paramount's relatively brief Vaudeville years and related community sing-alongs, which were revived.

THE MIGHTY WURLITZER (Stuart Fishelson Archives)

Robert Hope-Jones was the visionary who set out in England to transform the "King of the Instruments" heard for centuries in churches into something entirely different—a musical instrument (sadly) able to replace instruments and entire orchestras backing Silent Films by different technical means. An electrician by profession, employed by his nation's telephone company, formed after Alexander Graham Bell's and Thomas Alva Edison's invention of the telephone, Hope-Jones became an expat and through life circumstances sold his revolutionary new patent to a German American named Rudolph Wurlitzer in 1910, following the relocation in 1903 to Elmira, New York. Wurlitzer's original church organ factory was in Cincinnati, Ohio, where Hope-Jones secured work. By 1928, however, the factory had moved to North Tonawanda, a suburb of Buffalo, New York, where the Hope-Jones Unit Orchestra, which was essentially completed in 1890, joined other companies like Robert Morton, Adams, Etsy, Kimball, and Marr-Colton competing to satisfy the growing demand of two thousand movie theatres that employed them as accompaniment during the golden era of Silent Films...The Criterion among those in Harlem in 1913, for example, were designed by Samuel "Roxy" Rothapfel.

Not unlike the demise of Vaudeville, some twenty-eight thousand musicians lost their livelihoods after unit orchestras replaced orchestras, the Wurlitzer went out of vogue with the advent of the Talkies and live music heard on the radio. The upshot being that the Wurlitzer company was forced to retool and began profitably selling jukeboxes, violins, electric guitars, and recorded organ music still prevalent on merry-go-round carousels. Employing the body as a metaphor, however, to sketch some of the technical complexities of that totalizing musical instrument that not only essentially works on the principal of electric-magnetism to generate sound by manuals or stacked keyboards through forced air to detached pipes that essentially differentiates these from church organs, a useful summary by Hall (1961: 181–2) is a good launching pad for this discussion. His description of pipe organs as operating "by means of an intricate system of switches and relays, made in possible for every rank (pipes) to be played from every manual, and at different octave pitches...(and thus leading to new) ways to combine ranks into voices or stops...(as well as completely new solo voices)."

We begin this metaphor with the pentadactyl precision and power-gripping human hand, the result of millions of years of primate evolution, quintessential for playing our theatre's Mighty Wurlitzer's four keyboards (or manuals) consisting of half the pianoforte's eighty-eight keys stacked upon each other and displayed on a horseshoe-like curved wood framed structure decorated by colorful scrolls. For both hands not only are required to press down on 224 black and white keys but also pull down 247 levers individually named (and numbered) for specific musical instrument facsimiles, as well as pulling on a dozen or so buttons called pistons, also called resets, and six smaller button-like stops, also called shoes, that additionally are involved in the generation of sound. And lightly so, at least in the case of pianoforte-like keys, insofar a coin placed on any of the four keyboards, according to Puckett (ibid.), was all it took to cause booming!

In addition to hands on those four keyboards individually named from top to bottom as Bombard, Solo, Great, and Accompaniment for volume and such, the skilled organists' feet also work nineteen duckboard wooden swell pedals, vertically positioned side by side, which replace the pianoforte's dampening and sustaining pedals. Or, in the case of the Brooklyn Paramount's 4/26, which was shipped on June 30,1928, it required six months assemblage time. Those floor-board features are employed for what our other consultant, the skilled accordionist-cum-organist Joe Amato, calls or likens to strictly bass functions.

Continuing with this metaphor, the head or brains are vertically standing sound boards found in the organ's control room located behind loge seating facing stage right, which contain tiny magnets that ultimately relay signals through electrically wired transmissions and pneumatic switches originating from quadrupedal-like performers, who, in other words, do not technically produce music while playing, but rather send electric signals to the lungs, i.e., a blower still manu-factured by the Spencer Company in Connecticut, half the size of a jet engine, and housed in the basement said to match the equivalent of a twenty horsepower motor pushing an estimated five thousand cubic feet per minute of air along hidden ducts in the theatre to those two thousand pipes operating like ears and mouth, if you will. The latter, still stacked two-by-two and found in four rooms high atop both sides of the stage hidden by curtains and reachable only by daredevil technicians like the aforementioned Warren Librati, who probably broke insurance regulations by allowing me to follow him on two steep, mitered ladders to the top chamber whose verticality a moun-tain sheep might find daunting, and where only six hundred among those twenty-six ranks in 2009 were in working order. Naming those we find: English Horn; Clarinet; Saxophone; Solo String number one; Solo String number two; Gamba; Gamba Celeste; Viol D'Orchestra; Viol Celeste; Krumet; Concert Flute; Vox Humana (Main Chamber); Vox Humana (Solo); Tuba Mirabilis; Trumpet; Tuba Horn; Diaphonic Diapason; Open Diapason; Tibia Clausa (Foundation); Tibia Clausa (Solo); Orchestral Oboe; Kinura; Dulciana; Quintadena; Oboe Horn; Horn Diapason.

Before getting stuck further in the technical muck, our consultants remind us that the theatre organ's pipes require twelve volts of direct current and eight thousand amps dependent on box fans for cooling purposes, and that another clue toward any understanding of the Mighty Wurlitzer is by keeping in mind that "everything is dependent on wind pressure and valves and reservoirs that balance sound"…and what Amato, the retired NYC detective in charge today of repairs, and who keeps the Mighty Wurlitzer under strict lock and key, also wants known that it should be called a "the-a-ter" not a church organ, or else!

Nor should a second relay room in the basement (also facing stage right) be ignored, if only since it allows prerecorded organ music to be scored and programed in advance of usage, and that venetian-like vertical slats covered by curtains high on both sides of the orchestra also controlled the volume of sound. Whether an additional innovative feature of the Brooklyn Paramount or not, their actions were visibly illuminated in the darkened movie theatre.

Turning next to what originally were two thousand pipes ultimately responsible for the sound of music that replaced individual instruments. The pipes differed in thickness, height, and manufacture from bamboo and copper. Housed stage-facing right and left in four chambers stacked high above each other, those pipes housed stage-left facing and were called the Foundation atop the Main Chamber while on the opposite side of the stage there remains the Solo atop the "Orchestral Chamber" containing those assorted ranks.

Suffice, then, to note here that those are manufactured of bamboo and copper, the pencil-thin smallest of bamboo capable of reproducing flutes and piccolos, whereas the largest metal pipes, thirty-two feet tall into which a person could fit and necessarily held together with leather binding, captured the booming dynamics of brass instruments like the trumpet, trombone, French horn, etc. And along with the Mighty Wurlitzer's capability to reproduce reed-like European-manufactured musical instruments like the clarinet, oboe, and stringed instruments like the viola, violin, double bass, et al., in the stage-right-facing upper chamber activated by organists seated below in the orchestra, these additional features also deserve mention: so-called toys, for example, mimicking the glockenspiel, xylophone, marimba, vibraphone, sleigh bells, and chimes; traps, a complete drum kit with cymbals played with mechanical hands; and pipes in the left chamber capable of re-creating sounds that only an ethnomusicologist we dare say can discuss: the gamba and gamba celeste and other non-Western instruments. And finally, the Mighty Wurlitzer also was capable of dramatically accompanying Silent Films with the nonmusical sound of fire engines, doorbells, rain splattering on a roof, galloping horses, the calls of recognizably distinct species of birds (e.g., canaries), and the *vox humana*, Latin for "human voice," also effectuated by pulling a stop. Or, as Puckett (1928) also wrote: "When the organist is making the most of the instrument, the effect is the equivalent of an 800-piece symphony orchestra."

Turning now instead to reports about what the Mighty Wurlitzer and adjoining console played during our theatre's Vaudeville years and beyond, Henry Murtagh commanded that throne-like revolving Howard stool on opening night, while George Johnson played that second smaller Wurlitzer, whose sound was entirely dependent on the former, and unique because it could be removed from its separate lift stage-right facing and operated on stage. Those organists, as we also saw dueted on "Stars Are the Window of Heaven," while Murtagh, as reported in that typewritten manuscript about the Brooklyn Paramount's opening in our possession, additionally demonstrated "the various sounds a Wurlitzer could make, and in this apparent order": (1) sampled instruments from the Western symphonic orchestra (violins, et al); (2) a German band playing "Ach Du Leiber Augustine"; (3) a "workout on the Vox Humana," which reportedly began with a solo crooning lullaby; (4) a darky quartet humming "Suwannee River" that less offensively included tricks like bird calls, dogs barking, cats fighting, the harp, a drum, and bugle corps, a choo-choo train, three kinds of auto horns, steamboat whistles, Scotch bagpipes, calliope, the inevitable organ grinder's organ, the xylophone, and a marimba band; and finally (5) after he put them all together in the "Poet and Peasant Overture," the master organist was joined by Johnson on a rendition of "Stars and Stripes Forever"…a performance during which, according to the review of opening night found in *Variety* (op cit.), "the house shook with applause." Finally, along with being featured during the week of April 6, 1929, in an organ-versus-orchestra battle, Murtagh performed Christmas tunes in those years, whether or not sing-alongs.

Esther M. Morgan-Ellis (2018: 180) wrote "community sing-a-longs" and contrasted the Brooklyn Paramount with Manhattan-Paramount, which did not permit that era's karaoke. Moreover, she wrote that even before the lyrics associated with Mitch Miller's "follow the bouncing ball" community sing-alongs of the 1950s originated two decades prior by the screen animist Max Fleisher, and his innovation not only was projected onto the stage scrim by theatre projectionists in the balcony, but also were sold much like sheet music in the lobby ever since the Tin Pan Alley years in the 1920s. Dedicated Mighty Wurlitzer concerts were held before the first complete "vaude-cine" packaged shows.

Discounting the other borough's snobbery and our theatre management's continued family-like advertisement of place, *Exhibitor's Herald World* on February 1, 1930 (p. 54), for example, reported Bob West's sing-along during which audiences reportedly sang "My Fate Is in Your Hands," "Love Made a Gypsy Out of Me," and "Singin' in the Bathtub" accompanied by his playing—the latter pop tune with so-called projected gag slides and instructions that also called for "Everybody (to) get out In the aisle and dig." And one month prior, *Variety* (January 15, 1930) reported him having swiveled around on his risen seat and invited the theatre's audience to stick around for after-hours original radio programming on stage, with the implied or explicit come-on that their voices would therefore be heard nationwide.

Other concertizing teams over those years included West and Elsie Thompson (*Brooklyn Daily Times*, November 17, 1929); Thompson and

Don Baker reported on April 27, 1930, leading morning sing-alongs on both organs while Earl Abel "gives his organ concert at each show"; the world-famous Jesse Crawford, who made his debut here on July 10, 1931, and was also paired with Elsie Thompson; Stuart Barrie and Elsie Thompson, (September 9, 1933); Arthur Gutow and Joy Rush in 1933; Gutow and Deloris Del Rio, who usually performed on the neighboring Fox Theatre's organ; Merle Clarke and Tom Lillus (1933); Earl Abel and Elsie Thompson; Dick Liebert (the jolly prince of the organ) paired with Thompson; and finally Merle Clarke and Elsie Thompson (1933) during most of years 1931 and 1932, and who somehow did a puppet show on those keyboards, while on another occasion they performed a special arrangement of a popular song, "Rain on the Roof." Both organists "will demonstrate the various production and musical values of the two organs." But, also, they performed together on a piece titled *Home*, which was said to have signaled the onset of the stage show—a musical cue that, in lieu of an emcee, served to introduce the final Vaudeville act that evening, the "Romeo of Song," Russ Columbo.

Some examples of their combined playing researched in Morgan-Ellis (2018: 100–101) include Elsie Thompson and Earl Abel with a parody of the Civil War song "When You and I Were Young, Maggie" in 1930, which reportedly had the audience rolling, and six false starts by Thompson and Merle Clark in 1931 after introducing "Making Faces at the Moon" with a similar affect. She also wrote that from its opening, the rage among Brooklyn Paramount audiences in 1928 was singing the novelty song "I Faw Down 'n' Go Boom" (Morgan-Ellis, 2018: 152).

Returning however to Jesse Crawford, who often performed in tandem with his wife, he was a self-taught orphan born in Woodlawn, California, and performed in Silent Film theaters on the West Coast before moving to Chicago, where "The Poet of the Organ" met Helen Anderson, an organist as well working unit orchestras in the Windy City's movie palaces. And while, according to Morgan-Ellis (2018: 150), community sing-alongs and "song plugging was not (Jesse) Crawford's idea, as a Paramount employee, he was obliged to promote Paramount-Prolix products, including songs from Paramount films and music that was available at the theatre." All the same, he found ways of protesting sing-alongs by starting and stopping ballads otherwise performed as standalones (Morgan-Ellis, 2018: 153). Helen Anderson-Crawford was the opposite. For while her husband also preferred light operatic tunes, she turned Tin Pan Alley tunes like "Within the Passion of my Dreams" into hot or syncopated Jazz-like numbers. In that regard, Hall (1961: 185) cited *Variety*, which spoke about her encouraging audience requests for Jazz numbers during their previous stint at Manhattan-Paramount—Mrs. Jesse Crawford then ragging "The Black Bottom", a popular dance originating like so many others in Harlem, as well as "This Is My Lucky Day" and "Blue Skies." Presumably this also occurred on the other side of the East River in downtown Brooklyn, where the trade magazine reported on February 12, 1930, that he also played pop tunes like "A Love Tale to Alsace Lorraine," "All By Yourself in the Moonlight," "Marie," and "If I Had You"—the latter was recorded by Rudy Vallée in 1928. Another source, however, *Motion Picture News*, reported that on January 12, 1929, after Jesse performed "Cradle of Love" as a solo on the Mighty Wurlitzer, Helen teamed up with him on the smaller console and they both played "Ragging the Scales," a community sing-along that came with lyrics probably on decorative Maurice Workset–manufactured color slides projected onto the scrim for audience participation during their seven-minute Vaudeville portion. All the same, even though Morgan-Ellis also wrote that the common practice of song plugging was not Jesse Crawford's own idea, she reported he was "obliged to promote Paramount-Publix products, including songs from Paramount films and music that was made for purchase at the New York Paramount theater." It was a practice, as she also reminds us, found in all the major studios during the heyday of Vaudeville, so by inference also at the Brooklyn Paramount.

In any event, song fests continued here at least through the week of April 9, 1933, when Bob (The Man You'll Love to Sing With) West was once again reported leading them. Among his ways of engaging audiences, West reportedly might enjoin laughing contests as a result of special lyrics to "That's My Weakness Now" that replaced most words with 'ha-ha" as well as encouraged laughing contests between men and women in the audience. However, unlike the other organists, Bob West also reportedly introduced a new style of interaction with audiences: by turning around to face them and encourage their singing and employing the theatre's new public address system while standing alongside the console (Hall, 1961).

Here are additional words about the Mighty Wurlitzer and community sing-alongs that nonetheless marked the difference between Brooklyn and Manhattan-Paramount locations during their respective Vaudeville years.

First, *Variety*'s reminder of our theatre's "downtown fixture audiences...as family life" on January 15, 1930, and the trade magazine's additional characterization of Brooklyn Paramount "as line no other neighborhood crowd anywhere." And while also speaking about Bob West as the permanent solo organist and the man you love to sing with, its reviewer added: "From responses at the show reviewed, the billing seemed deserved. Via slides, West informed the full house that to become stage stars, they must also read Haas (slides) besides sing songs congregationally." Along with describing "one line for the girls and the next for the boys," he was prompted to jibe: "Sounded like a bunch of kids in kindergarten, so willingly did they follow the teacher." And, finally, he reported the theatrical manner during which "West turns around and uses his audience to talk and encourage better vocal outbursts. And they love it."

A second Mighty Wurlitzer wisdom story attached to place described Helen Crawford wearing her dress backward as if for comic effect while organists raised and lowered themselves on that unit orchestra still housed on a stage-left facing below the former orchestra floor deliberately for laughs.

And not only do we read in an unsourced journal about the booming power of the Mighty Wurlitzer created by only the placement of a thin dome on one of its four keyboards, yet another relevant factoid about our theatre's unique musical instrument was that its solo concertizing during Vaudeville was transmitted to the Hotel Paramount on Saturday evenings during the Paramount Radio Hour. During the week of January 3, 1930, we also read about a "novel radio broadcast accompaniment for the organ numbers."

Before turning to radio as another face of our theatre's earlier history, nearly a decade after Vaudeville at the Brooklyn Paramount had ceased and the Mighty Wurlitzer had been kept in storage (along with the theatre's valuable art and furniture collections), we read in the *Brooklyn Eagle* on December 26,1946, about that New Year's Eve anticipated "return of in-person entertainment...together with audience-participation singing led by Tom Avery at the organ at every performance beginning at 6:00 p.m.," i.e., prior to the final screening of *Blue Skies* starring Bing Crosby cofeatured with *Wife Wanted*. And whether or not a subsequent annual occurrence, six years later, another organist, Robert McCoombs, was similarly hired to entertain audiences on New Year's Eve in 1951.

Finally, we end this chapter with the words of master organist Tom Hazelton, about our theatre's Mighty Wurlitzer heard in a Voice of America production on July 26, 1996:

This organ was built to do one thing: accompany silent films. It was not really conceived to do anything else, but it does many other things beautifully. It plays orchestral type of music, show tunes, classical, and is really one of a kind.

CHAPTER 10

Radio Ears

The late sports broadcaster Art Rust Jr. used to speak about having *seen* boxing matches on the radio. Unusual as this chapter heading might seem, we borrow and paraphrase his viewpoint. Another explanation was Woody Allen's 1987 nostalgic family comedy *Radio Days*, which illustrated the power of that new medium and opened with a Jewish middle-class family in Rockaway, Brooklyn, gathered around that cabinetry-like furniture that, pre-TV, used to occupy a central living room place...listening to the plight of a child who'd fallen into a well. This title also refers to those lagomorph-like antennae used for improved TV reception during the early years of that succeeding type of mass media.

For radio, as E. B. White memorably noted about Guglielmo Marconi's 1897 invention of aerial telegraphy (radio) recalled in an essay titled *Sabbath Morn* in 1933 also figured prominently in the Brooklyn Paramount's earlier history, i.e., the electrical phenomenon, which posed a threat to Vaudeville's live entertainment on stage. White memorably likened radio to a chief pretender to the throne of God, after it regularly came into people's lives and homes. H. L. Mencken (2000: 559) traced wireless telegraphy's contribution to the making of

mass media in America following its development in Berlin in 1906...
how it was banned during World War I because of fear that the construction of the Eiffel Tower would allow radio to be used for sabotage
by Axis powers during the First World War.

Among the earliest American radio stations was WJZ in Newark. It
was owned by Charles B. Popenoe, and on July 31, 1927, in the *Brooklyn
Eagle* we were informed he set up shop with a five-hundred-watt gen-
erator on the roof of a building to broadcast the Dempsey-Carpentier
Heavyweight Championship bout in 1921 close by in Jersey City, New
Jersey. The World Series came one year later, and the idea of broadcasting baseball games joined live musical performances in capturing
the public's imagination. Then eleven years later, NBC set up shop in
Rockefeller Center, which was built in 1933, a year when fifty thousand
radios were reportedly found in American households. And soon after,
that figure dramatically increased to twenty-two million sets!

Issues regarding professional licensing that also occurred in
pharmacy, law, dentistry, and this author's profession were part and
parcel of radio's beginnings. Yet despite its original contributions by
ham radio operators while helping ships at sea with weather reports,
another early battle concerned radio's potential for broadcasting
mixed informational media. This included news and educational lectures opposed to its commercial potential. Madison Avenue, needless
to say, eventually triumphed over the Radio Fund Committee, which
formed in New York City in 1924 around the same time as the formation of CBS (the Columbia Broadcast System) followed by RCA, the
Radio Corporation of America, two years later (Hilms, 1997).

Print journalism somewhat surprisingly contributed to the popularity of early radio...with the *Chicago Tribune* apparently the first
major newspaper to take advantage of loyal readers' attachment to
daily reading of comic strips as well as broadcasts about the news
and scheduled hours of emergent popular radio programs. As a result,
Warner Brothers leapfrogged ahead of rival studios by purchasing
WKFB, a radio station in 1925, as well as their pioneering stride regarding sound in films and Vitascope features.

The same held true for one of the wonder theatres in downtown Brooklyn in that same year, the Mark Strand Theater, which on March 22, 1925, "brought to Brooklyn theatergoers last week...the first actual radio studio settings that have been presented on the stage of any theater." Not surprisingly, the fiercely competitive Adolph Zukor overcame initial suspicions about the damage radio might do to vaude-film houses in his sprawling chain of some 1,500 theatres here and around the world by directing Paramount officials to acquire its own station.

Moving ahead to November 25, 1928, then, the very day after the Brooklyn Paramount's opening, *The New York Times* reported a truce between Brooklyn's four warring stations, WCGU, WLTH, WSGH, and WBBC. "First terms of the agreement were WBBC's broadcast from the Paramount Theatre in Brooklyn last night between 8 and 12 o'clock should not be interfered." Or, so we read about those battles regarding the assignment of radio frequencies and scheduled programming. Moreover, the powerhouse founder of Paramount-Prolix was quoted in the *Brooklyn Eagle* promising that "all the varied resources of this great amusement organization will be utilized in fashioning the finest radio entertainment possible." In view of Zukor's mantra about the public always being right, i.e., the very title of his autobiography (Zukor and Kramer, 1953), it isn't surprising that he told a local reporter about a study of radio currently undertaken by his film studio with the purported hope of learning when we went on the air what we would do in a manner that would benefit not only the vast radio public but also the thousands of motion picture theaters throughout the country.

Then, one year after his business partner, Jesse Lasky, pledged to change over from Silent Films to the Talkies, the following banner headline appeared in the *Brooklyn Eagle* on August 25, 1929: "Zukor Announces New Radio Series on Columbia Chain." And with Paramount-Lasky's reported half interest in CBS, we additionally read about a "definite working arrangement between the two companies to bring radio, stage and screen together on a basis that will assure the public the best features of the amusement in these three great forms of entertainment."

This might be regarded as an additional face in our theatre's earlier history.

So, for example, we note that on September 21, 1929, the studio launched a series of one-hour Saturday-night types of entertainment originating in Hollywood that through telephones included Brooklyn Paramount performers like Jesse Lasky and Rubinoff as part of the Paramount Weekly Radio Hour between 10:00 to 11:00 p.m. Eastern time heard across the nation on the Columbia Broadcast System. Vaudeville sketches or playlets performed on stage drawn from accompanying films screened here also were rewritten for the radio listening pleasure of audiences at home with the "Publix Radio-Vue." For examples, the *Exhibitor's Herald World* on January 4, 1930, reported Harry Green leading a sing-along from the Brooklyn Paramount stage, and Crawford in the previous year accompanying scenes taken directly from *The Return of Sherlock Holmes* on the Mighty Wurlitzer during the week of October 18, 1929.

A second literal interface stems from the fact that big stars of Vaudeville presented on stage were advertised and based on their popularity on radio shows to potential audiences doubtlessly familiar with them. Duke Ellington's performances were transmitted by a wire from the Cotton Club on Mondays and Thursdays at 11:45 p.m. on WEAF in 1931. Or, as we read in the local tabloid on January 23, 1931: "This is Ellington's first stage appearance in Brooklyn since his rise to fame on radio." Ditto presumably as well for Cab Calloway on the basis of the Heidi-Ho Jazz bandleader's popularity on the "Lucky Strike Radio Hour Broadcast" in 1931 and 1932...a commercial sponsor, which notoriously in retrospect promoted cigarette smoking as a surefire way for women to lose weight and that resulted in sales of $14 billion in 1926, which nearly tripled by 1930 (Crisp and Stewart, 2024: 130).

Still other examples from those earlier years of Jazz history as part of Vaudeville weekly offerings included the Mills Brothers, billed as "Radio's Rhythm Entertainers" during their six appearances; that is, after having been initially heard as African American pioneers over

Cincinnati's fifty-thousand-watt radio station in the early 1930s, even though their racial identities were deliberately forbidden by commercial sponsors (Friedman, 2016: 41). Also Ethel Waters, who initially was heard on Rudy Vallée's "Fleishman's Hour" and violinist Ben Bernie's radio show singing "What Harlem Means to Me." She also recorded popular hits like "Dinah" and "Stormy Weather," having the distinction of being advertised as the "first colored girl to sing through the air," and the first African American woman to host her own radio show—the *Ebony Four Radio Hour* in 1933–1934, which moved from NBC to CBS and was renamed *The American Revue*, a coast-to-coast half-hour national broadcast at 7:00 p.m. ET. It was broadcast in front of a live audience on Sunday nights and sponsored by the American Oil Company between October 22, 1933, and February 25, 1934; that is, until being forced off air following pressure from Southern sponsors (Bogle, 2001: 83, 229).

As for those big star Vaudevillians, Belle Baker's appearance during the week of September 16, 1932, was advertised as "the singer heard on WABC on Sundays from 9:00–9:30 p.m.," a radio program sponsored by the American Safety Razor Company; and Kate Smith, whose radio show, sponsored by La Paloma cigars, expanded from one to five nights weekly during the 1930s on the basis of her increased popularity, and two stage appearances here were advertised as "The voice that cheers a million radio listeners" as she was dubbed First Lady of Radio.

Others advertised in terms of their radio successes included Jack Benny, who was billed as the stage, screen, and radio's new sensation during the week of May 27, 1932; Stoopnagle and Budd advertised as radio's funniest comedians; Fanny Brice as Baby Snooks heard on the *Philco Hour*, a long-running popular radio show that began on November 25, 1937, after having been reworked from her 1934 Ziegfeld Follies' stage persona as "Babykins" continued on radio through 1947 before flopping on TV (Goldman, 1992; 1997); and Burns and Allen, who followed their initial radio broadcast on the BBC in London in 1929 with guest spots two years later on Eddie Cantor's and Rudy Vallée's popular radio shows before appearing as regulars on broadcasts by another Vaudevillian who'd performed here, Guy Lombardo. Their long-running radio success included commercial sponsors like the Pandora Cigar Company, which George Burns famously employed as a prop on the comedy team's long-running TV show.

Indeed, such was the national celebrity—and notoriety—of the blackface/white Vaudevillian comics Amos 'n' Andy that their lone stage appearance at the Brooklyn Paramount during the week of May 15, 1931, not only was billed as containing rib-tickling (racist) humor, but also "pungent wit and mirth provoking trials and tribulations (that) have delighted radio listeners through the country." Resulting, it might also be mentioned, that only did our theatre's management sponsor a jingles contest about them, but also placed radios in the Grand Lobby and basement lounges to accommodate any fears anxious patrons had between on-stage appearances in Vaudeville of missing those nightly radio broadcasts by that "black-faced pair from radio land" whose shows originated in Chicago.

Similarly, David Rubinoff and his Magic Violin were billed as radio's maestro prior to bookings here, and Arthur Tracy, a. k. a. the Street Singer, whose WABC radio show was heard on Mondays and Wednesdays at 10:45 p.m., Fridays at 9:00 p.m., and Sundays at 12:00 p.m., whose appearances at the Brooklyn Paramount were promoted in 1932 as those of "radio's most thrilling versatile singer."

But so, too, were lesser-known (SMALL) Vaudeville performers billed in terms of their radio success: Roy Atwell, advertised as "Radio's Stuttering Star," and Jeanne Lang as "Radio's Singing Sensation" during their joint appearances during the week of September 1, 1933.

In some cases, however, the reverse held true.

Thus, Bing Crosby's transcendent world-famous success as a crooner was parlayed into his long-running thirty-minute radio variety show originally sponsored by Chesterfield cigarettes—871 half-hour programs totaling 368 hours from 1931 to 1952. The same was probably true with regard to Eddie Cantor who also became an iconic radio star as a result of his *Chase and Sandborn Hour* that ran for decades, and which, according to his biographer (Weinstein, 2018: 95), commanded 80 percent of this nation's radio listenership in the year 1930 alone! Still other examples include Jack Benny, whose 596 half-hour radio shows totaled 1,113 episodes, and Bob Hope, whose Pepsodent toothpaste's sponsored program, which lasted from 1938 to 1952 and totaled 416 hours.

Yet a third interface were radio promotions in which the newest makes and models were manufactured by the Kolster Radio Corporation in Newark, New Jersey. In that regard, a trade show was held in the Grand Foyer and so-called Grand Lounge under the radio company's auspices during the week of March 23, 1929, where radio receivers and reproducers were on display. One month later, the so-called "Father of Radio," Dr. Lee de Forest, was advertised as appearing in situ on April 20, 1929, at 2:15 p.m. Saturday afternoon, where he was said to bring along a prototype of a television, which threatened to obliterate the popularity of radio, much as were previous concerns regarding what the latter might do to live Vaudeville entertainment.

Another trade show was dubbed the Annual Christmas Radio Exposition. With advertised giveaways, it was held between December 13 and 29, 1929 (from 11:00 a.m. to 11:00 p.m.) and boasted two Bosch radios in the Florentine Foyer (basement lounge), presumably won during a drawing hosted by Rudy Vallée. Another radio trade show was advertised on September 25, 1930, as "Ludwig Baumann Day at the Brooklyn Paramount," as company employees appeared in formal attire from the manufacturer's lone store in our borough. According to the local tabloid, it created a "harmonious blend with the rich background of the Brooklyn Paramount Theatre, considered one of the finest in America," and whose promotion allowed older model radios to be turned in toward the (reduced) purchase price of $137.50 for the new and improved Majestic radio on display; and that was with only a small deposit of $2.50 expected during one of the first layaway monthly payment plans. Finally on October 16, 1931, we read that during the appearance of Vaudevillians Georgie Jessel and

Sophie Tucker on stage, Majestic radios on display in the theatre's basement (Granada Lounge) were given away free every day of that week, presumably during drawings.

Vaudeville playlets employing radio as themes comprised a fourth way in that new medium figured in our theatre's earlier history; the satirist/radio star Fred Allen quipped he preferred well done. TV's future megastar of the *Texaco Power Hour*, Milton Berle, was billed as "Radio's Comedy Sensation" when he appeared in *Radio Frolics* during the week of February 9, 1934. Similarly, Rudy Vallée starred in *Radio Romance* during the week of July 13, 1929. And also during those years, the relatively big Vaudeville singer Harry Richman (née Henry Reichman Jr.) was listed as emcee for the stage *divertissement* in our theatre as part of a highly amusing skit by Charles Webster and a novel radio broadcast accompaniment for the organ numbers.

Still another—fifth—way in which radio prominently figured in the Brooklyn Paramount's earlier history can be illustrated: On February 28, 1931, when we read about these advertised "Radio Stars in Person" headlining that week's Vaudeville portion, the popular crooner, John Morton Downey, nicknamed "The Irish Nightingale," reportedly sang Tin Pan Alley songs like "Just a Gigolo," "Wabash Mom," and an Irish lullaby. He was joined by the Bobby Sanford Ensemble, who curiously were advertised as "radio personalities predominated at the Paramount," appearing along with that week's film screened here: *Honor Among Lovers*.

Indeed, during the week of May 29, 1931, newspaper advertisements reported the Second Radio Revue said to feature favorite radio stars in person doing *Radio Land*. Here again, Morton Downey's name topped a long cast. One final example is that during the week of January 20, 1933, when, along with the featured film *Tonight Is the Night* (with Claudette Colbert and Fredric March), we read that the Vaudeville component not only featured Leo Carrillo advertised as "Hollywood's greatest one-man show," but also as an "Extra-Added Attraction" there were the Radio Rogues, singers billed as "Brooklyn's Own Radio Stars."

Live radio broadcasts of nationally popular syndicated programs were also held on stage at the Brooklyn Paramount. Examples from this sixth interface include two episodes of *The Kate Smith Radio Show*, which ran on radio from March 17, 1931 to August 1, 1958, a fifteen-minute show initially that was expanded to an hour. It launched the career of Abbott and Costello—dates of Smith's two live radio show broadcasts from our theatre occurred during the week of January 22, 1932.

Also, the Silent Film stars Bebe Daniels and her husband, Ben Lyons, a World War I ace-pilot-cum-actor, broadcasted their long-running *At Home With*—radio show on stage here live in a revue titled *Talk of the Town* for four nights, April 20, 22, 23, and 26, 1934. That was before they became expatriates and relocated to England following death threats from a stalker.

Another example was *The Breakfast Club*, an episode of that enormously popular long-running Chicago-based daily radio broadcast nationally from the Brooklyn Paramount theatre's stage on a Friday morning, May 1, 1947. Hosted by Don McNeil, this pioneering popular show was ordinarily heard daily at 9:00 a.m., the longest-running on this medium—from June 23, 1933 through December 27, 1968. It was said to offer unabashed sentiment, human interest, music, and song and evocatively also advertised in folksy terms in our borough's tabloid as a "get-together" for all of us who smile before breakfast and then can't break the habit all day long—a place to come "where a fellar needs a friend" (Weinstein, 2018). Fran Allison of the early TV series Kukla, Fran and Ollie fame was among the best-known performers on what essentially was an unrehearsed show that reportedly received one hundred thousand letters annually from fans and sold Eight hundred fifty thousand membership cards as well, including being a prototype for Arthur Godfrey and other morning hosts to this day. *The Breakfast Club*'s enormous popularity was a separate live broadcast of this touring radio show that also sold out Madison Square Garden!

During its formulaic "four calls to breakfast"—marking each

fifteen-minute interval of a one-hour allotment—Brooklyn Paramount audiences got to participate in the March Time, the third of segments which reportedly saw three hundred children in our theatre march up and down the aisles and then around the *Breakfast Club* cast seated at a table on stage. Whether or not those popular radio interviews were reprised with invited listeners, we learned that cast members sang while accompanied by the Mighty Wurlitzer. And probably as well sentimental letters from radio listeners read on air during "Inspiration Time," the fourth of those segments was joined by devotees who'd endured standing in lines that surrounded the theatre as fans were also said to have been drawn from the Nutmeg State (Connecticut)...anxious presumably to enjoy Jack Owens and Patsy Lee singing "Moon over Brooklyn," apropos, as well as "The Brooklyn Polka" performed by Eddie Ballantine's Breakfast Club Orchestra. Not for nothing, either, but the Brooklyn Paramount's full house that morning was also entertained by familiar cracks about our borough's hapless (in those years!) Brooklyn Dodgers baseball team... Like three-year-old Jackie Reichling, who showed up in a baseball uniform complete with mitt and was called to the stage by the radio host. But it should be noted that *The Breakfast Club* did its stint for racial integration in the year Jackie Robinson broke the color barrier in Major League Baseball by presenting the Vagabonds billed as one of the nation's greatest colored quartets (Dunning, 1998: 114–17).

Another radio show reprised on our theatre's stage was *Roxy and His Gang*. During the week of April 15, 1934, many alumni rejoined the mostly forgotten showman Samuel Lionel "Roxy" Rothapel (née Rothapfel), whose Sunday night pioneering radio show in 1922 and also was first to broadcast a symphony from a movie theatre. Its cast of two hundred were a national success, as David Melnick (1987) became "America's First Family Hour" captivated America's listening public in the late 1920s. Down on his luck after a career that saw the ex-Marine redesign several movie theatres, he was panned by critics for the lengthy opening stage shows he created at Radio City Music Hall, Adolph Zukor took pity and hired him for what became his final hurrah—the Roxy Radio Show gang's reunion and tour of Paramount theatres in 1934 that included ours. Among the most famous of its radio program who appeared on stage here on November 18 of that year including Eugene Ormandy, future conductor of the Philadelphia Orchestra; the Metropolitan Opera singing star Jan Peerce, whose familial conflicts regarding religious expectations and his desire to sing opera might well have provided the inspiration for *The Jazz Singer*; Mme. Henrietta Schuman-Schenk, an opera singer; even the ballerina nicknamed Gamby, who reportedly came out of retirement a second time to join her benefactor on our theatre's stage. Lesser-known performers included Yasha Bunchuk, who led the Brooklyn Paramount Orchestra on March 9, 1934; Harold Van Dusee, who reportedly sang "Laugh, Clown, Laugh"; and these additional former cast members: Viola Philo, Beatrice Belkin, Robert Weede, Colia Braaz, and Frank Moulin.

One final radio show was broadcast live on our theatre's stage: *The Benay Venuta Big WOR Radio Show*. It, in fact, was booked for fourteen consecutive Monday nights, commencing July 10, 1939. She was a former Silent Film star who'd also made the transition to the Talkies was otherwise heard on radio from 1935 to 1940 in the 8:30–9:10 p.m. time slot. Pauline Alpert, a pianist, and the Charioteers, a vocal group, and the Ernie Fiorito Orchestra were part of those live radio broadcasts headed on stage here by Benay Venuta (née Benvenuta Rose Crooke), who not only was the vocalist on radio's *Duffy's Tavern*, a decade-long popular show in the 1940s, but replaced Ethel Merman in *Kiss the Boys Goodbye* and *Annie Get Your Gun* on Broadway. Along with her subsequent appearance in a 1948 film about World War II titled *I, Jane Doe*, Benay Venuta also hosted a Saturday morning quiz show in that year that pitted celebrity children against their parents (Dunning, 1998: 80). Brooklyn Paramount's management also announced that the *Venuta Air Show* on stage at the Brooklyn Paramount would not increase the admission price because of this innovation (*Brooklyn Eagle*, July 7, 1939).

Mary Pickford's radio show titled *A Church Mouse* was included with its cast in the Vaudeville presentation during the week of February 2, 1934, in her advertised first and only Brooklyn appearance at the Brooklyn Paramount along with a screening of her film *All of Me* costarring Fredric March, and Miriam Hopkins.

Original radio programming, on the other hand, counted as another—seventh—vital part of our theatre's earlier history. *The Midnight Owl Frolic* were thirty-minute after-hour radio broadcasts from the stage at 11:30 p.m. on Tuesday evenings. Commencing January 14, 1930, the last of those audiences were invited on the following nine complete "vaude-cines" to stick around and enjoy additional performances by some featured performers as well as a few invited others—at no extra charge. Reportedly also carried over radio stations on CBS, at-home radio listeners got to enjoy some or all of these performers who appeared in what the local tabloid might not have been exaggerating—it advertised the latest and most elaborate of programs that are being created for ear as well as eye.

John Skinner poked fun in previewing those in his aptly named "Seeing What You Hear" radio column in the *Brooklyn Eagle* by reporting on January 4, 1930, that our theatre was advertising its original programming as "Hearing what you see..." Neglecting, thus, the fact that through microphones and loud speakers radio folks at home could similarly experience Lou Witten introducing assorted acts broadcast to two hundred Columbia Broadcast System stations. For, what we read in a subsequent column, "60,000 miles of wire connecting various microphones and control panels belonging to Columbia in and around New York." Then as if apropos, the journalist discussed a near mishap on this innovative radio program on February 4, 1930, when the Midnight Frolics were saved by a stagehand named Ev Hanlon, who employed a flashlight when the stage lights inexplicably went dim, thus reportedly rescuing the torch singer Lillian Roth and her piano accompanist about to perform "Sweetness Down Among the Sugar Cane" for the theatre's full house.

A proposed wisdom story from another Tuesday night after-hours radio broadcast hosted live on the Brooklyn Paramount stage involved

America's Boyfriend, Charles "Buddy" Rogers, Mary Pickford's second husband, whose appearance on February 18, 1930, was followed by woodshedding afterward with another pianist, Homer Phillips, banging away on their Steinways...on "dirty Jazz breaks," while on March 1, 1930, Rogers reportedly did a somersault off the piano before he played Jazz and also regaled theatre audiences and at-home radio listeners with tell-all adventures about his burgeoning Hollywood career. Yet another week saw—heard—debonaire Harry Richman singing "Puttin' on the Ritz" and Fanny Brice singing "My Man"...who another Tuesday night reportedly did her hilarious spoof on *Romeo and Juliet* reprised from her inaugural appearance at the Brooklyn Paramount. The saxophonist Benny Kreuger, recorded with the Original Dixieland Jazz Band in 1917, and who also led the Brooklyn Paramount Orchestra more than a decade later, stayed on to perform an after-hours duet with the violinist, Rubinoff, on "St. Louis Blues" (February 18, 1930).

Naming a few additional Midnight Frolic performers, for example Jesse Crawford performed light numbers, such as "In a German Garden," on the Mighty Wurlitzer. And also the largely forgotten star of London's revue *Wake Up and Dream*, Frances Shelley, reportedly sang Cole Porter's "What Is This Thing Called Love?" before tripping embarrassedly over her own skirt on her way offstage during her appearance on March 4,1930, in an after-hours radio broadcast emceed by early TV's future star of *Trouble with Father*, Stu Erwin, who replaced Lou Witten during a Tuesday night episode that included Mack and Moran identified as "blackfacers," as well as Elsie Thompson leading a community sing-along. She reportedly got laughs by demonstrating the orchestra pit elevator arrangement.

The invited guest, Ginger Rogers, who, whether fiction or fact, was said to have been strapped to a gurney and rushed to our theatre in downtown Brooklyn in an ambulance—with police escort—from the Broadway stage following her final bows in *Top Speed* at the Chanin Theatre at 11: 22 p.m., reportedly arrived twenty-two minutes later at 11:45 p.m. with three-quarters of a minute left for song on January 28, 1930, during one of her three appearances in our theatre's original radio broadcasting.

FILM STAR ON NIGHT OWLS FROLIC

Charles Buddy Rogers, film actor, who will be seen and heard in the program to be broadcast from the stage of the Brooklyn Paramount over WABC and the Columbia Broadcasting System tonight at 11:30 o'clock.

BUDDY ROGERS LITHOGRAPH (*The Brooklyn Daily Eagle*, February 25, 1930)

Similarly, we read about the appearance of newcomer Olive Shea on January 21,1930, the advertised singer adjudged as "radio's most beautiful girl" at the Radio's World Fair, and who was said to be making a Brooklyn combination stage and radio appearance on that following Tuesday.

A final note on original after-hours radio programming on our theatre's stage during the Vaudeville years. On January 15, 1930, *Variety's* man in downtown Brooklyn wrote the following about the *Paramount-Prolix Radio Hour*: "Love the weekly radio broadcast, and how the world can hear your voice. (For) Such good nature in an audience spells bucks for a theatre."

Continuing then with this eighth additional face of our theatre's earlier history, Ed Witten, who served as emcee of the Jimmy Durante Texaco-sponsored weekly radio show as well as an organ recital series on CBS radio, was additionally tasked with introducing—reintroducing—Vaudeville performers that night to those disparate Midnight Owl Frolics' audiences. Finally in this regard, John Skinner, a dialectician, so-called, also raved in his radio column about the comic dialectician, Henry Burbig, who appeared with Fanny Brice in that spoof by the Bard, writing he got as many laughs from the radio listeners as have ever been extracted.

Now we'll reference some films screened here that revolved around radio's popularity as a ninth interface during our theatre's Vaudeville history. Most notably among those was the first of four Paramount-Prolix's *Big Broadcast* films that played here during the week of October 14, 1932...whose theme was radio and featured several of its stars who also performed live during the Brooklyn Paramount's rich Vaudeville era. Such performers included Cab Calloway, Burns and Allen, the Mills Brothers, the Boswell Sisters, as well as Arthur Tracy and two other forgotten Vaudeville stars, Donald Novis and Frances Langford. Novis was billed as "Radio's Most Thrilling Singer" during his appearances in 1932, while Langford was billed as "radio's hottest torch singer" during her appearance in that same year.

Some ways in which radio crossed paths with other faces can be illustrated by the Boswell Sisters, who not only performed during our theatre's initial Jazz years as well as on stage in Vaudeville, but also on Bing Crosby's *Woodbury Radio Show*, originating in Hollywood, and Rudy Vallée's *Fleishman Hour* (Titus and Boswell Minnerly, 2014: 154–58).

Finally, we come full circle to that early debate of whether radio should be used for public service to enhance listeners' general education or to enrich corporate sponsors (not to mention performers' coffers as well). On December 15, 1930, the local tabloid spoke about this tenth way radio interfaced with our theatre's earlier history, noting an "entire radio program (devoted) to the Brooklyn Emergency Unemployment Committee." That is, ninety minutes of live programming broadcast from our theatre's stage reportedly throughout the land (world?) via relay to the Leverich Towers, Brooklyn Height's landmark hotel in those years, and also the home of the powerful radio station WLTH. Their airwaves carried an appeal that night about the goal of raising $500,000 at the start of the Great Depression for out-of-work residents in our borough. That plea for donations came with live entertainment supplied by Brooklyn Paramount Vaudevillians, who included its singing organist, Elsie Thompson, and the advertised orchestra leader, David Rubinoff, who led the Brooklyn Yankees, heard on Eddie Cantor's radio program one year later. May Joyce was listed as another featured artist that night.

As a postscript, however, we end this chapter about the quintessential importance of aerial telegraphy in all four faces of the Brooklyn Paramount's initial thirty-four-year history by signing off as did Roxy on his popular Sunday night weekly radio broadcasts heard on NBC:

"Goodnight, pleasant dreams, and God bless you!"

CHAPTER 11

Tom Mix, Freaks, Prudence Penny, Latin American Music, "Badminton, Anyone?" the Harlem Rens' and Brooklyn Dodgers' Hoops, Too: Extracurricular Events

These additional faces or extracurricular events in Brooklyn Paramount's earlier history will be grouped under five subheadings for discussion's sake: (1) Additional Music, (2) Rodeos, (3) Freaks, (4) Hoops and Other Sporting Events, and (5) Potpourri.

1. Additional Music

Financial concerns about the Brooklyn Paramount existed from the start. *Variety,* for example, on February 6, 1929, less than a year after the theatre's opening, reported that to boost attendance, there were "Paul Ash Whoopee Shows" in the Grand Lobby daily after 9:00 p.m. Another hint of those concerns occurred even earlier, when we read the following in the *Brooklyn Eagle* on January 12, 1929: that the house band's accordionist, Sammy Carr, had assembled two hundred similar musicians to perform for those lobby parties. And those extracurricular musical events were scheduled twice daily on weekday afternoons at 3:00 p.m. between vaude-pix offerings, as well as at 9:00 p.m., or after the completion of both. Carr was quoted in that tabloid echoing the Paramount studio's music supervisor, Boris Morros, and his expectation about lobby pianists that his aggregation should also provide mental relaxation for people (customers) who have weak arches. In any event, we also read a few months later on April 28,1929, about a dance party in the Great Hall following the final screening of *The Letter* (starring Jeanne Eagels) and Paul Ash's stage band featured in a Vaudeville production of John Murray Anderson's *Say It with Music.*

Continuing with those extracurricular-like musical events, the local tabloid reported on March 14, 1930, about piano and violin recitals...after each stage show during that entire week. Fritz Kane and Russell Hope provided additional musical fare in the Grand Lounge. *The Times-Union* reported nearly two weeks later on May 25, 1930, that another accordionist, Frankie Judnick, was teaming up with the organist Else Thompson (albeit on piano) and a violinist to offer additional musical entertainment at no extra cost every night in the Grand Lounge. Then in the following year, a late-night dance was reported on February 13, 1931, after *Stolen Heaven*, a Paramount Talkie starring Nancy Carroll, and Vaudeville and music provided by the new stage band's leader, Charlie Davis, who was dubbed Brooklyn's Own Friend came with his boys to informally entertain their new Brooklyn friends in the Grand Lobby.

Next, the *Brooklyn Citizen* reported another type of extracurricular musical activity in the following year: the same Frankie Judnick's after-hours appearance in the Grand Hall during the week of March 19, 1932, with his new club, the Judnickites, who were advertised as presenting "a new kind of community singing every morning before the first show." Whether or not accompanied by the Mighty Wurlitzer, their community sing-alongs were reported as a more intimate affair, sort of a friendly get-together for those who like to sing. But also consistent with the frequently advertised *heimische* or unique family-friendly atmosphere extolled in the Brooklyn Paramount by all the local tabloids from its inception came the following announcement: "Sweetheart Night" to be held in the summer in 1932, i.e., more Wednesday night dancing in the lobby advertised as well as a special program.

Another example of this additional face is apparent from a banner headline in *The New York Times* on February 3, 1929: "300 Banjoists Wanted." And its clarion call was for amateur, professional, elementary, or advanced musicians interested in joining a banjo orchestra under the direction of Sammy Carr, identified as the banjo soloist at the theatre. Plus, sweetening that open invite, he wanted it known that individual musical parts would be especially arranged to suit each player's ability.

Newspaper accounts two decades later reported cocktail-type pianists entertaining theatre-patron women (if not men as well) outside the Vauxhall Room, a. k. a. Lady's Lounge, overlooking the Great Hall. It offered free admission to subsequent shows, if theatre goers could stump Bob Novack with the names of requested songs.

The appearance of Justo Angel Don Azpiazú and His (Cuban) Habana Orchestra during the week of July 31, 1931, also belongs to this subheading. Azpiazú, who at the time enjoyed worldwide fame with *El Manisero*, "The Peanut Grinder Song," thus presumably introduced *son-pregon*, a Latin American rhythmic musical expression probably unknown to most if not all of our theatre's audiences...that popular tune featuring the call of a street vendor for that snack for sale while traveling Cuba's dirt roads and cobblestoned streets from barrio to barrio in Havana. And *El Manisero*, according to the famous timbale player Tito Puente, performed here during the 1950s, introduced the rhumba to the non–Latin American world...and that became so popular, "Rhumba-Fox Trot" was printed on 78s as if celebrating the new dance craze (Roberts, 1999). "The Peanut Grinder Song" also featured the peddler Antoine Machin's call and response from Julio Cueva's trumpet in Azpiazú's band, a song whose popularly not only was such that its melody was whistled by Groucho Marx in *Duck Soup*, screened here during the week of December 19, 1933, but it also inspired so-called Latin Jazz twenty years hence. Indeed, even an archconservative Midwestern WASP bandleader like Stan Kenton recorded *El Manisero* featuring Mario Bauza on alto saxophone.

Decades before multiculturalism entered the collective conscience in Anglo-America, we find these additional examples on stage at the Brooklyn Paramount: Paul Ash leading his Merry Pranksters during the week of January 29, 1929, in a Vaudeville sketch titled *Hot Tamale Blues* as advertised by our theatre's first publicist as "The Brooklyn Paramount goes Mexican this week!" And with the hype, if not hokum, we read about a galaxy of sizzling senoritas and syncopated toreadors helping the bandleader create a "fandango of scintillating entertainment," accompanied by management's advertised promise of a fiesta. They boasted that it made the most colorful show this theater has ever offered.

Ash, according to Hall (1961: 213–14), previously outfitted band members with Eskimo wear in simulated igloos as well as kimonos with pigtails during various skits at the Granada Theatre in San Francisco as far back as 1918. But illustrating that arguably thin line between genuine and spurious multiculturalism, we read in the *Exhibitor's Herald* on December 8, 1928, about the appearance of Little Ana Chang, a. k. a. "the pretty Chinese star of syncopation," during the second week of the Brooklyn Paramount's earlier history, who was also dubbed as a Chinese Blues singer and proffered two Tin Pan Alley songs—"That's All I Want to Know" and "There's a Rainbow Around My Shoulder," the latter recorded by Al Jolson in the 1928 film *Singing Fool* that never was screened here. All the same, we also read that Ms. Chang had won a fine hand and had to beg off calls for an encore while the African American crooner George Dewey Washington had a return engagement on that same night. It was reported he received a marvelous reception, subsiding only when the motion picture *Someone to Love* was started—that is, for his rendition of "The Spell of the Blues," whether or not with a call for an encore.

Another example of multiculturalism was the appearance of the exotic dancing beauty Ledova during the week of May 27, 1932, described as credited with popularizing the rhumba in this country. Or Armida (née Vendrell), a Mexican singing, dancing, and entertaining actress during the week of November 27, 1931. Or Joe Fong as part of the *Chinese Whoopee Revue* during the week of June 13, 1930.

The Hindu snake dancer Hasoutra (née Ryliss Barnes Simpson), who was born in Shanghai and made her debut on our theatre's stage during the week of January 10, 1930, and a troupe of Soviet dancers (March 16, 1934) were not unlike Nikita Balieff's dance troupe performing during the week of March 7, 1930, in colorful Russian costumes.

Jumping ahead to the 1950s, two decades after the demise of Vaudeville were dedicated concerts of authentic Latin American music performed on our theatre's stage. For example, Ismael "Esy" Morales's orchestra during the week of April 26, 1950, led by its Puerto Rican flautist, who'd worked with siblings during the 1930s in a dance band before forming his own *danza orquestra*. He was managed by George Goldner of Rock 'n' Roll fame who recorded them on Tico Records. And of related interest, the name of a *film noire* screened here during that same week in 1950 was *Criss-Cross*, which starred Burt Lancaster and featured Morales's band performing that number he wrote.

Then there was a Mambo Festival booked four years later. Thus, two shows on April 24, 1954—a Saturday night—featured Tito Puente (née Ernest Anthony Puente Jr.) at 8:30 p.m. and midnight as part of a Mambo USA tour, which opened at the Apollo Theater in Harlem. It was promoted by Morris Levy with whom the world-famous timbale player supposedly had a special friendship. A band member named Joe Conzo (2010: 172–73), however, wrote that his boss "was treated like shit." Featured on the Brooklyn Paramount stage that night along with Tito Puente was the Joe Loco Quintet led by a Nuyorican (née Jose Estevez Jr.); Pupi Campo, advertised as "Latin America's Mr. Personality;" "Babalu" Miguelito Valdes (née Jacinto Campillo), who worked in the studio band on *The Tonight Show* hosted by Jack Paar between 1954 and 1956; Myrte Silva (La Gorda de Oro), a transnational Nuyorican vocalist and composer advertised as the Sophie Tucker of

Cuba; Arsenio Rodriguez, nicknamed El Ciego Maravillioso and credited with having invented *son montero*, another distinctive rhythmic
component still found in Latin music; Mercedes Valdes; and finally
Candido, the percussionist who was part of Stan Kenton's second
gig here in 1954.

Part of that Mambo-Rhumba Festival was the appearance of the
Sevilla Fort Dancers said to be under the musical direction of Gilberto
Valdés, another highly regarded Cuban bandleader. The champion
Mambo-Rhumba dance team demonstrated the mambo for our theatre's audiences when that dance craze prompted the Arthur Murray
Dance School to send instructors to our theatre on two separate occasions in 1947, June 2 and August 6, offering free lessons in the lobby
with the hope of attracting customers for mambo and cha-cha-cha
lessons to studios.

Other examples of extracurricular musical events suggesting this
additional face of Brooklyn Paramount's rich earlier history can also
be added: the appearance of the Brooklyn crooner Ziggy Lane during
the week of December 23, 1948, for example. The former vocalist in
Chico Marx's Big Band who replaced Mel Torme not only opened
the Forsythia Room at the Granada Hotel near the theatre, but for a
brief while hosted his own TV Show called *Dinner Time* during the
1950s. The composer of "This Love of Mine," "Dear Mona," and "Have
You Read the Bible Today?"—the latter sung by the popular western
cowboy husband-and-wife team of Roy Rogers and Dale Evans—Ziggy
Lane, finally, was backed by a musical group called the Keynoters.

Four additional examples are also noted.

First, on March 9, 1932, a Friday night, Mme. Louise Tetrazzini,
who was advertised as a Metropolitan Opera singer, performed arias
from *La Traviata* and *Rigoletto*; this second example given the generic
nation of audiences occurred during the week of November 18, 1932,
when Maurice Spiegel, our theatre's second manager, presented
another famous opera star, Mme. Ernestine Schumann-Heink. The
program in her return engagement unfortunately wasn't reported.
The third example, however, qualified as genuinely multicultural—an

evening of Italian folk music on April 26, 1950, a Wednesday, featuring the so-called Italian Crosby, Nicola Paone, the Sicilian owner of an Italian restaurant on West Thirty-Fourth Street frequented by Broadway stars, and who appeared as part of Esy Morales's variety-type multiethnic show that included the return engagement of Jewish American comedian Henny Youngman.

Finally, and saved for last with authorial privilege, was the lone appearance of Pawnee Chief Charles Shunatona conducting the United States Indian Reservation Band in a performance of *Red Rhythm* during the week of February 7, 1930.

2. Rodeos

Separated by some thirty years were two rodeos. In the first of those, Thomas Edwin Mix, the iconic megastar who appeared in 291 silent Western films, including his own productions, appeared on a Saturday morning in 1929. A former United States marshal memorialized by Adolph Zukor (1953: 165) as a top cowpuncher and an authentic ripsnorter. The high point of the rodeo show was when Mix mounted on "Tony, the Wonder Horse" on our theatre's stage for the entire week commencing May 16, 1929, and six-shooters blazing at little clay things mounted on a target…he occasionally missed during what was advertised as a miniature rodeo. Mirroring the fact that animal acts were part and parcel of Vaudeville, the Pennsylvanian featured three cowboys and two additional horses that delighted youngsters during five shows, if only since seeing the grander rodeos booked in Madison Square Garden as well as playing cowboys and Indians at home—without realizing it was the US Calvary instead who fought America's First Citizens for territorial reasons. And since voice was required for radio, Mix's curiously was dubbed in his long-running radio series. *The Standard Union* (March 16, 1929) described his tinseled appearance as supported by two other cowboys who combined to give an exhibition of fancy roping, while the star carried on a confidential conversation with the audience.

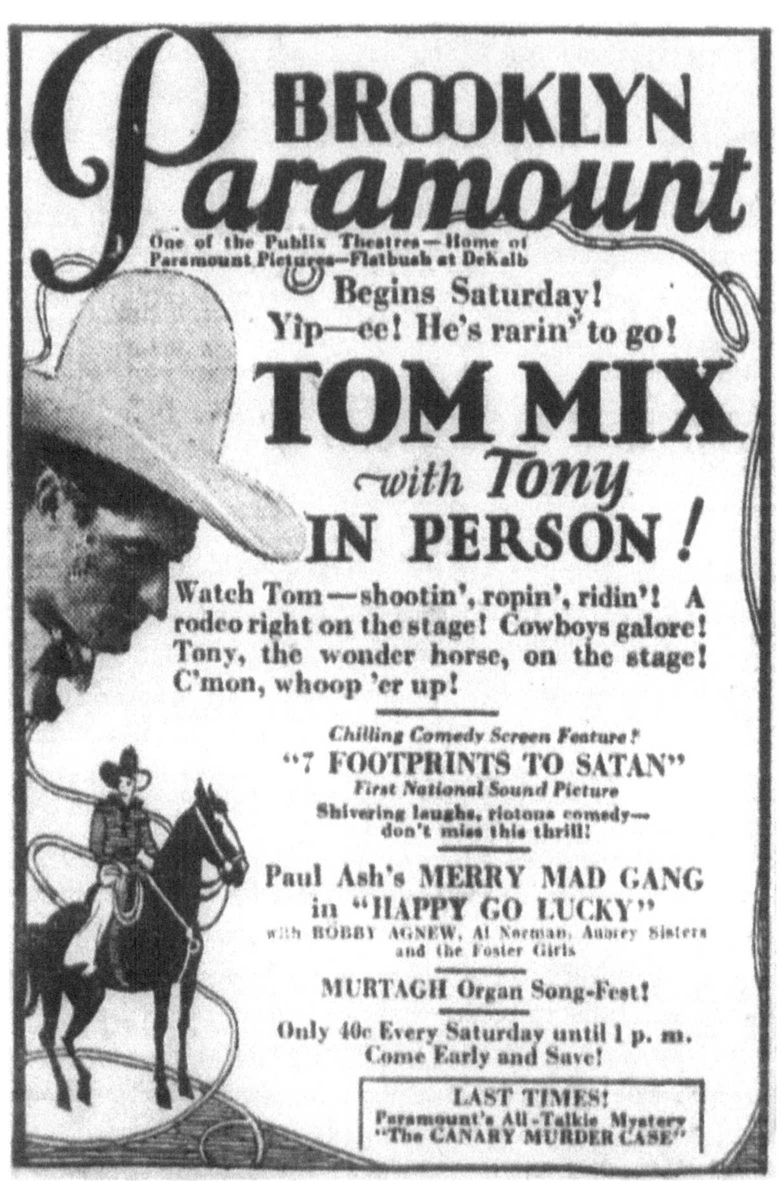

TOM MIX ADVERTISEMENT (*The Brooklyn Daily Eagle*/March 14, 1929)

Small talky-talk indeed, as the radio characters of *Vic and Sage* would have said, for while fondling his cream-colored ten-gallon hat, Tom Mix reportedly invited them to drop in anytime at his Bar

Circle A Ranch in Prescott, Arizona, and have supper with Mamma Mix and the little Tomasinos...whether or not having consulted Mrs. Mix. *Looping the Loop* was screened that week, a Silent Film made by Paramount-Prolix's UFA studio in Germany about a circus performer that was originally titled *Todesschleiffer* dubbed in English.

Finally, we note two museums and one airport named for Tom Mix, who also rode his horse during President Teddy Roosevelt's funeral procession in 1918; his visage also appears with other world-famous figures on the Beatles' "Sgt. Pepper's Lonely Hearts Club Band" LP; and Rudy Vallée sang "Empty Saddles" at Mix's funeral in 1935.

Time traveling two decades ahead, the second rodeo presented on stage at the Brooklyn Paramount was led by the gold-medal-winning Olympic-swimming-champion-cum-Sci-Fi-film-star of serialized episodes of *Buck Rogers* screened in other movie theatres, Clarence Linden "Buster" Crabbe III, who initially starred in W. C. Fields's *You're Telling Me*, released in 1933, and not only would be dubbed the Lion Man in *King of the Jungle* that played here during the week of March 3 in that year, but who was advertised as "the world's most perfect man." Crabbe followed Johnny Weissmuller in a Tarzan film, but so did the TV star of *Captain Gallant of the Foreign Legion* and host of a children's show as well ride his horse (named Smokey) on a Saturday morning, February 9, 1952, heading a second miniature rodeo two decades after Tom Mix that included the vocalists Whitey Carson and Beverly Wright...who yodeled cowboy songs, twirled their lariats, and shot clay pigeons, as described in the tabloids. That week's feature-length accompanying film could only have been planned in advance, insofar as *Wanted, Billy the Kid* starred Buster Crabbe in this first revisionist portrayal of the notorious New Mexico outlaw William H. Bonney.

3. Freaks

A third example of extracurricular events we apologetically subsume under that politically incorrect title is Singer's Midgets, better known as the Munchkins from *The Wizard of Oz*, who had to be rescheduled one week to the gala opening of the Brooklyn Paramount as a result of being held over at the New York Paramount. And so it was that during the week of December 1, 1928, they appeared here in a Vaudeville skit titled *Miniatures of '29*. Two of those little people posed in boxing gear in the display window of A and S on Fulton Street, as an advertisement for their Brooklyn Paramount debut—the sort of show business hype referenced when Fred Allen and Jack Benny squared off in pugilistic gear during their headline-grabbing fake feud, and more recently was used for self-promotion by Andy Warhol for his (painting) collaborations with Jean-Michel Basquiat.

A second example was found in *Variety* on April 2, 1930, which reported "a regular sideshow ballyhoo and barkers with circus atmosphere and freaks [*sic*] running from the usual fat lady and midgets to a sword swallower and fire eater." And its reporter not only described this extracurricular event as an outgrowth of lobby parties, but also wrote they were intended as an exploitative stunt aimed at diverting theatre patrons from Ringling Bros. and Barnum & Bailey's three-ring show circus scheduled to begin at Madison Square Garden on April 28 of that year.

The *Times-Union* (December 6, 1930) shockingly—offensive from our contemporary perspective, anyway—wrote about Rudy Vallée having tried something new in novelties on stage—making love to a petit-singer midget. And to which was added that the original and clever staged stunt was accompanied by six young ladies playing harps, etc.

In a not dissimilar vein, children of theatre patrons during the week of December 8, 1939, were invited to meet Little Santa, the so-called Talking Wonder. Who was he? A miniature Santa forty inches tall who reportedly answered questions posed by youngsters in the Grand Lounge prior to Christmas.

4. Hoops and Other Sporting Events

"The Brooklyn Paramount Theatre will present the first of a series of professional basketball games on its stage next Friday." Thus, we read in *Variety* on November 16, 1936, about this unique booking under the direction of Joe Lee, the Fabian Theatre manager otherwise appointed in 1935 following Paramount-Prolix's bankruptcy during the Great Depression, and who promised to revive Vaudeville for the new lease-holder. Profiled by Art Arthur in his featured column in the *Brooklyn Eagle* on August 29, 1934, "Doc" Lee, a former PR man for Tom Mix and Harry Houdini, dubbed the Barnum of Brooklyn, could only have been desperate when those plans went astray and he sought to uphold one of our theatre's slogans: "Get the women and children into the theatre and the rest will follow."

Regarding hoops, eight games between former-collegiate-all-Americans-turned-professional were played on stage in three seasons in front of packed houses on Thursday and Friday nights between 1936 and 1938. Despite advertisements that reported those were played on a regulation-sized court in two fifteen-minute halves—and broadcast over WMCA radio by the veteran sportscaster Richard Edward "Dick" Fishel, a former Syracuse University football star who played one season in the fledgling NFL—our stage measured smaller.

The Brooklyn Jewels played against New York University on February 14, 1936. And during that inaugural season, a battle of the *boros* pitted the world-famous Harlem Rens—representing Harlem's Renaissance Ballroom—against those Brooklyn Jewels on April 10, 1936, in an unusual racially mixed promotion...which they surprisingly lost. Nor are the results of a return game between those teams on November 16, 1936, known to us, and represented the same sort of sensationalism that accompanied all-colored orchestras led by Duke Ellington, Cab Calloway, and other African American Jazz musicians. Arguably of even greater voyeuristic interest to Brooklyn Paramount moviegoers, however, was the basketball game featuring the Brooklyn Jewels, coached by Ed Wilde, who defeated the Alabama Pitts on February 21, 1936, by a score of 32–27 in front of another reported full house, as the latter was comprised of visiting trustees from Sing Sing prison in upstate New York.

Then during the (expanded) ten-game season in the following year—launched on January 8, 1937—the Philadelphia Hebrews met the Dux, who included Arthur Kameros, formerly Long Island University's Blackbird's captain. Other participating teams in that pre-NBA year included Kate Smith's Original Celtics versus the Crushers, who were said to have been led by Ike "King Kong" Klein, listed as over six feet, two inches and tipping the scales at two hundred pounds. Still other teams from when the college game was more popular than the pros included the Kingston Colonels playing against Barney Sedran's sensational New York Whirlwinds, who were led by Phil Rabin, a former Long Island University standout on a team that listed Tiny Hearn as their six-foot, eight-inch center and that also featured Tony DePhillips from Fordham, Sol Kopitko from City College, Leo Bender and Bill Nash from Columbia, and Willie Rubenstein from NYU. But so, too, did Ossie Shechtman, another former great Long Island University basketball player on our legendary Blackbirds, and who scored the very first points in NBA history in 1946, lead the Jewels on February 5, 1937. Finally, during the third and last year of this innovation, the season kicked off with the House of David against the Brooklyn Dukes on January 7, 1938.

Of sociological interest was the willingness of Jewish basketballers to compete on their Sabbath, which commenced on Friday nights. It was clear evidence of their acculturation, if not their desire to achieve full assimilation in America's melting pot. In any event, the Newark Hebrews, led by Herb Cohen, described as a local Jewish boy who never shoots the ball with two hands—he emulated Stanford University Hank Luisetti's innovated one-handed push shot that replaced two-handed set shots in those years prior to the jump shot—were defeated on January 14, 1938, by the Original Celtics starring Joe Lapchick, the legendary star-cum-New-York-Knickerbockers'-head-coach. One can only wonder, however, why the local tabloid on November 24, 1937, announced that those weekly basketball games were being

pushed ahead from their original Thursday night slots before returning to that original game week night. Ethnicity also figured in the
composition of other teams...as was the case with the New York Gaels,
who were nicknamed the fighting Irishmen and boasted players with
names like McDermott, Dunleavy, McDonald, and Fitzpatrick.

The promotion-minded Fabian Paramount theatre manager
also booked Jim Barton's Tobacco Road Tramps against the Detroit
Clowns on a wintery pre-Christmas Wednesday night in 1936 in lieu
of Vaudeville...teams not unlike the Harlem Globetrotters described
as offering burlesques on basketball, football, fishing, and dentistry,
while wearing circus regalia when Joe Lee officially pronounced
Vaudeville dead in our theatre in a local tabloid on December 22, 1936.

Still talking hoops, we might also note that Zucker's so-called
Zouves, Brooklyn Paramount's ushers with their vaunted military-
like precision attributed to Roxy in other theatres, were allowed to
form teams that competed against other theatres on our stage three
years prior to Lee's experiment. Ben Hall (1961: 164) also wrote about
our theatre's squads of ten hoopsters who competed on stage at the
Brooklyn Paramount and posted their fifth consecutive victory against
the Prospect Park YMCA team by a score of 44–23 in front of an
audience on December 15, 1933. Teams comprised of ushers named
Rosenthal, Zuckerman, Bluestein, Welinsky, Younger, Levine, and
Hunter, who not only defeated the Bears Stearns basketball squad on
Governor's Island (by a score of 34–12) but enjoyed another unde-
feated season two years later after easily swamping the Radio City
Music Hall squad by a score of 37–11 during an away game on February
21, 1935, also played during their off-hours, needless to say.

And since our theatre's stage was also obviously too small to show-
case its ushers' football and baseball prowess, the only evidence about
the former we found stated Brooklyn Paramount's baseball squad
lost to the Parish in Bay Ridge on June 3, 1933, by a score of 9–3
on a Sunday afternoon game for which admission was charged, and
whose opponents included one of the greatest of all Negro League
baseball All-Stars, Buck O'Neill. Finally, seven years later, they lost to

the heavy-hitting Century Circuit Theater team by a score of 13–8 on April 23, 1941, on another Sunday afternoon in Marine Park, Brooklyn.

Before returning to basketball (and introducing other sports), we note that Vaudevillians were the second face of our theatre's earlier history. They joined with management personnel on a bowling team. On March 3, 1932, in the *Brooklyn Times-Union,* the following humorous account involved crooner Bing Crosby's appointment as captain of that year's squad...which included his brother Everett at right guard; the organist Merle Clarke listed as fullback; Don Hahn assigned to the set 'em up, i.e., nonautomated bowling pins; the theatre's publicist, Maurice Bergman (eyeshade and all) joined by his assistant, Henry Spiegel (without his gal) as substitute strikers; Les Kaufman appointed official scorekeeper, a. k. a. counter-upper; Minnie B. Eaton and George Ettinger relegated to the cheering squad; and Robert Weitman, the new theater manager said to have been recruited for moral support. Although the names of opposing teams were not given, strikes and spares were probably tallied at the Paramount Bowling Lanes, a two-story adjoining building on Flatbush Avenue Extension, whose lease would be terminated in 1950 after Long Island University took full control of both Paramount properties from which one or more lanes were used during this author's undergraduate years.

Doc Lee innovated two additional sports played on our theatre's stage to replace Vaudeville: badminton and table tennis.

Regarding Vincent Richards, a former tennis star who played against the great Bill Tilden in the 1920s—and lost—he was hired to demonstrate this rival lawn sport on our theatre's stage. And so it was that we read on March 23, 1936, a Monday night, Richards, who was identified as a world champion, by the scores of 15–9 and 15–12, defeated Arthur Ellis, who also represented a British athletic company that hoped to sell the necessities of badminton, i.e., rackets, shuttlecocks, and netting, used on the big stage at 10:40 p.m. Doc Lee's pledged to the local tabloids that in lieu of Vaudeville, there would be other sports. The Fabian Paramount's manager was forced to cancel three subsequent Monday-night badminton exhibitions for good sociological reasons…for, as we read in *Variety* (April 7, 1930), that lawn sport appeals only to a limited class. As, indeed, Lee was similarly forced to concede: "If response to the game of badminton is the criterion then Brooklyn is below the cultural status of the West Coast out where the Gowanus Canal begins and holds as much love in not less than croquet." The identical explanation, interestingly enough, given for the failure of the Russian dance company Chauve-Souris reported in *Variety* on March 15, 1930, reported they were over the heads of Brooklyn Paramount audiences, and arguably revelatory as well—badminton was to be more in accord with the "greater intelligentsia of Broadway's theatregoers!"

Table tennis, anyway? Doc Lee, on the other hand, successfully booked table tennis (ping pong matches) several Saturday afternoons on stage in the same year Vaudeville made a brief revival. Commencing on October 28, 1937, Brooklyn Paramount audiences were more familiar with this indoor sport as a result of membership in the borough's numerous "Y's" and were invited to watch films after watching matches that were part of New York State's Table Tennis Invitation Tournament in the early afternoon. The matches began on that Saturday at 2:00 p.m. and continued for several weeks before culminating in semifinal matches between Johnny Abrams and Sid Jacobs, and Barney Grimes (ranked fourth in the nation) against Henry Sigman, whereas the ultimate champion remains unknown to us.

Finally, hoops is our last example in this subheading of extracurricular faces. For nearly two decades after the last of those professional contests, our borough's beloved baseball team competed against—and defeated—four different professional teams during exhibition contests that also took place on our theatre's stage. Yes, those beloved "Boys of Summer" memorialized by Roger Kahn (1972) also entertained theatre audiences on four separate Monday evenings from 1949 to 1950.

Dubbed the Brooklyn All-Stars, Gil Hodges, Eddie Miksis, Don Newcomb, Rex Barney, and Ralph Branca comprised their original Fab Five—with "Campy," Roy Campanella, the baseball team's Hall of

Fame catcher listed as a "Sixth Man." According to *Variety* (December 21, 1949), the theatre was 75 percent filled on that previous Monday night when they narrowly defeated the Long Island Bombers by a score of 51–47 with leading metropolitan sportswriters like Jimmy Cannon from the *Post* and Frank Graham from the *Tribune* among management's invited honorary guests. Whether or not the same number of candy bars were sold in succeeding weeks, the count was three hundred during that first Monday night. The rebranded "Trolly Dodgers"-cum-Brooklyn-Robins were defeated by the Baltimore Colored Capitols by a score of 24–22 on the day after Christmas in 1949. They played in two fifteen-minute halves rather than four quarters.

BROOKLYN DODGERS BASKETBALL TEAM (*The Brooklyn Daily Eagle*/December 19,1949)

Then, on January 2, 1950, when their squad was joined by William "Dolly" King, the five-star athlete who was Long Island University's greatest sportsman, and who scored thirteen points a decade after graduation, the Brooklyn All-Stars defeated the Newark Mules by a score of 46–38 in the new year. While in the fourth and what proved to be the final of those exhibition games during a projected six-game season, "Da Bums" defeated the Washington Coloreds on January 9, 1950, by a score of 62–54; that is, after the screening of *Inspector General* starring Brooklyn's Danny Kaye paired with the B-film *Alias, the Champ.*

Understanding why this scheduled series negotiated by grown men and cut by two games was because of the baseball team's legendary general manager, Branch Rickey. He was the same man who convinced Jackie Robinson to help break its color barrier in 1947 and overrode that contractual agreement stating fear of injuries incurred during those players' off-season. Asked by a local journalist why the future Hall of Fame pitcher Don Newcombe would be willing to participate, he said in that era underpaid ballplayers were forced to secure off-season day jobs to support their families on paltry salaries. "Newk" sharply replied, "Show me how (else) I can make that much dough off-season for thirty minutes' work!" How much "dough"? One hundred dollars a game.

"New Hoopsters Replacing the Dodgers" was the *Brooklyn Eagle* headline on January 16, 1950, regarding what should have been game five of that curtailed exhibition series. Replacements for former collegiate standouts like NYU's Ralph Branca of the Brooklyn All-Stars narrowly defeated the rival borough's New Yorkers by a score of 45–42 on our theatre's stage. Along with acknowledging what could only have been yeomen efforts by Brooklyn Paramount stagehands while assembling and disassembling makeshift basketball courts weekly, i.e., following years of having to set up and take down trapezes and associated nettings weekly during the Vaudeville era, not unlike the crooner craze for Sinatra at the New York Paramount, frenzied teen-aged retro-bobby-soxers were said to have rushed to claim front-row orchestra seats in the Brooklyn Paramount to admire those brawny and handsome Brooklyn Dodger heroes who'd shed flannels for basketball's short shorts!

Also, *The Exhibitor* (November '43–May '44) reported yet another regulation basketball game recently in which the Marine division of Bendix lost to the ARMA Corps by a score of 24–20. The Brooklyn Paramount must also be viewed, as a local tabloid put it, functioning as a community center. Finally, the *Film Daily* also reported that Doc Lee booked a basketball game between two unnamed defense industry teams on our theatre's stage on November 27, 1943. Assuredly it was at least a patriotic exercise during the Second World War when hundreds of their employees were drawn to cheer their places of work, respectively.

5. Potpourri

These additional extracurricular events were also part of the Brooklyn Paramount's fabled earlier history.

A celebration of Russ Columbo's twenty-fourth birthday was held in the theatre's lobby on January 14, 1932. At that time, patrons, women only who shared the crooner's same birth date, were invited to write in fifty words or less why they thought he won the favor of Brooklyn theatregoers. Their reward? A slice of birthday cake baked by the popular local eatery in those years, Joe's, named for Joe Satori, its owner, proffered to twenty winners at 2:30 p.m. A friend could join them, and they were invited to see and hear the Vaudevillian's performance as well as that week's accompanying film, *This Reckless Age*. Birth certificates were required as well as accompanying photographs (*Brooklyn Times-Union*, January 2, 1932).

Then there was a birthday bash for Rudy Vallée with promised cake and autograph-signing as reported in the *Times-Union* on April 11, 1930. It was said to feature "no less than three jazz bands" for what was described as an "elaborately staged incident." A party was announced on February 15, 1931, during which Charlie Davis led his stage band in a program designed to entertain friends.

Still another potpourri-like event was an early Monday morning appearance on December 2, 1930, by Beth Brown who wrote the novel *Applause* about show business, and it starred Helen Morgan in its film adaptation screened during the week of November 29, 1929 (*Brooklyn Daily Times*). The author signed autographed copies of her book.

Similarly, the so-called commodification of beauty those years saw an extracurricular-like fashion show during the week of October 9, 1931. Titled "Ermines on Parade," it was advertised with this banner local newspaper headline: "Direct from Its Broadway Engagement." This million-dollar fur exposition involved a bevy of beautiful models wearing mink coats sold by I. J. Fox on Fifth Avenue in Manhattan and displayed on our theatre's stage. Moreover, whatever connection (if any) one might want or must make of the film screened that week titled *The Road to Reno* (starring the former silent screen western star William "Hopalong Cassidy" Boyd), that flick also featured Lilyan Tashman, who, as we saw, was among that septet featured in Paramount's *Manhattan Cocktail*, which opened our house, and who appeared in a Vaudeville sketch several weeks later during the week of February 12, 1932...the Brooklyn comedienne-actress also advertised as "the best dressed woman in show business" in the local tabloid as well as a "Popular Star Showing Latest Gowns." We also read about her shopping sprees in Paris that purportedly resulted in her being six months ahead of women's fashion in the United States.

Also under this subcategory was another example of political incorrectness. Our theatre's audiences back in the day were treated off-stage to the same entertainment this author vividly recalls provided by local firemen in PS 15 on the Lower East Side during the early 1950s: a miniature Punch and Judy show as reported in the local tabloid during the week of July 24, 1931.

Engle's Marionette Company was featured off-stage during Christmas week in 1934. Along with them performing "Hansel and Gretel" in the great hall following the matinee on Christmas Day, commencing on Monday in that year were the original puppetry creations like "The Circus." In addition to "Snow White and the Seven Dwarves" on Wednesday of that holiday week, Engle's Marionette Company offered other Grimm Brothers' children's favorites, e.g., "Goldilocks and the Three Bears," as well as another of their creations, "Queen of Hearts"—the latter performed on Saturday and with special requests allowed, if they were submitted in advance.

Magic shows, which according to Joe Laurie (1953), were alternatively dubbed as dumb or ABRACADABRA acts in Vaudeville lingo, were also booked on and off-stage as additional potpourri.

Nicola was advertised in the tabloids August 8, 1931, as the world's master magician when he appeared during what was called "Brooklyn Paramount Family Jubilee Week." He was reportedly able to make elephants disappear. And so, too, was the world-famous illusionist Thurston, booked on stage here—along with apparently demonstrating sleight-of-hand card tricks during the last week of October in that same year; however, those were seen in the balcony. His legerdemain included sawing a woman in half and making her whole again, shooting his associate from a cannon, and also magically causing her to float in midair. Laurie (1953: 197) further wrote that Howard Thurston was trained by the Great Kellar and reigned for forty-seven years as an undisputed champ. Hyped as well by our theatre's house publicist as "The World's Greatest Magician," he appeared at the Brooklyn Paramount with his company of fifty-two doing one hundred marvelous feats.

Yet another illusionist was Madame Lucia Eastman. She brought her extraordinary powers to our theatre's stage in 1931, and she was able to forecast the future as well as interpret the past. She could also read faces of willing patrons for repressed secrets off-stage.

Finally, four additional extracurricular events should be noted in this regard.

A graphologist, M. Gene Dennis was billed as the "Internationally famous Kansas Wonder Girl/She Tells All." She was booked for five consecutive weeks in 1929 and was curiously touted as already having answered more than ten thousand questions in her career. Sampled writing from theatregoers, however, had to be submitted in advance, according to the *Standard Union*, as this handwriting analyst, for reasons unknown, was also advertised as possessing golf skills as well as enjoying coast-to-coast drives in her high-powered car.

A second example also found and demonstrated in the basement lounges of our theatre was the lightning sketch artist Dorothy Dwin, who proffered her advertised skills at no extra cost to theatre patrons beyond the theatre's admission price during the week of April 27, 1930. And she returned for seven additional days in 1931 as an extracurricular attraction, albeit working the so-called "Music Room" on the Brooklyn Paramount's mezzanine.

This third example featured Howard Becker, who was hired during the week of August 17, 1930, to create silhouettes of theatre patrons as keepsakes. He worked every night outside the Music Room.

And this fourth and final example related to the screening of Mark Twain's major work *Huckleberry Finn* (during the week of August 7, 1931, and starring Jackie Coogan). A search was held for a boy to dress like Huck in association with the world premiere of the film.

Summing up, then, this chapter documented what was reported in the local tabloid during the Brooklyn Paramount's fourth anniversary celebration in 1932: "it was the first theatre in the country to extend to its thousands of patrons extra services, such as dancing, food exhibits, radio services, and serving tea and ice cream in the Grand Lounge during intermissions."

CHAPTER 12

Giveaways, Puzzles, Essays, and Other Writing Contests

Any number of extracurricular faces demarcate the Brooklyn Paramount's earlier textured history from most of the other wonder theatres in our borough. For, more than dinner plates in cereal boxes familiarly offered, we begin with these spectacular giveaways in what was arguably called the contest theatre.

Starting with Majestic radios awarded to theatre patrons selected from drawings in 1931, three separate and astonishing drawings were held on consecutive dates for a brand-new, sixty-horsepower, six-cylinder Chevrolet with Synchro-Mesh on December 10, 17, and 24, 1932—with the crooner Russ Columbo as part of the special Christmas cheer. The winners were announced from the stage, and even more astonishingly were eligible to win two or three more prizes, provided they kept returning and purchased admission tickets on all three dates. These advertisements were shown by blown-up photographs of models displayed throughout the theater! Columbo, on January 14, 1932, greeted the winner of a "fifty words or less" writing contest of "Why Russ Columbo Captured Brooklyn Theatregoers." The event was connected with his birthday celebration.

Distantly related to the car giveaway was an outdoors promotion that took place nearly two decades later. On July 10 and 11, 1948, Brooklyn Paramount patrons were invited for a sneak preview of the '48 Tucker on display in what originally was the Paramount Parking Terminal on DeKalb Avenue. In time, the free parking became a fabric factory before returning to a garage, which Long Island University purchased for faculty and staff in the 1970s. As we write this, it was being torn down to give way to another high-rise in this hot real estate market in downtown Brooklyn. "The first public showing ever!" was the come-on for that special promotion for the car, manufactured by the rogue manufacturer Preston Tucker, the subject of a 1988 Hollywood biopic starring Jeff Bridges.

Other original giveaways included one thousand copies of *True Detective* magazine awarded to the first one thousand theatre patrons on January 6, 1952, who also got to meet Horace McMahon, the costar (with Kirk Douglas) of *Detective Story*, a riveting film brought back from its initial screening during the week of January 30, 1950. Those giveaways were offered gratis before its 6:25 p.m. and 10:00 p.m. second run.

Yet another example was whatever the prize of the "Name It and Take It Contest" announced on stage more than a decade earlier, whose winner was announced on stage by Ed East, the WOR host of Benay Venuta's radio show on behalf of the sponsoring Cel-Ray beverage company (*Variety*, August 2, 1939).

Turning to another extracurricular event, the "Brains and Beauty Contest" was cosponsored with the *Standard Union* and announced weeks before the Brooklyn Paramount's opening. Launched on the steps of the borough's municipal hall on November 10, 1928, we read about a call for a dozen young nonprofessional women between the ages of eighteen and twenty-one, who also had to be Brooklyn residents as well as single and never divorced. Participants were invited to send along photographs to the local tabloid pursuant of a Hollywood acting career, and if they were unable to provide a photo, the sponsors of this contest promised assistance. Moreover, contestants additionally had to explain why they thought of themselves as temptresses, i.e., defined as a siren that is at times languorous, but possessing a fiery spirit that may easily be aroused. Sexist or not, twelve finalists had to await a final selection made by our theatre's first manager, J. L. McCurdy; their photos appeared in the tabloid along with others. The eventual winner was expected to undergo salaried training for forty-five dollars a week for twenty-five weeks while learning how to act and dance, etc., presumably at Paramount's Acting School in Astoria, Queens. And not only that, but the contestants were reminded that the winner would join two of the studio's leading ladies, Brooklyn's own Clara Bow and Manhattan's Hell's Kitchen starlet Nancy Carroll. She would spare the contest's losers' dismal fate of becoming stenographers, salesgirls, and secretaries.

By 1932, the "Brains and Beauty Contest" had apparently morphed into the so-called "Panther Contest" with more provocative perquisites, as only young unmarried Brooklynite women could apply, provided "they were simple, yet exciting, alluringly beautiful, and possessed with sensual beauty." They were also required to have a perfect figure, perfect teeth, and personality. And as if those attributes weren't enough, applicants were reminded they couldn't be blonde, brunette, or titian, and must, above all, have the true soul of an actress. Six finalists were presented during Screen Test Night on a Thursday on the Brooklyn Paramount stage. They got to meet "Smiling" Eddie Lowery, the Vaudevillian singing star of that week's program; the winner not only was also promised a gorgeous fall wardrobe valued at $250 by Loesser and Company but also the opportunity of being photographed by a professional cameraman as part of what proved to be a national competition. The ultimate winner was promised a role in the future Paramount Talkie following five weeks' training in Hollywood for two hundred dollars a week, where she would be taught the art of pantomime and drama by studio experts (*Times Union*, June 30, 1930). In that regard, twenty-one-year-old Miss Hirshorn of 632 Ocean Parkway in Brooklyn was the reported winner, yet she lost in the national competition. We read three years later on February 3,

1933, that Kathleen Burke, living in the Kings Borough, won the entire contest and got to appear alongside Richard Arlen and Charles Laughton in *Island of Lost Souls*, shown that week on our theatre's screen.

Similarly, a hairdressing contest was announced. Thus, on February 27, 1929, a call went out for fifty contestants willing to compete on stage for two days, and at 9:00 p.m. a winning prize would be awarded, but the date wasn't stated.

Nearly two weeks later, an "Anonymous Photo Contest" was announced on March 24, 1929. It sought the face of the most appealing young man or woman caught strolling down Brooklyn's streets unaware of a photographer hired by the theatre; here again, though the winning prize unfortunately was not indicated, those defined appealing faces of many finalists appeared in a local tabloid.

A so-called Moviegram contest next was announced on June 23, 1929, and its winner amazingly received free passage on a luxurious ocean liner to and from Paris from Manhattan's West Side piers as part of a two-week packaged deal...which additionally included the promise of sightseeing World War I battlefields for naming the Hollywood star in a film not more than four years old whose title was kept secret by our theatre's management. Whatever was that contest's second-place prize, a cutout of the four-door Buick sedan awarded the winner had been placed on display inside the theatre, while the prize for the third-place winner was an automatic-tuning Zenith radio in this giveaway contest advertised as more fun than solving crossword puzzles.

Then in the 1930s, the *Times-Union* on July 3, 1930, reported that Ed Kreisler had won the "Grin Contest" over Abraham Bidder and Clarence Brush—each of whose photographs appeared in that tabloid along with other contestants. As similarly described, a staff photographer with a "grinning camera" had been sent out on assignment to prowl the borough in search of "The Face with the Best Smile." The finalist was promised to meet Jack Oakie, Hollywood's film star in those years, also born in Brooklyn (218 Prospect Place), and who was invited to judge between ten to fifteen grins for free admission to a show in our theatre for the winner along with a twenty-five dollar cash prize presented on stage by that face-friendly popular actor whose grin (and ruddy visage), in fact, by recount was featured in twenty-two films screened here!

A related contest was for the most interesting face; it was posted during the week of February 5, 1932, as we read in the tabloid that a dual personality expert, William Benton, had been hired to analyze submitted photograph entries for that ultimate winner.

The initial winners of countless so-called opportunity contests were announced on January 14, 1931: Madeline Bowman of 4601 Eleventh Avenue, Brooklyn, who, for example, was selected on the basis of her winning song performed seated atop the Mighty Wurlitzer accompanied by Elsie Thompson on stage backed by the Brooklyn Paramount Orchestra.

Yet another contest hosted by the Brooklyn Paramount was similarly based on Neighborhood Amateur Hour–type competition, and whose eventual winner on January 31, 1931, was small blonde Edna Simpson, a seventeen-year-old aspiring vocalist who sang on stage backed by Charley Davis and His Merry Makers. Then again on September 6, 1931, we read in the *Standard Union* about another opportunity contest, which tallied several hundred applicants from "Neighborhood Frolics Groups" and whose winners were also feted on our theatre's stage on that following Wednesday night. Although their names weren't reported, Florence Newman of 1348 East Twenty-Eighth Street, Buddy Manners of 365 Pulaski Boulevard, and Vincent Calendro of 7612 Fourteenth Avenue also living in the King's Borough were cited as officers in two of those neighborhood clubs.

A few months prior, however, Ilson's Children's Department Store (474 Fulton Street) on June 13, 1931, sponsored "Free Weeks of Summer Camp for Children." In this giveaway contest, six Brooklyn children's winners, three boys and three girls, won ten weeks' free vacations away from the city's blistering heat in one of three camp-sites: Camp Stuts in Highland, Ulster County, New York State; Camp Lian in Fish's Eddy, Delaware; and/or the Cuheca Culture and Health

Camp in Waterford, Connecticut. The latter was reportedly run by Mr. and Mrs. Henry Schact, who also directed the Culture and Health School in Brooklyn throughout the rest of the year. And that is what was advertised as ten happy weeks of summer vacations valued in toto at $2,000 promised to winners whose names would be drawn on stage again by our theatre's bandleader, Charley Davis—a contest in which theatre patrons were invited to vote as many times as they desired, provided they paid full admission on each separate date as part of this special promotion by the Brooklyn Paramount.

The "Sky Bride Contest," on the other hand, came with its own unique reward. Engaged couples willing to be married during an airplane flight were invited during the week of April 22, 1932, to submit their names for the drawing...and not just to be married in another large lumbering trimotor Fokker like the one that flew back and forth over our theatre on opening day, either. Those nuptials were to take place in an eighteen-seat Eastern Air Transit Candor, whose flight plan was charted between New York and Delaware. Harry Blech and Shirley Pearlman, eventual winners, not only got to tie their marital knot in midair, but they also received fifty dollars in gold, a diamond-studded ring from L. B. Parman in Manhattan, and other gifts from participating sponsors. They were also promised free admission to *Sky Bride*, a Paramount new release starring Richard Arlen and Jack Oakie screened that week in our theatre.

What, no honeymoon? Unable to answer that question, we can, however, report these two caveats of "The Sky Bride Contest." As applicants were first and foremost reminded: "You furnish the girl and the license, and the Brooklyn Paramount furnishes the plane!" And second, they were also reminded not to forget their photo. All the same, since even the best-laid marital plans can be waylaid, that aerial wedding ceremony was postponed from Saturday until the following Wednesday. The reason wasn't at all religious or on account of inclement weather, either, but rather an unforeseen complication that arose when Brooklyn's city clerk refused to issue a marital license in lieu of information about the winners' future residency—a dilemma rectified only when the one and/or other (or both hopefully) agreed it would be Brooklyn before they were finally allowed to exchange sacred vows while flying between Queens and Philadelphia. If only for the marital record's sake, we can also report that Mr. and Mrs. Harry Blech were pronounced man and wife while flying directly over Bay Ridge, their intended future place of residence in what the tabloid added was the first Jewish Sky Wedding.

The annual "Miss Christmas Seals Contests" held between 1946 and 1956 also made the news. On November 21, 1956, contestants had to be registered nurses and graduates of any of our borough's seventeen accredited nursing programs; they had to be at least eighteen years old; and for whatever reason, they could not be connected with the Brooklyn Tuberculosis Association. After eliminating contestants presumably in those nursing schools, the winner that year got to appear on the Brooklyn Paramount stage on November 23, 1956. Curiously as well hailed as the new "Queen of the Brooklyn TB Association," the winner also received a $350 outfit from any of the five leading department stores in downtown Brooklyn. Notably, our theatre's manager, Eugene Pleshette, was listed as the medical organization's director.

Still another giveaway contest was titled "First Baby Born in the Borough in the New Year, 1947." Its prize for winning parents? A twenty-five-dollar United States Savings Bond, conditional not only on the birth and submission date, but also on a required copy of the infant's time and date of birth verified by the attending obstetrician and/or any residing hospital official. Here again, whether by coincidence or mere mortal design, this giveaway contest was also thematically related with a film screened the week of October 2, 1947: *Welcome Stranger*, which starred Bing Crosby, Joan Caulfield, and Barry Fitzgerald.

Still another giveaway contest during the following decade was the "Mrs. America Contest of 1955," whose winners—yes, plural— were promised $15,000 in prizes, during a national promotion by Paramount Pictures, which in this instance staged a runoff competition for the top draw of a $400 gas range as part of the awarded $1,200 kitchen with additional appliances that included a free trip to Florida with the winner's husband. Those over-the-top doings were accompanied by the zaniness of Martin and Lewis in *Three Ring Circus* cofeatured with Gene Kelly starring in *Crest of the Wave* during the week February 11, 1955.

During the 1950s we read on May 24, 1952, that Mrs. Catherine Lenuso had won a TV for identifying a well-known male celebrity as part of a "Name the Face Contest." Then six years later, we read about an extraordinary giveaway: Theatre patrons on July 13, 1956, were challenged to identify five famous faces on display in the lobby to win $35,000 in prizes, which included an Aeolian Spinet; two hundred Alsol Car Beauty Kits; thirty-six free vacations; and twenty-five thousand Ro-Zee Vacation Guide Books, presumably for other theatre patrons. Desperate times toward the end of our theatre's early history included waning attendance, which prompted the Brooklyn Paramount's final manager, Gene Pleshette, to guarantee every adult who entered would receive a prize. It was a futile situation that Pleshette directly addressed. *Slightly Scarlet* and *The Bold and the Brave* were cofeatures screened that week in the Brooklyn Paramount.

Yet another of those contests was dubbed "Who Is the Oldest Mother in the Borough?" Announced on November 12, 1929, soon after the opening of our wonder theatre, its winner was reportedly allowed to join with all her children and her close friends…(and) be entertained by Paul Ash, with free admission.

Onto essay-writing contests discussed in reverse order from this chapter's title. The first of those advertised in the *Standard-Union* on March 13, 1929, was "Why I Am Kind to Animals?" The tabloid apparently reported its winner sharing the stage with Tom Mix, who brought rodeo to our theatre.

We also read about an essay contest whose theme was "Pet Superstitions"…which again was probably held in conjunction with the screening of *Knock on Wood*, a screwball comedy starring Brooklyn's Danny Kaye, which opened on July 7, 1954. The twenty winners were promised free admission for the best essays answering this question: "Why I Believe in My Pet Superstition?" (*Williamsburg News*, July 9, 1954).

Another of those was "The Model Mailman in Brooklyn Contest." Contestants were invited to submit photographs of their selections, along with reasons why they recommended those federal employees. The thirteen highest vote-getters reported on August 17, 1939, not only were invited to a luncheon in swanky Manhattan Beach in Brooklyn, but the highest voter received a thirteen-day cruise with a companion and hotel stay in Miami Beach. The fifth winner received season passes for two to the Fabian (Brooklyn) Paramount. Whether or not job-related, the ninth- through thirteenth-highest vote getters received pairs of high-quality shoes from Marks Brothers on Delancey Street in Manhattan. Mailmen were broadly defined to include postal clerks as well as letter carriers.

Yet another essay contest bore the theme "Love at First Sight." Contestants were expected to submit essays between fifty and one-hundred words during the week of March 4, 1932, thereby hoping to win a pair of free admissions to another of the theatre's thematically related screenings: *Strangers in Love*, a Paramount flick, starring Fredric March and Kay Francis. Among those winning essays, we read that Mrs. W. J. Poit wrote about falling in love at first sight with her future husband no sooner than having unpacked during a summer vacation when she saw him casually standing on the veranda.

A related theme was the "Happy Husband Contest" (*Brooklyn Times Union*, March 9, 1932). Still other contests dealt with these far-ranging topics: "What Would I Do for the People If I Were President?" "How Can I Amuse Myself on a Rainy Day?" "Describe a Queer Character." "What Do You Admire Most in Shakespeare's Plays—The Humor, the Tragedy, Delineation of Character, or His Choice of Words?"

The newspaper columnist Elaine Jean instructed young dues-paying members in her dispersed club to "Write on any subject that appeals to you!" Given their ages, prior parental permission was initially required.

Another essay-writing contest offered a cash prize of fifty dollars in 1931 for theatre-paying customers willing to divulge their funniest experiences. Those 100–150 words, which had to be submitted to the *Brooklyn Daily Times* (540 Atlantic Avenue) by the assigned date c/o the great comic Eddie Cantor, who appeared on stage here during that same week of September 18, 1931. He was willing to read entries and select first, second, and third prize winners with promised cash prizes of fifteen dollars, ten dollars, and five dollars,

Other essay contests on other dates bore titles like "How I Met My Wife," "What I'd Do If Elected President," and "If I Had a Million." The latter was advertised on January 9, 1931, in the *Brooklyn Times Union* during some of those darkest days of the Great Depression. Still others came with cash prizes for winners of writing contests concerned with themes like "Ways to Improve Homes for an Aged Parent," "Self-Discovery Connected with World Travel," "Future Educational Goals," and even "Fantasized Clothes-Purchasing Sprees." Edward Smolowitz of 732 Snediker Avenue in Brooklyn, for example, won for nobly expressing his intention of using prize money from the "If I Had a Million" to build recreation centers for poor kids—ironically or not held during the week of January 5, 1933, when probably the Brooklyn Paramount screened "If I Had a Million," starring Gary Cooper, George Raft, and Charles Laughton.

"Why I Think Brooklyn Is the Best Place to Live" was another related essay contest subject. We also read about contestants invited during the week of February 26, 1934, to answer the blatantly sexist question posed by James Cagney in his tough-guy role in *The St. Louis Kid*—whether or not "girls go for the assertive type of man, a man who won't hesitate to put a woman in her place if he feels it necessary or, is it the quieter, more attentive and meeker male whom girls lost their hearts to?" Those twenty-five winning essays in seventy words or less were each awarded two free passes to that coming attraction.

Two final thematically related essay-writing contests that doubtlessly were designed to attract customers away from other deluxers during the 1940s and 1950s can also be documented: "Why I Prefer a Mountain Vacation," in which twenty-eight winners who'd written in one hundred or fewer words during the week of June 20, 1948, why they hoped to escape this city's sweltering summer heat were promised two weeks gratis with spouse or friend a stay in an upstate participating Catskills Mountain hotel (*Motion Picture Herald*, July–August 1948). While in that seasonal converse held one decade later—"Why I Prefer a Miami Beach Vacation" was announced February 26, 1954, the seven winners of which were promised two weeks all-expenses-paid vacations away from winter's brutal cold in any of these participating Florida hotels: the Cadillac, Delano, Ocean Turf, and four others in Miami Beach. The names of those seven winners of this "Vacation Contest," incidentally: Mrs. Edna Goldstein; Mrs. Lucy Havron; Mrs. Richard Snodgrass; Morris Nussbaum; Alan L. Smith; Matthew Forbes; and James Brennan, each of whom, once again, were permitted to bring along one guest, whether significant other or another. All the same, here again we probably shouldn't be surprised that one of the film offerings in the Brooklyn Paramount during "The Vacation Contest" held during the week of February 22, 1950, was *Dear Wife*, a comedy starring Joan Caulfield and William Holden based on the Broadway play *Dear Ruth*. Another "Miami Beach Vacation" contest announced these seven winners on April 8, 1955: Mrs. Edna Goldstein, Mrs. Lucy Havron, Mrs. Richard Snodgrass, Morris Nussbaum, Alan L. Smith, Matthew Forbes, and James Brennan (*Williamsburg News*).

But also we read in a place-based essay contest that Ana Boxer of 39 Turner Place had won first prize on October 22, 1929, for her composition titled "Brooklyn, the Paramount City's Paramount Borough."

And while we're still at it, we also read two decades later on March 31, 1951, that Gene Pleshette had won a $500 first prize award for his participation in a film contest sponsored by United Artists titled "So Young, So Bad." Our theatre's formidable manager reported this campaign angle "Modern girls...are they better or worse than women of previous generations?"

While in yet a different writing contest, Janet Sonnenstrahl of 36

Plaza Street in Brooklyn won one hundred dollars for her rhyming couplets on October 13, 1931, in what was dubbed a call for "The Best Original Advertisement for Brooklyn's Paramount." Her reported entry titled "Kingdoms for Sale" went like this:

Undoubtedly the Kings of old
Despite their jewels, their lands, their gold
Were far less fortunate than you.
My dears, their lives were drab, it's true.
They couldn't forget that care exists,
Or blow their sorrows to a mist
And live three precious hours a night
In magic worlds of new delight.
Riches, romance, youth...at will,
Life for part of a dollar bill!
We pity them who never thought
A priceless privilege could be brought.
Oh, Paramount, throw wide your portals
To these lucky modern mortals.

A greater prize of $1,000 was posted under the "Eagle-Zain Ad Contest" on November 13, 1931, for the person selected as having written forty-one best ads for a variety of products (like Drake's cakes) and companies (like Domino's Sugar). Still another similar writing contest during the Depression years called for the best jingle regarding those nationally prominent Caucasian Persuasion controversial-today blackfaced radio and screen comedians, Amos 'n' Andy, who appeared on stage here during the week of May 15, 1932. The winner was promised a twenty-five-dollar cash prize, as well as guest passes to view their show, provided the jingle must contain a last line referencing Amos 'n' Andy's Paramount film, *Check and Double Check*. Second-place winners not only would have their entries published in the *Brooklyn Times*, but two daily winners also received free theatre tickets.

Distantly related to those writing contests was the *Standard Union's* Spelling Bee for Eighth Graders. Announced on April 28, 1932, its competition was held in the Grand Lounge on Tuesday and Thursday afternoons, May 3 and May 10, between 5:00 and 5:30 p.m. with the winner promised to be announced on stage. A trip to Bermuda was the apparent prize for that whiz kid in that familiar contest supervised by Brooklyn's Superintendent of the Board of Education, Margaret Rae. Moreover, some wag came up with the clever idea of staging a contest for the best misspelled word...an oxymoron, surely, yet the winner nonetheless was promised two courtesy passes to our palatial cinema for submission of a word or words that defies this author's intelligence.

Turning next to the spate of puzzle-like contests sponsored by our movie theatre, we begin with the call for anagrams involving the names of major film stars and/or big Vaudeville performers held in association with their staged appearances....and with free admission to their performances as prizes for winners amassing the largest number of three-letter words found in the dictionary based on those entertainers' names. The rules were no homonyms allowed, and contestants were also judiciously forewarned: "No cheating allowed!" However, that rule was enforced, Pola Negri and George Jessel were only two of many names from which anagrams had to be extracted from their names in alphabetic order. Still other examples included the famous husband-and-wife Crawford Mighty Wurlitzer team during the week of May 6, 1932; the phrase "Hot from Harlem" during the week of April 21, 1931, pertaining both to Cab Calloway and Bill "Bojangles" Robinson, whose Cotton Club revues were respectively advertised as such.

To spur attendance, we read on October 16, 1931, that a really Big Vaudeville star, Sophie Tucker, who was the subject of an anagram contest, received press during another "Home Talk Paramount Word Puzzle" devoted to George Jessel's birth name, in which she was quoted with these mistaken four- and five-letter words derived from Jessel—jeer, and gorge in this contest, which called for three words, and whose winners got to see their Vaudeville show titled *Some of These Days* featuring both Big Vaudeville stars in thirteen dazzling scenes on stage on October 19, 20, and 21 in their revue commencing October 19, 1931.

Handsome Star Provides Fans With Puzzle Pieces in Theater Contest for Paramount Seats

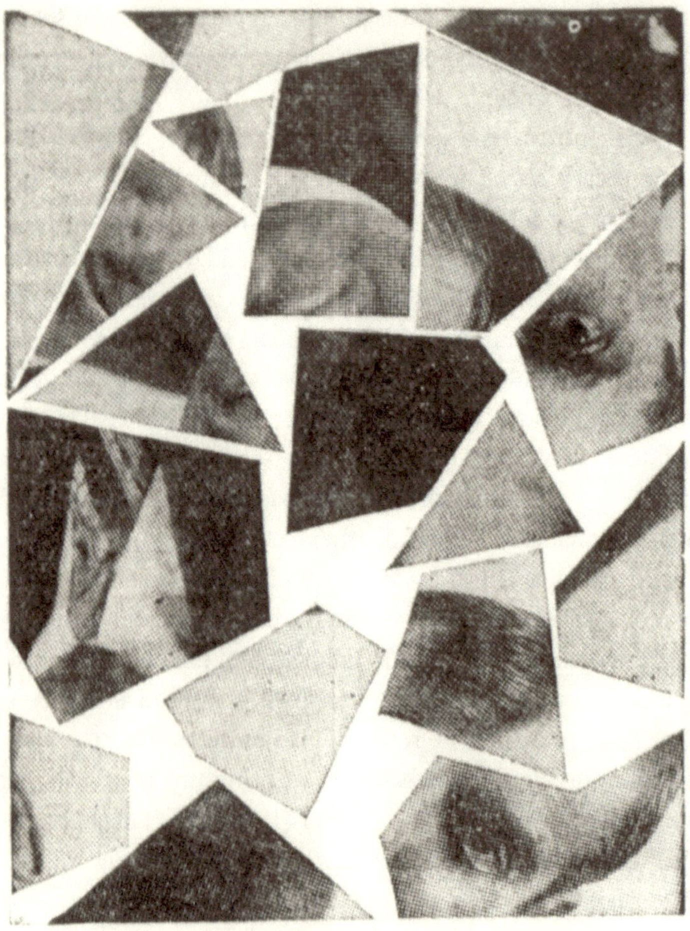

HOME PUZZLE (*The Brooklyn Daily Eagle*/January 4, 1933)

Additional puzzles were announced under the rubric "Home-Talk Paramount Contests." So, for example, interested theatregoers were invited to dissemble and reassemble portraits of celebrities like "Smiling" Eddie Lowery for free tickets to one of his Vaudeville appearances in 1932, as we shudder to recall identical instructions issued by intimidating matron like public school elementary teachers regarding our homework assignments that "neatness counts!"

Leave it to Fred Allen with his acerbic wit to quip about his dissembled portrait contest held on May 20, 1933, "The *Brooklyn Eagle* jigsaw puzzle looked like a Wasserman test to me!" (McCarthy, 1966: 259)

Moving ahead into the 1940s, however, an entirely different contest held in the Brooklyn Paramount was announced by the *Brooklyn Eagle*: a "Ten Best Film" challenge during which participants were invited to pit their selections from 164 printed releases in 1940 against the list of *Film Daily* mavens—with prizes for winners with the closest number of matches curiously sorted by gender, as in the two top women received free passes to the Albee or to our theatre, whereas both top men got to select either the Fox or Loew's Metropolitan. Oh, and sixty-five runners-up also received free admission to the distant RKO Century in Bushwick, which originally was a Vaudeville house and went out of business showing films in the 1970s.

Of an entirely different nature, though nonetheless interactive between management and theatre audiences all the same, were the "MVP, Most Popular Player," and the "MPP, Most Colorful Player" contests held at our rebranded Fabian Paramount and the Fabian Fox involving Brooklyn Dodgers' players in 1942. And so it was that Dolph Camilli, a left-handed twelve-year veteran first baseman compiled the highest number of votes for MVP—19,754—while the baseball team's catcher, Fred "Dixie" Walker, won the more subjectively imagined MPP with 22,443 votes. The same person who ironically circulated the infamous anonymous petition seeking signatures from teammates willing to join his racist boycott against Jackie Robinson several years later in 1947—the Dixiecrat's alleged excuse was fear of losing customers in his grocery store back home in Birmingham, Georgia, if forced to play alongside the immortal number forty-two—a racist action which resulted in his trade!

But there was yet another interesting aspect of that contest. For, not unlike the usurpation of rights of those Brooklyn Dodgers players who chose to compete against professional basketball players in their off-season, the baseball team's president, Lee McPhail, informed the press why he was pulling both contest winners from a dinner at the Granada Hotel on September 26, 1941—for which fans had already shelled out three dollars per ticket to meet and greet both winners—his seemingly absurd quoted reason being concern lest they get upset by pummeling of fans and other demonstrations, and hence be unable to play in the forecasted coming World Series against their dreaded rival New York Yankees. All the same, Peter Golenbock (1984) wrote that those players were presented with Bond suits and Hamilton wristwatches separately on the stages of the two theatres leased to the Fabians in those years at different scheduled times, i.e., our Paramount at 8:00 p.m. and the Fox on the other side of Flatbush Avenue Extension several blocks south at 9:30 p.m. with time allowed for walking that short distance.

Among our favorites, however, was the "Who Is He?" contest. In 1936, its contestants were invited to guess the identity of a pair of celebrity figures whose portraits appeared in the local tabloid, whose five winners in that so-called "Word Puzzle" contest received pairs of complimentary tickets to view *The Big Broadcast*, screened in our theatre that week, after they were also expected to submit their impressions of the famous radio team, as well as provide their show's theme song...said to have been based on the only clue given, a bawdy poem by Robert Burns in 1782, "Comin' Thru the Rye," which down the road inspired the title of J. D. Salinger's only novel, *Catcher in the Rye*...whomever those were.

Coming full circle and closing on the last years of the Brooklyn Paramount's thirty-four-year run as a movie theatre, we conclude this chapter with these spectacular giveaways. The first announced by the local tabloid on December 20,1957, as such: Many Prizes for

Paramount Patrons. And for that drawing scheduled on the following day, ticket holders in attendance of *The Story of Esther Costello* (with Joan Crawford and Rossano Brazzi) paired with Victor Mature and Diana Dors in *The Long Haul* were eligible to compete for prizes ranging from free membership in the Rozee Vacation Club; vacations in various hotels on the eastern seaboard ranging from Quebec in the north through the Catskills south to Miami Beach, Florida; Broil-Quik rotisseries; travel trunks; as well as membership in the Sterling Health Club—a package amounting to $25,000.

This final giveaway was advertised in the local tabloid that previous year in 1956: "Everyone who enters will receive a prize." But that is, only after producing a box top or label from Borden's Instant Milk, Good Luck margarine, a Hoffman beverage, or Ipana toothpaste. As reported in *Variety* (May 16, 1956), all ticket holders were eligible, provided they spent at least $1.50 toward the purchase of any of those products.

Skimming past the No-Cal Beauty Contest reported on July 24, 1959, in the *Williamsburg News*, whose preliminaries were held on stage here on succeeding Wednesday nights between July 29 and August 19—for the prize of a modeling career—we close with this Trivial Pursuit–type bittersweet question posed within weeks of our theatre's closing date by *Variety* on April 12, 1962, involving our theatre's manager, who clearly was forced to resort to desperate straits for attracting audiences to keep this dying swan alive: "Name the only managing director of a wonder theater whose daughter became a motion picture actress and starred in a Hollywood film shown in the old man's house." Hint: The title of the film was *Rome Adventure* and the actress's name was Suzanne Pleshette!

Finally, in that regard, we note that contestants were also instructed to submit entries to "The Home Talk Office" (4806–08 Fourth Avenue) no later than on that following Monday, so that the thirty theatre patrons with the largest and most nearly correct lists of words might receive courtesy tickets to the Brooklyn Paramount Theatre during the subjects' stage appearances.

CHAPTER 13

A Community Center as Well?

Cambria and Falge (1929: 890), in their study of the unique lighting in our theatre, anticipated by more than a century the familiar tripartite division of texts employed by postmodern literary scholars (Krupat, 1989): The opening of the Brooklyn Paramount Theatre by the Publix Theaters Corporation (the operating organization of the Paramount Famous Lasky Corporation), they wrote, could well have been marked as a national event rather than a local one, and certainly an international one to people. Adopting that framework, we featured these additional extracurricular faces in our theatre's initial incarnation in those three terms, which allow us to hypothesize that ours functioned as a community center as well.

A. Local Extracurricular Events

So, for example, the *Evening Herald and Moving Picture World* on December 29, 1928 (p. 62) reported within a month of the theatre's opening a midnight benefit hosted by Paul Ash. Said to play Santa for proceeds directed toward local needy kids, we also read that Edward Paul led the Brooklyn Paramount Orchestra in the overture to *La*

Traviata followed by an aria sung by a contralto named Stella Powell. Then, after George Murtaugh played "Hail, Hail, the Gang's All Here" on the Mighty Wurlitzer, the redheaded wunderkind Ash introduced fourteen Big and Small Vaudeville headliners...who included the future Toastmaster General George Jessel, Helen "Betty Boop" Kane, Milton Watson, Karavieff, as well as Paramount film stars like Richard Dix joining that charitable cause.

The Knights Before Christmas, a fraternal order organized by a newspaper columnist named Edward Zeltner, also sponsored the Christmas fundraiser for the borough's local needy kids. On December 15, 1929, we read that they hosted children from unnamed social agencies who were given gifts as well as the chance to see that week's film offering, *The Marriage Playground*, as well as a specially designed Vaudeville show.

Another report speaks about those dancers led by the ingenue Maria Gambarelli. Then one decade later, we similarly read on December 26, 1939, about another annual Christmas charitable extracurricular event cosponsored again by the Brooklyn Paramount and the Knights Before Christmas...with stocking-filled gifts for forty local needy children distributed on that Saturday.

Indeed, on March 25, 1956, the Knights Before Christmas was still staging pre-Christmas benefits with gifts for hundreds of handicapped and needy youngsters (*Brooklyn Eagle*, March 23, 1956). As was the case on December 12, 1959, when the wives of another fraternal order identified as "Eves" were reported wrapping thousands of Christmas toys in the theatre for poor youngsters in the borough; they were also treated to a lavish dinner and special show at Ben Maksik's Town and Country Club, Brooklyn's most famous (and largest mob-connected) nightclub, formerly located near Mill Basin (*Williamsburg News*, December 4, 1959).

Poverty-stricken children in the King's Borough were also feted during annual Easter fundraisers. For example, when we read the following in the local tabloid on March 27, 1937, some 12,624 poor kids received seats to see *Maid of Salem* (starring Fred MacMurray and Claudette Colbert) paired with *Her Husband's Secretary* in our theatre under the supervision of licensed police matrons hired to control the behavior of out-of-school children on holiday. Indeed, Si Fabian, identified as "General Manager of the Brooklyn Paramount Theater," was quoted several months later on July 11, 1937, in another context discussing the possible use of the theater that summer for groups of children who did not have the means nor were fortunate enough to enjoy a few cool hours away from the hot city streets. His additional comment about philanthropy thereby underscored our view—hypothesis—that the Brooklyn Paramount might just as well also be conceived as a community center.

Here again time travel into the future allows us to read in the *Williamsburg News* on May 25, 1956, about another fraternal lodge, the Knights of Columbus, that was involved in another fundraising event for the collection of gifts for hundreds of handicapped and needy local youngsters to be distributed that Easter, when theatre ticket prices were raised from $2.50 to $10.00 for this extracurricular event featuring various stage, screen, and TV personalities. That charitable organization's sixth annual production was headed and organized by Gene Pleshette, our theatre's manager, aided by Mort Curtis, listed as theatrical manager, and who was said to have been involved with the recruitment of volunteers to distribute gifts among hundreds of handicapped and needy youngsters.

Yet another local extracurricular charitable event involved the Brooklyn Paramount's partnership with the Thirteenth Regiment Armory located on Sumner and Putnam Avenues in the King's Borough.

We read in the *Brooklyn Eagle* (December 21, 1929) that the tabloid partnered again with the theatre manager by hosting after-hours fundraisers for the tabloid's "Forty neediest cases from the Eagle Fund," a charitable midnight event, which in this instance saw the bandleader of those Merry Pranksters come out of retirement for that Saturday and lead them. The stars included Paramount's actor Charles Ruggles as well as Vaudevillians for the admission price of one dollar. The proceeds were targeted for the borough's unhappiest families. All the same, theatre patrons were instructed to enjoy themselves.

The United Parents' Association hosted a special holiday local program for children. As reported on December 30, 1929, in the local tabloid, needy children convened at the Brooklyn Paramount at 9:30 in the morning. Some three thousand youngsters were said to be representing nearly every school in the borough. And while it remains moot whether those kids who reportedly filled the house were permitted to view the featured film that week—*Pointed Heels*, a Paramount melodrama about show business, starring the blonde sex kitten Carole Lombard—they got to see selected comedies and were also entertained by Rudy Vallée on stage, presumably singing and playing his alto saxophone along with contributions from other Vaudevillians.

Thus, on March 2, 1929, we once again read about Paul Ash leading a bevy of unnamed Vaudevillians on stage during an after-hours late-Saturday-night charity ball. John L. McCurdy, the theatre's first manager, reached out to the president of the prestigious Montauk Club, William English, for financial support. English's defining role in the construction of the Brooklyn Paramount is discussed in the final chapter of this book.

Still another local charitable event was the second annual movie party benefit for the Anthonian Hall. So, from June 3 to June 7, 1929, Miss Madeleine Walsh, president of that Roman Catholic residence for blind women located near our theater on 105 Greene Avenue, and Mrs. William G. Strieb, cochair, sent out calls for members from their rental space on the second floor of the Brooklyn Paramount's adjoining eleven-story office building to help with regard to what was advertised as a nonsectarian event.

Additional local charitable causes that involved our theatre can also be documented. So, for example, *The New York Times* on June 5, 1949, reported we entertained children from various settlement houses on that previous day. Although no reason was given, some three hundred children as well as twenty crippled kids from St. Giles Hospital in the borough were carried in and out of these premises by specially assigned local policemen to satisfy what the sociologist

Robert Merton would have termed as the Brooklyn Paramount's latent function, i.e., contrasting with the theatre's manifest function as an entertainment parlor. And once again, the Knights Before Christmas, an organization of business and professional men, was reported in the *Williamsburg News* six years later on May 23, 1956, planning an all-star benefit on stage two days hence, the proceeds from which were said to be intended to purchase gifts for hundreds of handicapped youngsters, as personalities from stage, screen, and TV were advertised as expected to donate their time.

Still another local extracurricular event that remains part of our cinematic-like palace's earlier history was reported on May 30, 1950, when Eugene Pleshette, the theatre's manager, played host to children from settlements, orphanages, and hospitals for this charitable function said to be devoted to preventing juvenile delinquency as a result of the stated alarm of a group of benevolent business and professional men willing to address that new social problem. Thus, a cohort of supposedly at-risk kids were selected from eleven local social service agencies, such as the Red Hook Community Center for Children, St. Joseph's Female Orphans Home, etc., who along with homebound handicapped children were reportedly transported by the Brooklyn Red Cross Motor Chapter to our theatre, where they got to enjoy one of the last Marx Brothers' films, *Love Happy*. They also got treated to boxed lunches. No mention, however, was made if they got to see the cofeature that week, *Davy Crockett*, which we can safely conclude they did.

Indeed, decades before Rock 'n' Roll was blamed for juvenile delinquency in America during the 1950s, we report again about Mary Pickford's lone appearance on our theatre's stage. In 1934, she appeared in a sketch from A *Church Mouse*, the actress's NBC radio program re-created on stage; her visit presumably connected with the return engagement of her (second) husband, Charles "Buddy" Rogers, in a starring role that week in the Brooklyn Paramount's Vaudeville offering...an appearance that made the front-page news of our local tabloid on February 6, 1934, for which she was photographed with the head of the Flatbush Boys Club and a few of its honor youngsters, whose lives were reportedly saved from their ongoing membership. Her social conscience as noted, marked by the fact that Lew Leslie's *A Rhapsody in Black* accompanied her appearance, which contained the Berry Brothers as well as twelve instrumentalists who call themselves the Sepia Syncopating Misses.

So-called "Good Cheer Clubs" were also involved in local civic-minded ways...as we read that during the week of December 22, 1928, thousands of poor kids received bags of candy, nuts, and ice cream provided by the Reid Ice Cream Co., the Mason-Peaks Company, and Joe Sartori, the owner of a local popular restaurant near our theatre. And lest we be remiss by failing to report that Al Jolson's hit song "There's a Rainbow Round My Shoulder" was performed by Don Baker on the Mighty Wurlitzer for those challenged children on that pre-Christmas morning who also got to view *The Haunted House* thanks to the cosponsorship of a local tabloid, an apparent charitable cause reportedly supervised by the Brooklyn Paramount's head usher and his staff, as well as the house assistant general manager, Stephan L. Barutto.

And speaking of ice cream, the *Times-Union* reported on June 4, 1930, that all theatregoers were invited to the Great Lounge for an all-you-can-eat treat. That indulgence was sponsored by an out-of-state New Jersey dairy after the afternoon's screening of *Safety in Numbers*, a musical directed by Victor Scherzinger, who wrote the two pre-Code songs heard in *Manhattan Cocktail*.

A final club needs to be mentioned: the Brooklyn Paramount Athletic and Social Club, which was reported in the tabloid on February 10, 1933, "entertain(ing) their friends at their clubrooms tomorrow night." Whatever its nature, Frank Carreccia recently from the Club Saxon headed up the entertainment committee. The creator of the fallaway dance apparently hired the Club Paramount Orchestra and relied on some of the foremost radio stars for entertainment.

Yet another community-minded local extracurricular event was the allowance of telegraphs sent from the basement lounge by theatre patrons during intermissions at the discounted price of twenty cents per word, as reported on February 5, 1930.

While another local charitable cause evidenced in our theatre's multivariate earlier history was the Community Milk Fund, whose 140 members hosted parties at the theatre from Monday through Friday during the week of April 4, 1940, during which five hundred blocks of tickets were purchased as part of their fifteen-year-old charitable organization's good works. They were Brooklyn women from Crown Heights and Flatbush who previously raised money during card parties that resulted in 150 bottles of that essential nutrient annually provided daily to needy children in the borough. There was also a movie benefit on December 15 of that year with Mrs. Rhoda A. Weissman and Mrs. Eleanor Jeffers, who were in charge.

We also note the appearance of Brooklyn's Borough President John Cashmore on Monday morning, April 27, 1942, between 9:00 and 9:30 a.m., in recognition of three blind citizens who attained outstanding achievements during our nation's Second World War civilian home front. Hizzoner, accordingly, also praised the work of Mrs. Marion Lefcourt, president of that organization; Mrs. Cecil Keller, veep; Mrs. Minnie Lester, treasurer; Mrs. Rosalie T. Rosen, secretary; and Mrs. Frances Greenberg and Mrs. Jean Taubin listed as cochairs. The celebration of Brooklyn's Annual Week of the Blind in our theatre was also reported on March 2. 1946, with Dixie Walker, the controversial baseball catcher on the borough's beloved Brooklyn Dodgers who presented savings bonds to several blind residents.

Still talking disabilities, we take additional delight recounting our theatre's response to the needs of another group with special needs during its earliest years. For, as the local tabloid reported, Lou Goldberg, its theatre manager, supervised the installation of thirty Bell Telephone Laboratories headphones on the backs of mezzanine seats accompanying a device that came with a pencil-shaped potentiometer manufactured by Western Electric for hearing-challenged patrons to provide them with auditory assistance. The device allowed full enjoyment of the Paramount feature film screened during the week of July 21, 1929, *River of Romance* (starring Buddy Rogers). *Variety* (July 17, 1929) picked up on this philanthropic gesture by additionally reporting that the device received a 67 percent approval rating by the American Federation of the Deaf.

Needless to say, issues pertaining to the quality of sound became quintessential to all movie theatres following the tumultuous change-over from Silent Films—if indicated only by the title of a featured column "Hearing What You See" by John Skinner in the *Brooklyn Eagle*. Apropos, Skinner found fault with our theatre's projectionists in one column, blaming union membership for their alleged laziness on the job. All the same, an advertisement in the *International Projectionist* on October 31, 1933, applauded the various Publix Theatres projection departments, especially the staff of the Brooklyn Paramount, whose personnel were singled out: Morris Heller, Nat Hewitt, William Parker, John Hurley, John Timmerman, William Garbade, Charles Lippman, George Van Deura, and I. Sherman.

Continuing in this vein, the United Parents' Association gathered here during the week of March 23, 1929, for an outing coordinated with the screening of *Redskin*, a powerful social-issues Paramount Silent Film directed by Victor Schertzinger, to which dialogue was added, that starred Richard Dix, who dramatized the plight of what sociologists called "the marginal man," i.e., the return of an Eastern-boarding-school-educated Navajo in this instance to the sprawling Navajo Reservation, who initially was rejected by tribal members for acquiring non-Indian ways. Advertised as a beautiful love story, the protagonist of this film with its objectionable title (according to today's standards) not only wins acceptance by discovering oil, but in the end also gets to marry a beautiful woman...an indigenous woman, needless to say.

Then, too, there was Brooklyn on Parade, a local talent show originating in Bensonhurst, Williamsburg, Coney Island, Bushwick, and Flatbush, which formed Paramount Neighborhood Frolic Clubs. The names of these finalists among sixteen runners-up on our theatre's stage, all singers, were: Tom Lillis, Vincent Calendo, and Gladys

Gambling, during the week of November 18, 1931, as part of an "All Brooklyn" program.

There were evenings devoted to local sports teams as part of the Brooklyn Paramount's dedicated community-minded local events.

For example, "The Brooklyn Robins Night" was held on May 26, 1929, a Tuesday, when this second annual extracurricular romp brought together players on the soon-to-be-renamed Brooklyn Dodgers baseball team in our house. The Paramount inaugurated Robins Night. Or, so we read about that year's welcoming event to players on the team named in those years for its manager, Wilbert Robinson. And not only would the borough's tabloid list their names, but off-season jobs were indicated as well. Hank DeBerry and Dave Bancroft, for a pair of examples, were said to own and operate shoe stores in Savannah, Tennessee, and Superior, Wisconsin, respectively.

Another sports-related extracurricular event was the screening of *Scenes of Erasmus v. Manual Training High School* on November 5, 1934, a Monday night. Billed as an exclusive Brooklyn showing, one can easily infer that the interscholastic borough rivalry was a very big deal in those years. The *Paramount News* filmed the entire gridiron match for special screening of what the tabloid called a sort of preparatory rally for both teams' gridiron meeting the following afternoon at Ebbets Field, and in addition to those players, the Brooklyn Paramount also hosted the entire Brooklyn Dodgers professional football team.

Still another of those was devoted to recognition of Brooklyn's outstanding high school football players in 1931…who were presented on stage, where they received trophies from our theatre's organist, Merle Clark, on that Friday night, December 12. From among those eleven so-called huskies selected by the *Brooklyn Times-Union* staff—in collaboration with the Brooklyn Paramount's management—we not only extracted the name of the Long Island University five-sport standout William "Dolly" King, a six-foot, three-inch, two-hundred-pound gridiron star residing at 883 Green Avenue, but also these two locals who went on to greater sports heights: Marty Glickman, who lived at 2141 Seventy-Fifth Street in our borough, who was banned from the 1936 Olympics in Berlin because he was Jewish, and Sid Luckman who lived at 2501 Cortelyou Road and became a legendary Chicago Bears professional quarterback, who also for the record was listed at five foot eleven and 190 pounds.

In yet another sports-related local extracurricular event, the tenth anniversary of Lafayette High School was celebrated here nearly two decades later. Arranged by the Brooklyn public school's alumni as a theatre party in 1949, it saw donation boxes placed in various locations at the Brooklyn Paramount for nearly an entire month, i.e., between January 17 and February 2, with the stated goal of raising money to support team sports whose athletic programs boasted the Hall of Fame great pitcher for the Brooklyn-cum-Los-Angeles Dodgers, Sandy Koufax.

Returning yet again to basketball games held on our theatre's stage, there was also Saturday morning competition between kids belonging to various settlement houses, mostly in our borough. Held before the feature films and commencing on December 15, 1939, we read that the Final City Basketball Game was scheduled at 10:00 a.m. on March 9, 1940, between kids weighing no more than 135 pounds. Among those local participating teams were the Brooklyn Navy Yard Boys' Club, which remains a short walking distance from our theatre and whose team one Saturday played against the University Settlement House representing the Lower East Side of Manhattan. Theatre patrons willing to come out early got to stay on for both ensuing films. But so, too, were there local basketball games between girls representing the CYO (Catholic Youth Organization) and Jewish Community House of Bensonhurst. Chick Baker was named coordinator of youth basketball at Brooklyn's Paramount, and the former heavyweight boxing champion Jack Dempsey reportedly was set to toss up the opening ball during one such game (November 27, 1939).

Yet another community-minded extracurricular event was a treasure hunt for kids from the Brooklyn Navy Yard Boys' Club held in our theatre on October 8, 1950—with pirate costuming, which was a prerequisite for participation.

Of an entirely different nature, we further note a local columnist named Prudence Penny answering women's questions about domestic matters on stage as part of a Monday afternoon series that commenced on December 20, 1929. Our theatre's *nom de plume*, who was one of different women columnists supplying that social service in Hearst papers throughout the nation, might well have been Mrs. Mabel Burridge, a forty-two-year-old widow called Mother and Aunt, as well as home economist in her local radio program in the *New York Journal-American*. "An Afternoon with Prudence Penny" and "Prudence Penny Parties" were how those appearances here were advertised. Their startup time of 3:30 p.m. on those weekday afternoons was obviously when young mothers had enough time to pick up their kids after school and hurry over with them to the Brooklyn Paramount for tendered advice on nagging questions confidentially submitted in advance.

These additional diverse examples of what we are calling local extracurricular community-minded events were also documented.

On May 22, 1934, we read in the tabloid about "100 prominent Jews" from the borough who were in attendance to fete the Odessa-born composer and former musical director of Yiddish theater, Alexander Olshanetsky, who was said to have been making his English debut. The new conductor of the Brooklyn Paramount Symphony Orchestra (as it was crowned) had precociously graduated from the Russian Imperial Conservatory at the age of sixteen and went on to conduct Yiddish operettas and musical comedies. Maestro Olshanetsky had just completed a four-week residency at the Manhattan-Paramount.

Another of those was the Kiwanis Klub Kabaret [*sic*] hosting a theater party on February 28, 1934, under the auspices of Thomas A. Clarke, who had invited forty artists willing to donate their time as entertainers for that unspecified benefit.

Celebrity fan clubs were part of the Brooklyn Paramount's local extracurricular calendar. The Joan Blondell Fan Club, for example, was headed by Jean Galasse, who lived at 134 Ashland Place, a block east of our theatre. She had summoned one hundred members on

September 18, 1934, to attend the opening of *Dames*, a Busby Berkeley choreographed musical starring their heroine, who began as part of a sister act in Vaudeville.

And Good Cheer Clubs were frequent players. Their founder tendered advice to youngsters in her daily newspaper column and periodically roused club members to participate in essay-writing contests with family-based themes. One such winner got to meet Mary Pickford and received gifts as well. Yet another of those was Aunt Hetty's Club, whose "Junior Eagle" members belonging to her Rainbow Club were rewarded guest seats to see *Skippy*, a Paramount film starring the child actor Jackie Coogan at a Gala Christmas Party held on December 2, 1934, that was also advertised as a special promotion. But those sixteen-year-old members had to first submit thirty *Brooklyn Eagle* newspaper coupons in a self-addressed, stamped envelope to Aunt Hetty in her office on Fulton Street. "Remember, children," she cautioned against disappointment in advance of another self-promotion, an Easter gathering, reminding them in her daily column that if not selected, "I expect you to be very sweet and obedient and if your mother asks you to stay at home and she invites a friend of hers to this party, then that will be your Easter gift." Or else the "Merrie Little Elf...be very angry."

Another example was Elsie-Jean's Happy Times Club, said to number more than forty-one thousand boy and girl club members, established in 1935. They were invited to write in for tickets to attend the birthday celebration of George Washington on February 23. Indeed four thousand members of her Happy Times Club were promised Sun Dial kazoos on October 27, 1933, for their attendance of the premiere of *The Emperor Jones*, which starred the great African American college-athlete-cum-actor-singer/activist Paul Robeson in a filmed dramatization of Eugene O'Neill's Broadway play, about which a *Times-Union* reviewer described its dramatization of a power-crazed Black dictator as a classic of Negro humanity. Those noisemakers, however, were distributed to enliven the mad jamboree that followed the film during a birthday party for our theatre's new stage bandleader, Stan Myers.

A third and final example dates a few years earlier when Rudy Vallée entertained one hundred Uncle Henry Rainbow Club members, who the local newspaper wrote, "they wanted to see this talented young man in a Sherlock Holmes picture, to say nothing of listening to the exquisite music."

And surely, too, another extracurricular local event, which had nothing to with the Brooklyn Paramount's original charter, was the Staff Party held on December 15, 1934, a dinner dance with food, music, and entertainment, held in the Great Hall. Whether or not an annual event, these names of Brooklyn Paramount employees were reported on that date as members of its organizational committee: Murray Greenbaum, Louis Olshansky, Murray Weber, Fred Mendelsohn, Dan Dumblusky, Sam Hellerstein, and Lou Levy.

While hardly a planned event, there also was an occasional litigation against the theatre for accidents as well as union-related controversies that also qualify as local extracurricular events.

Despite an estimated three million paid customers over the theatre's initial thirty-four-year history, the only example of the former involved thirty-year-old Mary Praia of 1329 East Fourth Street in Brooklyn, who, despite her attorney's claim for $50,000 in damages to cover the cost of her surgically repaired fractured hip said to have resulted, was severely injured in the mezzanine balcony on May 15, 1931. The case was initially thrown out of Justice Steinbrink's courtroom alleging "there was no evidence to show faulty architectural or building fault." Two years following appeals, the Appellate Court on March 6, 1934, overruled that initial judgment and held the Brooklyn Paramount accountable.

With regard to labor–management disputes, the only instance we found involved the firing of projectionists in 1949. Thus, after Nat Hewitt and Steve D'Inzillo were let go and a job action followed, Robert Weitman, the Manhattan Paramount manager, when pressed for an explanation by the press gave incompetence as the reason for their dismissal—based on the alleged fact that they inserted the wrong reel during a recent screen offering. Pleshette's mentor, however, refused to answer countercharges that they'd instead been fired for protesting Weitman's working hours extensions from midnight to 2:00 a.m. sans recompense...which, for the record, followed those projectionists joining Local 306 of the Motion Pictures Machine Operators Union. But so, too, did Harry Garfman of that union, who was interviewed during the related job action on Times Square where fellow projectionists picketed in front of Manhattan's Paramount. They blamed the strike on a lockout of members of their union by the Brooklyn Theater. Pickets led by Mrs. Frank Fimano outside the Brooklyn Paramount's adjoining eleven-story office building, however, had nothing to do with the theatre—they were against the BMT, which rented office space for having joined the Transport Workers Union (December 12, 1954).

Turning next to the local police blotter as it remotely pertains to additional faces of the Brooklyn Paramount, we begin with a robbery that occurred during the theatre's inaugural Vaudeville show.

Thus, while Marie Gambarelli was doing her thing on stage at noontime on November 24, 1928, someone broke into the star ballerina's dressing room and stole $234 from her purse. The culprit was an African American named Harry Walker, age thirty-four, who did what criminals so often compulsively do, i.e., revisit the crime scene soon thereafter. Walker was then arrested and charged with the original break-in following a stakeout on that following morning and after $222 had been planted in another Vaudevillian's dressing room. Apprehended on the fire escape behind the theatre overlooking de-mapped Hudson Avenue, which we called Pigeon Alley, the second-story burglar humorously quoted what he once again was doing up there: "I just wanted to get into the theater to see the show" (*Brooklyn Eagle*, November 29, 1928).

Incomparably worse was what occurred more than a year later. On December 30, 1929, a Saturday night, we read about the cold-blooded murder of a motorcycle cop in Woodside, Queens. Officer Joseph Joekel responded to a call about a drugstore robbery in Maspeth (Queens), while on his way to work that night; he identified the stolen taxicab following a police radio report that said it had been hijacked in front of the Brooklyn Paramount when its owner was awaiting a pickup. He unfortunately paid with his life—shot three times in the head by one or more of those four desperados. The taxi was owned by Louis Rosenberg, who was forced to drive them from downtown Brooklyn into the adjoining borough.

In another synchronicity, the mother of that tragically young first defender motorcycle cop, who tragically left behind four young children, happened to be attending a Christmas party on that Saturday night close enough to that drug stop to sadly identify the body of her slain son.

This second, more local police blotter item was benign by comparison. It involved two pairs of sisters from Manhattan arrested for creating a public disturbance in the Great Hall of our theatre. As reported on February 11, 1929, they shouted, "Don't Push, Shove!" They were probably bored and frustrated standing in line inside the theatre and anxious to get to their seats. Fortunately, no one was injured, although the newspaper reporter who covered the story commented about the near-pandemonium and its potential for leading to a sort of house of cards. From his terse reportage, we also read: "Somebody screamed. Somebody neither shoved nor pushed but punched. Somebody called the Poplar St. police station." The Brooklyn Paramount manager identified those four young women (in their early twenties) to six cops who promptly arrived at the scene, resulting in the arrest of Kitty and Tessie Laura, and Rose and Minnie Ferra, charged with causing a disturbance. Need we also editorialize by adding that *Sins of the Father* starring Emil Jannings was the Paramount film screened that night?

Our theater's next local police blotter item in chronological order saw the arrest of Joseph Milone for having stolen a loudspeaker from the theatre after he attempted to sell it for $125 to the owner of a candy store on Metropolitan Avenue in Brooklyn. The owner, Emile Guisto, then called the police and identified the culprit who got arrested (*Standard Union*, December 15, 1931).

Next we read in *The New York Times* (November 7, 1945) about the supposed theft of a woman's large black handbag inside our theatre. It belonged to Mrs. Frances Di Donna, who dutifully reported the missing brown wallet with $750 to management. She, however, changed her story when the police arrived to investigate. She admitted that she had absentmindedly left the purse in a telephone booth after placing a call and hurriedly returned to the married couple's seats following a hectic afternoon of furniture shopping with her hubby, Raymond, a World War II veteran, home minus an arm. The title of one of those films in the Brooklyn Paramount they'd dropped in to see was *Scotland Yard Investigator*!

Still another local police blotter was serious. As reported on New Year's Eve 1951, two men purchased tickets for the 1:17 a.m. late night/ early morning showing of *Let's Dance* and *The Hidden City* and then slipped inside the manager's office and made off with part of the holiday receipts. Their haul was $4,000, and thankfully none of those seven staff members taken hostage were harmed. Two of them were women whom they locked up along with five men inside a washroom. Those bandits made off with the loot during a reported full house of 4,200 moviegoers, otherwise oblivious to that real-life off-screen drama (*The New York Times*, January 1, 1951).

Then two years later, *The New York Times* on July 7, 1953, reported another Brooklyn Paramount Theatre–related crime. It involved the nefarious doings of the Packard Gang, comprised of two teenagers and an older accomplice in his late twenties who owned that American manufactured sturdy cruising car. They'd intercepted a forty-eight-year-old Black porter named Moses Cain on Third Avenue and Warren Street in our borough while on his way to work in our theatre and took him hostage in their hideaway at 577 Drew Street. They beat information out of him regarding the location of the overnight theatre earnings. While one gang member was left behind to keep watch over the terrified porter, the other two brazenly walked into the theatre's employee entrance at Hudson and DeKalb claiming they sought work at 10:00 a.m. An usher who joined Long Island University's Security headquarters years later then walked to Assistant Manager Angelo Calderado's office. He had been threatened with a brandished gun before making off with the previous day's gate receipts of $2,500 and left both behind bound and gagged though otherwise uninjured.

A footnote to this robbery was that a laundry mark on the clean shirt Cain was given to replace his blood-stained shirt provided the clue that broke the case, thereby allowing the police to trace the former back to those criminals' attic and promptly arrest them. Also of related interest was that those captured gang members additionally confessed to having successfully burglarized two other cinematic-like palaces (*The New York Times*, July 7, 1953).

Then six months later, *The New York Times* (December 18, 1955) reported another place-based crime: two men having taken a dentist hostage after he'd dropped off his daughter in front of our theatre. They forced Eugene Raicus, DDS, to drive them to his dental office on Eastern Parkway and took $275 from their hostage's wallet along the way. When they discovered the absence of additional cash, his family members' lives were threatened, lest he deliver an additional $5,000 on the following (Saturday) morning. Instructed by telephone at his home in Belle Harbor, Queens, to deliver the money to our theatre, those extortionists, however, were duly apprehended in the lobby by detectives whom Dr. Raicus riskily contacted.

Yet another extracurricular local crime-and-punishment story involved the seeming entrapment of a twenty-year-old Hispanic male named Robert Cruz, who, according to *The New York Times* (April 4, 1961), was apprehended by three undercover detectives with a stash of marijuana. Claiming to have obtained it from a seaman aboard a South American ship, Cruz explained he hoped to sell twelve thousand manufactured joints at $1.25 each, hardly chump change in those years.

Two bomb incidents were also part of what we identify as the theatre's extracurricular local earlier history.

In the first of those, *The New York Times* reported on April 23, 1949, that someone set off two harmless stench bombs in the orchestra during what the reader shouldn't be surprised by now to learn that that panic occurred during the screening of *Incident*, a film starring John Payne (not Wayne). Had it not been for the clever action of an employee, as the newspaper explained, a stampede among 2,100 patrons would surely have occurred. Perfume was sprayed into the vents during what was also disclosed as the Brooklyn Paramount beset by labor problems. This was evidenced by ten union members from the Motion Picture Machine Operators Union picketing outside to protest the firing of two of the theatre's projectionists for having joined the AFL chapter. Miraculously, only 107 theatregoers fled and received ticket refunds.

Several years later, however, a real bomb went off. It was planted inside a Wakefield-Hayward orchestra seat, and several patrons were injured on December 2, 1956, at 7:50 p.m. during a screening of *War and Peace*. And that dastardly deed was directed initially by a disgruntled Con Edison employee in Manhattan. George P. Metesky was his name, and the aptly called "Mad Bomber" was victimized by an industrial accident and fired without compensation, not unlike the Son of Sam during the 1970s, who terrorized our city. He'd planted thirty-two homemade bombs for sixteen years between 1940 and 1956 in other prominent public places as well, e.g., Grand Central Station and Radio City Music Hall, and even Manhattan's Paramount. Miraculously no one ever died, though six persons in our theatre were, like others, injured when a homemade metal-pipe bomb was set off. Among them was Abraham Blumenthal, a thirty-six-year-old Brooklyn postal clerk who reportedly got blasted into the air from his seat, and the Russo Sisters, Doris and Joyce, who were also injured. The other three victims also reported by *The New York Times* (December 3, 1956) were only psychologically terrorized. Here, as before, the astute action of management prevented a stampede, as Assistant Brooklyn Paramount Manager Horatio Tedesco fortunately calmed the audience by (somehow) convincing them that the explosion was only a firecracker. Metesky, who usually alerted authorities about his next target—by handwritten notes or telephone—was finally apprehended and tried, then released from prison several years later as a rehabilitated terrorist (*The New York Times*, February 20, 1957).

B. National Extracurricular Events

The first of these was a midnight fundraiser for the NVA, the National Vaudeville Association, an after-hours show held on April 20, 1929, a Saturday night, which introduced the great tap dancer Bojangles to our theatre for the first time. Another performer was Trixie Friganza (née Delia or Orphelis O' Callahan), a leading actress and operetta singer. Indeed, twenty-nine Vaudevillians provided entertainment for separate admission following the evening's complete vaude-cine offering for that noble cause of helping out-of-work performers in that live entertainment already a dying occupation, and whose fate would be permanently sealed as a result of the Great Depression.

"American Week" was another national extracurricular event. For seven days, commencing February 26, 1940, Catholic and Jewish World War I veterans were feted during the screening of *Fightin' Caravans,* an apropos war film starring James Cagney and Pat O'Brien, popular enough before our nation's entry into the Second World War to reportedly have drawn 113,227 theatre patrons after being held over for a second week.

A third example was Red Cross month. Held in 1953, some five hundred flying saucers made of lightweight paper were released from the roof of the Brooklyn Paramount Theatre on March 2 of that year as part of a $7 million national fundraising campaign to help the humanitarian relief organization founded in 1881.

"Boys Scouts of America Day" was another national extracurricular event, with Rudy Vallée in 1929 leading the famous Boy Scout Band during "the first in a series of concerts at the Brooklyn Paramount Theater." The crooning maestro of the Connecticut Yankees, so-called, was also said to have wielded his baton while leading seventy-five Boy Scout musicians in a special twenty-minute-long concert that began exactly at 7:00 p.m. Then six years later in 1935, Charley Davis also led the Brooklyn Boy Scout Band on Monday, Tuesday, and Wednesday nights during one week in support of that national organization's goal of raising $250,000.

The New York Times two decades later on February 20, 1955, wrote about our theatre's celebration of George Washington's 223rd birthday...which drew the attendance of Boy Scout troops from the various boroughs in our city and others invited to view a color, feature-length film about their convention in 1953 titled *Jamboree* during the week of February 25, 1955—a national event since it was coordinated with the National Council of Boy Scouts of American, while its documentary was advertised as a first showing in New York City.

Yet another example saw the red-carpet treatment on a Monday night during the week of August 28, 1932, of celebrities for the opening of *Secrets of a Secretary*, a Paramount film that starred Claudette Colbert, who was said to have driven with her husband, Norman Foster, from a summer vacation in Montauk, Long Island, to attend. Indeed, they reportedly arrived in a black touring car during what was advertised as "Brooklyn Gone Hollywood" when the night sky was flooded with beams, i.e., presumably Klieg lighting, as music of an unstated nature was additionally blasted outdoors from amplifiers within the Brooklyn Paramount also announcing the arrival of other celebrity-filled vehicles for that studio-type preview—including Paramount-Prolix's Jesse Lansky, who motored over from the studio's headquarters on Times Square in Manhattan. Of additional relevance, however, were index cards distributed to street onlookers by our theatre's management soliciting suggestions for types of new films they felt the studio ought to make in the future—that is, anticipating by nearly two decades the autobiography title in 1953 of the film studio's founder and half-century CEO, Adolph Zukor, *The Public Is Never Wrong*.

A final example were programming interruptions for radio broadcasts of national import...as reported on February 21, 1942, about that coming Monday's 10:00 p.m. address during World War II.

C. International Extracurricular Events

Under this final rubric, we begin by referencing an international controversy between our theatre and Cuba about the Paramount musical film starring George Raft (as a dancer) titled *Bolero* that played here during the week of February 16, 1934. Probably resulting from their government's objection to erotic matieral following its screening in Havana, Cuba not only threatened our theatre manager with destruction of their rental copy, but also with a ban against all Paramount films in the country.

Along with the presentation of foreign Vaudeville stars like Maurice Chevalier and others, beginning on March 7, 1930, the internationally renowned Nikita Balieff led the *La Chauve-Souris* ballet on stage here.

Yet another international extracurricular event was a special concert for the Maimonides Chapter of Hadassah under Mrs. Florence Gordon, president. During the week of January 22, 1940, some portion of donated proceeds was promised to the Hadassah Medical Organization for its emergency projects for Palestinian Jews. Then one year later, the Eastern Parkway Division of the American Jewish Congress (AJC) announced a theatre party at the Brooklyn Paramount on January 20, 1941, on behalf of their international organization's mission as a protective arm and shield for Jewry throughout the world.

Another thematically related example pertaining to the largest number of diaspora Jews in Brooklyn as well as anywhere in the United States was held by the Adela Goldstein Chapter of the Mizrachi Women's Organization of America on March 16, 1942—a weeklong benefit in the Brooklyn Paramount as part of the Zionist organization's global fundraising efforts aimed at the relief of Palestinian Jews (*The New York Times*, March 16, 1941).

Still another example of an extracurricular international event that went far beyond our theatre's original *raison d'etre* as an entertainment venue was our theatre manager's invitation to the Israeli men's touring soccer team, seventeen in number, for a viewing of *Beyond Glory*, a film that starred Alan Ladd. and which opened on October 9, 1948.

Finally, and if any additional illustration of the big-heartedness of the world's first motion picture theatre built expressly for the Talkies is required, we cite this blockbuster benefit for two borough residents left permanently disabled in the aftermath of the Second

World War—an event which satisfies all three extracurricular territorial place-based criteria. We then read on April 19, 1947, about that star-studded all-night show, which sought to raise what sounds today like a paltry figure, $30,000, but in that year was the cost of installation of two accessibility ramps for both paraplegics, that would emable them to leave V. A hospital beds and achieve independent living in brand-new housing built on King's Highway in our borough.

Since synchronicities figure in all aspects of this book, check out these final examples regarding those wounded warriors, Murray Solomon and Joseph Kremetz. They were born in the same Brooklyn hospital five days apart in October 1925; grew up on the same block (St. Johns) in Park Slope, Brooklyn, though without knowing each other; and enlisted on nearly the same day in 1943, but were incredulously also nearly fatally wounded on the same day close to each other in Southern France in 1944!

In any event, the Cornell med school dropout and former Brooklyn Paramount manager, Robert Weitman, from his new perch at Manhattan-Paramount teamed with his protégé, Gene Pleshette, and cobbled together a program of top entertainers to perform on stage at the Brooklyn Paramount on that Saturday night. The partial list included the Jimmy Dorsey Orchestra; Martin and Lewis: Jerry Winchell and Paul Mahoney (a popular ventriloquist team); the comedians Myron Cohen and Morey Amsterdam; two former world-champion boxers, Max Baer, a heavyweight, and "Slapsie Maxie" Rosenbloom, a light-heavyweight; as well as dozens of lesser-known Vaudeville performers like Julie Shins, Mary Small, Lynn Shirley, Pat Henning, Coke and Poke, and Fred and Elaine Barry among others.

The biggest star that evening, however, proved to be the youngest member of the Boswell Sisters, who performed here twice in separate weeks in the 1930s during the third face of our theatre's earlier history, Jazz. Entirely wheelchair bound, Connee Boswell, according to the tabloids, "got a thunderous ovation for her songs" while reigning that night as Queen of the Charitable Show. It was sponsored by the Utica-Parkway–St Johns' Merchants Associates who contributed toward the

$36,000 for that humanitarian event with those glamorous Conover Girls selling autographed copies of programs before and after the all-night show to raise additional money.

By way of bringing closure to this hypothesis, a letter to the editor in *The Exhibitor* (November '43–May '44) regarding "Doc" Lee's impact is reprinted:

> Brooklyn-Paramount held a regulation basketball game recently in which the marine division of Bendix lost to ARMA Corps by a score of 24–20. This was hailed as an example of the many functions which (movie) houses can perform as community centers.

And finally, *The Coney Island Times* reported on December 21, 1957, that during Christmas week, all theatre patrons were invited to participate in another "Guess the Name" contest with prizes totaling $25,000 including hotel stays in Quebec, Canada, and Florida in the United States, as well as Broil-Quik Rotisseries, travel trunks, and other advertised items.

PART IV

CONCLUSION(S)

CHAPTER 14

Two Trains Running: Or, When Long Island University Met and Purchased the Brooklyn Paramount in 1950

We titled this chapter with the name of a film to examine what at first glance might seem to be another apple-and-orange example, i.e., of the similarities and differences between the Brooklyn Paramount Theatre (BPT) and Long Island University (LIU), which ran along parallel tracks from their near-identical birth dates until they merged in 1950. Our discussion is also informed by what is termed the "controlled comparative method" in anthropological studies (Eggan, 1954). The presentation seeks similarities and differences with regard to their respective histories and is subdivided into five shared components: (1) origins; (2) increased prices; (3) bankruptcies; (4) property sales; and (5) scandals. And if there are any doubts about its possible heuristic value, surely the fact that our theatre's manager, Gene Pleshette, was invited to discuss "The Motion Picture Industry" at our alma mater's business school in 1958 should eliminate those (*Williamsburg News*, October 12, 1958).

1. Origins

LIU and the BPT came into existence within two years of each other. On January 26, 1926, a wealthy Brooklyn lawyer and founder of the Manufacturers Bank Company named Ralph Jonas anonymously put up the initial capital to create a private university during a meeting of the borough's powerful committee of 111 he headed. The benefactor felt the second-largest city in the nation should house a private university after they'd voted on the public-funded Brooklyn College. Notwithstanding the confusion of our alma mater's geographically inspired name, LIU not only was given to avoid confusion with that other higher educational institution containing the borough's name, but also because the King's Borough is joined with Queens while extending some one hundred miles eastward to Long Island's north and south ends...a confusion that could have been avoided if America's great poet, Walt Whitman, had been listened to and those continuous lands should be called by their indigenous people's name, Paumanok. Never mind the fact that a rector of the Roman Catholic Church of Nativity, Monsignor John Belford, had previously voiced fear that atheists and agnostics would consequently corrupt the minds of students in the public college. Jonas, not unlike the founder of Paramount Pictures, Adolph Zukor, also staked personal wealth to his dream and more—his pledge of an additional million if other donors contributed $900,000 for the private educational venture across the East River from Manhattan's Paramount, something which never occurred (January 22, 1926).

LIU's initial rental headquarters for its inaugural class of 317 was in a landmarked high-rise today on 75 Livingston Street, the Brooklyn Chamber of Commerce/Court Chambers Building between Remsen and Montague near Brooklyn Heights in 1927, before its acquisition in 1929 of 300 Pearl Street; the six-story commercial building was forced to sell during our alma mater's first bankruptcy. Occupation of three floors of the Con Edison Building at 380 Pearl Street seemed to move closer and closer to the BPT, before that purchase date in 1950 (Mary Lai 2014 interview; Steinberg, 2016: 43). Whereas the BPT remained in situ since its opening date two years later on November 24, 1928.

2. Increased Prices

It probably should go without saying that since the cost of most everything in our modern industrial world kept increasing over time, tuition at LIU and ticket prices at the BPT similarly rose during their respective early histories—with exceptions in the case of the movie theatre.

Thus, LIU undergraduates initially paid seven dollars per credit in 1926, a figure that rose until this author's family paid twenty-five dollars per credit between 1959 and 1963 for my tuition…and continues upward to astronomical, unaffordable costs even as I write. The same essentially held true at the BPT, whose patrons initially paid twenty-five cents until its admission cost reached two dollars and fifty cents per seat in 1962, albeit with a few noticeable exceptions: *Billboard*, for example, notifying its readers on August 8, 1928, to expect a price war resulting from construction of the Brooklyn Theater (ours) with other deluxers in the oversubscribed theatre situation in downtown Brooklyn, which included the Albee, Strand, and Loew's Metropolitan. It was unlike LIU, after prices had risen to thirty-five cents until 1:00 p.m., as reported on January 4, 1929, and then went up forty cents a week later (also with time restrictions). On the following New Year's Eve we read that midget prices were announced, i.e., reductions to twenty-five cents until 1:00 p.m. and thirty-five cents until 5:00 p.m. Then after rising to sixty-five cents from 5:00 p.m. they dropped to fifty-five cents after 1:00 a.m., and which dropped back to fifty-five cents for all seats from 1:00 a.m. until dawn. Yet *Variety* two years later reported on October 25, 1930, that increased ticket prices had once again been dramatically lowered from seventy-five cents during the Great Depression. Indeed, one year later, we also read on October 2, 1931, that the BPT's low price had dropped even further from twenty-five cents to fifteen cents, again during restricted hours. The same held true regarding admission price volatility evidenced a year later, when all patrons were charged twenty-five cents until 2:00 p.m. and thirty-five cents from 2:00 p.m. to 5:00 p.m. Even more dramatic was the announcement on November 26, 1939, that children paid fifteen cents while adults paid thirty cents. Another example occurred during the Second World War, when increased admission ticket prices were once again dramatically slashed to twenty centers plus three cents (for the war tax) during Monday–Friday matinees for a total of twenty-three cents, while Saturday and Sunday patrons paid twenty cents plus four cents for a total of twenty-four cents until 5:00 p.m., and those rose slightly to twenty-five cents plus five cents for a total of thirty cents until closing hours (*Film Daily*, July 3, 1941). Finally, we note another contrast with the still-increasing tuition costs at LIU—discounted theatre seating prices for World War II soldiers, commencing July 7, 1941, provided they arrived in uniform.

3. Bankruptcies

David Steinberg (ibid, 39–47), LIU's longest-serving president thus far—twenty-seven years—wrote in his history of the school from 1927 until 1967 about its paltry endowment from the outset. Two bankruptcy filings of our tuition-driven, financially challenged private university led to the closing of the Pearl Street during the Great Depression and belt-tightening measures through the Second World War, when its predominantly white male population either were drafted or enlisted. For, as Steinberg (ibid: 48) also wrote: "To prevent closing an arrangement was struck that lasted until 1947." And part of those measures, according to what LIU's comptroller, Mary Lai, told us involved its president at the time, Tristram Walker Metcalf, reducing the number of Ivy League hires and reliance instead of adjuncts. In any event, after those hard times when LIU's student population of one thousand dropped by one-third, a turnout followed World War II. Then it's skyrocketing student population reached six thousand, which not only led to the purchase of the Brooklyn Paramount, but also to the acquisition of a second campus, the 123-acre C. W. Post estate in Long Island.

Mary Lai, among LIU's first women graduates and who returned to became CFO and an alumni fundraiser until her recent passing, told us that Ralph Jonas and LIU's entire board went underwater following the stock market crash of October 24, 1929. But such was not the case with Paramount. Despite its reported all-time-high earnings of $100 million, a precipitous drop to $15,857,444 occurred four years later on January 27, 1932. The suicide watch placed on Jesse Lasky (1957) when he was fired and reportedly lost eight million dollars while the film studio and its various subsidiaries sued each other, Adolph Zukor reported a combined salary from 1927 to 1932 of $858,000, along with cash bonuses totaling $750,000, as well as additional ownership of ten thousand shares of stock in the studio he built (*Brooklyn Eagle,* October 27, 1933). Even so, the reduction of employee salaries between 2 percent and 5 percent and the reduction of Vaudeville costs between $15,000 and $20,000 weekly for those changing weekly shows and salaries of big and small stars to $4,000 or $5,000. Additional savings could only have resulted from the studio's immediate divestment of half its 1,500 owned and/or leased movie theatres during a mandated reorganization by the feds. Zukor was quoted in the tabloid on January 31, 1931, as saying that he not only was willing to sell the BPT, but also the Kings, Pitkin, and Valencia similarly built in Brooklyn in the 1920s following the studio's expansion.

Yet we also read about wow weeks at the BPT during those challenging years...with *Variety* (January 30, 1929), reporting the Paramount film *Interference* netted $27,000 during the week of February 6, 1929; and two weeks later it was reported elsewhere that *The Wolf of Wall Street* tripled that figure—$71,000 during the week of February 16, 1929; and three years later, even deeper in hard times caused by the Great Depression, Cecil B. DeMille's film *This Day and Age,* whose controversial intimations about the coming spread of fascism in those years much like these, was reported doing brisk business at the BPT on August 29, 1933. *Variety* also previously reported on February 7, 1933, that "the Brooklyn Paramount...(was) holding up better than its sister house on Broadway."

Rudy Vallée (1962: 104) also reported hitting $40,000 average weekly grosses at the Brooklyn Paramount Theatre. But according to the *Brooklyn Eagle* on April 18, 1933., Vaudeville was dropped.

Despite our theatre's summer closings in 1933 and 1934, no matter those forced operational savings, William Greve had everything to do with the construction of the BPT. He was quoted in the local tabloid on October 19, 1935, after the studio's bankruptcy hearings got resolved, as saying that the theatre not only hadn't earned a profit since the opening date in 1925 [*sic*], but also that it amassed a debt of $1,574,000 through June 1933! And that's before Si Fabian, two years later, reported Paramount earned more than two million paid admissions, discounting thirteen thousand freebies to orphans and poor children (September 3, 1935).

4. Property Sales

Whereas LIU did not attempt to sell its Brooklyn campus until 1967 to CUNY, the subject of Steinberg's study and what led to successful student-faculty-alumni protests that effectively blocked that proposal, the *Brooklyn Eagle* on October 27, 1933, reported that the BPT was on the chopping block. However, Judge Robert A. Inch of Brooklyn's Appellate Court rejected all three bids in the following year, declaring the sales price was undervalued. All the same, Simon Fabian, whose offer of $75,000 doubled from his own funds was allowed on November 4, 1934, to lease our wonder theatre as well as the Fox and Strand in downtown Brooklyn. And so it was that the Fabian Brothers, who were upstate New York movie theatre circuit brokers, ran all three rebranded theatres for a decade. They also secured films for screening from Warner Brothers as well as the Paramount; that is, after the proposed mortgage of the BPT was lowered by two million dollars from $4,800,000 (October 31, 1935). The Fabian Paramount would then be returned to the reorganized (and refinanced) new entity United Paramount by the feds on February 20, 1945.

We also contradictorily read of the Paramount's Title 11 voluntary bankruptcy petition in 1931 as a result of reportedly being unable to liquidate and meet its obligations, while on the other hand the studio's attorney nonetheless was quoted in the press saying "Paramount Publix was bankrupt only in the sense of possessing assets worth less than liabilities." Then the Fabian Brothers reported annual profits of $65,000 against $58,000 presumably for all three theatres alongside property taxes assessed at $135,000. Yet despite their failed efforts to revive Vaudeville in 1934—and substitution instead of a double film policy and sporting events on stage here—Simon Fabian's parting words in 1945 proclaimed "great faith in the future of the borough and especially the locality in which the property is located." Apart from their installation of an RCA High Fidelity Sound system in 1937 for $25,000, however, these dramatic structural changes did not occur until full ownership to Paramount was restored: (1) removal of ginormous signage from the roof of the adjoining eleven-story office building, fully restored and attached by Live Nation BPT today; (2) replacement of carpeting as part of that $250,000 makeover; (3) removal from storage and restoration of the theatre's art and furniture collection valued at two million dollars in 1928; and (4) the revival of the Mighty Wurlitzer and restoration of community sing-alongs, which also ended with the demise of Vaudeville.

George Currie's Brooklyn column in the *Brooklyn Eagle* (February 5, 1945) is trenchant in this matter, insofar as he divulged secret plans in the works that might have launched a new era in Brooklyn theater entertainment. And so, too, did our theatre's manager in that year wax rosy with optimism about the coming future. As quoted in the press on December 20, 1945, Eugene Pleshette stated, "Brooklyn Paramount is planning to spend about $250,00 in refurbishing the theater." And toward that end, the *Brooklyn Citizen* one year later reported on March 5, 1946, that Hal Periera had been "borrowed from Hollywood" and sent east with the assignment of redecorating the theatre. Indeed, *Variety* (March 13, 1946) one week later broke the news that our fabled movie theatre's art treasure had been removed from storage and was once again placed on exhibition in lounges and lobbies, while the *Brooklyn Daily Eagle* one year later also announced on August 5, 1947, that the Mighty Wurlitzer was once again being played. Also in line with the one million dollars Paramount would spend in 1958 for the refurbishment of its Brooklyn theatre and its impact on theatre, Pleshette was quoted as saying:

> The location of the Brooklyn Paramount continues to prove familiar to many thousands of entertainer seekers each week and we feel the upright signs can be sacrificed in the upgrading of Downtown Brooklyn.

Then with greater significance to what instead occurred, Pleshette stated:

With the startling changes made by Long Island University, plus the construction of modern apartment developments bringing in thousands of middle-income families.

One year later in 1954, we read that "the Brooklyn Paramount Theatre and office building (were) on the block for sale." A rumored transaction reportedly said the sale "would not affect operation of the big downtown house." Whether hopeful that additional new housing like the Kingsview Coops built in 1953 and what came to be called University Towers was sold to LIU soon thereafter not only would save the BPT, these facts also remain: first, that Eugene Pleshette in August 1953 offered Boro Patrons the opportunity of winning a $500 certificate toward the purchase of a co-op apartment in the former, which consisted of five buildings with 292 apartments; and second, while the latter comprised three buildings with 550 apartments, their combined occupants would scarcely fill the BPT on a single night. And yet, in 1958, he was still waxing optimistic about a new era in Brooklyn theatre entertainment about to occur. For, as Eugene Pleshette told the *Journal American* in that year, "We feel modernizing and stream-lining the familiar exterior of the Downtown Brooklyn showplace… can be sacrificed to the upgrading of Downtown Brooklyn."

In any event, whether contradictory or not, the Glastet Corporation entered negotiations with the Hollywood studio to purchase the BPT, a two-year period from 1947 that culminated in what *The New York Times* on September 25, 1949, identified as "one of the largest of its kind in recent (New York City) history." For, along with those apparent corporate raiders' acquisition of our theatre and its adjoining eleven-story building, the troika of Alfred R. Glancy Jr., Roger L. Stevens, and Ben Tobin had put together an "all-cash deal" in which they also purchased the Empire State Building; one-half interest in Manhattan's Taft Hotel; a large printing plant in that borough; and some 9,500 vacant lots in Queens for development. But not for long... or at least as BPT was concerned, anyway. Because eight or so months after Glastet purchased Realty Associates and Realty Associates Securities, which held the theatre's mortgages and related bonds, they flipped both properties to LIU in 1950.

"Theater Building Sold to University" was the banner headline in *The New York Times* on August 3, 1950. Glastet's purchase price for 385 Flatbush Avenue Extension (Section 7/Block 2085/Lot 1). And according to what our primary consultant at LIU Mary Lai said, from the sales price of the Paramount was set at $1,351.000.33. With a mortgage initially evaluated at $1,800,000 for taxation's sake, the price was lowered to $1,673,524. Moreover, she recalled that LIU put down $200,000 on the closing date of August 24, 1950, and signed off on a payment schedule that called for quarterly sums of $31,500 at 4 percent interest, commencing January 1, 1951. The targeted final payment was set for April 1, 1963. Our primary consultant also told us about an additional $1.3 million spent on other required renovations to transform the eleven-story office building into classrooms and administrative space following the departure of commercial tenants, the last of whose lease was terminated in 1953.

Of greater relevance for our interests in the earlier history of the BPT, however, was an internal power struggle within LIU regarding the purchase of the BPT in 1950 that pitted the wealthy real estate tycoon William Zeckendorf, chairman of our alma mater's board of trustees in those years, against the LIU's popular president, Tristram Metcalf...a heated debate, as she recalled, having to do with the availability of an additional seven and one-half acres directly behind (east) of those four acres of what would be called Paramount Plaza, and which became the deal-breaker. But since the battle involved an unreported scandal that preceded the infamous "Scandal of '51" and payola scandal in 1959, which further substantiates our metaphor of two trains running on parallel tracks, here are some few preliminarily words about gossip and scandal.

5. Gossip and Scandal

The British social anthropologist Max Gluckman (1963) argued that those linked phenomena were found in every society. Likening gossip to sociological thermostats that regulate tensions, while on the other hand, scandals threaten the very existence of societies. Those remain not unlike the lyrics of a Frank Sinatra song that metaphorically link love and marriage with a horse and carriage.

Tracing at least as far back as Benjamin Franklin's "Busy Body" newspaper columns in 1728 in the *Pennsylvania Gazette* chronologically through nationally syndicated columnists like Hedda Hopper and Walter Winchell, Gluckman (ibid: 312) describes gossip not only as society's "principal manner in which internal struggles are fought" but as that which also provides social definitions of membership. This author's favorite example comes from a short story by Dorothy Parker, a member of the famous Algonquin Hotel circle of literary wits, who wrote the following in "The Diary of a Lady" published in 1933:

> Miss Rose came about noon to do my nails, simply covered in *the* most divine gossip. The Morrises are going to separate *any minute*, and Freddy Warren *definitely* has ulcers, and Gertie Leonard simply won't let Bill Crawford out of her sight even with Jack Leonard *right there in the room*, and it's all *true* about Sheila Phillips and Babs Deering. It couldn't have been more thrilling. (Crick and Stewart, 2024: 159)

More relevant examples for our concerns can be found in Martin Dickstein's writing—gossiping—in the *Brooklyn Eagle* on April 27, 1933, about the BPT's initial rumored sale: "This department has it on good authority that the Publix Theater Corporation, former operators of the Paramount, has relinquished its lease on the house, thus making it available either to some other theater chain or an independent exhibitor." Finally, we note that Neal Gabler (1994) used the word *gossip* in the title of his biography of the influential journalist, Walter Winchell, who appeared on stage here during the Vaudeville years.

Turning next to scandal, about which Gluckman (ibid: 312) also trenchantly wrote that "the more inclusive a social group is, the more will its members gossip and scandal about each other," ignoring what this author can add to sociological generalization to gossip and scandal in academia, arguably no better example of the latter can be found in Richard Sheridan's *School for Scandal*, required reading in a British drama class, and which opened on January 25, 1932, at the Majestic, the legit theatre near ours in which every single character's mission in that comedy/farce was the destruction of close friends' reputations through malicious lies. For, as the dramatist has one character cynically observe: "I believe there never was a scandalous tale without a foundation."

Notwithstanding the *Variety* story on September 5, 1956, titled "USA, Scandals (In Hollywood) Ain't What They Used To Be," the filmmaker Kenneth Anger (1975) not only recounted a litany of sordid tales of sex, drugs, and scandals—no Rock 'n' Roll yet!—during the Golden Age of Silent Films, but which also were documented in the Talkies that blemished Paramount as well as the other major Hollywood studios. The oft-recited Fatty Arbuckle, for example, who was (falsely) accused of murdering a starlet, and the scandal surrounding the "It Girl" Clara Bow, whose career largely ended as a result of her otherwise devoted secretary's violation of the controversial actress's trust by publishing her lurid memoirs, can serve as two examples. Indeed, Jesse Lasky (1957: 157) wrote the following in his memoir with amazement about those *cause celebres*: "I wouldn't have believed that the company could weather the loss of such a fantastically valuable trio, especially under circumstances that stigmatized Hollywood in general and our studio in particular."

Before turning to what were three scandals that linked the BPT and LIU, we note that George White's annual Broadway productions were called *Scandals* and found their way into Vaudeville programming in our theatre, albeit shortened. As did Earl Carroll's *Vanities*; the latter producer deliberately had himself arrested outside the Manhattan theatre named for him and imprisoned for showing indecent pictures as a way of attracting audiences (Crisp and Stewart, 2024: 91). And so, too, did several films screened here appropriate that title, if not subject matter, during our theatre's earlier history: *The Scandal Sheet* during the week of February 6, 1931; *The Billion Dollar Scandal* (January 27, 1933); *The Big Town Scandal* (January 22, 1948); and *Scandal in Sorrento* (March 8, 1950). And while the scandalous life and times of that sexual provocateur Mae West alone could illustrate this subject, these two additional examples involving other players whose reputations were above board might also be noted:

First, the Vaudevillian Jack Benny, whose publicist and biographer, Irving Fein (1976; 80–81), wrote about an incident that nearly ended the comedian's career: his arrest for unwittingly having failed to declare a jewelry item at customs purchased in Paris for his wife from a scoundrel, which proved to be stolen property, while Benny was returning home from abroad in 1938. And a second example that resulted in imprisonment was Rock 'n' Roll's foundational figure Chuck Berry's arrest for transporting an underage Apache woman across state lines, whether for illicit sex, employment in his amusement park, or both.

Ignoring other examples that also literally scarred the faces of other performers, our discussion of three scandals that linked the BPT with LIU can briefly begin with those two previously reported examples:

First, the so-called "Scandal of '51," which, as Gluckman warned, can and largely did destroy college basketball...involving point-shaving and possible dumping by players on Clair Bee's legendary Blackbirds, which won both the NCAA and NIT in the same year, understandably though unfortunately centered on the highly touted nineteen-year-old African American LIU sophomore Sherman White, who led the nation in scoring as a freshman and was imprisoned for six months after the illegally gained $2,000 was ironically found unspent hidden in his mattress at the local Y, when other players on the Blackbirds and in other colleges faced only suspension (Rosen, 1991; Sperba, 1998; Cohen, 2001; Gilbea, 2013).

As for the payola or pay-for-play scandal of 1959, despite the fact that Shaw (1974: 269) wrote that this practice extended in other forms as far back as the era of Tin Pan Alley and song pluggers, Alan Freed, like Sherman White. proved to be a scapegoat for other deejays (like Tommy "Dr. Jive" Smalls). Charged initially with a misdemeanor on May 19, 1960, for illegally accepting $116,580 and found guilty two years later of commercial bribery after admitting guilt, his life and livelihood ended (Morthland, 1980: 103).

Returning to college basketball, which is not unlike Rock 'n' Roll did not destroy our society but in fact came back stronger than ever. The hitherto ignored scandal linked the educational institution with the theatre. It involved seven and one-half acres that became part of the deal, and to understand what happened, we begin with a WEVD radio Town Hall forum on March 5, 1951, veritably on the eve of the Scandal of '51.

LIU's board chair William Zeckendorf came across as altruistic by warning about the dangers of gamblers and gambling known to be prevalent in big-time collegiate basketball. Since his message was carried in the local tabloid on that following day, however, we instead allude to that article titled "How Can We Clean Up College Sports?" In it, he railed against the so-called Mecca of Basketball, Madison Square Garden, which he claimed—complained—returned only $86,000 annually from unstated large(r) gate receipts generated by the success of LIU's men's basketball teams those years, that is, when, incredulous as this might sound, the college game proved to be the larger draw financially and otherwise than the subsequent merger of the ABA with NBA.

Students of *Freakonomics*, however, will have to explain the printed spreadsheet that alleged LIU's basketball program cost $186,000 per

annum, including the Blackbird coach's reported salary of $20,000—
for multiple sports coached by Bee—as well as trifling other expenses,
such as towels and laundering services given at $800 per annum,
for example. "Then we could have the Blackbirds play their home
games in front of 4,000 screaming students instead of 18,000 rabid
gamblers at the Garden," the future (twice) bankrupt developer was
also enigmatically (if not incredulously) quoted as fitting that round
peg into a square, so to speak.

Returning to our three interviews with the Greenpoint grocer's
amazing daughter, Mary M. Lai, who in 2014 recalled what initially
transpired. After likening Zeckendorf's additional lament about
having been betrayed by the head of BAM, the Brooklyn Academy of
Music, with whom he was also quoted in print saying they'd shaken
hands about the (alleged) sale of that magnificent Beaux Arts building to LIU for $500,000, to the idle-like boasting of little boys, she
recalled a heated debate between LIU's trustees' board chairman and
president:

> Mr. Zeckendorf was on the Board at the time—was elected Chair right
> away because of his clout... Anyway, since he and Robert Moses were
> on close terms, so, when those seven and a half acres of land behind
> the Paramount became available at a fair price, Mr. Zeckendorf offered
> to pay out-of-pocket for those—but only on conditions that his gift go
> unreported.

And so, too, did Steinberg (2014: 65) similarly write:
William Zeckendorf was very close to the remarkable Robert
Moses, an American version of a Roman pro-consul who built massive
infrastructural bridges, tunnels and housing in New York.

That internal squabble resulted from a debate whether to move
from three rented floors in the Con Edison Building at 380 Pearl Street,
which was on the market, and Mrs. Lai further recalled that it had
more footage than both adjoining Paramount properties. So, unless
Metcalf was opposed on ethical grounds to those forced evictions,

his reason remains unclear. Life-threatening surgery, compounded by Metcalf's recovery, only to return to work and find a copresident had been installed, got resolved when Metcalf accepted a home on the C. W. Post estate pending retirement. The sale also eliminated the School of Pharmacy's "home court" containing six hundred seats when the Brooklyn Paramount accommodated four thousand seats.

Robert Moses (Caro, 1975) was New York City's powerful parks and highway commissioner in charge as well of what was less provocatively termed as urban renewal. And while the Fair Deal was part of President Truman's answer to FDR's New Deal, it was enacted by the 1949–1950 Congress as PL 81–71 a decade after New York City tackled slum clearance in the surrounding Brooklyn Naval Yard area.

"Unveil Model of Fort Greene Clearance Plan At Dime Bank" was the banner headline in the *Brooklyn Eagle* on February 18, 1954. Its accompanying story included an architect's rendering of the Fort Greene Clearance Plan almost immediately adjacent to the BPT and contained a photo of two other key developers who would benefit financially from permission to construct high-rises: Louis H. Pink and Fred Trump. But not only was Zeckendorf absent representing LIU from that photo, but so too does the accompanying story neglect fifty-four on-site tenants living and working on those very same seven and one-half acres in the proposed urban renewal catchment area. Never mind whether LIU's board of trustee chairman made good on his pledged donation of $75,000 for those acres; the *Brooklyn Eagle* in a subsequent story dated August 20, 1954, described the Fort Greene designated Slum Clearance Project as acres of unsanitary cold-water tenements, factories, vacant lots, junkyards, and automotive services.

In that regard, two community-minded activists, Ben LeRoy Still and Anna May Mason, wrote the following nearly two decades prior on July 28, 1937, about those in a letter to the editor of the *Brooklyn Eagle*: "There is no area in Brooklyn that needs cleaning up more than the section known as the Navy Yard." Their discussion of sixty blocks containing substandard frame houses under the Old Tenement Law, i.e., lacking fire escapes, air shafts, et al., also anticipated the demolition of some 250 homes near Brooklyn's Navy Yard and construction of the Ingersoll-Willoughby Housing Center—a. k. a. the Fort Green Housing Project. Those reformers further lamented the rate of infant mortality twice the borough's average, and even higher incidences of diseases, such as TB. Then singling out what would became those contested seven and one-half acres they characterized as the very worst of the worst:

> The section at the southerly district adjacent to shopping district... (which) consists of sixteen small blocks about seventeen acres, adjoining Fort Greene Park on the west and bounded on the north by Myrtle Avenue, to the east by St. Edwards and Raymond Streets...(contains an area) on the south by a line running parallel to and about one hundred and fifty feet north of DeKalb and on the west by DeBevoise Place and Flatbush Avenue Extension called "the Jungle"...(an area reportedly so bad that) twenty-four police were assigned to special patrol duty.

Now, if only since linguists time and again have demonstrated that language not only defines but can also determine perception, we note Mary Lai's view of seven and one-half acres as anything other than a wretched slum. Additionally recalling those in her office in the financial building named for her on the C. W. Post campus of LIU in 2014, she stated:

On what became our ballfield there were nice homes like those brownstones you'd see today and going small businesses, parking lots, and warehouses.

Charged with aiding some if not all of those fifty-four on-site residents to find alternative housing, our primary consultant, for example, told us about the cat lady who literally had so many felines that, like the proverbial woman living inside a shoe, she didn't know what to do, but also about the owner of Paramount Bowling in one of those targeted buildings outraged that his two-story building was declared a slum and refused to move...and which was part of LIU. And more: the wife of William "Buck" Lai, who coached the freshman basketball squad under Clair Bee and twelve years after the "Scandal of '51" restored Division I hoops under Operation Rebound by converting the orchestra floor into a gymnasium, further recalled:

> I can also remember how upset was the owner of La Paloma, a nice Italian restaurant near Cumberland Hospital we heard Kate Smith and other Vaudevillians used to like to eat in after those shows when he was told he had to go!

Brownstones or not, notwithstanding the tabloid's story on June 17, 1954, that spoke about vacant lots and parking fields as well as structures, which LIU was required to demolish within three years, *The New York Times* reported a scandal we add to our list with this headline: "Suit Would Bar Clearing Slum Site for LIU." That is, those fifty-four on-site tenants formed the Boro Hall Corporation Owners of 365 Flatbush Avenue Extension and hired an attorney named John Flynn to block their anticipated eviction.

Their counsel, however, failed to convince Judge Charles N. Cohen that Brooklyn's tax base would consequently experience a serious financial loss as a result of lost revenue from mortgages, rents, and taxes on those seven and one-half acres...because of exemptions granted to private universities. Judge Ughetta probably then ruled against the Fort Green 54, some of whose residents might well have lived there before or during the gala opening of the BPT in 1928. In any event, following the city planning commission's vote on December 2, 1950, that upheld that judicial ruling, the matter was next sent to the board of estimates, which fixed a final eviction date on January 13, 1951.

Finally, notwithstanding a reported last-minute snafu caused by the assessors' inability to clearly demarcate the property lines between the BPT and its adjoining eleven-story office building, we read in the *Motion Picture Herald* in 1962 about these items additionally obtained by LIU along with eight miles of carpet following the Glastet Consortium's sale to LIU, which ended our metaphor of two trains running on parallel tracks with their resultant merger: (1) assorted stage projection and lighting equipment; (2) two Wurlitzers; (3) two grand-sized pianos; (4) twenty-eight Gallaher music stands (some silver, some gold); (5) four swivel piano stools (one broken); and (6) three ticket shredders. And whatever the fate of the movie theatre's invaluable art and furniture collection, whether another scandal or not, it is reserved for the Epilogue. Now, however, we turn to another contested matter in the final chapter of our book, "Who built the Brooklyn Paramount?"

CHAPTER 15

So, Then, Who Really Built the Brooklyn Paramount?

It wasn't until the Manhattan Bridge was completed in 1903 that the Flatbush Avenue Extension (FAE) in downtown Brooklyn became a major roadway in the borough. Effectively thus linking Manhattan's City Hall with bustling Fulton Street and its elevated subway, the FAE also figured prominently in this history of the beginnings of the Brooklyn Paramount Theatre (BPT) as a result of various plots of land that attracted tenants to what more than a quarter of a century later became the world's first motion picture theatre built expressly for the Talkies and its adjoining eleven-story office building.

William Hamilton English was a key player in what for metaphoric reason suggests another film title, *Six Degrees of Separation*. Because, after joining his father's manufacturing firm in Manhattan—which, for example, printed banking ledgers, he dabbled in speculations, i.e., primarily the importation of coffee beans from Panama. But he also purchased real estate...of relevance for our concerns Lot #57-#59-#61, a 54-foot-by-100-foot plat obtained from Thomas J. Murphy on February 18, 1905; and another property that came with a four-story brick building obtained from Mary J. Nolan, whose address was given as 64

DeKalb Avenue, additionally demarcated as "between Debovoise and Hudson." Both properties, as well as other small lots, became the site called Paramount Plaza and the future home of the BPT, which opened slightly more than two decades later in 1928, but that is, only after those and other tenants were initially bought out. And that unseemly task befell Brooklyn's future powerful developer in 1922, Harold E. Wittemann, a second of those proverbial six degrees of separation, who not only leased those properties from English and hired fellow real estate brokers to buy out fourteen tenants in all between 1924 and 1926, but purportedly also built the BTE. The tabloid from those years frequently spoke about the utmost secrecy because Manhattan's Paramount was under construction, hence the suggested fear about word getting around about the interest of Paramount-Lasky's head, Adolph Zukor, and the expansion of their empire into Brooklyn, thus prompting demands for more than what was being offered for eviction, if not flat-out refusals to move. William English's position as chairman of the powerful finance committee of that powerful studio was another decisive element in the birth of the BPT.

Of additional relevance was the so-called church plot. Our Lady of Mercy was a Roman Catholic church built during the Civil War and had to be moved (to Schermerhorn Street) because its 385-foot frontage on the anticipated FAE roadbed was in the way. As a result, this property, the address of which was given as "Fleet Street and the corner of DeKalb," introduces yet a third of those six suggested key players, William Greve, who for plenty good reason was nicknamed the "Landlord of the Brooklyn Paramount." He obtained that property from another key player, Charles F. Noyes, president of Prudence Bonds, which was one of forty subsidiary-holding companies controlled by Paramount and that ultimately issued municipal bonds for the theatre's construction. But so, too, did Greve head Realty Associates, among Brooklyn's powerful firms, which was established in 1901 and whose complex finagling and connections with other financial institutions whose directors sat on interlocking boards while remaining beyond the task at hand nonetheless were also relevant to the question of who really built the BPT. Before focusing on Wittemann, the Ibsenian master builder who supposedly built the BPT and whose ground-breaking date on both adjoining properties was July 23, 1927, and completion was sixteen months later. An additional hint of the importance of William English, who also served on most boards, can also be discerned from the fact that he obtained a copy of Paramount's *The Love Parade* (starring Maurice Chevalier) for a New Year's Eve private dinner party in 1930 hosted by the Montauk Club, which remains located in Brooklyn's Park Slope and was comprised at the time of the borough's powerful business leaders of which he served as president for decades. That privileged gift for private screening came along with a slate of Vaudeville performers additionally sent over from Manhattan's Paramount, presumably by Jesse Lasky, who still headed the film production of the powerful studio.

Back to Wittemann, who was raised in a large family of Dutch descendants on Staten Island, penniless after the First World War, the tall, handsome, young man built the Hippodrome on Staten Island before shifting to three outdoor markets in Brooklyn. But also during his rapid rise and fall, Harold Wittemann purchased properties with another developer, Samuel Agelof.

So, for example, both would file plans on June 20, 1922, to construct a two-story commercial building on English's leased land, i.e., the future site of the BPT. By summer's end, we also read on September 14, 1922, that they hired an architect to draw up plans for a commercial building on that site with a buff brick effacement and limestone trimmings for what they hoped would contain twenty-four stores—six of them facing FAE with three-hundred-foot frontage, three with 110-foot frontage facing DeKalb, and showroom space for additional business as well as on its second floor...with the projected cost given as $125,000 sans mention of possible on-site tenants. The frequently quoted, self-promoting Wittemann typically informed the local tabloids that his project would "greatly improve this fast-growing (downtown Brooklyn) business center" and, more, was expected to be built above an anticipated subway line. Indeed, the airplane photo of downtown Brooklyn that appeared in the *Brooklyn Eagle* in 1927 was credited to Harold Wittemann, and if only since one of his brothers owned an airplane hangar, one can wonder if he also coincidentally flew the trimotor Fokker over the BPT on opening day.

Of greater relevance for our concerns, however, was the additional tabloid information on June 22, 1922, when we read the terms of Harold Wittemann's lease with William English for that commercial property: twenty-one years at the estimated aggregated sum of $420,000. Even so, it is also important to point out that the Sandborn Fire Insurance Map of 1921–1922 not only depicts fourteen individual "households" on that site, but also curiously contains the words "movie house" on a property on the northwest corner of FAE and DeKalb. Be that as it may, by 1928, Wittemann's partner was apparently out of the picture (pun unintended)—a scandal-ridden figure whose daughter apparently innocently introduced her French boyfriend to Leon Trotsky in Mexico through her sister, who happened to be the Russian revolutionary's secretary and consequently was assassinated by him.

Back to their commercial property, we not only read four years later on February 17, 1926, that Wittemann purchased forty thousand square feet on Paramount Plaza with the stated intention of improving the land, but also that the anticipated height of that two-story commercial property had risen to fourteen stories...and now with open talk of that anticipated movie house. Notwithstanding additional newspaper reportage about the team of real estate brokers assembled by Wittemann, who reportedly bought out seventeen (not fourteen) of those householders between 1924 and 1926, we also learn about a suit by Amos Lamphear against the master builder for his promised commission of $72,000, whether English or Greve or Wittemann's money. A suit incidentally that for reasons not explained eliminated Mark Slocum (*Daily News,* June 27, 1927).

All the same, the *Brooklyn Standard-Union* reported on July 14, 1926, that they successfully purchased from many individual owners an accumulated forty-four thousand square feet through Amos S. Lamphear on which Harold E. Wittemann intended to erect a high-class office and theatre building on the plot. And with its construction cost for both properties on Paramount Plaza now reported at $2,5 million by the *Brooklyn Eagle* one week later on July 22, 1926 it was also ballyhooed, which ballyhooed it as "the largest real estate transaction ever consummated in the boro." That real estate transaction was described as having been completed on that Thursday, and it came with a twenty-five-year lease surrendered to "Famous Players-Lasky" for the anticipated staggering construction cost of $15 million! The height of the projected adjoining office building was now given as thirty-two stories, i.e., one fewer than Zukor's recently completed flagship Manhattan-Paramount. Unless we are supposed to believe that on-site tenants neither read newspapers nor were construed to learn about those anticipated matters through rumored gossip, if not word of mouth!

Be that as it may, the tabloid further reported that several old buildings on Hudson Avenue would have to be demolished on what formerly was Jackson Street, a. k. a. Irishtown during the Civil War, a thoroughfare linking the Brooklyn Navy Yard with Fulton Street, hence would prove quintessential for the delivery of props and wardrobes in back of the BPT, and that is, what also was described at that time for a single purpose: to make way for the theatre...similar to the Manhattan-Paramount, and which was expected to have a larger seating capacity while equipped with valuable paintings and tapestry hangings in its lobby. Rapp and Rapp, furthermore, were reported as having been hired to design the theatre, whose project office building/skyscraper was also projected to contain an identically crowned tower illuminated at night. It was built by Paramount-Lasky's Chicago-based in-house architects who replaced the firm of Murray Klein in Brooklyn Heights who were previously engaged by the Wittemann-Agelof team.

Ignoring yet another news article, which mistakenly stated that the BPT's adjacent office building would even be two stories taller than the Times Square thirty-three-story skyscraper, we now can turn to numerous citations that purport Harold E. Wittemann built the BPT.

So, for example, we read in the *Brooklyn Times-Union* on July 14, 1926, about final plans being drawn by architects and engineers hired by Wittemann for a high-class office and theatre building on the intersection of FAE, DeKalb, and Hudson Avenues, or as that local tabloid's banner headlined the accompanying story read: "Harold Wittemann To Erect Playhouse and Office Building." We'll skip past its construction cost for the moment given as $1,250,000, and which was said to have been obtained from a temporary ground loan from Charles Noyes of Prudence Bond…because one week later, *Variety* on July 21, 1926, spoke about final theatre plans for a twenty-two-story office building topped by a ten-story roof tower planned to be built by the Flatbush-DeKalb Corp. of which "Harold D. [*sic*] Widdemman [*sic*]… (is) principal factor." The proposed movie theatre was to be named the Brooklyn and cost $2.3 million while overall construction of this project was estimated at $7 million, according to that trade magazine.

Yet another seeming confirmation that Harold Wittemann built the BPT is dated six months later. On December 1, 1926, the *Brooklyn Times-Union* reported "the consummation for Harold E. Wittemann of leases aggregating $15,000,000, covering space in Mr. Wittemann's 35-story [*sic*] building now in the course of construction at Flatbush ave extension, DeKalb ave. and Hudson ave." And we also learn that six of those top floors or sixty thousand feet were expected to yield an aggregated rental figure of $2.5 million to the film studio from its rental agreement with the BMT, the Brooklyn Manhattan Transit subway line, which like the Brooklyn City Railway's expected rental of an additional ten thousand feet for $500,000 projected over time was also part of those negotiated long-term leases.

And while the *Standard Union* essentially carried that same story on another date, it also contained these purported new facts: (1) the new skyscraper would be called "the Wittemann," (2) four elevators were expected to provide ready access to seats for theatre patrons, (3) patrons wouldn't have to step outdoors as a result of the promise by the BMT head that one of its subway lines would stop below both properties, and finally (4) this deal transacted with Famous Players-

Lasky (Paramount) for the movie theatre involved "Wittemann (who) was expected to build both the office building and movie theatre at a cost of $12 million without a loan."

Additional purported evidence comes from a portrait of Brooklyn's master builder that appeared in the Sunday supplement to the *Brooklyn Eagle* one year later on January 16, 1927, titled "The Prevision to Build Skyscrapers." We read that "Mr. Wittemann closed the deal for the lease of the theater and later completed arrangements for the construction of the large building." Indeed, and as if responding to his interviewer's recitation of the new projected cost of $15 million for construction of the forty-eight thousand feet of those adjoining properties, Wittemann, with transparent conceit, not only took credit for the entire project but with less than full disclosure charged tenants on English's leased land with stalling tactics, as in the refusal to accept what accurately enough was termed bribe money to vacate. For, as the master builder (outrageously) was lamenting:

> Assembling an entire block so that I can put a big skyscraper on it is no easy task. Unless the purchases of plots goes on slowly and at intervals there seems always to be some obdurate person who will hold out for money, stopping the path of progress for selfish gain [*sic*]. Sometimes, rather than pay the exorbitant prices demanded by such persons, I have sold all my buildings in a block and started in to assemble one nearby or elsewhere.

But so, too, after lamenting that "three years of careful buying... (were) necessary to assemble the Flatbush Avenue Extension-DeKalb Avenue block," alongside immodestly being quoted boasting his intention "to build Brooklyn's largest office building," Wittemann's exact quoted words were as follows:

> I built the Fulton Street Market in Fulton Street and Nostrand Avenue, on what was previously a coal yard; then the Flatbush Market, At Church and Flatbush avenues; then the Bay Ridge Market; then bought

the Crescent theater and leased it; then became interested in other theater properties, and hence came to the conclusion, when I *contemplated*
the huge thirty-two-story building on Flatbush Avenue Extension at De
Kalb Avenue, that I ought to include a theater as part of it. I have already
leased it for a period of 25 years for the annual rental of $260,000.

Yet another proof that Harold E. Wittemann built the BPT comes
from the local tabloid on November 27, 1928, three days after the
gala opening of the BPT, in which the prominent Brooklyn builder
was similarly said to have "erected the new Paramount Theater in
Flatbush Avenue Extension."

Additional ex post facto news items of the same can readily be
cited. For example, the *Brooklyn Citizen* on February 24, 1929, within
weeks after the BPT's opening, also identified Harold Wittemann as
"the borough's leading builder who built the Paramount." As did these
additional articles in the business section of our borough's leading
newspaper in that same year report what we shall debunk as another
myth unfortunately associated with the BPT's earlier history: on January 6, 1929; June 19, 1929; and June 30, 1929. Indeed, four years after
its opening date, the *Brooklyn Eagle,* in an entirely different context
reported on January 4, 1932, about Harold Wittemann's "first big
operation in the vicinity (...) the Paramount at DeKalb Avenue and
Flatbush Avenue Extension."

Two final alleged proofs will be given. *The New York Times* on February 28, 1935, spoke about it having been erected in 1928 by Harold
Wittemann, while more than a decade after the BPT's opening, a
Brooklyn Citizen reporter caught up with the convicted felon on July
23, 1938, in Manhattan who'd served four years in federal prison for
income tax evasion that followed five and one-half months in alimony
jail prior for failing to satisfy court-mandated divorce payments to his
wife, and not only wrote that "one time one of the most active builders
in Brooklyn...rated as a millionaire...(who) among other structures...
built the Brooklyn Paramount Theatre."

In line with the previous chapter's discussion about the suggested relevancy of gossip and scandal along with the applied use of the anthropological-controlled limited comparative method, we include Wittemann's messy (or aren't they all?) divorce, which was splashed all over the local tabloids. These random tangential lines of evidence that along with other investigatory lines cast real as well as inferential doubts regarding the allegation that Wittemann built the BPT: (1) the fact that he got hauled into divorce court for the first time on December 4, 1926, that is, immediately after the land on which it was built got cleared of tenants, hence presumably his need for ready cash; and (2) the accompanying emotional damage that could only have resulted from two years' custodial battles regarding their two daughters; (3) additional time spent—arguably lost—in court regarding his finances: (4) the previously cited suit filed against Wiittemann's DeKalb-Hudson Firm on June 29, 1927, in Brooklyn's Supreme Court, virtually moments before the BPT's groundbreaking charging him with failure to compensate Albert Lohman a promised $72,000 for securing a twenty-one-year lease with Famous Players-Lasky of what could only have been William English's land; (5) additionally presumed psychological damage associated with Wittemann having been hauled into family court three days prior to the BPT's gala opening for failure of alimony payments, which resulted in custody jailing in Manhattan from October 17, 1932 to March 31, 1933; and (6) as if that combined stress wouldn't have been debilitating enough, the divorce-related loss of his regal Victorian home on Beverly Road in Ditmas Park and anticipated sale of his island retreat in Alexandria Bay that came with a yacht, butler, and mistress, and whose value would be given at $8 million during divorce proceedings.

Yet another related story in the *Brooklyn Times* on that day apparently sheds additional light by reporting that Lohman's inability to close that deal prompted him to subcontract another real estate broker, Mark Slocum, who was promised one-third of that commission. However it got resolved, we can only wonder who that third party was?

Ignoring what was also published regarding Loehman's promise to divide the $72,000 with two other scoundrels subcontracted to misinform fourteen or seventeen on-site tenants bribed to move from William English's leased land, a spate of contradictory and outright negative evidence found in the same local tabloids prove that someone other than Harold Wittemann built the BPT.

Toward that quest, in advance of its construction date we read on March 6, 1927, the following banner headline in the *Brooklyn Eagle*: "Allied Owners Take Witttemann Plot for Theatre." Then, two days later, the *Brooklyn Citizen* reported that the other house, that is, other than the one Kings and Pitkin and Valencia also built by Paramount in Brooklyn, "will be located in Flatbush ave. extension and DeKalb ave....(as) was recently purchased from Harold E. Wittemann."

Additional disconfirming evidence was reported on July 31, 1927, that four days after work had begun on the BPT, Wittemann invested heavy in land along Flatbush Avenue for a theatre designed in the style of the Paramount Theatre in Manhattan, but that its land was owned by the Allied Owners Corporation.

Skipping a few months to December 15, 1927, the banner headline in Brooklyn's *Standard Union* stated: "Paramount-Lasky Deal Wins Praise for Greve." He was head of the real estate company (Allied), which held the mortgage for William English intended for Paramount to build the Brooklyn Paramount Theatre. The accompanying story not only praises Greve's involvement but quotes a Thompson-Starrett vice president stating his company was erecting the structure for the Allied Owners Corporation.

Staying with William Greve for another moment, he was described several years later on October 19, 1935, as head of New York Investors, which controlled forty or more subsidiaries owned and controlled by Adolph Zukor for theatre-building purposes. An instructive portrait of Greve appeared in that local tabloid more than a decade earlier on September 22, 1923, who, unlike three of the other major arrivistes, was a single-minded, bold young man who defied his wealthy father's wishes and refused to obtain a college education, insisting it amounted to nothing more than four wasted years from what counted most in life: amassing wealth. No matter that what would have amounted to perfect symmetry had William Greve specifically refused to attend LIU, he, in any case, (admirably) started at the bottom of Realty Associates and rose to the presidency of that real estate firm formed in 1901, which, for example, held the mortgage to the church plot joined with the land leased by William English to Harold Wittemann—a real estate firm grown by Greve to $44,543,692, whose personal wealth estimated six years later at $24 million. But of greater importance for our concerns, that wheeler-dealer served reciprocally on various boards with other important players like Louis J. Horowitz, whose construction firm, Thompson-Starrett, built the BPT. Before closing more of that circle, however, these additional facts about Greve illustrate his holdings of financial backing of Harold Wittemann's DeKalb-Montague firm must now be discussed.

First the *Standard Union* wrote on March 11, 1927: "Greve-Wittemann Fulton Street Sale Involves $3,500,000." Unrelated to the BPT, the accompanying story concerned a ten-story commercial building that Wittemann's firm was invited by that financial tycoon to construct near the Brooklyn Academy of Music (BAM). And while that project was never realized, the three-story Wittemann Building (354 FAE) that remains on the southwest corner of FAE and Nevins went up in 1927 as a result of their collaboration—a commercial property large enough to accommodate an eighteen-hole miniature golf course, and that also advertised the world's largest Chinese restaurant as well as dozens of smaller retail stores.

A second vital fact is that Wittemann had inside information a few years earlier about Paramount's intention to launch an "invasion of our boro"—as its president, Sam Katz, was quoted saying in the *Brooklyn Eagle*. Thus with Greve's presumed financial backing, the master builder purchased and disposed of two potential rival theatres as part of his role in clearing the way for one of the anticipated new movie theatres in our borough, the BPT: (1) the so-called "historic old Montauk" built by Colonel Sinn in 1895 and forced to move about two hundred feet from its location on the southeast corner of DeKalb directly opposite what became Paramount Plaza as a result of the coming FAE…moved to 409 FAE and Fulton. It was originally run by the famous Vaudeville impresario B. Keith before its complex history saw it become the New Crescent after being leased to a Silent Film company in 1915 followed by its sale to the famous Shubert Brothers of Broadway fame in 1919. When the Schubert-Crescent was sold four years later to Wittemann in 1923, commencing a relatively long tenure that saw the renamed Werba sold by Wittemann to Mark Strand, reportedly earning him a substantial profit on his investment, which created a new interest in the locality among Manhattan investors, i.e., Zukor's Paramount empire (July 2, 1926); and (2) Wittemann's purchase in the following year of the original Montauk, which was built as a dramatic theatre by Brooklyn's state senator William H. Reynolds on April 25, 1895, between Livingstone Street and Hanover Place, and whose manager, Louis F. Werba, as reported on March 21,1925, was willing to rent for twenty years for commercial purposes or to continue as a theatre. According to *The Chat*, it was sold to Wittemann on August 8, 1925, for a figure that a local tabloid amusingly wrote "touched $1,000,000." Whether or not with William Greve's financial backing, which seems likely as a result of rumors that Warner Brothers was interested in opening a vaude-pix theatre in the area, and who promptly resold it on March 24, 1926, to a Bronx syndicate, they demolished it, and that hole-in the-ground property intended to become a six-story office building was purchased from the City of New York by none other than William Greve.

Stronger than inferential evidence that Harold Wittemann did not build the BPT can now be offered.

So, for example, the *Brooklyn Times-Union*, which on November 14, 1928, contained praise tendered toward Greve by George McLaughlin, president of Brooklyn's chamber of commerce, during a luncheon attended by Zukor and other Paramount officials in Brooklyn Heights two weeks prior to our theatre's opening under the newsprint heading "Movie Leaders Get Welcome in Brooklyn" as president of Realty Associates, and while whether or not Wittemann attended unfortunately remains unknown, all the same proof positive that Louis Horowitz's firm built the BPT was found in that local tabloid nearly one year prior. Thus, on December 15, 1927, we read:

> ...the Thompson-Starrett Company...of 250 Park Avenue in Manhattan is doing the actual building of the plot on which the Brooklyn Paramount Theatre is now rising...(That is, According to L. J. Fisher, Vice-President and General Manager of the Thompson-Starrett Company)...which is erecting the structure for the Allied Owners Corporation...the Brooklyn Paramount Theatre (which) will seat 4,188 patrons, making it the largest theatre in seating capacity in Brooklyn.

Indeed, the *Standard Union* a year before completion of the Brooklyn Paramount explicitly reported on November 20, 1927, "Thompson-Starrett Company are the builders. A similar story in the *Brooklyn Eagle* not only identifies Thompson-Starrett doing the actual building while otherwise crediting Harold Wittemann who first assembled the plot by purchasing eighteen [*sic*] separate parcels of land."

Then, too, definitive testimony given during bankruptcy and reorganization/refinancing hearings of the film studio on October 26, 1933, cited Francis T. Pender as the head of William Greve's Allied Associates having "testified that Allied Owners was incorporated in February 1927 to finance the construction of theatres for Paramount-Prolix."

Pender was also quoted saying its "formation was the result of negotiations between Paramount, Greve and Louis H. Horowitz," the latter described as "a director of New York Investors, and of the Thompson-Starrett Company," which "acting for the latter...built (theatres like the) Loew's Pitkin and the Valencia of Jamaica...including the Brooklyn Paramount."

A final proof that it was Louis Horowitz, president of Thompson-Starrett, and not Harold Wittemann who built the BPT, can also be found in the *Standard-Union,* in an article whose nameless reporter wrote that for all the contentiousness and entanglements of those reported contentious hearings, he not only felt the pieces of that jigsaw puzzle would ultimately fit together, but also added:

> Greve testified that at the time of the formation of Allied he was (also) a director of the Thompson-Starrett Company, the B. M. T. and of the Brooklyn Trust Company, as well as head of the New York Investors. He denied that any pressure had been exerted on Harold E. Wittemann, who had assembled the Brooklyn Paramount site with financing from the Brooklyn Trust to transfer the realty to Allied.

And still more revealingly:

> Allied was to do the financing and holds title to the theatres; Thompson-Starrett to build them; and Paramount to buy them with monthly payments over a fifteen-year period. The purchase price agreed upon was approximately 200 percent of all costs, including a promotion and financing fee paid to New York investors, the old Realty Associates (of Brooklyn) of 11 and one-half percent.

Doubtless Wittemann surrendered his lease on William English's land to Greve, who, as we shall see, was controversially nominated by Horowitz to serve on the three-member triumvirate created by bankruptcy court to oversee the refinancing of the rebranded United Paramount. He also self-reciprocally served on the board of Thompson-Starrett and was subsequently charged with theft of federal bailout funds for the movie studio.

But first this portrait of the rags-to-riches Louis J. Horowitz, which appeared in the *Brooklyn Daily Eagle* (November 24, 1912 and October 7, 1923), and was retold in his autobiography (Horowitz and Sparkes, 1937). They told the story of the Eastern European Jewish immigrant, who was born in 1875 in Czestchowa, Poland, arrived with his father in the United States virtually penniless as a seventeen-year-old in 1892. After settling in Brooklyn, his was a mercurial rise from stock boy in a shoe store to real estate builder, whose primary interest, it turns out, was public utilities. All the same, after that mathematical genius ascended to the presidency of Thompson-Starrett, his sound business acumen by 1912 soon boasted $50 million projects nationwide that included Chicago's Sears Tower, the Hotel Montreal, and in Manhattan the Woolworth Building, Waldorf-Astoria, Algonquin Hotel, American Stock Exchange, and municipal center on Worth Street. Included was an exclusive contract with Paramount, which prompted Horowitz to write about his firm's role in the construction of many theatres for his (Zukor's) company (Horowitz and Sparkes, 1937: 222–24).

At the same time, however, Horowitz also wrote about having turned down a seat on the film studio's board of trustees because "the enterprise (reportedly was) so complicated, so spread out with all its more than one thousand theaters and its tangle of ownership ramified through about four hundred corporations." Unfortunately, however, this scrupulously honest individual does not mention the BPT in his memoir. But we might well infer what he felt about the gig gleaned from Horowitz's objections to the Manhattan Paramount, whose completion by Thompson-Starrett occurred while he was vacationing in Europe. For, as Horowitz also wrote, he confronted Adolph Zukor following his return home about that monstrosity, which contained needless marble and tons of gingerbread bronze and objectionable glass mosaics and lush velvet hangings. His employer's beloved flagship theatre was additionally inexplicably lamented as the one job I am ashamed to acknowledge. Thankfully, though, at least he didn't destroy both as Ayn Rand has her protagonist Howard Roark do in her 1943 novel *The Fountainhead* when he objected to changes in what were his design!

In any event, we end this book by not only introducing that final character in this metaphorical word game of six degrees of separation, but also a moot final scandal. Archibald Palmer was clearly an idealistic crusading attorney who took on those five other powerful players during bankruptcy hearings in 1933 on behalf of stockholders he hired to represent, charging them with fraud through their operating practices and inarguably worse when it came to William Greve.

Long story shortened, two years after Paramount-Prolix-Lasky's declaration of bankruptcy in 1931, which prompted many of its forty subsidiaries created under New York investors to sue each other, after the studio's cumulative debt was reduced from $345 million to $70 million in that bailout, Palmer on October 10, 1933, convinced the Brooklyn Supreme Court judge to assess financial damages against William English and the others for profiting to the tune of $494,977.16 during the first three months of 1930 alone that ought to be paid back. He not only railed against them for earning more than United States Supreme Court justices and the American president, but made more serious accusations: first against conflict of interest framed as his opposition to Horowitz's recommendation that Greve be allowed to join the triumvirate responsible for Paramount's reorganization; and far worse than his conflict-of-interest charge that the latter would have to be a superman to function as trustee in the best interests of creditors of Allied Owners on land owned by Allied, Palmer's accusation of his unscrupulously pocketing $9,250,000 from the loan of $20 million tendered by the RFA to bail the film company out of bankruptcy!

"It is about time that the Greves and…(others) of the world learn that Mr. Roosevelt's new deal is here, and that the day of holding that the public should be grateful to people who lose their money is past," the crusading attorney thus was passionately quoted on October 10, 1933. In the *Brooklyn* Eagle, then one month later, after the court overlooked Palmer's warning about proverbially allowing a wolf in sheep's clothing entry in their pen, he also lamented on a subsequent date, "I think when we learn the story of what became of that $20 million it may make our hair stand on edge" (November 4, 1933).

Be that as it may, after Archibald Palmer grilled Greve during bankruptcy hearings two days prior on November 2, 1933, regarding whether he felt any undue pressure had been exerted on factotum Harold E Wittemann, particularly with regard to the lease on William English's land, he clearly surrendered that which allowed Thompson-Starrett to construct the BPT, and William Greve responded with a Melvillian thunderous "NO!" The bankruptcy hearing's presiding judge ruled in favor of that transaction with these words:

The deed, later introduced in evidence, showed the property turned over by Wittemann for $1 and other valuable considerations.

While hardly proof in any social scientific sense, these two additional circumstances might also be adduced as supportive evidence of our argument: (1) Wittemann's divorce, which was still pending on November 22, 1928, two days prior to the opening of the BPT, and whether fortunately or not for him, was court adjourned for an entire week; and (2) trespassing on human psychology, the fact also remains that not unlike Dostoyevsky's masterful illustration of Raskolnikov's guilt in *Crime and Punishment*, our person of interest, Harold E. Wittemann, returned to his own crime scene three days after the gala opening of the BPT. Quoted again in the local tabloid, he informed its journalist through demonstrable, transparent conceit about having (allegedly) been approached by a nationally known picture firm with theatres in Manhattan, Chicago, and San Francisco. Toward what end? It purportedly wanted him to build a $4 million movie theatre in downtown Brooklyn...and not just another cinematic-like cathedral close to the Brooklyn Paramount, mind you. For, as Wittemann was quoted in the tabloid, an unnamed individual had "seen the great crowd around the theater waiting for the doors (of the Brooklyn Paramount) to open" and was also told "that at eight o'clock in the evening more than 16,000 [*sic*] persons had entered the theater." Finally, the *Brooklyn Eagle* reported in lieu of evidence that the BPT's putative builder had him attend the gala opening, whether such was the case, Wittemann, apparently self-centered, added that the mysterious other had also told him about having come away "convinced Brooklyn could stand several more houses of the kind without damaging the business of the other theaters."

The End? Not!

A local newspaper photograph displayed on August 22, 1962, a day after the Brooklyn Paramount's closing, depicts a workman named Ray Cannavaro standing atop a tall ladder after he'd slipped those six letters "THE END" on our theatre's famous wraparound marquee. And those familiar bittersweet words flashed on the screen on that previous night, August 21, 1962, a Tuesday, when three hundred patrons, according to *The New York Times*, were sent home after having attended the final screening of *Hatari*, a Frank Buck-like "bring 'em back alive" romantic comedy starring John Wayne that instead dealt with the capture of large game for American zoos. Whether they were returnees or not from opening night in 1928, we also read that the dust-cloaked Mighty Wurlitzer was raised on its lift seemingly as well for the last time, and Bob West, who'd led community sing-alongs during the 1930s, played *There's Honey on the Moon* on what could only have been a nostalgic night.

THE END? The *Daily News* on March 28, 1962, similarly reported a private backstage farewell staff party hosted by Eugene Pleshette, the Brooklyn Paramount's manager since 1946, who was quoted dramatically (if not caustically) saying the following: "With its final hour fast approaching," he lamented the landlord had exercised "their option not to renew the lease (with Paramount Studios) and (so) there is nothing we can do about it." Indeed, that showman would even tweak our alma mater for its foolish decision not to renew the twelve-year lease with the Hollywood studio that reportedly guaranteed Long Island University an annual income of $60,000 by allowing films to be shown daily between 3:00 p.m. and midnight, not to mention the potential income in the future as was the case with Rock 'n' Roll and Jazz shows booked in the tuition-driven/financially challenged educational institution since the beginning.

Pleshette, moreover, placed a full-page goodbye in *The New York Times* on August 19, 1962, titled, "How Do You Shake the Hands of 2,627,319 People?" This was a curious figure to be sure, as we saw when Si Fabian leased the bankrupt theatre for a decade in 1935 and reported attendance at the renamed Fabian Paramount of 2,114,625 by the end of his second year alone. Or, for that matter, we read that a decade later Robert Weitman, in 1945, reported 3,951,764 allegedly were counted during its opening year. Not to mention the *Standard Union* on November 9, 1929, which reported another impossible figure, 3,951,764 in that year alone.

The proverbial last of the toughies/first of the softies, Eugene Pleshette, with whom our primary consultant, Mary Lai, spoke of having a warm relationship, would not only nobly join with other Brooklyn movie theatre operators on the steps of Brooklyn's city hall in 1954 to protest the 5 percent proposed municipal tax added onto ticket prices during TV's challenge, which already saw the closing of half the borough's three hundred movie houses, but also complained as such in a letter to the editor of the *Brooklyn Daily Eagle*.

Here is what Pleshette was quoted saying in that full-page advertisement in *The New York Times*:

I'd like to (thank you), because that's the way I feel about you people of Brooklyn, and what you've done, year in and year out, to make the Brooklyn Paramount a glamorous downtown showplace with a family touch.

As you've probably heard, Long Island University, which owns this theatre, is taking it over in its expanded educational program. The professors will take over from the pictures. And that will be the end of a theatre—and an era.

But I'm sure you feel as I so do that all the warmth and drama and love and laughter and joy in living that flowed from our screen and stage into so many hearts, that all this can't entirely be erased, as from a blackboard, that the Brooklyn Paramount will be remembered affectionately for a long, long time by many, many people.

And so, a final thank you for everything and goodbye to a wonderful people in a fabulous borough.

THE END? Numerous other obituaries about the theatre's four major faces can also be found. Within a year of its opening, *The Wall Street Journal* on October 29, 1929, reported that "The De Luxe Publix (Vaudeville) Units were permanently disbanded." However, while further claiming "only the great flagships—the Paramount in New York, the Metropolitan in Boston, the Chicago in Chicago" maintained live entertainment, it indicated "locations where pride and local customs demanded live stage shows along with the movies...kept up any semblance of the glory that was once Publix." Vaudeville at the Brooklyn Paramount continued here until the fall of 1934.

And death notices were similarly pronounced over Rock 'n' Roll... as Ted Goia, a Rock historian, wrote, "Gone are five shows a day at The Apollo, and the long lines at the Brooklyn Paramount!" Numerous examples can be given about the deterioration of our wonder theatre. Renee Smith, whose poetic description of the dilapidated and frankly depressing state to which the theatre had fallen in the early 1970s probably wrote after having attended a Mighty Wurlitzer Sunday afternoon organ concert:

Ancient tack
Ugly.
Confused.
Hellenistic art,
Baroque Rococo.
Arms, heads
Of naked women.
Posing-mermaids.
Dragons, fish, fantasy
Faces in pairs.
Never ending linear patterns, shapes,
and volumes of eclectic eccentric evolving in time.
Dark—in need for a little polish-grunge.
Cooling zones.

Quite a contrast, needless to say with this glowing encomium found in another anonymous source about our theatre built expressly for the Talkies. For, as we read in the "Pollyanna Department" of another local tabloid regarding what now must be called the Brooklyn Paramount's initial incarnation:

Romance is not all dead in Brooklyn. Spires of steel and stone rise overnight; subways scuttle on this speedy ways; radio loud-speakers bark at you from diverse doorways; Western Union and postal telegraph youths have new uniforms, gone Joseph urban, and you can see the sign—now red, not white—of the Brooklyn Paramount building from the Manhattan side of the Brooklyn Bridge.

THE END? Notwithstanding what the great wit Fred Allen comically penned on August 2, 1935, about Jesse Crawford, arguably the greatest of all Mighty Wurlitzer performers, in a letter to a fellow screenwriter at the time, Herman Wouk, the author of *The Caine Mutiny* ("You can never trust an old organ"), the Theatre Organ Society of America (TOSA) noted as it has given dozens of Sunday afternoon Mighty Wurlitzer public concerts with these accomplished performers since 1962: Dr. Charles Parameter; Hector Oliver and Dave Kapp during the 1970s; Carl Weiss, Dick Smith, Don Thompson, and Ron Rhode as part of bicentennial celebrations joined by the Harlem Boys' Choir under Barbara Eliot, whose husband, Donald Eliot, was chairman of Long Island University's board of trustees at the time, and a close family friend; and in the 1980s, Wurlitzer masters like Gary Phillips, and John Cook, a finalist in TOSA's young organist competition; Walt Strong and Simon Gledhill in the 1990s—a decade marked by the two additional instances of water damages from busted pipes that fortunately prompted generous donations from organ aficionados toward needed repairs; and a British organist, Carol Williams, who concertized here on September 26, 1999.

TOSA also sponsored Sunday concerts in the new millennium featuring these additional performers: Charlie Bough, Ralph Bache, Barry Baker, Juan Cardona Jr., Lee Erwin, Bob Maidhood, David Messines, Ashley Miller, Lew Williams, Nathan Avakian, Barry Baker, Ron Rhode, and Tom Hazleton.

THE END? Not with TOSA technicians devoting time to keeping the Mighty Wurlitzer functioning: with our other consultant, Warren Laliberte, an electrician with the BMT in charge from 1998 to 2005, whose death was followed nearly a decade later by one of the last of those Sunday afternoon concerts on May 18, 2014, dedicated to his memory and featuring Richard Hills Laliberte, who had been trained by Bob Walker, who divided his time at an advertising agency from the 1970s to 1997, and who in turn had been trained by Clem Young... not to mention our close associate Joe Amato, NYPD retired detective, waiting in the bullpen, as it were, to assume that responsibility and who is expected soon to collaborate with Live Nation in getting our so-called unit orchestra back again for performers like Bernie Anderson Jr. to accompany Silent Film masterpieces like *Phantom of the Opera*, as he did on October 28, 2012, and whose thunderous sonorities it remains difficult not to believe weren't responsible for Hurricane Sandy, which struck immediately after the concert.

THE END? Not when there was a glorious night on July 4, 1963, when these five legendary Rock-'n'-Roll-cum-Soul singers appeared on stage less than a year after the Brooklyn Paramount's closing: Sam Cooke, Lloyd Price, Jackie Wilson, Otis Redding, and Wilson Pickett. All five for the unimagined single price admission of five dollars!

THE END? Same as when a colleague and close friend in media arts, Farhard Farhadi, told Fishelson and me about having seen the folk singer Theodore Bikel in concert on April 17, 1963.

And the same held true for what we documented one year later: the indefatigable promoter, Sid Bernstein, who famously presented the Beatles at Carnegie Hall and Shea Stadium, and who was responsible for booking Eric Burdon and the Animals on what might have been a makeshift stage on September 4, 1964.

THE END? What a shame the scheduled concert on July 27, 1967, of Jim Morrison and the Doors and Chuck Berry, for unknown reasons, had to be canceled...their names revealingly billed in that order evidencing the change in what formerly was dubbed as race music into what followed in the music's evolution.

The Isley Brothers in 1969 returned from one of Alan Freed's eight vaunted Rock 'n' Roll Jubilees to our theatre's nonexistent stage. And so, too, were Tommy James and the Shondells ("Crimson and Clover") booked here three years later on July 15, 1972, as headliners by Morris Levy with the Grass Roots on a Saturday night.

Nearly a quarter century after Freed's first so-called anniversary Easter Jubilee in 1955, the *Daily News* cosponsored a "Tribute to the Golden Age of Rock 'n' Roll" with the Atlantic Avenue Merchants' Association in downtown Brooklyn in the so-called Paramount Gym... A nostalgic night on May 15, 1999, emceed by the legendary Joe Franklin of TV's *Memory Lane* who introduced these advertised "Alan Freed Original Acts" inducted into what was being touted as "Brooklyn's Rock 'n' Roll Hall of Fame": returnees from those glory years like LaVern Baker; Herb Cox and the Cleftones; the Harptones (still featuring Willie Winfield); as well as newcomers Norman Fox and the Rob Roys ("Tell Me Why") and the Bobbettes, whom the show's coproducer Richie "O" (for Orenstein) recalled with about our former classmates at Seward Park High School, who, talk about censorship in the music business, their controversial lyrics to "I Shot Mr. Lee" about a teacher, we incorrectly thought was our history teacher. Those lyrics nonetheless were changed to, "Look at Mr. Lee." In any event, that memorable evening was hosted by Cousin Brucie, the legendary WABC radio celebrity Bruce Morrow. And lest I forget another synchronicity that informs this book, one of the Bobettes' daughters took the last anthropology class I taught before retirement.

THE END? Not as long as there was another Rock 'n' Roll concert memorializing the former "Moondogger" held at the Brooklyn Paramount. On Easter Sunday, Deborah Nader commemorated Alan Freed's 1955 Easter Jubilee with some of those very performers:: The Penguins, who, yes, sang "Earth Angel"; Johnnie and Joe ("We Go Together"); the Drifters; the Teenagers, who also reprised some of their million-sellers with a substitute lead singer; Little Anthony (Gourdine) and the Imperials, also returnees though from another Jubilee; and the newcomers Bobby Lewis ("Tossin' 'n' Turnin'") and Kenny Vance and the Planotones, who hopefully still are "Looking for an Echo," their signature song. A retro event, which was no April Fool's day, either, for much as if history had stopped, others stood in a line that wound around the block as belated teenagers-cum-seniors, some of whom were also celebrating their golden wedding anniversaries, returned to hear those legendary performers as well as second-generation Rock 'n' Rollers.

THE END? Not when Duke Ellington returned to the Brooklyn Paramount on May 3, 1971, to perform at a fundraiser hosted by Long Island University's board of trustees in what was renamed Founders Gym.

THE END? Having also referenced the infamous Point-Shaving Scandal of '51, we might note that when Division I basketball was fully restored in 1964, another sign that the Brooklyn Paramount wasn't entirely dead, were performances of the Mighty Wurlitzer by the organist Eddie Layton. He took time off from gigs at Madison Square

Garden backing the New York Rangers and Knicks for eighteen years, and Yankee Stadium, where he was heard in four World Series, and the Nassau Coliseum, where he encouraged the Islander ice hockey team, to travel to downtown Brooklyn. He encouraged the Blackbirds, coached by Ray Haskins in the 1990s, by performing on the Mighty Wurlitzer for students, faculty, staff, and outside cheerleaders (*The New York Times*, February 2, 1997). Layton was followed by a medical student, Dr. Larry Smith, and James Leafe, who grew up on the Cattaraugus Iroquois Reservation near the Wurlitzer factory in Western New York State. The Seneca fell in love with their unit orchestras, and also entertained our bleacher creatures by performing familiar Rock 'n' Roll and Pop songs.

THE END? Not when Bob Maidhof and Dave Messineo recorded *Christmas in New York* albums on our 4–26 Opus #1984. Another Wurlitzer master organist, Billie Naille, can still be heard on *Big, Bold and Billy*, a performance similarly recorded in situ.

THE END? Not when Don Baker, who, like Duke Ellington, would in the biblical sense also return forty years later and record a tribute album for the noted movie theatre historian and author Ben Hall (1961) following his tragic death. That was after Baker told us in its liner notes how the Wurlitzer Company in Manhattan had sent him in 1928 to witness the construction of the larger and smaller consoles sold for parts, and he also got to play the unit orchestra in 1928!

THE END? Not when Jelani Eddington was invited in 2006 to play the Mighty Wurlitzer as part of the ninetieth birthday celebration of Doctor Bob, a benefactor and lifelong organ aficionado, in the Paramount gym. Or when Don Baker forty years later recorded a tribute record album following the senseless murder of Ben Hall!

THE END? Not before May 7, 1962, when *The New York Times* reported one hundred organ fanciers like Mrs. Leonard MacLain from as far afield as Niagara Falls to Richmond, Virginia, were invited to play licks on the Might Wurlitzer. It was the last time before that week's film was among the last few screened here.

THE END? Following my misunderstanding with Clay Cole, I

called him with an invitation to celebrate his Rock 'n' Roll Christmas shows in 1960 and 1961 and appear on a panel with knowledgeable writers and other performers from those years. He initially declined my offer...the misunderstanding was because I didn't know he was Art Rucker Jr., and Clay Cole was his stage name. After my apology for thinking I'd dialed the wrong number, when things got sorted, he happily reconsidered and announced, "I guess that means Clay Cole is alive again!"

THE END? The same held true for our four one-credit academic courses celebrating the Brooklyn Paramount's faces and glory years, we opened to the general public. It included prominent speakers in panel discussions that were followed by musical offerings as well:

Remembering Jazz at the Brooklyn Paramount on October 15, 2004;

Remembering Vaudeville (April 25, 2008);

Clay Cole Returns? Remembering the Rock and Roll Years at the Brooklyn Paramount (March 27, 2009); and

Magnet for the Masses, a symposium on April 15, 2011, that discussed films screened here.

Each was recorded and sold by Jeff Gold Enterprises in boxed sets that today unfortunately are difficult to obtain.

Despite Mack Gordon's Tin Pan Alley composition "There Will Never Be Another You," no matter how exciting these days with what Live Nation advertises as the second chapter of the Brooklyn Paramount, nothing can bring back D. G. Pollock, DDS, who occupied Offices on the second floor of the theatre's adjoining eleven-story building and whose rental agreement with Paramount was $143.75 a month, came with advertisements for "beautiful lifelike sets of teeth at lower than clinic prices, as well as extractions and fillings." And the same remains true for the medical doctors Samuel A. Stein (Offices 202–203) and Sol Fleisher (204), whose rents were also $143.75 and $75 a month, respectively.

No more haircuts were available in the future from A. J. Marino (205—$1,200 rent per annum) for that matter...or federally guaranteed loans offered by the Bankers Commercial Corporation, which rented Office 206 for $3,300 per annum; or the possibility of Live Nation collecting rent from the board of transportation, who occupied the third and fourth floors and paid $27,025 yearly to the building's original owners, and the railroad, which rented the fifth through the eleventh floors for $138,000 per annum.

Finally, the Boro Academy College Preparatory Institute, which, too bad for our tuition-paying parents, wasn't around for tutoring when this author and Stuart Fishelson lacked the high school average grade of eighty-four that would otherwise have allowed us to attend CUNY for free!

The same held true for commercial enterprises in Brooklyn Paramount's adjoining eleven-story office building whose leases were terminated by Long Island University when it took full possession between 1950 and 1953: the Winfred Beauty Supply Store; Standard Plumbing Fixtures, which advertised "the most advanced designs at 353–379 Flatbush Avenue Extension in the Paramount Building"; the Rembrandt Photograph Studio, whose services in this new age of selfies obviously would not be required; the Delco-Heat Automatic Oil Burner Company; and Paramount Chemists, which would make a hit today as a result of its advertisements for genuine Texas Mineral Water Crystals.

A case couldn't be made for the need of free consultations and hearing tests administered in Suite 205 by the Metropolitan Center... not with Long Island University's renowned Speech and Hearing Center on the same floor. However, the Haber Brothers Motors Company, whose address was 375–379 FAE and who occupied the ground floor of the Paramount office building and paid $4,500 for rent annually. While the Paramount Oasis, Inc., is gone forever, their address was 381 Flatbush Avenue Extension and they paid $1,920 per year for whatever services they provided, same as the terminated lease by Long Island University in 1953; and, finally, there were the services of Theresa Gagliardi and Joseph Scala, a cosmetologist and barber, who apparently shared a lease for $1,980 per annum that expired in 1954.

Also gone forever is the Moulin Rouge, whose address was 350

FAE, a supper club adjacent to the theatre advertising the best floor show in its ballroom, and where for five dollars per person and suppers at seven dollars and fifty cents were offered until 1930, when a fire forced its relocation. Ditto the Turf Restaurant, the Tropical Isle, and Rossman's Kosher Restaurant, whose address was 392–393 Flatbush Avenue Extension, and which advertised attendance by world-famous stars of stage and screen in October 1933...with forty-five-cent lunches—beer included—as well as eight-course dinners for sixty cents; that is, also with free suds following the repeal of Prohibition.

Granted a BMW and/or Jaguar distributorship might more likely thrive today in this booming real estate market on the spot previously occupied by S. M. Rose's Desoto-Plymouth distributorship that also sold used cars across from the Paramount, i.e., a familiar advertising ploy that played off the fame of our fabled theatre. It seems unlikely for the return of a Texaco or other gas station on the triangular-shaped island currently housing a gigantic sculpture of the Brooklyn Bridge on Flatbush Avenue Extension and Debevoise Place and Fleet Street. While another dining car close by where we used to eat lunch might likely make a comeback, it is not likely that Cushman's Bakery will return. However, the sandwich that shop became Enduros, a nightclub, and, in 1950, Junior's world-famous deli.

Antiquarian though our interests in the earlier history of the Brooklyn Paramount Theatre might be, the whereabouts of the art and furniture collection valued by *The New York Times* in 1928 at $2 million remained disappeared since the sale of Glastet to Long Island University. Along with the expensive European furniture, all we could find about that mystery was a clause in the contract, which curiously or not speaks about the sale of the sculpture, the furniture and art sold for one dollar. Surely one of those sellers, a major figure in establishing the Kennedy Center as well as being a Broadway figure, would have learned about Romanelli marble sculptures like *The Triumph of Venus*, *Three Brothers*, and *Cupid and Psyche*. Without meaning to cast aspersion. The purchase price of the art collection our theatre's first manager was quoted saying not only would pay for a Packard but McCurdy also told a visitor that $25,000 worth of furniture was more than his annual salary of $2,500.

Not to be ignored or neglected is our curiosity for statuary and furnishings and two paintings by world-famous artists that went missing following Long Island University's purchase of the Brooklyn Paramount from the Glastet Corporation in 1950. They were valued at $3 million in 1928. Starting with *Portrait of Erla de Facci Negrati*, a portrait of the ten-year-old wealthy former Erla Howard, a member of one of Brooklyn's reputed oldest families, painted by the American master William Chase Merritt, which along with the rest, Frank Cambria purchased in 1928 during an estate sale, including an unknown-as-yet canvas by the French impressionist painter Jules Joseph Lefebvre, a pair of sculptures by Romanelli (*Three Brothers* and *The Triumph of Venus*), and invaluable furniture in both lounges.

Speculate though we might about their fate, the only clues were found in the documents regarding the theatre's sale from Glastet to our alma mater, we were also permitted to see two contracts. Each of which alludes to the sale of personal property and equipment catalogued on April 15, 1936, after Fabian's ten-year lease with the studio, and Realty Associates Securities, holder of the theatre's mortgage, obtained for one dollar from Long Island University. Whatever inference one can draw from that otherwise friendly property transfer, the safer one is by ending what began as an elegiac history about our former deluxer that escaped the wrecker's ball and miraculously has recently been transformed into a vital entertainment parlor. It is our hope that tour bus docents no longer will mistakenly announce to the folks from Peoria that Frank Sinatra played the Paramount, when they should have indicated it was Manhattan's, nor misinform visitors that Jerry Lee Lewis set fire to a piano during his lone appearance on stage here during Alan Freed's eighth and final Rock 'n' Roll show in 1958. Whether or not our hypothesis that Tommy Dr. Jive Smalls should instead deserve credit for having introduced that new African American genre called Rhythm and Blues in 1954 on the Brooklyn

Paramount stage six months prior to Freed's more famous Easter Rock 'n' Roll Jubilee here in 1955 will ultimately be proved. A further stretch would be that visitors to our great city will learn that Louis Horowitz built the Brooklyn Paramount, not the other reputed master builder from those years.

We cite these two final wisdom type stories: a synchronistic conversation in the bleachers of the Steinberg Wellness Center in 2006 with the father of Long Island University's former basketball coach, Jim Ferry Sr., a retired transit police officer, who was also similarly quoted discussing the importance of the Brooklyn Paramount as such in *Newsday* (February 18, 2005):

> This was the place... There was Broadway's Paramount and then there was THE Brooklyn Paramount. You went there on dates, hoping to impress your date, it was so grandiose. I know I did... Took her up in the balcony, where I must have impressed with place because we married a short time afterwards.

A second and final wink acknowledges what an admired former colleague in the history department of our alma mater, Joe Dorinson, on whose shoulders we proudly stand, often told journalists who randomly telephoned showing occasional interest about what began with Joe's preliminary research: "The Brooklyn Paramount isn't only a landmark, it's also a national treasure."

We now close off...not with those two fateful words, THE END, regarding those 1,909 films, 279 Vaudeville revues, twelve dedicated Jazz concerts, and the entirely lucky number of thirteen Rock 'n' Roll shows along with the miscellany rest as such: with our hope that today's postmillennials interested in purchasing tickets to see performers and bands, whose names and music we scarcely know, don't call Trafalgar 4-9172, because that phone number for the resplendent redone Brooklyn Paramount Theatre has been changed!

References

Abel, Allen. 1995. *Flatbush Odyssey: A Journey Through the Heart of Brooklyn.* McClelland & Stewart.

Amburn, Ellis. 1995. *Buddy Holly: A Biography.* St. Martin's Press.

Anderson, John Murray. 1954. *Out Without My Rubbers: The Memoirs of John Murray Anderson as Told to Hugh Abercrombie Anderson.* Library Publishers.

Anger, Kenneth. 1975. *Hollywood Babylon.* Straight Arrow Books.

Anka, Paul, and David Dalton. 2013. *My Way: An Autobiography.* St. Martin's Press.

Astor, Vincent. 2019. "Recycled Rapp and Rapp," 10–19, *Marquee* 51, no. 1.

Basso, Keith H. 1996. *Wisdom Sits in Places.* University of New Mexico Press.

Baxter, John. *Hollywood in the Thirties.* London: A. Zwemmer Limited, 1968.

Bennett, Stephanie, and Thomas D. Adelman. 2019. *Johnnie B. Bad: Chuck Berry and the Making of HAIL! HAIL! ROCK 'N' ROLL.* Rare Bird Books.

Bennett, Tony. 2012. *Life Is a Gift: The Zen of Bennett.* Harper.

Bennett, Tony, and Scott Simon. 2016. *Just Getting Started*. Harper.

Bennett, Tony, and Will Friedwald. 1998. *The Good Life*. Simon & Schuster.

Benny, Jack, and Joan Benny. 1990. *Sunday Nights at Seven: The Jack Benny Story*. Warner Books.

Bernstein, Sid, and Arthur Aaron. 1993. *It's Sid Bernstein Calling*. Jonathan David.

Berry, Chuck. 1987. *The Autobiography*. Simon & Schuster.

Bogle, Donald. 2001. *Heat Wave: The Life and Career of Ethel Waters*. Harper.

Bragg, Rick. 2014. *Jerry Lee Lewis: His Own Story*. Harper.

Brooklyn Times-Union. 1928. "Disrobes atop Flagpole: Actress Dares Pneumonia in Paramount Theatre Publicity Stunt." November 7.

Calloway, Cab, and Bryant Rollins. 1976. *Of Minnie the Moocher and Me*. Thomas Y. Crowell.

Calt, Stephen. 2002. "The Anatomy of a 'Race' Music Label," 86–111. In *Rhythm and Business: The Political Economy of Black Music*, Norman Kelley, ed. Akashic Books.

Cambria, F., and F. M. Falge. 1929. "Theatre Lighting, Its Tragedies, Its Virtues," 890–907. In *Transactions of the Illuminating Engineering Society* XXIV.

Carlin, Richard. 2016. *Godfather of the Music Business Morris Levy*. University Press of Mississippi.

Caro, Robert A. 1975. *The Power Broker: Robert Moses and the Fall of New York*. Vintage.

Carter, Richard G. 1994. *Goodnight Sweetheart, Goodnight: The Story of the Spaniels*. August Press.

Chandler, Charlotte. 2009. *She Always Knew How: Mae West, a Personal Biography*. Simon & Schuster.

Charles, Ray, and David Ritz. 1978. *Brother Ray: Ray Charles' Own Story*. Da Capo.

Christgau, Robert. 1980. "Chuck Berry." In *The Rolling Stone Illustrated History of Rock and Roll*, Jim Miller, ed. Random House.

Clements, Cynthia, and Sandra Weber. 1996. *George Burns and Gracie Allen: A Bio-Bibliography*. Greenwood.

Cohen, Harvey G. 2010. *Duke Ellington's America*. University of Chicago Press.

Cohen, Stanley. 2001. *The Game They Played*. Da Capo.

Cohodas, Nadine. 2004. *Queen: The Life and Music of Dinah Washington*. Pantheon.

Cole, Clay. 2009. *Sh-Boom! The Explosion of Rock 'N' Roll, 1953–1968*. Morgan James.

Coleman, Rick. 2007. *Blue Monday: Fats Domino and the Lost Dawn of Rock 'N' Roll*. Da Capo.

Collis, John. 2002. *Chuck Berry: The Biography*. Aurum Press.

Conzo, Joe, and David A. Pérez. 2010. *Mambo Diablo: My Journey with Tito Puente*. Backbeat Books.

Cott, Jonathan. 1980. "Buddy Holly." In *The Rolling Stone Illustrated History of Rock and Roll*, Jim Miller, ed. Random House.

Crafton, Donald. *The Talkies: American Cinema's Transition to Sound, 1926–1931*. Vol. 4 of History of the American Cinema, edited by Charles Harpole. Charles Scribner's Sons, 1997.

Crisp, Helen, and Jules Stewart. 2024. *Strike Up the Band: New York City in the Roaring Twenties*. Reaktion.

Cullen, Frank, Florence Hackman, and Donald McNeilly. 2006. *Vaudeville Old and New: An Encyclopedia of Variety Performers in America*, vol. 1 and vol. 2. Routledge.

Dahl, Linda. 1984. *Stormy Weather: The Music and Lives of a Century of Jazzwomen*. Pantheon.

Dannen, Frederic. 1991. *Hit Men: Power Brokers and Fast Money Inside the Music Business*. Vintage Books.

Deloria, Philip J. 1998. *Playing Indian*. Yale University Press.

Del Valle, Cezar. 2010. *The Brooklyn Theatre Index*, vol. 1 (2010), vol. 2 (2010), and vol. 3 (2014). Theatre Talks.

DeWitt, Howard A. 1985. *Chuck Berry: Rock 'N' Roll Music*, 2nd ed. Pierian Press.

Diamonstein-Spielvogel, Barbaralee. 2005. *The Landmarks of New York: An Illustrated Record of the City's Historic Buildings*. The Monacelli Press.

Douglas, Ann. 1995. *Terrible Honesty: Mongrel Manhattan in the 1920s*. Farrar, Straus & Giroux.

Douglas, Tony. 2001. *Jackie Wilson: Lonely Teardrops*. Routledge.

Driggs, Frank, and Harris Lewine. 1982. *Black Beauty, White Heat: A Pictorial History of Classic Jazz, 1920–1950*. Da Capo.

DuciBella, Joseph R. 1997. "Vertical Signs," 24–25. *Marquee* 29, no. 1.

Dunning, John. 1998. *On the Air: The Encyclopedia of Old-Time Radio*. Oxford University Press.

Eames, John Douglas. 1985. *The Paramount Story: The Complete History of the Studio and its 2,805 Films*. Crown Publishers.

Easton, Carol. 1973. *Straight Ahead: The Story of Stan Kenton*. William Morrow.

Eggan, Fred. 1954. "Social Anthropology and the Method of Controlled Comparison." *American Anthropology* 56, no. 5: 743–63. https://doi.org/10.1525/aa.1954.56.5.02a00020.

Erenberg, Lewis A. 1981. *Steppin' Out: New York Nightlife and the Transformation of American Culture, 1890–1930*. University of Chicago Press.

Evanier, David. 2011. *All The Things You Are: The Life of Tony Bennett*. Wiley.

Eyman, Scott, 1997. *The Speed of Sound: Hollywood and the Talkie Revolution, 1926–1930*. Simon & Schuster.

Fein, Irving A. *Jack Benny: An Intimate Biography*. New York: G. P. Putnam's Sons, 1976.

Fetrow, Alan G. 1992. *Sound Films, 1927–1939: A United States Filmography*. McFarland and Company.

Fields, Armond. 2003. *Sophie Tucker: First Lady of Show Business*. McFarland and Company.

Friedman, Douglas E. 2016. *Four Boys and a Guitar*. Booklocker.

Friedwald, Will. 2020. *Straighten Up and Fly Right: The Life and Music of Nat King Cole*. Oxford University Press.

Fuchs, Otto. 2016. *Bill Haley: The Father of Rock 'n' Roll*. Wagner Verlag.

Fuller-Seely, Kathryn H. 2017. *Jack Benny and the Golden Age of American Radio Comedy*. University of California Press.

Gabler, Neal. 1988. *An Empire of Their Own: How the Jews Invented Hollywood*. Crown.

Gabler, Neal. 1994. *Winchell: Gossip, Power and the Culture of Celebrity*. Alfred A. Knopf.

Garofalo, Reebee. 2002. "Crossing Over: From Black Rhythm and Blues to White Rock 'n' Roll," 112–137. In *Rhythm and Business: The Political Economy of Black Music*, Norman Kelley, ed. Akashic Books.

Giddins, Gary. 1985. "Joe Turner: Unmoved Mover," 92–94. In: *Rhythm-a-ning: Jazz Tradition and Innovation in the '80s*. Da Capo.

Giddins, Gary. 1998a. "Louis Armstrong/Mills Brothers (Signifying)," 23–26. In *Visions of Jazz: The First Century*. Oxford University Press.

Giddins, Gary. 1998b. "Ethel Waters (The Mother of Us All)," 51–58. In *Visions of Jazz: The First Century*. Oxford University Press.

Giddins, Gary. 1998c. "Duke Ellington (Part 1: The Poker Game)," 102–117. In *Visions of Jazz: The First Century*. Oxford University Press.

Giddins, Gary. 1998d. "Count Basie/Lester Young (Westward Ho! and Back)," 170–183. In *Visions of Jazz: The First Century*. Oxford University Press.

Giddins, Gary. 1998e. "Ella Fitzgerald (Joy)," 196–203. In *Visions of Jazz: The First Century*. Oxford University Press.

Giddins, Gary. 1998f. "Charlie Parker (Flying Home)," 261–282. In *Visions of Jazz: The First Century*. Oxford University Press.

Giddins, Gary. 1998g. "Dizzy Gillespie (The Coup and After)," 283–97. In *Visions of Jazz: The First Century*. Oxford University Press.

Giddins, Gary. 1998h. "Sarah Vaughan (Divine)," 298–307. In *Visions of Jazz: The First Century*. Oxford University Press.

Giddins, Gary. 1998i. "Bud Powell (Strictly Confidential)," 318–23. In *Visions of Jazz: The First Century*. Oxford University Press.

Giddins, Gary. 1998j. "Stan Kenton (Big)," 327–29. In *Visions of Jazz: The First Century*. Oxford University Press.

Giddins, Gary. 1998k. "Miles Davis (Kinds of Blues)," 339–54. In *Visions of Jazz: The First Century*. Oxford University Press.

Giddins, Gary. 1998l. "Nat King Cole (The Comeback King)," 402–406. In *Visions of Jazz: The First Century*. Oxford University Press.

Giddins, Gary. 1998m. "Stan Getz (Seasons)," 407–412. In *Visions of Jazz: The First Century*. Oxford University Press.

Giddins, Gary. 1998n. "Dinah Washington (The Queen)," 425–30. In *Visions of Jazz: The First Century*. Oxford University Press.

Giddins, Gary. 1998o. "Art Tatum (Sui Generis)," 439–43. In *Visions of Jazz: The First Century*. Oxford University Press.

Giddins, Gary. 1998p. "John Coltrane (Metamorphosis)," 476–89. In *Visions of Jazz: The First Century*. Oxford University Press.

Giddins, Gary. 2000. *Faces in the Crowd: Musicians, Writers, Actors, and Filmmakers*. Grand Central Publishing.

Giddins, Gary. 2001. *Bing Crosby: A Pocketful of Dreams, The Early Years (1903–1940)*. Little, Brown.

Gildea, Dennis. 2013. *Hoop Crazy: The Lives of Clair Bee and Chip Hilton*. University of Arkansas Press.

Gillespie, Dizzy. 1979. *To Be or Not...to Bop*. Doubleday.

Gluckman, Max. 1963. "Gossip and Scandal." *Papers in Honor of Melville J. Herskovits/Current Anthropology* 4, no. 3: 307–316. https://doi.org/10.1086/200378.

Goldberg, Marv. *Marv Goldberg's R&B Notebooks*. Originally published in Discoveries #113, October 1997. © 1999, 2009. https://www.uncamarvy.com/Clovers/clovers1.html

Goldman, Herbert G. 1992. *Fanny Brice: The Original Funny Girl*. Oxford University Press.

Goldman, Herbert G. 1997. *Banjo Eyes: Eddie Cantor and the Birth of Modern Stardom*. Oxford University Press.

Goldrosen, John, and John Beecher. 1987. *Remembering Buddy: The Definitive Biography of Buddy Holly*. Penguin Books.

Golenbock, Peter. 1984. *Bums: An Oral History of the Brooklyn Dodgers*. Putnam.

Gould, Stephen Jay. 1992. *The Panda's Thumb: More Reflections in Natural History*. W. W. Norton.

Gourse, Leslie. 1994. *Sassy: The Life of Sarah Vaughan*. Da Capo.

Groia, Philip. 1983. *They All Sang on the Corner: A Second Look at New York City's Rhythm and Blues Vocal Groups*. Phillie Dee Enterprises.

Grossman, Barbara W. 1991. *Funny Woman: The Life and Times of Fanny Brice*. Indiana University Press.

Guralnick, Peter. 1980. "Fats Domino." In *The Rolling Stone Illustrated History of Rock and Roll*, Jim Miller, ed. Random House.

Haines, Elaine M. 2017. *Queen of Bebop: The Musical Lives of Sarah Vaughan*. Ecco.

Haley, Bill Jr., and Peter Benjaminson. 2019. *Crazy Man, Crazy: The Bill Haley Story*. Backbeat Books.

Hall, Ben. 1961. *The Best Remaining Seats*. Da Capo Press, Inc.

Hansen, Barry. 1980. "Doo-Wop." In *The Rolling Stone Illustrated History of Rock and Roll*, Jim Miller, ed. Random House.

Haskins, Jim. 1977. *The Cotton Club*. Random House.

Haskins, Jim. 1987. *Queen of the Blues: A Biography of Dinah Washington*. William Morrow.

Haskins, Jim, and N. R. Mitgang. 2000. *Mr. Bojangles: The Biography of Bill Robinson*. Welcome Rain Publishers.

Hershorn, Tad. 2011. *Norman Granz: The Man Who Used Jazz for Justice*. University of California Press.

Hilms, Michele. 1997. *Radio Voices: American Broadcasting, 1922–1952*. University of Minnesota Press.

Hittman, Michael. 2009. "The Father Says No?" *American Indian Culture and Research Journal* 33, no. 1: 119–30. https://eric.ed.gov/?id=EJ835824.

Hittman, Michael, and Don Lynch, ed. 1997. *Wovoka and the Ghost Dance*, 2nd ed. University of Nebraska Press.

Hofstadter, Richard. Anti-Intellectualism in American Life. Alfred A. Knopf, 1963.

Horowitz, Louis J., and Boyden Sparkes. 1937. *The Towers of New York: The Memoirs of a Master Builder*. Simon & Schuster.

Isacoff, Stuart. 2012. *A Natural History of the Piano: The Instrument, the Music, the Musicians—from Mozart to Modern Jazz and Everything in Between*. Vintage.

Jackson, John A. 1991. *Big Beat Heat: Alan Freed and the Early Years of Rock and Roll*. Schirmer.

Jackson, John A. 1997. *American Bandstand: Dick Clark and the Making of a Rock 'n' Roll Empire*. Oxford University Press.

James, Etta, and David Ritz. 2003. *Rage to Survive: The Etta James Story*. Da Capo Press.

James, Tommy, and Martin Fitzpatrick. 2010. *Me, the Mob, and the Music: One Helluva Ride with Tommy James and the Shondells*. Scribner.

Jasen, David A. 1988. *Tin Pan Alley: The Composers, the Songs, the Performers and their Times*. Donald I. Fine.

Kahn, Roger. 1972. *The Boys of Summer*. Harper & Row.

Kanfer, Stefan. 2006. *Stardust Lost: The Triumph, Tragedy, and Mishugas of the Yiddish Theater in America*. Alfred A. Knopf.

Kaplan, Michael, ed. 1983. *Variety Film Reviews, 1907–1980: A Sixteen Volume Index to Titles*, vol. one. Garland Publishing.

Katz, Ephraim. *The Film Encyclopedia: The Most Comprehensive Encyclopedia of World Cinema in a Single Volume*. 2nd ed. HarperPerennial, 1994, 45.

Kaufman, J. B. 1990. "Fascinating Youth: The Story of the Paramount Pictures School." *Film History* 4 (2): 131–51.

Kay, Karyn, and Gerald Peary, eds. 1977. "Interview with Dorothy Arzner," 153–68. In *Women and the Cinema: A Critical Anthology*. E. P. Dutton.

Kenly, William S. 1987. "Paramount: The Early Sound Years." *MoMA* 44: 6–7. https://www.jstor.org/stable/4381023.

Kenney, William Howland III. 1986. "The Influence of Black Vaudeville on Early Jazz." *The Black Perspective in Music* 14, no. 3: 233–48. https://doi.org/10.2307/1215064.

Koch, Stephen. 2014. *Louis Jordan, Son of Arkansas: Father of R&B*. The History Press.

Koszarski, Richard. 1983. *The Astoria Studio and Its Fabulous Films: A Picture History with 227 Stills and Photographs*. Dover Publications.

Krupat, Arnold. 1989. "Local, National, Cosmopolitan Literature," 202–2 32. In *The Voice in the Margin: Native American Literature and the Canon*. University of California Press.

Laing, Dave. 2010. *Buddy Holly*. Indiana University Press.

Lang, Rocky, and Barbara Hall, eds. 2019, *Letters from Hollywood: Inside the Private World of Classic American Moviemaking*. Abrams.

Lanza, Joseph, and Dennis Penna. 2002. *Russ Columbo and the Crooner Mystique*. Feral House.

Lasky, Jesse L., and Don Weldon. 1957. *I Blow My Own Horn*. Doubleday.

Laurie, Joe Jr. 1953. *Vaudeville: From the Honky Tonks to the Palace*. Henry Holt and Company.

Leider, Emily Wortis. 1997. *Becoming Mae West*. Farrar, Strauss & Giroux.

Leigh, Spencer. 2019. *Buddy Holly: Learning the Game*. McNidder & Grace.

Lewis, Steven. 2012. "'Untamed Music': Early Jazz in Vaudeville," thesis. The Florida State University College of Music. https://repository.lib.fsu.edu/islandora/object/fsu:204554/datastream/PDF/view.

Locke, Alain, ed. 1925. *The New Negro: Voices of the Harlem Renaissance*. Touchstone.

Louvish, Simon. 2005. *Mae West: It Ain't No Sin*. Thomas Dunne Books.

Louvish, Simon. 2019. *Monkey Business: The Lives and Legends of the Marx Brothers*. Interlink Publishing.

Loza, Steven. 1999. *Tito Puente and the Making of Latin Music*. University of Illinois Press.

Mahar, Karen Ward. 2006. *Women Filmmakers in Early Hollywood*. The Johns Hopkins Press.

Marcus, Greil. 1980. "The Girl Groups." In *The Rolling Stone Illustrated History of Rock and Roll*, Jim Miller, ed. Random House.

Marquis, Donald M. 2005. *In Search of Buddy Bolden: First Man of Jazz*. LSU Press.

McCarthy, Joe, ed. 1966. *Fred Allen's Letters*. Doubleday.

McClean, Albert F. Jr. 1965. *American Vaudeville as Ritual*. University of Kentucky Press.

Melnick, Ross. 2012. *American Showman: Samuel "Roxy" Rothafel and the Birth of the Entertainment Industry*. Columbia University Press.

Mencken, H. L. 2000. *The American Language: An Inquiry into the Development of English in the United States*, 4th ed. Alfred A. Knopf.

Miller, Jim, ed. 1980. *The Rolling Stone Illustrated History of Rock and Roll*, Random House.

Momaday, N. Scott. 1987. *The Names: A Memoir*. University of Arizona Press.

Morgan-Ellis, Esther M. 2018. *Everybody Sing! Community Singing in the American Picture Palace*. University of Georgia Press.

Morris, Edmund. 2019. *Edison*. Random House.

Morrone, Francis. 2001. *An Architectural Guidebook to Brooklyn*. Gibbs Smith.

Morros, Boris. 1959. *My Ten Years as a Counterspy*. Viking.

Morthland, John. 1980. "The Payola Scandal." In *The Rolling Stone Illustrated History of Rock and Roll*, Jim Miller, ed. Random House.

Naylor, David. 1991. *American Picture Palaces: The Architecture of Fantasy*. Prentice Hall.

Nemeck, Paul L. 1969. *The Films of Nancy Carroll*. Lyle Stuart.

Norman, Philip. 1996. *Rave On: The Biography of Buddy Holly*, Simon & Schuster.

Nye, Russel B. 1970. *The Unembarrassed Muse: The Popular Arts in America*. Dial Press.

Ogren, Kathy J. 1989. *The Jazz Revolution: Twenties America and the Meaning of Jazz*. Oxford University Press.

Palmer, Robert. 1980. "Rock Begins." In *The Rolling Stone Illustrated History of Rock and Roll*, Jim Miller, ed. Random House.

Pegg, Bruce. 2002. *Brown Eyed Handsome Man: The Life and Hard Times of Chuck Berry*. Routledge.

Powdermaker, Hortense. *Hollywood: The Dream Factory*. Boston: Little, Brown & Company, 1950.

Puckett, Raymond. 1928. "Organ Equals 200-Piece Symphony Calling upon 800 Instruments." *Pep-O-Grams* 5, no. 2: 10. https://ia601503.us.archive.org/7/items/paramountpepograo5unse/paramountpepograo5unse.pdf.

Powdermaker, Hortense. 1950. *Hollywood: The Dream Factory*. Little, Brown.

Rachlis, Kit. 1980. "The Everly Brothers." In *The Rolling Stone Illustrated History of Rock and Roll*, Jim Miller, ed. Random House.

Ribowsky, Mark. 2020. *The Big Life of Little Richard*. Diversion.

Roberts, John Storm. 1999. *Latin Jazz: The First of the Fusions, 1880s to Today*. Schirmer Trade.

Rosalsky, Mitch. 2000. *Encyclopedia of Rhythm & Blues and Doo-Wop Vocal Groups*. Scarecrow Press.

Rosen, Charley. 1999. *Scandals of '51: How the Gamblers Almost Killed College Basketball*. Seven Stories Press.

Rust, Brian, and Malcolm Shaw, ed. 2002. *Jazz and Ragtime Records, 1897–1942*, vol. 1. Mainspring Press.

Said, Edward. 1978. *Orientalism*. Vintage.

Sapir, Edward. 1921. *Language: An Introduction to the Study of Speech*. Harcourt, Brace & World.

Sapofsky, Irv (Rabbi). 1994. "Al Jolson, the Jazz Singer, and the Jewish Mother Who Became My Mammy." *Judaism: A Quarterly Journal of Jewish Life and Thought* 43 no. 4: 424–31.

Schatz, Thomas. 1988. *The Genius of the System: Hollywood Filmmaking in the Studio Era*. Pantheon.

Seldes, Gilbert. 2001. *The Seven Lively Arts*. Dover Publications.

Shapiro, Mitchell E. 2007. *Radio Network Prime Time Programming, 1926–1967.* McFarland & Company.

Shaw, Arnold. 1974. *The Rockin' Fifties: The Decade That Transformed the Pop Music Scene.* Hawthorn Books.

Shaw, Arnold. 1978. *Honkers and Shouters: The Golden Years of Rhythm & Blues.* Collier Books.

Shaw, Arnold. 1986. *Black Popular Music in America.* Schirmer Reference.

Shaw, Greg. 1980. "The Teen Idols." In *The Rolling Stone Illustrated History of Rock and Roll*, Jim Miller, ed. Random House.

Shearing, George, and Alyn Shipton, ed. 2004. *Lullaby of Birdland: The Autobiography of George Shearing.* Continuum.

Shipton, Alyn. 1999. *Groovin' High: The Life of Dizzy Gillespie.* Oxford University Press.

Shipton, Alyn. 2001. *A New History of Jazz.* Continuum.

Simon, George T. 1981. *The Big Bands*, 4th ed. Schirmer Books.

Slide, Anthony. 1998. *The New Historical Dictionary of the American Film Industry.* Fitzroy Dearborn.

Smith, R. J. 2022. *Chuck Berry: An American Life.* Hachette Books.

"Smith, Ruth Bingaman." 1991. AMICA Honoraries, *The Amica News Bulletin: Automatic Musical Instrument Collectors Association* 28, no. 4: 43, July/August. https://stacks.stanford.edu/file/druid:yh866wb6902/28-04.pdf.

Snyder, Robert W. 1989. *The Voice of the City: Vaudeville and Popular Culture in New York.* Oxford University Press.

Sobel, Bernard. 1961. *A Pictorial History of Vaudeville.* Citadel Press.

Sparke, Michael. 2010. *Stan Kenton: This Is an Orchestra!* University of North Texas Press.

Sperber, Murray. 1998. *Onward to Victory: The Crisis That Shaped College Sports*. Henry Holt and Co.

Stearns, Marshall, and Jean Stearns. 1994. *Jazz Dance: The Story of American Vernacular Dance*. Da Capo.

Steinberg, David J. 2016. *"Preface to the Future": A History of Long Island University Through the Turbulent Sixties*. CreateSpace Independent Publishing.

Taylor, Robert. 1989. *Fred Allen: His Life and Wit*. Little, Brown.

Thomson, David. 2010. *The New Biographical Dictionary of Film*. Alfred A. Knopf.

Tisserand, Michael. 2016. *Krazy: George Herriman, A Life in Black and White*. Harper.

Titus, Kyla, and Chica Boswell Minnerly. 2014. *The Boswell Legacy: The Story of the Boswell Sisters of New Orleans and the New Music They Gave to the World*. CreateSpace Independent Publishing.

Tosches, Nick. *Hellfire: The Jerry Lee Lewis Story*. New York: Dell Publishing, 1982.

Tucker, Mark, ed. 1993. *The Duke Ellington Reader*. Oxford University Press.

Tucker, Sophie. 1945. *Some of These Days: The Autobiography of Sophie Tucker*. Garden City.

Vail, Ken. 2002. *Duke's Diary: The Life of Duke Ellington, 1927–1950*, part 1. Scarecrow Press.

Vail, Ken. 2002. *Duke's Diary: The Life of Duke Ellington, 1950–1974*, part 2. Scarecrow Press.

Vera, Billy. 2019. *Rip It Up: The Specialty Records Story*. BMG.

Vieira, Mark A. 2019. *Forbidden Hollywood: The Pre-Code Era (1930–1934), When Sin Ruled the Movies*. Running Press.

Waksman, Steve. 2022. *Live Music in America: A History from Jenny Lind to Beyoncé*. Oxford University Press.

Wald, Gayle F. 2007. *Shout, Sister, Shout! The Untold Story of Rock-and-Roll Trailblazer Sister Rosetta Tharpe*. Beacon Press.

Ward, Ed. 2016. *The History of Rock and Roll, Volume One (1920–1965)*. Flatiron Books.

Waters, Ethel, and Charles Samuels. 1951. *His Eye Is on the Sparrow: An Autobiography*. Doubleday.

Weinstein, David. 2018. *The Eddie Cantor Story: A Jewish Life in Performance and Politics*. Brandeis University Press.

West, James L. III, ed. 2002. *Tales of the Jazz Age: The Cambridge Edition of the Works of F. Scott Fitzgerald*. Cambridge University Press.

Wexler, Jerry, and David Ritz. 1993. *Rhythm and the Blues: A Life in American Music*. Alfred A. Knopf.

Whiteside, Jonny. 1994. *CRY: The Johnnie Ray Story*. Barricade Books.

Whitfield, Eileen. 1997. *Pickford: The Woman Who Made Hollywood*. University Press of Kentucky.

Whitmore, Will. 1928. "A Journey Through the New Brooklyn-Paramount Theatre," 40–42, December 22. *Exhibitors Herald and Moving Picture Theatres*.

Willensky, Elliot. 1986. *When Brooklyn Was the World (1920–1957)*. Harmony.

Winner, Langdon. 1980. "The Sound of New Orleans." In *The Rolling Stone Illustrated History of Rock and Roll*, Jim Miller, ed. Random House.

Young, David E., and Jean-Guy Goulet, eds. 1994. *Being Changed by Cross-Cultural Encounters: The Anthropology of Extraordinary Experience*. University of Toronto Press.

Zukor, Adolph, and Dale Kramer. 1953. *The Public Is Never Wrong: The Autobiography of Adolph Zukor*. G. P. Putnam's Sons.

Acknowledgments

I begin these acknowledgments with administrators, colleagues, and students at Long Island University, my alma mater, and happily still home of the Brooklyn Paramount Theatre, which unlike other wonder theatres in downtown Brooklyn that either (sadly) have been demolished or used for other purposes. Our cinematic-like cathedral however, has remarkably been restored of late by Live Nation and continues to present top-flight entertainment for postmillennials. From the top down, as it were, the late President David Steinberg, a visionary for twenty-seven years, who, while he often viewed our interests in the place as "antiquarian," nonetheless was kind enough to read the penultimate chapter of this book and offer critical feedback. Vice President Jeffrey Kane also chipped in with invaluable psychological support and friendship. On the ground closer to home, Gale Stevens-Haynes, a former-student-cum-university-attorney, was always there for us with financial support and timely advice in her role as provost of the Brooklyn campus. The late Connolly College Dean David Cohen, a fellow undergraduate and basketball buddy, not only honored me with the nickname "favorite pest" but also came through with funds that allowed us to purchase photographs from various archives and support by backing one-credit courses about the Brooklyn Paramount referenced in the Epilogue. To Assistant Dean Kevin Lauth I owe eternal gratitude for recommending me to host a weekly NPR Jazz radio interview series at the station on the former Southampton (Long Island) Campus purchased by Dr. Steinberg, which in every way has had everything to do with the salvation-like historic project that gave rise to this book—a strategy not unlike my training as an ethnographer and researcher among Native American communities that led to prior books and whose indigenous teachings instruct this "intimate portrait" of the Brooklyn Paramount referenced in the Prologue. Associate Vice President for Capital Projects Peter Tymus deserves at least honorary mention, if only because no one loved the theatre more than Pete, who told about stopping weekday afternoons on his way home from Brooklyn Tech High School along DeKalb Avenue musing about the theatre's restoration, and sadly died a few years before that work he otherwise supervised in that capacity could begin. Finally, the late Mary Lai, an LIU lifer like Fishelson and me, who negotiated contracts with Alan Freed and other promoters and rented what was also her alma mater for a decade of memorable concerts commencing in 1950 when LIU purchased the Brooklyn Paramount, while loyally serving ten presidents as CFO. She was a devoted employee for seventy years and not only welcomed us in her office in the building on the CW Post named for Mary Lai on three separate occasions for taped video, included interviews between 2004–2014 as our invaluable consultant, but also generously shared information while allowing us access to what unfortunately were only a few remaining of those and other contractual documents.

On to an intermediate level, as it were, colleagues and students, our Brooklyn Paramount academic events wouldn't have been possible without the help of Bob Barr from A/V, who rescued us with equipment and their malfunction too many times to count. Farhadi Farhadi a. k. a. "Fred," a photographer in his own right, helped us mount photographic exhibits and the museum-like showcases containing paraphernalia like an original usher's uniform and cap and their like we obtained for display in the theatre's former Grand Lobby. Alisa Yalan of IT designed creative posters for Brooklyn Paramount related to academic events as well as provided computer assistance and a million and one other "small" favors without which our efforts wouldn't have been successful. She, like Fred, was also an alumnus of Long Island University, the school of "second chances," as Provost Stevens-Haynes used to promote it.

Turning next to other boots literally on the ground, the "Friends of the Brooklyn Paramount" were colleagues and alumni who remain too many to list, but their generous (solicited) donations to the Brooklyn Paramount Theatre Fund helped, for example, raise enough money to produce a short video titled "Welcome to the Brooklyn Paramount" narrated by Don K. Reed of radio Doo-Wop broadcasting fame found on our website, if not YouTube. In similar regard, my boyhood friend, the late Joseph K. Fassler, was kind enough to fund a dinner for the thirty-three Jazz musicians who performed in "Remembering Jazz at the Brooklyn Paramount," which was advertised as "three bands for $25" containing some of the music of legendary Jazz musicians heard on stage here back in the day. Performance date was October 15, 2004, a memorable Friday on a makeshift stage in our theatre that *AllAboutJazz* immodestly reviewed as an "historic event." A few hundred copies distributed for educational purposes at no cost are still available. If nothing else, Joey's contribution from his business operation, Restaura, Inc., helps to discredit the ongoing cynicism unfortunately still heard among some Jazz club owners that Jazz musicians neither should be paid—union scale in this instance—nor fed what proved to be a delicious catered meal in the former Grand Lobby of the Brooklyn Paramount renamed Luntey Commons at the time.

The names of students in our respective classes who helped with this project no longer can be retrieved...though three of them do happily spring to mind: (1) Elizabeth Maroni, who created splendid murals connected with our museum-like showcases; (2) Jun Chun, who helped this author assemble a PowerPoint still used for public presentations about our cinematic-like cathedral; and (3) Edwian Stokes, who not only engineered many episodes of *In My Pocket*, my radio show, but currently is busy creating a Brooklyn Paramount podcast.

Turning next to others encountered on this journey who profoundly impacted our project, the late Ron Hutchinson, who purchased the Vitaphone archive, generously gifted us with memorabilia referenced above as well as with the photos of Vaudeville performers who performed on stage here during those halcyon pre-TV years that provided continuous entertainment, which for better or worse, accelerated the downfall of that "old gal." Another stalwart was Dave Harmon, a Rock 'n' Roll promoter of retro-concerts in Florida, who not only introduced us to several of those old-timers from those golden years of what was controversial music at the time, but he helped them with financial advice. A third friend was the late Doctor Bob, Robert Waldheim, a retired cardiologist and organ enthusiast—and donor—whose ninetieth birthday we happily hosted in our theatre with a Mighty Wurlitzer concert, who sadly died before seeing the restoration of the Brooklyn Paramount, something our dear lamented friend longed to see.

Additional photos found in these pages were gifted by Eddie Bert, the Jazz trombonist who worked in Alan Freed's Big Band. We acknowledge innumerable reference librarians in the mid-Manhattan Branch of the New York Public Library, the Grand Army Plaza Library in Brooklyn, the Library of Performing Arts at Lincoln Center in Manhattan, the Brooklyn Historical Society, and more recently, the Rutgers Street Library on the Lower East Side. Finally, thank you to the Floyd Memorial Library in Greenport, New York, whose reference librarian Christopher Bianci helped me secure many of the books itemized in References, and Ian Fleury, the IT wiz, who bailed me out of innumerable computer problems while also helping me locate assorted archival sources online.

Speaking of the latter, the *Brooklyn Daily Eagle* was downloaded online halfway through my library investigations, saving these comprised eyes the drudgery of hours of microfilm and microfiche research at the Brooklyn Public Library and Forty-Second Street Library in

Manhattan. I use it extensively throughout these pages with and with citations other than dates, but when I cite other invaluable tabloids, those written sources are usually named: *The Brooklyn Times, The Brooklyn Standard-Union,* and Manhattan's tabloids like *The New York Times.*

A special shout-out also to John Fontillas, H3's managing partner, who was kind enough to share an invaluable manuscript about opening night at the Brooklyn Paramount as well as a Zip drive containing thousands of informational pages about Paramount Studios.

I must thank other readers of its various chapters—Joe Amato on the Mighty Wurlitzer; Keith Wlosek from Arcadis, responsible for the theatre's amazing restoration, and who was kind enough to help me with technical details about the theatre's architecture; Craig Morrison, theatre historian, for reading the Introduction; my buddy and colleague, the sociologist Arthur Kimmel, who laboriously proofread and reported errors; and my close associate in Native American studies, Alex Ruuska, who provided additional reading before this delayed submission date for reasons found in the Prologue. Any errors that remain, needless to say, are mine.

I also want to acknowledge Leigh Altshuler and Costa Damaskos for directing me to Scribe.

Yet another deserved shout-out goes to Meryl Singer, my wife who half a century later had to live through more years of detached preoccupation required to complete a book; and oldest daughter Julie whose background in publishing got me through technical questions associated with this initial nonacademic manuscript.

And, finally, my brother-in-arms in all things Brooklyn Paramount, Stuart Fishelson, the royal "we" in this book's text, who sadly died in 2023 after a horrific bout with scleroderma while Live Nation commenced asbestos abatement preparatory for its amazing restoration. Not a nicer or sweeter person left his footprints on this troubled planet. I dedicate this book to Stuart's memory, with the curious synchronicity that his undiagnosed disease was finally treated at Johns Hopkins, thanks to Norman Steinberg's friendship with the comedian Bob Saget, whose sister unfortunately died of the same disease.